Industrial Heritage and Regional Identities

In many heritage sites, non-spatial forms of identity are interlinked with spatial ones. This book provides the first global survey of how regions of heavy industry grapple with their industrial heritage and what it means for regional identity. It explores how region-branding seems to determine the ultimate success of industrial heritage, a process that is closely connected to the marketing of regions to provide a viable economic future and attract tourism to the region.

Drawing on international case-studies from coal- and steel-producing regions, the chapters explore how heritage has developed powerful links to regional and local identities, from class, gender, religion, ethnicity, race and culture. It highlights both the commonalities and differences in the strategies employed towards a regions' industrial heritage, and draws a range of powerful conclusions about the path dependency of particular forms for post-industrial regional identity in former regions of heavy industry. This book will appeal to students and scholars in the fields of heritage, tourism, geography and cultural studies.

Christian Wicke is Assistant Professor in political history at Utrecht University.

Stefan Berger is Professor of Social History at Ruhr University Bochum and director of the Institute for Social Movements.

Jana Golombek is a doctoral student and a research associate at the German Mining Museum in Bochum and is working as a researcher and curator at the LWL-Industrial Museum in Dortmund.

Routledge Cultural Heritage and Tourism Series
Series editor: Dallen J. Timothy
Arizona State University, USA

The *Routledge Cultural Heritage and Tourism Series* offers an interdisciplinary social science forum for original, innovative and cutting-edge research about all aspects of cultural heritage-based tourism. This series encourages new and theoretical perspectives and showcases ground-breaking work that reflects the dynamism and vibrancy of heritage, tourism and cultural studies. It aims to foster discussions about both tangible and intangible heritages, and all of their management, conservation, interpretation, political, conflict, consumption and identity challenges, opportunities and implications. This series interprets heritage broadly and caters to the needs of upper-level students, academic researchers and policy makers.

www.routledge.com/Routledge-Cultural-Heritage-and-Tourism-Series/book-series/RCHT

Valuing World Heritage Cities
Tanja Vahtikari

Waterways and the Cultural Landscape
Edited by Francesco Vallerani and Francesco Visentin

Heritage of Death
Landscapes of Emotion, Memory and Practice
Edited by Mattias Frihammar and Helaine Silverman

Industrial Heritage and Regional Identities
Edited by Christian Wicke, Stefan Berger and Jana Golombek

Industrial Heritage and Regional Identities

Edited by Christian Wicke,
Stefan Berger and
Jana Golombek

LONDON AND NEW YORK

First published 2018
by Routledge
2 Park Square, Milton Park, Abingdon, Oxon OX14 4RN

and by Routledge
711 Third Avenue, New York, NY 10017

Routledge is an imprint of the Taylor & Francis Group, an informa business

© 2018 selection and editorial matter, Christian Wicke, Stefan Berger and Jana Golombek; individual chapters, the contributors.

The right of Christian Wicke, Stefan Berger and Jana Golombek to be identified as the authors of the editorial material, and of the authors for their individual chapters, has been asserted in accordance with sections 77 and 78 of the Copyright, Designs and Patents Act 1988.

All rights reserved. No part of this book may be reprinted or reproduced or utilised in any form or by any electronic, mechanical, or other means, now known or hereafter invented, including photocopying and recording, or in any information storage or retrieval system, without permission in writing from the publishers.

Trademark notice: Product or corporate names may be trademarks or registered trademarks, and are used only for identification and explanation without intent to infringe.

British Library Cataloguing-in-Publication Data
A catalogue record for this book is available from the British Library

Library of Congress Cataloging-in-Publication Data
A catalog record for this book has been requested

ISBN: 978-1-138-24116-9 (hbk)
ISBN: 978-1-315-28117-9 (ebk)

Typeset in Times New Roman
by Apex CoVantage, LLC

Contents

List of contributors   vii

   Introduction: industrial heritage and regional identities   1
   CHRISTIAN WICKE

1 **Mining memories: Big Pit and industrial heritage in South Wales**   13
   LEIGHTON S. JAMES

2 **Looking back: representations of the industrial past in Asturias**   32
   RUBÉN VEGA GARCÍA

3 **Regional identity and industrial heritage in the mining area of Nord-Pas-de-Calais**   56
   MARION FONTAINE

4 **A post-industrial mindscape? The mainstreaming and touristification of industrial heritage in the Ruhr**   74
   STEFAN BERGER, JANA GOLOMBEK AND CHRISTIAN WICKE

5 **Contested heritage and regional identity in the Borsod Industrial Area in Hungary**   95
   GYÖRGYI NÉMETH

6 **Identity and mining heritage in Romania's Jiu Valley coal region: commodification, alienation, renaissance**   119
   DAVID A. KIDECKEL

7 **Regional identity in the making? Industrial heritage and regional identity in the coal region of Northern Kyūshū in Japan**   136
REGINE MATHIAS

8 **"There needs to be something there for people to remember": industrial heritage in Newcastle and the Hunter Valley, Australia**   168
ERIK EKLUND

9 **From mills to malls: industrial heritage and regional identity in metropolitan Pittsburgh**   190
ALLEN DIETERICH-WARD

10 **Regions of heavy industry and their heritage – between identity politics and 'touristification': where to next?**   214
STEFAN BERGER AND PAUL PICKERING

Index   237

Contributors

Allen Dieterich-Ward is Associate Professor of History at Shippensburg University. He completed his PhD at the University of Michigan in 2006 and specializes in urban, environmental and political history. He is the author of *Beyond Rust: Metropolitan Pittsburgh and the Fate of Industrial America* (2016). His current work focuses on the relationships between regional identity and landscapes of production/consumption.

Erik Eklund is Professor of History and Director of the Centre for Gippsland Studies at Federation University Australia. His major works include *Steel Town: the making and breaking of Port Kembla* (2002), and *Mining Towns: making a living, making a life* (2012). From 2015 to 2016 he was Keith Cameron Visiting Chair in Australian History at University College Dublin, Ireland. He held an appointment at the University of Newcastle from 1994 to 2007, and maintains a close interest in the city's history and heritage.

Marion Fontaine is lecturer (Maître de conferences) at the Université d'Avignon (France) and member of the Research Centre "Centre Norbert Elias". She is interested in the social and political history of the European working-classes and in the history of the deindustrialization process. She recently published *The Racing Club de Lens et les gueules noires. Essai d'histoire sociale* (2010) and *Liévin 74. Fin d'un monde ouvrier* (2014).

Leighton S. James is Associate Professor of European History at Swansea University. He studies at the universities of Cardiff and Glamorgan. His research interests include the industrial history of the South Wales and Ruhr coalfields and the social and cultural history of warfare in the eighteenth and nineteenth centuries. His previous works include *Witnessing the Revolutionary and Napoleonic Wars: German Central Europe* (2013) and *The Politics of Identity and Civil Society in Britain and Germany: Miners in the Ruhr and South Wales, 1890–1926* (2008).

David Kideckel is professor emeritus of cultural anthropology at Central Connecticut State University. He recently published *Getting by in Post-Socialist Romania: Labor, the Body, and Working Class Culture* (2008) with a companion video, "Days of the Miners: Life and Death of a Working Class Culture".

He recently embarked on a project considering "Regional Responses to the Decline of Coal and the Transformation of Energy Practice" comparing circumstances in communities and economic institutions in the Jiu Valley, Romania and southern West Virginia.

Rubén Vega García is Professor at the Oviedo University, responsible for the Oral Sources Archive for the Social History of Asturias. He has worked on the Francoist and democratic periods, following research lines focused on working cultures, labor unionism, social unrest and de-industrialization processes.

Paul Pickering is Director of the Research School of Humanities and the Arts, Australian National University. He has published extensively on commemoration, memory, re-enactment and social and political culture in the Anglophone world. His latest book is *Sounds of Liberty: Music, Radicalism and Reform in the Anglophone World 1790–1914* (with Kate Bowan) published by Manchester University Press in 2017. He is currently working on a study of the evolving urban-industrial landscape and the politics of heritage in Manchester and Salford over the past two centuries to be published in Routledge's Museums in Focus Series in 2019.

Regine Mathias is Professor Emerita of Japanese History, at the Ruhr-University Bochum. Her main field of research is Japanese social and economic history, with a focus on Japanese mining and labor history. Major publications include: *Industrialisierung und Lohnarbeit – Der Kohlenbergbau in Nord-Kyshū und sein Einfluß auf die Herausbildung einer Lohnarbeiterschaft (Industrialization and Wage Labor. Coal Mining in Northern Kyūshū and its Influence on Labor)* (1978); *Japanische Bergleute im Ruhrgebiet (Japanese Coal Miners in the Ruhr area)* (co-edited with Kataoka; Meid; Pascha; Shimada) (2012); Female Labour in the Japanese Coal-mining Industry in Janet Hunter (ed.) *Japanese Women Working – Past and Presence* (1993); Picture Scrolls as a Historical Source on Japanese Mining in Nanny Kim, Keiko Nagase-Reimer, Anke Scherer (eds.) *Mining, Monies and Culture in Early Modern Societies: East Asian and Global Perspectives* (2009); Japan in the Seventeenth Century: Labour Relations and Work Ethics in *International Review of Social History* 56, Special Issue (2011); The Nation at Work: Gendered Working Patterns in the Taishô- and Shôwa periods in Andrea Germer et al. (eds.) *Gender, Nation and State in Modern Japan* (2014).

Györgyi Németh has been associate professor in industrial history and industrial archaeology at the University of Miskolc, Hungary. Her research interests include the theory and practice of industrial heritage conservation as well as the evolution of heavy industrial landscapes publishing: *Growth, Decline and Recovery: Heavy Industrial Regions in Transition* (2008). She has contributed recently to *Industrial Heritage Re-tooled: the TICCIH Guide to Industrial Heritage Conservation*.

Introduction
Industrial heritage and regional identities

Christian Wicke

The making of industrial society has often been historicized as integral to the transition to modernity in the West.[1] This transition towards mass society, some scholars of national identity have maintained, involved the loss of communal memory and the functional need for new constructions of collective memory.[2] Yet, the methodological nationalism in the history of industrialization has obscured the unevenness of this development at the regional level. Regions, rather than nations, might be the more useful spatial categories for historical studies of industrialization.[3] Any traveler crossing highly industrialized nations such as England, Germany or the United States in the 21st century would be able to confirm this observation: the concentration of the modern does not necessarily correspond to the concentration of the industrial. Some parts of these nations have been affected by industrialism much more profoundly than others. In the course of the industrial revolutions, large-scale industries including coal and steel production had irreversibly transformed the landscape and culture of particular regions around the world. Urban and rural infrastructures, ecological and agricultural systems, class and gender relations, labor and ethnic migration, customs and dialects, aesthetics and memories have all been affected by heavy industries particularly in areas of high concentration. The industrial region became a foreign country.[4]

Similarly, regions of heavy industry have often been subject to dramatic processes of deindustrialization, which have affected cultures and landscapes of such regions in virtually all spheres of life.[5] Forms of pre-factory deindustrialization have certainly happened already in pre-modern times and in spaces outside of the industrialized West.[6] Since the mid-20th century, however, energy transitions and increasing economic globalization have left urbanized regions in highly industrialized countries, especially those centering on the 'old' industries of coal and steel, extremely vulnerable. While global market mechanisms have had great impact on local deindustrialization processes, national economies and political cultures had some power to determine the speed and timing of such processes. The European example well illustrates these discrepancies: neoliberal Thatcherism, for example, in the 1980s showed little patience for the unprofitable coal mining industries in Great Britain, and the downfall of state socialism in Central and Eastern Europe around 1990 triggered wide-reaching deindustrialization measures. The Rhenish capitalist model, in contrast, allowed for a 60-year (i.e. 1958–2018) transition period out of black-coal mining in the Ruhr, which for so many years has received enormous federal subsidies.[7] A historical comparison between deindustrializing regions therefore is a challenging exercise as the regional temporalities within the same period may be greatly different. This also holds not only with regards to the economic management of deindustrialization as such but also to the memory politics and 'cultural-trauma management' that deindustrialization automatically brings to the scene. As this comparative volume will show, industrial heritage initiatives have experienced very different degrees of financial support, from billions to nothing.

Industrialization and deindustrialization, thus, are uneven processes. This also holds when we lower the level of abstraction and look more closely into the deindustrializing region. Assuming entire regions were turning completely postindustrial would be an overly holistic approach,[8] as particular sectors, communities, classes, families and individuals within regions will always be influenced much more than others.[9] Against this patchy picture, the study of deindustrializing regions risks unnecessary shortcomings when 'regions' are treated essentially as unitary social objects. Like national identities, regional identities are profoundly based on a unifying imagination transcending different social groups without necessarily solving their tensions.[10] Regional identities in many ways are consumed reflexively by individuals in the public through many kinds of historically charged symbols, sites and rites that may appear as banal but fulfill an important function in the social, cultural and political organization of society, and ultimately also for personal identities.[11] The way regional identity is constructed, however, is discursive and not consensual.[12] In a transformative society, where individual and mass identities seem to have ontologically merged, the selective articulation of memory and representations of aesthetic judgment are collective processes that cannot operate without contestation.[13] Regional identity, like society, is so amorphous and multifaceted that, ultimately, in the same region there is more than just one regional identity, which not only is dependent on the internal complexities but also on the regions' embeddedness in fluid national, transnational and global networks.[14]

To be sure, this book does not attempt to define what regional identity actually is, and the authors may therefore employ very different perspectives in their chapters that will hopefully stimulate further work in the field. The editors study regional identity from a constructivist point of view,[15] and we invite every reader to individually re-think the meaning of regional identity. In this volume on regional identity and industrial heritage, the relationship between constructions of collective spaces (regions) and collective pasts (industrial heritage) is of primary concern, while personal experiences and identifications for example with the labor that shaped the deindustrializing region remain secondary.[16] This would require systematic surveys and interviews which we cannot offer here.[17] When we discuss identity and heritage, we are primarily interested in the public representations of regions, specifically in the form of History (with capital H) that serve a purpose, either functionally or intentionally.[18] We are especially hoping to get a better sense of *how* regions, and social and individual agents within the regions, selectively produce and use their heritage in relation to the (self-)representation of 'regionhood'. Regions, like nations, not only are administrative or economic units; they also are imagined communities reliant on historical narratives and visions for the future that legitimize their continuous existence as spatial entities.[19]

In theory, history is always open and changing over time as we cannot know how the past will be articulated in the future; in practice, however, it appears as if the History of regions often also has been somewhat path-dependent: regional identities rely on a relatively limited historical repertoire from which memories can be selected, reformed, rearranged and estranged from previous meanings, though not endlessly. Regions' historical cultures, moreover, are bound to what is socially acceptable, politically possible and financially realizable. Their opportunities are constrained, for example, by mainstream perceptions of authenticity and aesthetic legitimacy within and outside of the particular region, and increasingly by the globalizing political economy of heritage with its international funding bodies and tourism streams.[20] The aesthetic appeal of industrial heritage has changed greatly over the last decades. Regional identities often emerged in modern Europe in combination with the tourism industry offering escape from urbanized and industrialized spaces.[21] Today de-industrial sites themselves have the potential of attracting thousands of tourists. Changes from below are dependent often on visionary civil society groups, which risk constructing 'un-authorized heritage',[22] and are willing and able to reform the practical articulation of historical consciousness in society (i.e. *Geschichtskultur*/historical culture).[23] But, once discovered as a potential source of income, the valorization of industrial heritage becomes engrained in the region-branding from above. Looking at nine case studies of this volume, it is fascinating to see the very different degrees of legitimacy industrial heritage has been endowed with over time, and how differently the actor's levels – comprising individuals and institutions from many different sections of society – have appeared from region to region.

An extensive amount of literature on industrial heritage has been produced by conservators, local historians, museums and public institutions, and scholars associated with such networks.[24] The industrial archeology movement that emerged in the 1950s in Great Britain and pioneered in this field was followed by the increasing establishment of the history of technology in faculties.[25] That industrial heritage today is being taken seriously by academic scholarship, and is a subject taught at so many universities, has been due to the instituting of Heritage Studies across the humanities, social sciences and geosciences. While the industrial heritage discourse over the last fifty years or longer has centered predominantly on material objects, there seems to be a trend now to move beyond the tangible. In the Nizhny Tagil Charter for the Industrial Heritage from 2003, it is very broadly defined as consisting "of the remains of industrial culture which are of historical, technological, social, architectural or scientific value. These remains consist of buildings and machinery, workshops, mills and factories, mines and sites for processing and refining, warehouses and stores, places where energy is generated, transmitted and used, transport and all its infrastructure, as well as places used for social activities related to industry such as housing, religious worship or education".[26] Material culture offers us important insights into the changing social meaning of the past in deindustrializing regions. Studying such meaningful manipulation of the world of things helps us to better understand the manifold imaginations and practices of the cultural and political elites in a region. Industrial sites such as steel plants and mining complexes may, for example, be forgotten, abandoned or demolished. They may also be preserved, museumized, commercialized and/or touristified.[27] Once engrained in the region's official heritage, the relic infrastructure of the coal and steel industry may also acquire its own agency in the evolution of regional identity, for example, in the form of monumental landmarks.

The definition above is too restrictive, however, for the purpose of this volume, and every reader should feel encouraged to also reconsider the meaning of industrial heritage. Among the many different kinds of scholars working on industrial heritage, there seems to be a wide consensus that industrial heritage comprises more than just 'big stuff' but also many forms of more subtle, intangible forms of heritage that have no direct connection with material culture.[28] After all, many forms of immaterial culture can provide us with similarly important insights about the relationship between imaginations of the past and the region. Think of prolonged usage, for example, of workers' traditional songs, idioms and leisure activities in formerly industrialized regions, especially where the professional identities of the miners or steel workers have merged with overall representations of regional identities. I can also not see any reason why more progressive forms of creative expression evoking industrial pasts, such as Asturian Hip Hop or Punk songs, should be excluded from the industrial heritage discourse.

The particularity of the forms of heritage and historical cultures in (de)industrial regions constitutes an intriguing tension once we lift the level of abstraction again to a more global, or at least Western, perspective. Despite the unevenness of industrializing and deindustrializing processes, one cannot overlook the commonalities and transnational influences in the economic and cultural performances of coal- and steel-producing regions. Think of the machinery, terminology, work process, environmental transformation, labor migration, timing, sound and smell: industrial culture has connected regions around the world. The industrial lifeworld rapidly unfolded its global character in the modern era. And, while it is quite surprising to see how differently these regions have been managing the public memory of their industrial past, during this project we have witnessed the connectedness of a transnational industrial-heritage movement and the great urge of activists, public servants, politicians and scholars from (de)industrial regions to learn from each other's experiences. There might be another factor, in the near future, which relativizes the regional particularities against the global. There is an increasing realization that the relics of modernity associated with the burning of fossil fuel since the invention of the steam engine also represent the making of anthropocentric climate change.[29] As scholars have suggested re-conceptualizing notions of human history vis-à-vis planetary history, the industrial heritage discussed in this volume may acquire new meaning.

The idea for this volume originated in Bochum, a former black-coal mining town that developed around a large cast-iron plant, the Bochumer Verein.[30] Located in the heart of the Ruhr region, Germany's former industrial powerhouse, the university has become the city's largest employer since General Motors shut its Opel plant in 2014. Around the same time, the Director of the Institute for Social Movements at the Ruhr-Universität Bochum (RUB), Stefan Berger, brought this project into being to expand on the institute's research tradition in the comparative regional history of de-industrialization, including questions of heritage and identity.[31] Berger gained funding for two years from the State of North-Rhine Westphalia and the Regionalverband Ruhr and was able, with the enthusiastic support from Jana Golombek and myself, to establish an international network of wonderful scholars in this field. As there is an overwhelming amount of (de)industrial regions, we started the project focusing on regions that have experienced, like the Ruhr, a dominant coal or steel industry and have shown a relatively high degree of polycentric urbanization. We were particularly interested in the question of to what extent the cultural landscape of the Ruhr really is *the* shining example of industrial heritage in the world, and why the industrial-heritage movement in this region has been so incredibly successful in comparison to similar regions around the world. The RUB Research School has assisted us in bringing scholars of various disciplines to conference panels and workshops to the Ruhr, and many of them have decided to continue working together within a working group of the newly founded European Labour History Network. This volume is based on a workshop held in Bochum in late October 2015. Unfortunately, not all cases discussed in this project can be published in this particular volume.[32] Its content, chapter by chapter, follows a zigzag travel east. Starting in western Europe, in Wales, the journey slowly goes via Spain, France and Germany to Hungary and Romania. From eastern Europe it takes a long flight to Japan, at the other end of Asia, and from there to the eastern coast of Australia. It finishes with a case study in North America.

In the first chapter, Leighton James takes us to the industrial heritage of South Wales, where regional, national and working-class identities have been strongly intertwined. Through examination of museum catalogues, reports, interviews and questionnaires, he explores the development of industrial heritage in this region with particularly reference to the Big Pit National Coal Museum. James places the experience of industrial heritage in the region within the context of debates surrounding the purpose of industrial heritage and the tense, often competitive, relationship between community expectations, the economic aims of various governmental institutions and the creation of an "authorized heritage discourse".[33] In this case, the interpenetrations of national and regional discourses are highly developed, as the initiatives for industrial heritage in the region over the last century have been bound to the growing sense of Welsh national identity. James shows that the more urbanized and industrialized South Wales, with its increasingly anglicized and more heterogeneous mining communities, had a complicated and strained relationship to a representation of Wales that had been essentially agrarian and Welsh-speaking. The decline of the mining industry in the post-war period, according to James, has not lead to a complete dissolution of the industrial Welsh-working class that was particular to the region within the nation. It remains doubtful, nevertheless, whether the region's industrial heritage has the capacity of maintaining a sense of its working-class identity as there is an irreversible loss of the generation with lived experience of the mining industry.

Rubén Vega García further discusses this generational dimension in Asturias. Over the last decades of the 20th century, the slow decline of mining and other industries has led to social tensions and a mental change among wide sections of the regional society. For him, the generational changes in industrial heritage and regional identity under conditions of deindustrialization are of great importance. As the new generations' lifeworld is fundamentally different to the older ones, the rich industrial heritage of the region, both tangible and intangible, is being reinterpreted while at risk of disappearing. Vega García is interested in this relationship between continuities and ruptures in the historical culture of Asturias. As mines and factories have closed, he shows how the cultural heritage of industrial Asturias has become a powerful source of inspiration for artistic performance among sections of 'post-industrial' generations. Brought up in a fundamentally transformed landscape to the one they consult as their ethical reference, they nevertheless act as vociferous agents in constructing memories of the industrial era that is rarely reflected in the touristic representations of Asturias. Recently the presence of the mining and industrial past in, for example, literature, audiovisual fiction and documentaries, music and the arts has grown stronger, while articulating the feelings of loss and uncertainty about the future of the region. The intangible heritage of the industrial era, and most importantly its decline, forms the underlying narrative to the youngsters' artworks, which often is politically radical.

Studying the former mining basin of Nord-Pas-de-Calais in France, Marion Fontaine explains that the official recognition of the industrial heritage in the region has led to a sanitization of its industrial past and not necessarily to a reliable reflection of the regional and historical identity of the region. In 2012, the regional mining basin was added to the list of UNESCO World Heritage sites. The UNESCO status, Fontaine argues, has been widely perceived as a form of 'consecration', which epitomizes the major role that industrial heritage today plays in the region. This valorization, however, is problematic: those who celebrate the region's mining in the official heritage discourse also perceive it also as stigmatizing and burdensome, and as indicative to the region's social and political problems. Fontaine discusses how, after the closure of the mines beginning in 1969/70, the region has moved from a strong urge to 'erase' the industrial past entirely, to its encompassing valorization towards 2012. She demonstrates how a network of regional, political, cultural, educational and workers' associations has been engaged with the idealization and ultimately successful institutionalization of the industrial past, the representation of which, however, remains strongly selective as the quest for erasure of what is felt to be onerous remains dominant.

Berger, Wicke and Golombek subsequently analyze the 'success story' of industrial heritage in the Ruhr, which also contains a large UNESCO site around the Zollverein mining complex that is part of infrastructural network of a unique industrial-heritage landscape between Dortmund and Duisburg. The chapter shows that the initiatives for industrial heritage in the region started as a critical movement from below. It was institutionalized, however, by an impressive system of stakeholders from regional associations, public companies and the state government. With a large-scale urban renewal program between 1989 and 1999 industrial heritage became virtually inescapable to any local or traveler in the region. The industrial past, thus, has become the most dominant time layer permeating most representations of the Ruhr's regional identity. At the same time, the critical heritage discourse became overshadowed by regional image campaigns and efforts for touristification. The material remains of the industrial era have become strongly aestheticized objects, imparting few insights into the environmental and labor exploitation in the Ruhr's history, which leaves the region's industrial heritage appearing somewhat de-historicized.

Györgyi Németh offers insights into the first post-Socialist region of this volume, that is, the Borsod Industrial Area in Northern Hungary around Miskolc and Ózd. She offers a very different narrative of the region, which in the interbellum has also been referred to as the 'Hungarian Ruhr'. The regional identity of this area was strongly defined by the class and professional identity of miners and iron workers. During the Socialist period after the Second World War, the coal and steel industries were controlled by the Socialist government and the industrial identity of the region appreciated. This, however, was followed by deep-cutting processes of privatization and deindustrialization from the 1990s. Unlike in the 'actual' Ruhr, the industrial heritage subsequently was, in the eyes of the regional institutions, of no value. Little of the rich material culture that could have represented the industrial past, which had been formative to the region, was therefore preserved. As the decay of the region's industrial heritage is progressing, and the industrial past remains negatively charged, there seems to be no political opportunity for a de-privatization of post-industrial sites and no sustainable basis for the regional identity of the Borsod Industrial Area.

David Kideckel contributes a second chapter on a post-Socialist mining region. Similar to Northern Hungary, in the urban conglomeration of the Romanian Jiu Valley there has been little initiative to preserve the declining industrial heritage. Kideckel argues that the decline in mining and the associated heritage has been facilitated by a strong movement of regional businesses, political leaders, officials, property owners and members of the middle-classes towards valorization. The consequence has been an alienation of (former) working people from their home region and heritage. Kideckel points to another problem, reminiscent of the situation in Northern Hungary: the legitimacy of industrial heritage has been undermined by what is perceived as the 'dark heritage' of both socialism and post-socialism. This negative perception and antipathy towards mining heritage has led to a fragmentation of the Jiu Valley's regional identity. Kideckel, however, believes that the regional identity also contains seeds for a heritage revival, as there have been some attempts by local artists and intellectuals to save some mining sites. By registering industrial heritage with cultural officials and organizing activities to reconnect local groups to their heritage, they seek to counter the movement for commodification.

Regine Mathias focuses on the Japanese coal and steel region, Northern Kyūshū, which from the mid-19th century became an industrial powerhouse. Emerging workers' communities across the region then developed proud professional identities, combined with experiences of social discrimination, rather than one coherent regional identity. Similar to the Ruhr, from the late 1950s the region was deeply affected by the decline of the coal industry, and the impact of the oil shocks of the 1970s and 1980s on the steel production led to large-scale deindustrialization processes. Political efforts were taken in Northern Kyūshū to restructure the regional industries, and there were attempts to preserve the local culture and memories of the coalmining industry which however were originally not successful. Mathias shows that industrial heritage in Japan has subsequently been placed predominantly in the framework of the national narrative on the country's modernization, rather than regional identity. After the foundation of Japan's Industrial Archaeology Society (*Sangyō kōko gakkai*) in 1977, the idea of preserving industrial sites began to spread. Since the 1990s remnants of coal mines, blast-furnaces, harbor structures, factories and other buildings have been put on the national preservation list. In 2015 several sites in Northern Kyūshū became even part of a large UNESCO World Heritage project titled "Sites of Japan's Meiji Industrial Revolution".

Erik Eklund's chapter covers an important mining and industrial region in Australia, centered on the former 'steel city' of Newcastle and its hinterland, in the state of New South Wales. Eklund explains that industrial heritage in Newcastle and the Hunter Valley developed an uneasy and 'ambivalent' relationship to regional identity, and that both deindustrialization from the 1960s and later reindustrialization processes have added to this ambivalence. Parts of the population had a more future-oriented vision for the region's post-industrial identity which they sought to disassociate from its industrial foundations, whereas others did celebrate its industrial past. The return of large-scale coal mining from 2001 further challenged representations of a coherent regional identity. This incoherence is also reflected in the urban space. While there are industrial heritage sites in the region, they do not represent an integrated heritage landscape. The recognition of industrial heritage for the regional identity, thus, remains very limited and uneven. This lack of acknowledgement for the region's industrial past was exemplified best by the complete demolition of the BHP steelworks site in the early 2000s, which had operated in Newcastle throughout most of the 20th century.

Allen Dieterich-Ward contributes the final case study to this volume, that is, on Greater Pittsburgh in the United States. Dieterich-Ward shows that from the late 1970s, industrial heritage in the region was recognized as a measure for urban renewal. While postwar urban renewal sought to erase the industrial buildings from the cityscape, the industrial past was successively recognized though not directly for heritage motives. Themed sites, building rehabilitation, riverfront trails, and historic buildings and quarters were placed in the context of industrial heritage to create a more appealing regional identity that would facilitate the deindustrializing region's economic appreciation and gentrification by the 'creative' and middle classes. As urban spaces thus experienced a remarkable renewal through conservationism, including environmental rehabilitation, the traditional working-class communities suffered from ongoing industrial and demographic decline, and industrial-heritage conservation remained subordinate to the leading market motive of neoliberal urbanism.

Stefan Berger and Paul Pickering complete this volume with some stimulating reflections, reminding us once again of the great changes the industrial heritage discourse has undergone over the second half of the 20th century until now. The specific constellation of particular deindustrialization processes, agent networks for heritage and identity politics have regionally differed around the world, which has not made it possible everywhere to protect important testimonials of the industrial age. Nevertheless, there is a common trend perceivable driven by the prospect of valorizing industrial heritage and regional identities. The neoliberalization and touristification of deindustrializing spaces has ultimately promoted the authorization of industrial heritage around the world. Berger and Pickering conclude that future comparative histories of industrial heritage should not ignore the many voices that have been silenced through this movement from above.

Notes

1 Gellner, Ernest. 1964. *Thought and Change*. London: Weidenfeld and Nicolson; Hobsbawm, Eric. 1962. *The Age of Revolution: 1789–1848*. London: Weidenfeld and Nicholson.
2 Nora, Pierre. 1989. Between Memory and History: Les Lieux De Mémoire. *Representations* 26: 7–24.
3 Sidney Pollard. 1973. Industrialization and the European Economy. *The Economic History Review* 26: 636–648. For the importance of regions in the study of industrialization, see also various chapters in Czierpka, J., K. Oerters and N. Thorade, Eds. 2015. *Regions, Industries, and Heritage: Perspectives on Economy, Society, and Culture in Modern Western Europe*. Basingtoke: Palgrave Macmillan.
4 Chargesheimer and Heinrich Böll. 1958. *Im Ruhrgebiet*. Cologne: Kiepenheuer & Witsch.
5 See e.g. Jefferson Cowie and Joseph Heathcott, Eds. 2003. *Beyond the Ruins: The Meanings of Deindustrialization*. Ithaca, NY: ILR Press.
6 Christopher H. Johnson 2002. Introduction: De-industrialization and Globalization. *International Review of Social History* 47: 3–34.
7 Stefan Goch. 2002. Betterment without Airs: Social, Cultural and Political Consequences of De-industrialization in the Ruhr. *International Review of Social History* 47: 87–111.
8 Cf. Daniel Bell. 1973. *The Coming of Post-Industrial Society: A Venture in Social Forecasting*. New York: Basic Books; Touraine, Alain. 1971. *The Post-Industrial Society: Tomorrow's Social History: Classes, Conflicts and Culture in the Programmed Society*. New York: Random House.
9 See, e.g. Valerie Walkerdine and Luis Jimenez Gender. 2012. *Work and Community after De-Industrialisation: A Psychological Approach to Affect*. Basingtoke: Palgrave Macmillan.
10 Benedict Anderson. 1991. *Imagined Communities: Reflections on the Spread and Origin of Nationalism*. 2nd ed. London: Verso.
11 Michael Billig. 1995. *Banal Nationalism*. London: Sage; Hobsbawm, E. and T. Ranger, Eds. 1982. *The Invention of Tradition*. Cambridge: Cambridge University Press.

12 Stuart Hall. 1996. Who Needs Identity?, in S. Hall and P. du Gay, Eds. *Questions of Cultural Identity*, London: Sage, 1–17.
13 Norbert Elias. 2001. *Society of Individuals*. New ed. London: Bloomsbury Academic; Halbwachs, Maurice. 1992. *On Collective Memory*. Chicago: University of Chicago Press; Bourdieu, Pierre. 1987. *Distinction: A Social Critique of the Judgment of Taste*. Cambridge, MA: Harvard University Press.
14 Dorreen Massey. 1984. *Spatial Divisions of Labour: Social Structures and the Geography of Production*. New York: Methuen; Massey, Doreen. 1994. *Space, Place, and Gender*. Minneapolis: University of Minnesota Press.
15 See, e.g. Aansi Paasi. 1986. The Institutionalization of Regions: A Theoretical Framework for Understanding the Emergence of Regions and the Constitutions of Regional Identity. *Fennia* 164: 105–146.
16 Cf. John Kirk and Christine Wall. 2011. *Word and Identity: Historical and Cultural Contexts*. Basingtoke: Palgrave Macmillan.
17 Cf. Detlef Briesen, Rüdiger Gans and Armin Flender, Eds. 1994. *Regionalbewußtsein in Montanregionen im 19. Und 20. Jahrhundert: Saarland – Siegerland – Ruhrgebiet*. Bochum: Universitätsverlag Dr. N Brockmeyer.
18 Prasenjit Duara suggests that history written to serve the construction of nationhood should be spelt with capital H. I suggest this is also applicable to constructions of regional identities. Prasenjit Duara. 1995. *Rescuing History from the Nation: Questioning Narratives from Modern China*. Chicago: University of Chicago Press.
19 I am grateful to Linde Egberts for sharing her wonderful dissertation with me, which has just been published as Linde R. Egberts 2017. *Chosen Legacies: Heritage in Regional Identity*. London: Routledge.
20 Tim Winter. 2011. The Political Economies of Heritage, in H. Anheier and Y. Raj Isar, Eds. *Cultures and Globalization: Heritage, Memory and Identity*, London: Sage, 73–81.
21 See Eric Storm. 2018 (forthcoming). Tourism and the Transnational Construction of Regional Identities, in X. Manoel Núñez and E. Storm, Eds. *Regionalism and Modern Europe: Identity Construction and Movements from 1890 to the Present Day*, London: Bloomsbury.
22 Laurajane Smith. 2006. *The Uses of Heritage*. Oxford: Routledge.
23 Jörn Rüsen. 1994. Was ist Geschichtskultur? Überlegungen zu einer neuen Art, über Geschichte nachzudenken, in J. Rüsen, T. Grütter and K. Füßmann, Eds. *Historische Faszination: Geschichtskultur heute*, Cologne: Böhlau, 3–26.
24 For a helpful overview, see James Douet. 2013. *Industrial Heritage Re-Tooled: The TICCIH Guide to Industrial Heritage Conversation*. Lancaster: Carnegie.
25 Wolfhard Weber. 1980. Von der "Industriearchäologie" über das "Industrielle Erbe" zur "Industriekultur". Überlegungen zum Thema einer handlungsorientierten Technikhistorie, in U. Troitzsch and G. Wohlauf, Eds. *Technik-Geschichte*, Frankfurt: Suhrkamp, 420–447.
26 ICOMOS www.icomos.org/18thapril/2006/nizhny-tagil-charter-e.pdf (accessed 1 July 2017).
27 Philip Feifan Xie. 2015. *Industrial Heritage Tourism*. Bristol: Channel View Publications.
28 Yahaya Ahmad. 2006. The Scope and Definitions of Heritage: From Tangible to Intangible. *International Journal of Heritage Studies* 12(3): 292–300.
29 Dipesh Chakrabarty. 2009. The Climate of History: Four Theses. *Critical Inquiry* 35(2): 197–222.
30 David F. Crew 1980. *Town in the Ruhr: A Social History of Bochum, 1860–1914*. New York: Columbia University Press.
31 See, e.g. Klaus Tenfelde Ed. 2003. Strukturwandel aus vergleichender regionaler Perspektive nach 1945. *Mitteilungsblatt des Instituts für Soziale Bewegungen* 30, http://moving-the-social.ub.rub.de/index.php/Moving_the_social/issue/view/41 (accessed 1 July 2017); Tenfelde, Klaus, Ed. 2008. Raumbildung als mentaler Prozess: Schwerindustrielle Ballungsregionen im Vergleich. *Mitteilungsblatt des Instituts*

für soziale Bewegungen 39, http://moving-the-social.ub.rub.de/index.php/Moving_the_social/issue/view/52 (accessed 1 July 2017).
32 See also Christian Wicke, Stefan Berger and Jana Golombek. Eds. 2017. special issue of *The Public Historian* Vol. 39 No. 4 ; Berger, Stefan, Ed. Forthcoming. *Constructing Industrial Pasts: Industrial Heritage Making in Britain, the West and Post-Socialist Countries*. New York: Berghahn.
33 Smith, Laurajane and Emma Waterton. 2017. Constrained by Commonsense: The Authorized Heritage Discourse in Contemporary Debates, *The Oxford Handbook of Public Archaeology*, Oxford: Oxford University Press.

Bibliography

Ahmad, Yahaya. 2006. The Scope and Definitions of Heritage: From Tangible to Intangible. *International Journal of Heritage Studies* 12(3): 292–300.
Anderson, Benedict. 1991. *Imagined Communities: Reflections on the Spread and Origin of Nationalism*. 2nd ed. London: Verso.
Bell, Daniel. 1973. *The Coming of Post-Industrial Society: A Venture in Social Forecasting*. New York: Basic Books.
Berger, Stefan, Ed. (forthcoming). *Constructing Industrial Pasts: Industrial Heritage Making in Britain, the West and Post-Socialist Countries*. New York: Berghahn.
Billig, Michael. 1995. *Banal Nationalism*. London: Sage.
Bourdieu, Pierre. 1987. *Distinction: A Social Critique of the Judgment of Taste*. Cambridge, MA: Harvard University Press.
Briesen, Detlef, Rüdiger Gans and Armin Flender, Eds. 1994. *Regionalbewußtsein in Montanregionen im 19. Und 20. Jahrhundert: Saarland – Siegerland – Ruhrgebiet*. Bochum: Universitätsverlag Dr. N Brockmeyer.Chakrabarty, Dipesh. 2009. The Climate of History: Four Theses. *Critical Inquiry* 35(2): 197–222.
Chargesheimer and Heinrich Böll. 1958. *Im Ruhrgebiet*. Cologne: Kiepenheuer & Witsch.
Cowie, Jefferson and Joseph Heathcott, Eds. 2003. *Beyond the Ruins: The Meanings of Deindustrialization*. Ithaca, NY: ILR Press.
Crew, David F. 1980. *Town in the Ruhr: A Social History of Bochum, 1860–1914*. New York: Columbia University Press.
Czierpka, Juliane, Kathrin Oerters and Nora Thorade, Eds. 2015. *Regions, Industries, and Heritage: Perspectives on Economy, Society, and Culture in Modern Western Europe*. Basingtoke: Palgrave Macmillan.
Douet, James. 2013. *Industrial Heritage Re-Tooled: The TICCIH Guide to Industrial Heritage Conversation*. Lancaster: Carnegie.
Duara, Prasenjit. 1995. *Rescuing History from the Nation: Questioning Narratives from Modern China*. Chicago: University of Chicago Press.
Egberts, Linde R. 2017. *Chosen Legacies: Heritage in Regional Identity*. London: Routledge.
Elias, Norbert. 2001. *Society of Individuals*. New ed. London: Bloomsbury Academic.
Feifan Xie, Philip. 2015. *Industrial Heritage Tourism*. Bristol: Channel View Publications.
Gellner, Ernest. 1964. *Thought and Change*. London: Weidenfeld and Nicolson.
Goch, Stefan. 2002. Betterment without Airs: Social, Cultural and Political Consequences of De-Industrialization in the Ruhr. *International Review of Social History* 47: 87–111.
Halbwachs, Maurice. 1992. *On Collective Memory*. Chicago: University of Chicago Press.
Hall, Stuart. 1996. Who Needs Identity?, in S. Hall and P. du Gay, Eds. *Questions of Cultural Identity*, London: Sage, 1–17.
Hobsbawm, Eric. 1962. *The Age of Revolution: 1789–1848*. London: Weidenfeld and Nicholson.

Hobsbawm, Eric and Terence Ranger, Eds. 1982. *The Invention of Tradition*. Cambridge: Cambridge University Press.
ICOMOS www.icomos.org/18thapril/2006/nizhny-tagil-charter-e.pdf (accessed 1 July 2017).
Johnson, Christopher H. 2002. Introduction: De-Industrialization and Globalization. *International Review of Social History* 47: 3–34.
Kirk, John and Christine Wall. 2011. *Word and Identity: Historical and Cultural Contexts*. Basingtoke: Palgrave Macmillan.
Massey, Doreen. 1984. *Spatial Divisions of Labour: Social Structures and the Geography of Production*. New York: Methuen.
Massey, Doreen. 1994. *Space, Place, and Gender*. Minneapolis: University of Minnesota Press.
Nora, Pierre. 1989. Between Memory and History: Les Lieux De Mémoire. *Representations* 26: 7–24.
Paasi, Aansi. 1986. The Institutionalization of Regions: A Theoretical Framework for Understanding the Emergence of Regions and the Constitutions of Regional Identity. *Fennia* 164: 105–146.
Pollard, Sidney. 1973. Industrialization and the European Economy. *The Economic History Review* 26: 636–648.
Rüsen, Jörn. 1994. Was ist Geschichtskultur? Überlegungen zu einer neuen Art, über Geschichte nachzudenken, in J. Rüsen, T. Grütter and K. Füßmann, Eds. *Historische Faszination: Geschichtskultur heute*, Cologne: Böhlau, 3–26.
Smith, Laurajane. 2006. *The Uses of Heritage*. Oxford: Routledge.
Smith, Laurajane and Emma Waterton. 2017. Constrained by Commonsense: The Authorized Heritage Discourse in Contemporary Debates, in *The Oxford Handbook of Public Archaeology*, Oxford: Oxford University Press.
Storm, Eric. (forthcoming). Tourism and the Transnational Construction of Regional Identities, in X. Manoel Núñez and E. Storm, Eds. *Regionalism and Modern Europe: Identity Construction and Movements from 1890 to the Present Day*. London: Bloomsbury.
Tenfelde, Klaus, Ed. 2003. Strukturwandel aus vergleichender regionaler Perspektive nach 1945, *Mitteilungsblatt des Instituts für Soziale Bewegungen* 30, http://moving-the-social.ub.rub.de/index.php/Moving_the_social/issue/view/41 (accessed 1 July 2017).
Tenfelde, Klaus, Ed. 2008. Raumbildung als mentaler Prozess: Schwerindustrielle Ballungsregionen im Vergleich, *Mitteilungsblatt des Instituts für soziale Bewegungen* 39, http://moving-the-social.ub.rub.de/index.php/Moving_the_social/issue/view/52 (accessed 1 July 2017).
Touraine, Alain. 1971. *The Post-Industrial Society: Tomorrow's Social History: Classes, Conflicts and Culture in the Programmed Society*. New York: Random House.
Walkerdine, Valerie and Luis Jimenez Gender. 2012. *Work and Community after De-Industrialisation: A Psychological Approach to Affect*. Basingtoke: Palgrave Macmillan.
Weber, Wolfhard. 1980. Von der "Industriearchäologie" über das "Industrielle Erbe" zur "Industriekultur". Überlegungen zum Thema einer handlungsorientierten Technikhistorie, in U. Troitzsch and G. Wohlauf, Eds. *Technik-Geschichte*, Frankfurt: Suhrkamp, 420–447.
Wicke, Christian, Stefan Berger and Jana Golombek, Eds. 2017. special issue of *The Public Historian* Vol. 39 No. 4 (November, *Deindustrialization, Heritage and Representations of Identity*).
Winter, Tim. 2011. The Political Economies of Heritage, in H. Anheier and Y. Raj Isar, Eds. *Cultures and Globalization: Heritage, Memory and Identity*, London: Sage, 73–81.

1 Mining memories
Big Pit and industrial heritage in South Wales

Leighton S. James

Introduction

In 1935, Thomas Jones, the educationalist and founder of the journal *Welsh Outlook*, angered at the sense of hopelessness that infected South Wales during the economic depression, suggested satirically that the mining valleys should be evacuated and turned into an industrial museum.[1] Coal mining in South Wales survived the 'devil's decade', but a brief flowering of the industry in the immediate post-war period masked long term economic decline. The region was hit by waves of pit closures in the 1960s and again in the 1980s and 1990s. In January 2008, the oldest continuously worked deep coal mine and the last in South Wales, Tower Colliery, shut its gates. This marked the end of an industry that had dominated South Wales for almost two centuries.

Today, mining in the region is restricted to small-scale private drift mines that are but a pale shadow of the industry which at its height employed over 270,000 men. Yet, although the industry is effectively dead, it is not forgotten. Attempts to capture some of South Wales's industrial past through industrial heritage sites began in the 1970s with the establishment of the South Wales Miners' Museum, but the best known and larger sites are Big Pit at Blaenavon (Figure 1.1) and the Rhondda Heritage Park. The former forms part of the Blaenavon World Heritage site, which was inscribed in 2000. Other industrial heritage sites relating to the South Wales's coal mining past include Cefn Coed Colliery at Neath and the Waterfront Museum in Swansea. The open air Museum of Welsh Life at St. Fagans has also begun to incorporate more buildings relating to Wales's industrial past, such as the Oakdale Workmen's Hall. South Wales might not have been evacuated, but in some respects Thomas Jones's suggestion that the mining valleys be turned into an industrial museum has been realized.

The relationship between heritage, history and class identity has, since the 1980s, promoted significant debate between historians, cultural commentators and those involved in the heritage industry. For some commentators, such as Patrick Wright, heritage served as an essentially conservative political project that appealed to national identities as a cover for deindustrialization.[2] Similarly, Robert Hewison decried the heritage industry in Great Britain for foisting a nostalgic and superficial cultural economy on communities and for contributing to a 'climate

Figure 1.1 Wales Big Pit Blaneavon

of decline'. Hewison shared Wright's criticism, but he also addressed industrial heritage specifically. He criticized it as more often the result of economic weakness and questioned the accuracy of the past presented. In the context of South Wales, he pointed to the irony of the closure of the Lewis Merthyr pit and plans to offer on the same site "a total mining experience, [where] ex-miners will re-enact their redun".[3] In fact, fears that industrial archaeology would turn South Wales into "a nation of museum attendants minding the world's biggest mausoleum" had been voiced at the start of the 1980s.[4] J. Geraint Jenkins, historian and former curator of the Welsh Folk Museum, echoed these concerns by emphasizing the denatured situation of some preserved industrial buildings. The complexes they had once been part of had been bulldozed, leaving them standing incongruously on otherwise bare plots of land. Similarly, he questioned what visitors could learn from the sanitized nature of the Big Pit museum, writing,

> because they [the visitor] can walk comfortably upright along well-lit corridors the reality of coal mining can hardly be presented to them. . . . If the visitor relies on impressions of the coal industry gathered from a visit to Big Pit, then he or she will hardly understand why coal miners throughout history fought employer and government over the wretched conditions of work in the mines.[5]

Such critiques appear to afford little hope for heritage to maintain and transmit working-class identity in a post-industrial age. In the 1990s, however, Raphael

Samuel challenged the idea that heritage is essentially reactionary and offered a more positive vision of its role.[6] He regarded it as a popular rather than hierarchical, top-down process and argued that it was symptomatic of a breaking down of class divides. He praised industrial heritage for "enlarging the notion of historic monument" and recognizing that the process of deindustrialization in the 1960s and 1970s was as momentous as the Industrial Revolution.[7] Samuel's support for heritage was a reaction to the criticism it had received at the hands of Wright and Hewison in the 1980s, but he also regarded it as a way of forwarding a Socialist or anti-Thatcherite political agenda of community cohesion in the face of privatization and economic liberalism.

Laurajane Smith has charted a route between Hewison's pessimism and Samuel's optimism. While broadly welcoming the heritage movement, she has pointed to the potential problems in the creation of authorized heritage discourses (AHD) imposed by state agencies on industrial communities. She has highlighted the contested nature of heritage as different groups and actors negotiate the creation of heritage narratives. She points to the importance of individuals and communities exercising control in the heritage process, "because of the political and cultural power of 'heritage' to represent and validate a sense of place, memory and identity".[8]

This chapter argues that this contestation of heritage has been evident on several levels in Wales. First, there were the tensions between Welsh national identity and that of the South Wales coalfield. Early heritage initiatives in Wales were tied to expressions of Welsh national identity often rooted in the Welsh language. During much of the 20th century, however, this sat awkwardly with a more specific, regional working-class identity in a South Wales coalfield decisively shaped by the experience of industrialization and its attendant social and political changes. Early heritage produced an AHD that essentially excluded the industrialized, Anglicized and, by the inter-war years, Labour voting, South Wales coalfield in favor of an idealized rural, Liberal, Welsh-speaking past. Second, when industrial heritage did emerge in South Wales in the wake of the decline of the mining industry it was subject to the tensions identified by Smith between local communities' desires to conserve and commemorate and state agencies emphasis on economic revitalization and attempts to impose an AHD. Some heritage sites, such as the Rhondda Heritage Park, seemed to conform to Samuel's depiction of heritage as a bottom-up movement aimed at maintaining community cohesion, but were later co-opted by state agencies, which saw them as a means of economic regeneration.[9]

The chapter uses the example of Big Pit, South Wales's premier industrial heritage site, to challenge Samuel's idea of heritage as necessarily about community action, whilst at the same time demonstrating that attempts to impose an AHD are complicated by the role of the guides who are able to draw on their own experiences as working miners and of the decline of the industry. It will argue on the basis of tourist surveys, interviews with staff members at Big Pit and visitor questionnaires that there continues to be a complex relationship between representation of industrial South Wales and broader Welsh national identity. Although the two share commonalities, the primary sources point to continued tensions between the different visions of Wales outlined above. Finally, industrial heritage has an ambiguous relationship with working-class identity in a post-industrial setting, but it nevertheless plays a crucial role in transmitting a sense of South Wales's industrial history to a wider audience.[10]

The industrialization of South Wales

The coal industry decisively changed the character of the South Wales valleys and the adjoining coastal plain. Although coal mining in Wales dates back to the Roman period, the rapid expansion of industry began only in the late 18th century. Early coal production in the region initially served the iron and steel works, which themselves developed to serve demand created by Britain's wars with France in the eighteenth and early nineteenth centuries. Peace post-1815 witnessed an economic slump, but the industry was given a further boost by the expansion of the rail network and the transition from sail to steam locomotion in shipping. The latter was particularly important for the coal industry in South Wales. Although the western edge of the coalfield produced anthracite, which was largely destined for domestic production, much of the coal produced in the eastern and central valleys was particularly suited for the production of steam. Welsh 'steam' coal supplied the growing merchant navy and its coaling stations worldwide. By the end of the 19th century, it had also become the preferred supplier to the Royal Navy. Consequently, steam coal became a commodity in its own right and the development of sale coal for steam production in the last half of the 19th century saw coal mining surpass the early metal industries to achieve its hegemonic position in South Wales.

The expansion of the coal industry transformed the South Wales valley from a predominantly rural and agriculture region into one of the most important industrial centers in Britain. As a labor-intensive industry the coal companies required an influx of migrants to meet its demand for labor. Early waves of migrants were initially drawn from the surrounding Welsh counties, a process which Brinley Thomas has suggested initially strengthened the Welsh language and culture.[11] This immediately available pool of labor had been largely exhausted by the last quarter of the 19th century and thereafter the labor force, particularly in the eastern valleys, was drawn increasingly from the English counties bordering Wales. In the first decade of the 20th century, migration into South Wales was second only to that into the United States of America. Brinley Thomas's thesis has been challenged for underplaying the impact on industrialization on rural Welsh communities. Research has also suggested that linguistic shifts were complex.[12] Nevertheless, the growing complexity in the social composition of the population of the industrial Valleys and decline of the Welsh language were to have important repercussions for early heritage initiatives.

This rapid population growth resulted in parallel rapid urbanization of the valleys. The topography fostered the development of a distinctive pattern of urban settlement. Narrow ribbon-shaped streets with rows of terraced housing climbed the valley sides, whilst the pit and railway networks occupied the valley floor.[13] The Church of Wales failed to keep up with this rapid urbanization, and various Nonconformist denominations filled the religious and cultural vacuum. The less hierarchical structure of Nonconformity encouraged the active involvement of the population and the chapels became important social as well as religious spaces within the mining communities. The chapels, their choirs and their local *eisteddfodau* (cultural festivals composed of music and poetry recitals celebrating the Welsh language) formed a crucial part of the initial strengthening of Welsh identity in the early to mid-19th century. Nonconformity continued to play a significant role in the cultural and community life of the South Wales valleys well into the 20th centuries. However, as a sign of the increasing Anglicization of the eastern and central mining valleys, by the late 19th century and early 20th century many chapels had switched to the use of the English language. They, along with the pubs, miners' institutes and sporting clubs, provided a vibrant cultural space for the mining communities by the end of the 19th century.[14]

The political life of the 19th-century South Wales mining valleys was dominated by the Liberal Party, which appealed to a middle and growing working-class electorate on the basis of their shared Nonconformity and Welsh identity. By the later 19th century, however, the interests of miners and the middle-class professionals, industrialists and 'shopocracy' of small tradesmen that dominated the leadership of the Liberals increasingly diverged. The growth of the trade unions and more combative industrial relations led to increasingly vocal calls for working-class representation, a process accelerated by the establishment of the South Wales Miners' Federation (SWMF) in 1898. In the late 19th century, tensions within the Liberal party were addressed through the acceptance of working-class electoral candidates and the emergence of 'Lib-Labism', which sought to marry traditional Liberal concerns with trade unions' demands regarding wages and working conditions. Yet the Federation, with its federal structure of local miners' lodges, was deeply rooted in the local communities and contributed to the development of a political creed, Labourism, distinct from Liberalism or Lib-Labism. The fragile alliance of middle-class and working-class interests was undermined by a wave of industrial unrest from 1910. Meanwhile, the newly-formed Labour Party made increasing inroads in the mining valleys, particularly in local politics, a process facilitated by the affiliation of the SWMF to the party in 1906. Labour finally achieved its breakthrough at Parliamentary level after 1918, and in the inter-war period it supplanted the Liberals as the dominant political party of the South Wales coalfield. The region remains a Labour stronghold.[15]

The industry reached its peak in the early 20th century. Its preeminent position can be encapsulated in a few figures. By 1913 South Wales was the largest British coalfield in terms of production, producing 56.8 million tons in that year. The mining workforce reached its highest level in 1920 when 271,500 men were employed in the industry. Thereafter, however, the industry contracted in face of competition from cheaper energy sources, the growth of other industries that provided alternative sources of employment, and as the result of government policies. By 1981, there were just 37 deep collieries and 28,000 men employed in mining. In the aftermath of the 1984/85 miners' strike, these remaining mines were progressively closed.[16]

The economic and social impact on a region that had been so dependent on one industry was devastating. Between 1981 and 2004 some 27,200 jobs or 97 per cent of coal mining jobs were shed in South Wales. This represented 21 per cent of all male jobs in the area. Other industries, such has manufacturing, had expanded in South Wales after 1945, but they could not hope to replace the mass employment once provided by the pits. Only 19 per cent of jobs lost in coal mining had been replaced by employment in other sectors by 2004.[17] One of the staff at Big Pit, Huw, recalled the mining industry as a social service in that it provided work for those who struggled in other sectors. "Everybody had a purpose" and therefore a sense of worth.[18] The coalfield also suffers from higher than average indices of long-term health problems and high levels of out-of-work benefit claimants.[19] Industrial decline and the attendant fraying of the social fabric of the mining communities were evident before the 1980s, however. In 1964 the Conservative Government felt that the image of Wales itself was hindering economic diversification and dynamism. Russell Lewis, Conservative activist and future publicity officer for the party, wrote in a pamphlet titled *Wealth for Wales* that it was "time we Welshmen killed the myth of Wales as a land of slag heaps, populated by wild men in cloth caps and mufflers, unredeemed save by the enthusiasm for rugby football and song"[20]. Despite a variety of industrial policy initiatives aimed at revitalizing the economy of South Wales, ten years later the education director of the Mid Glamorgan County Council wrote bluntly to the Secretary of State for Wales, "The Valleys are dying".[21]

Heritage initiatives and visions of Wales

Although heritage took off as the industry declined, ideas for industrial heritage actually have a long pedigree in South Wales. The preservation of Wales's past had become an issue in the late 19th century and early 20th century and can be seen as part of the 'rebirth' of Welsh national identity. Rhiannon Mason has argued that it had its roots in attempts to carve out increased autonomy and representation for Wales against the background of economic prosperity based on heavy industry. This effort was encapsulated in a range of initiatives, including the establishment of national institutions, such as the National Library and the University of Wales. Plans for a national museum were mooted in the 1870s, but the National Museum of Wales (NMW) was finally established by Royal Charter in 1907. Its opening was delayed by the First World War until 1922. The importance of Wales's industrial history was recognized in its original charter and early plans included a model coal mining gallery. The initial collection, however, was comprised of patron donations and the holdings of the older Cardiff Museum and focused on natural history and the decorative arts. The archaeological collection, Welsh Bygones, neglected the more recent industrial past in favor of a focus on its agricultural past.[22]

The same was true of the Welsh Folk Museum which opened in 1948 and was later to become St Fagans National History Museum. Iowerth Peate, curator at the

National Museum, member of Plaid Cymru and one of the driving forces behind the museum, took his inspiration from folk museums in Scandinavia that focused on agricultural life. He envisaged the Folk Museum as representing "all the elements of Welsh life". His focus, however, was on rural life and artisanal production. In his 1948 pamphlet, *Folk Museums*, there was no reference to industrial Wales or the miner. Instead, rural craftsmanship was privileged and Peate hoped that the museum would play a role in "reinvigorating Welsh culture" by supporting artisanal production.[23] The craftsman, for Peate, was central to Welsh identity. He wrote in a guide to the Welsh Bygones collection that

> Anyone who knows the real Wales well can estimate the importance of these craftsmen to the life of their communities, and with the decline of the demand for their services comes the disintegration of small societies of folk which are of real value in a civilised state.[24]

He also emphasized the importance of the Welsh language, arguing that all the staff at the Folk Museum should be Welsh-speaking, "for without this key to our tradition, he cannot be competent to carry out his duties".[25]

This emphasis on the rural, Welsh-speaking past as the 'real' Wales had a long tradition. Prys Morgan has argued that since at least the 18th century those seeking to preserve and resurrect Welsh culture have looked to rural Wales as the true representation of Welsh identity.[26] The industrial Valleys, by contrast, were depicted by some inter-war Welsh writers, such as H.W.J. Edwards in *The Good Patch* and Rhys Davies in *My Wales*, as denatured and degraded. Both authors used distinctly sexual metaphors in their descriptions and depicted Glamorgan as "the whore of the family of Wales who sold herself to English industrialism".[27] This representation of Wales was deeply influenced by the image of the *gwerin*. The *gwerin* were depicted as a rural, thrifty, sober, learned, Dissenting and largely classless society with close relationship to the soil and bound by a common linguistic and religious culture.[28] There was little room for the more disputatious, heterogeneous and Anglicized mining communities with their often bitter industrial disputes. This *gwerin* imagery, however, was gradually supplanted by the idea of the Welsh working class after the First World War, a process represented politically by the rise of Labour and the eclipse of the Liberals as the dominant party of Wales.[29] Yet, the idea of the *gwerin* remained remarkably durable and influential on cultural institutions and actors, despite the industrialization of South Wales. Even the location of the NMW was disputed by some of the Welsh intelligentsia, on the basis that as a new city with a heterogeneous population based on the export of coal, it was the very antithesis of Welsh *gwerin* identity.[30]

This tension between facets of Welsh identity still has echoes today and was referenced by a staff member at Big Pit interviewed by the author. Huw commented that

> The Welshness of the valleys comes from the closeness of the communities. I feel as Welsh as anybody and proud, but I also think Welsh-speaking Wales

is a different country . . . that is more so in this part of the coalfield because it is closer to England.[31]

Similarly, Ceri Thompson highlighted the differences between industrial South Wales and the rest of the country, commenting, "The working class identity in Wales . . . was sort of very different from the rest to Wales".[32] He also pointed to St. Fagan's continued emphasis on the *gwerin*, although he suggested that particular representation of Wales had been, at least partially, supplanted by a (post) industrial vision.

> If you look at St. Fagans there's very much a Welsh identity. . . . It was basically looking at the *gwerin*, mid-Wales, north Wales, the farming areas. . . . Whereas today many people see Welsh identity as coal mines and coal tips, valley housing, what have you.[33]

It was not only the different visions of Wales and its people that influenced the development of industrial heritage. Mason has pointed out that in the 1940s, coal mining and heavy industry generally were "perceived to be still so modern and culturally dominant" that they did not required preservation.[34] Nationalization in 1947 and increased investment seemed to secure the future of the industry. There were also practical problems incorporating the large machinery associated with the industry in the existing museum buildings. Interest grew from the end of 1950s in tandem with the growth of industrial archaeology in Britain generally. Bella Dicks has argued that the eventual emergence of industrial heritage represented an elision of the *gwerin* image of Wales and the regional, industrial and Anglicized Wales.[35] Thus, the history of industrial South Wales, and the mining industry in particular, which had hitherto been largely excluded from heritage representations of Wales, has now been subsumed into images of the Welsh nation. As Peter Wakelin of CADW, the Welsh heritage body, commented to the *Times* in 1999, "The winding-frame was as much an icon of Wales as the leek, the daffodil and the rugby ball".[36]

A Department of Industry was eventually established in 1959 and a model of a coal mine opened in the National Museum. But it was in the 1970s, within the context of the decline of the industry, that the first industry heritage initiatives were undertaken. In 1974, a Welsh Industrial and Maritime Museum (WIMM) was established in Cardiff Docks. The emphasis on large machinery at the WIMM, however, was criticized for falling prey to "shiny machine syndrome" and for depicting a history of "work without workers".[37] Visitor numbers were also relatively low, numbering only 39,000 in 1990 compared to 100,000 at the adjacent hands-on science museum, Techniquest.[38] Nevertheless, the closure of the museum in 1998 when the site was sold to the Cardiff Bay Development Corporation provoked criticism of the National Museum, particularly as no alternative site for the artefacts had been identified. The threatened loss of the collection promoted a press campaign to save the institution. In an example of the merging of the specific identity of industrialized South Wales and wider representations of

Wales, the *South Wales Echo* demanded that the NMW "Preserve our Past!".[39] The Welsh Affairs Committee also asked the directors of the NMW pointed questions about a lack of investment in industrial heritage and whether they had "lost credibility as guardians of Wales' industrial and maritime past".[40]

Earlier heritage initiatives had explicitly been linked to Welsh identity, but new economic imperatives also contributed to the emergence of industrial heritage. As the Welsh Tourist Board's report, *Realising the Tourism Potential of the South Wales Valleys*, made clear, heritage was now regarded as a potential economic replacement for industry. Since the 1980s, a series of strategies for tourism have been published by the Welsh Tourist Board and later by the Welsh Government.[41] These initiatives emerged both from the NMW and from local communities. For example, the first mining museum in Wales, the South Wales Miners Museum at Cynonville, was opened by volunteers in 1976 and originally consisted of a miner's cottage and displays of objects and photographs. Other smaller heritage sites also emerged as the industry declined, such as Cefn Coed Colliery Museum at Crynant, Neath. The hopes for economic recovery pinned on these sites have not, it seems, been met as the numbers of visitors remains low. Cefn Coed received 18,671 visitors in 1983, but this had fallen to 12,000 by 1993, whilst the South Wales Miners' Museum received 34,338 and 33,827 in the same years.[42] The latter site was subsequently expanded, but a 2010 report on regeneration in the Afan Valley noted that its finances were fragile despite success in obtaining grants. Its location has also counted against it, a resident stating, "you're not going to come out of your way to come and visit it, that's the trouble".[43] Recent research by Andrew Jones and Kathryn Flynn has suggested that such smaller industrial heritage sites provided fewer economic and community benefits. They require fewer staff, create fewer jobs and have found it difficult to access funding. They are, claim Jones and Flynn, therefore regarded with a degree of cynicism and apathy by local communities.[44]

Big Pit and the Welsh working-class identity

These smaller attractions were ultimately overshadowed by Big Pit at Blaenavon, which provides an example of the institutionally driven conservation activity. The NMW and the Welsh Tourist Board (WTB) approached the National Coal Board (NCB) in the early 1970s with proposals to preserve a pit. At the end of the decade, the NCB identified Big Pit as a potential site because it was not too deep and enjoyed natural ventilation and drainage, thereby reducing maintenance costs. Big Pit closed in 1980 and became a Charitable Trust. It was run initially by Gwent County Council and Torfaen District Council, but development was slow as the local authorities were unable to meet the costs of supporting Big Pit due to the financial constraints caused by the decline of the industry.[45] Big Pit was ultimately taken over by the NMW and its wider regional regeneration remit seemed to be partially realized through the creation of the Blaenavon World Heritage site in 2000, which encompasses not only Big Pit, but the remains of the Blaenavon Ironworks, the Workmen's Hall and the Heritage Railway.[46] Big Pit also won the Gulbenkian Prize for Museum of the Year in 2005.

Big Pit was held up in the media as an example of how to conduct industrial heritage in other former heavy industrial areas in Britain.[47] It was initially hoped that the site would become self-sustaining as a going concern by attracting some 250,000 visitors a year.[48] Visitor numbers have fallen far short of this optimistic level, although these numbers are not far short of the expectations of the original Joint Steering Group of 150,000 per annum.[49] In 2014, Big Pit received 149,087 visitors, while in 2015 it received 147,085, a decline of 1 per cent.[50] Visitor numbers declined again between April 2015 and March 2016 to 144,813, a fall of 7.7 per cent from 2014.[51] Moreover, despite elision of the *gwerin* and industrial image of Wales identified by Dicks in the heritage movement, research conducted by the WTB into tourism trends between 2006 and 2016 points to visitors' greater interest in Wales's medieval than its industrial past. Some 20 per cent of day visitors to Welsh attractions interviewed by the WTB gave visiting a castle or similar historic attraction as the specific reason for their visit. This compares with only 8 per cent who gave visiting an industrial heritage attraction as the purpose of their visit. A higher percentage of overseas visitors (17 per cent) gave visiting an industrial heritage attraction as a specific reason for visiting Wales, but some 61 per cent cited castles as the main attraction.[52] The visitor figures for both industrial heritage sites and castles are in turn dwarfed by visitor numbers to Folly Farm, a theme park and zoo in West Wales, which welcomed 500,000 tourists in 2013.[53] Visitor numbers have increased markedly since free admission to national museums was introduced by the Labour Government in 2001. Prior to that visitor numbers to Big Pit were more modest. Between 1983 and 1998 they peaked in 1992 at 120,387, just 48 per cent of the planned operating capacity.[54] Ironically, the fall in visitor numbers was linked to the decline in the coal industry, while its privatization in the 1990s meant that it could no longer look to the National Coal Board (NCB) for technical support.[55]

The nature of the attraction has also evolved over time. Initially, there was little presentation or interpretation of the history of the working-class mining communities of South Wales. Instead, the emphasis was on the underground experience. The 'shiny machinery' fetish was also evident. Ceri Thompson recalled that when he was first appointed curator at Big Pit that "there was a feeling I should only be collecting technical items" and he had to challenge actively the belief that "mining in Wales can only be represented by large machinery and small hand tools". The site subsequently broadened to encompass representations of the social, political and cultural life of the mining communities.[56]

The difficulties faced by Big Pit in the 1990s were compounded by competition from the opening of the Rhondda Heritage Park in 1990 on the site of the former Lewis Merthyr colliery. The Park represents an example of a heritage site that had its origins in local community activism, but which was later taken over by institutional agents. Bella Dicks has examined the history of the Heritage Park and shown how this community initiative was taken over by the Welsh Tourist Board and Welsh Development Agency. These bodies drafted in outside consultants to develop the exhibitions and tensions developed over the Park as a site for "local popular representation (whether as memorials for place-identity or spaces for local amenities) and entrepreneurial regeneration (the exhibition of community for the tourist gaze)". The result was a tourist attraction with a simulated underground experience, rather than a museum.[57] One interviewee hinted at similar tensions at Big Pit, commenting that it is, "all about numbers, and somehow it can be too much about numbers, not the experience".[58] Moreover, as with the other industrial heritage sites, the economic hopes for the RHP have not been realized. Visitor numbers peaked in 1996/7 at 75,689, but had fallen to 36,911 by 2014/5.[59]

Big Pit nevertheless appears to have had more of an economic impact on local communities than smaller sites.[60] One interviewee, however, questioned whether the local community regarded the proximity of the museum as an economic benefit.[61] "The town probably doesn't think Big Pit is a big asset. They think we should promote Blaenavon a bit more". He also expressed the view that tourism represented the 'last gasp saloon' and asked what would replace tourism if that failed.[62] Big Pit currently employs 50 full time and part time staff, the majority of them with some experience of working underground.[63] However, as with the South Wales Miners' Museum, transport links between the major population centers on the coastal plain to Big Pit remain problematic. In light of this, Huw commented that "the fact that we get 150,000 people to come to the top end of Blaenavon is an achievement in itself".[64]

Finally, industrial heritage also poses some specific challenges. While Big Pit boasts a unique underground experience, the maintenance of the shaft, tunnels and machinery requires specialist knowledge and skills. The maintenance of the machinery is particularly demanding. The ropes that support the cage, for example, require replacement every 10 years in a demanding and highly skilled operation. To date, the necessary skills have been provided by the practice of recruiting ex-miners, who have the technical skills to maintain the exhibit. Apprenticeships offer a way of maintaining these skills, but are limited in number. Historic machinery conservators also have responsibility for equipment at a variety of industrial sites. The preservation of the fabric of the sites as the ex-miners retire will therefore pose a significant challenge. As Huw pointed out, "if we lose the underground part, the museum loses a heck of a lot".[65]

The eventual retirement of guides who have a lived experience of the mining industry also raises questions regarding the changing nature of the visitor experience, issues of authenticity and the role of the museum in maintaining working-class identity. Research on whether industrial heritage sites can maintain working-class identity following de-industrialization is somewhat mixed. As noted above, Dicks has pointed to the difficult relationship between the desire to commemorate, on the one hand, and to commodify the industrial past at the RHP, on the other. She has also pointed to the role of ex-miners as tour guides at RHP and the ambiguous nature of their performance. The emphasis of the exhibitions is on the resilience and perseverance of communities that do not and cannot exist in the same form. "Ultimately, the individual performer is alone on stage: able to evoke only echoes of collective power".[66]

Early surveys of visitors to Big Pit, moreover, suggested that the attraction mainly appealed to those from non-manual backgrounds. Research conducted by the Welsh Tourist Board in 1984 found that three out of ten visitors came from a professional or managerial background. A further third came from non-manual households. The same survey showed that a quarter of visitors gave education as the reason for their visit and only one in seven gave an interest in industrial archaeology as their rationale. Some three quarters gave the reason for their visit as "to see how coal is mined".[67] Research into the backgrounds of visitors to the Rhondda Heritage Park in 1993 suggested that some 70 per cent of the visitors came from non-working class backgrounds. However, a survey conducted by Bella Dicks just two years later at the same attraction suggested that just over half (51 per cent) of visitors came from manual occupations.[68]

In order to assess visitors' reception of Big Pit the author conducted a survey of visitors by questionnaire in September 2016. Thirty-six visitors to Big Pit completed the questionnaire over a week in September 2016. Visitors were asked for their thoughts on Big Pit and the impression the attraction gave of the South Wales's industrial history. They were also asked whether exhibits led them to reflect on their own experiences or family history and whether industrial heritage sites had a role in maintaining a sense of working-class identity. Respondents were asked their level of educational attainment and their employment status in order to gauge their social background. The survey suggests that the profile of the visitors is slightly tilted towards those with higher educational attainment. Of the 36 visitors, almost half (15) held a university degree or a postgraduate qualification. By contrast, just four had vocational training only, while seven held GCSEs or equivalent. The survey also highlighted the older age profile of the visitors. Just over 53 per cent were retired compared to 28 per cent in full time employment. Finally, the sample contained few local visitors. Just two respondents came from Wales, compared with 20 from England. Thus, over 55 per cent came from England. Big Pit also attracts many overseas visitors. Eight visitors interviewed came from overseas, predominantly North America, but also from as far afield as Australia and the Philippines.[69]

The above survey, therefore, portrays the average visitor to Big Pit as university educated, English and retired. This snapshot raises questions about the extent to which Big Pit contributes to sustaining a Welsh working-class identity. The survey, however, does suffer from several limitations. First, its sample size is small. Second, the results are likely also colored by the timing of the survey, in that it occurred during the school term in early autumn. Surveys conducted at different times could well produce different results. Some 60 per cent of school trips to the attraction during the school year come from France, for example.[70] Moreover, although the visitors were predominantly not Welsh, around 17 respondents agreed that Big Pit nevertheless led them to reflect on their own experiences or their family history. Many of these respondents referred to family members who had worked as miners or in other industries or industrial regions.[71]

Finally, when the visitors surveyed were asked directly whether Big Pit and other industrial heritage sites help maintain a sense of working-class identity, all but two of 36 replied positively. Although most interviewees responded with a simple yes, some provided more expansive answers. When asked about whether

Big Pit could maintain working-class identity, one female visitor commented, "absolutely. It is possibly one of the few ways to give the public any understanding of working-class life". Another woman emphasized the importance of the museum for transmitting knowledge and a sense of working-class history and identity to younger generations "Definitely – our children need to know this".[72] Another visitor highlighted the importance of heritage to children, commenting, "with 6 years olds in mind" that the site gave the sense of "a different time". Staff have also pointed to the cultural and educational importance of Big Pit, particularly for children, through schemes involving those from deprived areas and difficult backgrounds. Huw commented, "Because of the way the guides have become they can collar (i.e. engage) 90 per cent of them [kids]".[73]

This sense of a different time referred not only to the underground tour, but also to the surface building, particularly the pit head itself. The pithead gears and the tips that characterized the South Wales coalfield have largely disappeared and have been replaced by green hillsides. This has been a positive phenomenon. The Aberfan disaster of 1966 in which a colliery spoil tip collapsed and engulfed a school, leading to the deaths of 116 children and 28 adults, revealed the potential dangers in that industrial landscape. But there are implications for the cultural memory of the coalfield as the physical indicators of the industry disappear. One of the interviewees, Huw, commented on the changes in the landscape since the end of the industry and highlighted the importance of Big Pit in maintaining the iconic image of the mine in that physical landscape. Asked about the importance of Big Pit he responded,

> Massive, massive, I think in an area like this there is not a lot evidence of mining in south Wales. In a few years time, people won't know what a head gear looks like. . . . You rarely see a coal tip. It's a totally different place.[74]

The visitors unanimously praised the attraction, with several describing it as "thought provoking and eye opening", "informative" and "enlightening". The guides form a crucial part of the experience. Currently, they draw heavily on their own experiences to inform their tours of the underground workings. This is a dynamic process in which the guides judge the attitudes of the tour group and tailor their accordingly. Paul described the process thus,

> You are assessing people the minute your party comes to you. . . . You find out what kind of tour they want by asking them questions as you take the contraband from them. . . . You pitch your talk to whatever group you've got. . . . A lot of the tour is about the men and their stories.[75]

Several researchers had pointed to the importance of this tour guide 'banter' for transmitting a sense of authenticity.[76] The staff interviewed by the author also pointed to the central role of 'banter'. Paul commented, "You feel it straight away. It is exactly the same feeling as a pit. The same feeling, the same banter. That comes over to the visitor, except the bad language".[77] Bethany Coupland, however, has pointed to the complexities of the relationship between the living memory embodied in the tour guide talks and heritage narratives. She argues that the autobiographical memories of the ex-miners emphasized far more the loss of community that accompanied deindustrialization than the "romanticised discourse encountered in the language associated with heritagisation".[78]

Several of the heritage initiatives were also envisioned as changing the perception of the Valleys. The authors of *Realising the Tourism Potential of the South Wales Valleys* argued that tourism offered the opportunity to change the image of the region and that "past suffering has led to problems of self-image, of lack of pride, and even lack of respect for people in the Valleys".[79] Two of the interviewees, Huw and Ceri, articulated the same sense of decline identified by Coupland. Although identification with concepts of Welsh identity and to South Wales as a region appears to remain strong, both interviewees suggested that the traditional working-class culture strongly associated with mining and the Labour Party that characterized the mining valleys is on the wane. Huw felt that there was a lack of respect in the de-industrialized communities of South Wales and that 'working-class ethics' had collapsed in the deprived valleys, whilst Ceri pointed to the support the UK Independence Party has recently received in South Wales and wondered whether the people were "becoming more individualistic than in the past".[80]

Yet, vestiges of the militancy and workers' solidarity so often associated with the South Wales miners are still evident. In March 2016 museum staff went on strike in protest against cuts in extra pay for weekend work. Ceri commented "It was as though they [the Big Pit staff] were re-enacting 1984/85 and I think the rest of the union within the museums saw these as the storm troopers because they knew what to do . . . so that thing is still alive here".[81]

The question of how the ex-miner guides will be replaced is, therefore, particularly problematic and raises questions relating to authenticity and the transmission of a regional, working-class identity. All the interviewees pointed to the importance of succession planning and speculated on the consequences of employing guides without experience of mining as a living industry. Ceri pointed out that "guiding had changed flavour anyway" because older guides with experience of different working practices have retired. However, he also stated

> at the moment what's a nice thing is if someone asks a question they can answer it from their own experience. . . . Otherwise you will just have a guide who will say "they did this" and "they did that", rather than, you know, we did this or we did that.[82]

It is possible to employ private contractors to cover the maintenance needs of the museum, but all interviewees stated a preference for more apprenticeships to allow a younger generation of guides to be trained in mining techniques. Not only would this be economically advantageous to local communities, but would preserve a link to the Valley's industrial past. As Huw commented, "I feel particularly in the mines context, although they may not have direct experience of mining there will be family contexts . . . that's the type of people we should be recruiting".[83]

Funding, however, remains the main barrier to the employment of a large number of apprentices and recent budget cuts make that an unlikely prospect in the near future. Ceri argued that "it is not the visitor flow but the amount of money to pay staff".[84] One possible solution is the return to paid entry. The Welsh First Minister, Carwyn Jones, has committed the Welsh Government to maintaining free entry, however.[85] The staff at Big Pit also expressed concern at how a return to paid entry might affect not only visitor numbers, but also their social background. Huw reflected this concern when he stated, "there is something here worth paying for, but then you start influencing the social class of the visitors".[86] The already ambiguous role Big Pit has in maintaining Welsh working-class identity would be weakened if the visitors became increasingly drawn from middle-class backgrounds, whilst the residents of deprived local communities were unable to access the heritage site.

Conclusion

The desire to preserve some of South Wales's industrial past has a long history. That history has, however, been dogged by a tension between the long-standing *gwerin* image as the real Wales and the different portrait of Wales offered by the industrialized Valleys. Early proponents of heritage, such as Iowerth Peate, looked to preserve the agricultural and artisanal past of Wales and neglected its industrial history. Although attitudes began to change in the post-war period, traces of this bifurcated image of Wales are still evident today. It was only from the 1970s that industrial heritage sites proliferated in South Wales from a mixture of cultural, political and economic reasons. Although industrial heritage was subjected to a range of criticism in the 1980s, much of it seems unwarranted. In particular, the early criticisms of Big Pit for being inauthentic are unjustified. By their very, nature industrial heritage sites cannot be authentic as they are no longer working industrial concerns. Health and safety concerns usually preclude visiting working mines whose raison d'être is economic production not the maintenance of cultural memory. One may as well criticize medieval castles for no longer fulfilling a military function.

On the other hand, some of the hopes attached to industrial heritage have not been realized. The preservation of the industrial past was only one justification for the development of industrial heritage. Sites like Big Pit were also meant to fulfil a compensatory role for the dwindling coal mining industry by providing jobs opportunities and revitalizing the local economy. Big Pit has continued to draw large numbers of visitors, but the expectations of industrial heritage as an engine of job creation have, in the main, not been met. Ironically, early industrial heritage was linked to the fortunes of the mining industry generally. All the sites referred to here appear to have suffered a decline in visitor numbers following the decline of the industry in the late 1980s, with numbers climbing following governmental support and the introduction of free entry.

This necessity for government funding appears to challenge Samuel's interpretation of industrial heritage as community driven and anti-statist. Indeed, it is possible to see the history of industrial heritage in south Wales as an insurgency that was ultimately co-opted and neutralized by state agencies by being included in an enlarged AHD. Yet, the two agendas of industrial heritage, of preserving the past and economic regeneration, have not always been easy bedfellows. The two trends are encapsulated in the figure of the ex-miner guide, an individual with a lived experience of the industry, who now makes his living explaining the history of that industry to others. They form a crucial part of claims to authenticity in Big Pit and elsewhere. This research largely corroborates the studies of Dicks and Coupland, which have highlighted the complex relationship between commodification of the working-class experience and memories of the guides. The emphasis on unity, solidarity and resilience in the AHD is often undermined by oral histories that stress decline and the loss of community. Finally, the interviews with the Big Pit staff suggest that the elision of the *gwerin* image of Wales and industrial South Wales is not as complete as Dicks has suggested. Although there is greater overlap than was evident in the immediate post-war period, there still remains a sense that Big Pit represents a different vision of Wales.

The survey of visitors also highlights the ambiguous role Big Pit plays in maintaining a regional, working-class identity in a post-industrial age. Many of the visitors had older family members who had worked in coal mining or another heavy industry, but few were working class, whilst most were English or from overseas rather than Welsh. But class identity is a malleable concept. High educational attainment or a white-collar occupation does not preclude identification with the working class or with its history. Both the visitors and the staff interviewed felt strongly that industrial heritage, and Big Pit in particular, does have a role in supporting a working-class identity that remains intimately bound with the representation of the South Wales coalfield as a region.

Succession planning, however, poses difficult challenges. The replacement of guides who are ex-miners with 'green' labor raises two issues. The first concerns the preservation of the necessary technical skill to maintain the site itself. The second revolves around the transmission of working-class history and identity to the visitors. To what extent will a new generation of guides without experience of mining as a living industry be able to transmit a sense of past, to validate a sense of 'place, memory and identity'? Much depends on how this transition is handled and whether there is the political will to support it. Huw summed up the mixture of hope and anxiety for the future of Big Pit by asking "is it our right to leave it fail".

Notes

1 Thomas Jones's essay, What's wrong with South Wales, was printed in Thomas Jones, *Leeks and Daffodils* (Newtown: Welsh Outlook Press, 1942), 111.
2 Patrick Wright, *On Living in an Old Country: The Nationalist Past in Contemporary Britain*, 2nd ed. (Oxford: OUP, 2009).
3 Robert Hewison, *The Heritage Industry: Britain in a Climate of Decline* (London: Methuen, 1987), 97.

4 Hywel Francis cited in Robert Merrill, Cefn Coed Coal and Steam Centre: The Interpretation of a Mining Community, *Interpretation* 17 (1981), 13.
5 John Geraint Jenkins, *Getting Yesterday Right: Interpreting the Heritage of Wales* (Cardiff: University of Wales Press, 1992), 83.
6 Raphael Samuel, *Theatres of Memory: Past and Present in Contemporary Culture*, 2nd ed. (London: Verso, 2012).
7 Raphael Samuel, *Theatres of Memory: Past and Present in Contemporary Culture*, Volume 2 (London: Version, 1994), 176.
8 Laurajane Smith, *Uses of Heritage* (London: Routledge, 2006), 297.
9 See Bella Dicks, *Heritage, Place and Community* (Cardiff: Cardiff University Press, 2000).
10 The author interviewed Ceri Thompson, the curator at Big Pit and two members of staff, referred to here as Paul and Huw. Thirty-six visitors were surveyed via a questionnaire. The author would like to thank Ceri Thompson, Katherine Jenkins and Big Pit for their co-operation during the research for this chapter. I would also like to thank Dr. Christian Wicke and Dr. Richard Marsden for reading earlier drafts of the chapter.
11 Brinley Thomas, The Migration of Labour into the Glamorganshire Coalfield, 1861–1911, in Walter Edward Minchinton (ed.), *Industrial South Wales, 1750–1914: Essays in Welsh Economic History* (London: Frank Cass, 1969), 37–56.
12 For an overview, see Colin H. Williams, The Anglicisation of Wales, in Nikolas Coupland (ed.), *English in Wales: Diversity, Conflict and Change* (Clevedon: Philadelphia, 1990), 19–47 and W. T. R. Pryce, Language Zones, Demographic Changes, and the Welsh Culture Area 1800–1911, in Geraint H. Jenkins (ed.), *The Welsh Language and Its Social Domains* (Cardiff: University of Wales Press, 2000), 81–100.
13 See Philip N. Jones, *Colliery Settlement in the South Wales Coalfield, 1850–19126* (Hull: University of Hull, 1969) and Malcolm J. Fisk, *Housing in the Rhondda, 1800–1940* (Cardiff: Merton Priory Press Ltd., 1996), 30–47.
14 That community is evoked in Hywel Francis and Dai Smith, *The Fed: A History of the South Wales Miners in the Twentieth Century* (Cardiff: Cardiff University Press, 1998).
15 This process is described in Chris Williams, *Democratic Rhondda: Politics and Society, 1885–1951* (Cardiff: Cardiff University Press, 1996).
16 For the post-war history of the mining industry, see Ben Curtis, *The South Wales Miners, 1964–1985* (Cardiff: Cardiff University Press, 2013).
17 Christian Beatty, Stephen Fothergill and Ryan Powell, Twenty Years on: Has the Economy of the UK Coalfields Recovered?, *Environment and Planning A* 39 (2007): 1660 and 1663.
18 Huw (Big Pit staff member), interview by Leighton S. James, 1 September 2016.
19 Some 9.8 per cent of the South Wales population are deemed in bad or very bad health in the 2011 census compared with 5.6 per cent across Great Britain, while in 2013 17 per cent of the working age population claim benefits compared to 10.9 per cent nationally. Cited in Mike Foden, Steve Fothergill and Tony Gore (eds.), *The State of the Coalfields: Economic and Social Conditions in the Former Mining Communities of England, Scotland and Wales* (Sheffield: Centre for Regional Economic and Social Research Sheffield Hallam University, 2014), 16 and 22.
20 Russell Lewis, *Wealth for Wales* (London: Conservative Political Centre, 1964).
21 Martin Johnes, *Wales since 1939* (Manchester: MUP, 2013), 72 and 127.
22 Rhiannon Mason, *Museums, Nations, Identities: Wales and its National Museums* (Cardiff: University of Wales Press, 2007), 109–146.
23 Iowerth Peate, *Folk Museums* (Cardiff: University of Wales Press, 1948), 57 and 55.
24 Iowerth Peate, *Guide to the Collection of Welsh Bygones: A Descriptive Account of Old Fashioned Life in Wales* (Cardiff: National Museum of Wales and University of Wales Press, 1929), 1.
25 Peate, *Guide*, 59.
26 Prys Morgan, From a Date to a View: The Hunt for the Welsh Past in the Romantic Period, in Eric Hobsbawm and Terence Ranger (eds), *The Invention of Tradition* (Cambridge: CUP, 1983), 43–100.

27 Derrick Price, Gazing at the Valleys: Representation and the Cultural Construction of South Wales (PhD diss., University of Birmingham, 1992), 99. See H. W. J. Edwards, *The Good Patch* (London: National Book Association, 1938), 91 and Rhys Davies, *My Wales* (New York: Funk & Wagnalls Co., 1938), 14.
28 Prys Morgan, The Gwerin of Wales: Myth and Reality, in Ian Hume and W. T. R. Pryce (eds.), *The Welsh and Their Country* (Llandysul: Gomer Press, 1986), 134–152.
29 Gwyn Williams, *When Was Wales?* (London: Penguin, 1985), 137–140.
30 Alexandra Ward, Archaeology, Heritage and Identity: The Creation and Development of a National Museum in Wales (Cardiff: PhD diss., University of Cardiff, 2008), 101.
31 Huw, interviewed by Leighton S. James, 1 September 2016.
32 Ceri Thompson (Curator), interview by Leighton S. James, 1 September 2016.
33 Thompson, interview.
34 Mason, *Museums, Nations, Identities*, 162.
35 Bella Dicks, *Heritage, Place and Community* (Cardiff: Cardiff University Press, 2000), 85–102.
36 *The Times*, 8 June 1999.
37 Kath Davis. Cleaning Up the Coal Face and Doing Out the Kitchen: The Interpretation of Work and Workers in Wales, in Gaynor Kavanagh (ed.), *Making Histories in Museums* (London: Leicester University Press, 1996), 105.
38 Tim Caulton, *Hands-On Exhibitions: Managing Interactive Museums and Science Centres* (London: Taylor and Francis, 2006), 6.
39 *South Wales Echo*, 17 June 1998.
40 HMSO, Welsh Affairs Committee, House of Commons, *Session 1998–99 1st Report. 16 February: The Closure of the Welsh Industrial and Maritime Museum* (London: The Stationery Office, 1999) www.publications.parliament.uk/pa/cm199899/cmselect/cmwelaf/258/8102610.htm.
41 Andrew L. Jones and Kathryn Flynn, Flogging a Dead Horse or Creating Cultural Capacity: The Development and Impact of Mines as Alternative Tourist Destinations: A Case Study of South Wales, in Michael V. Conlin and Lee Jolliffe (eds.), *Mining Heritage and Tourism: A Global Synthesis* (London: Routledge, 2011), Kindle edition.
42 J. Arwel Edwards and Joan Carles Lourdes, Mines and Quarries: Industrial Heritage Tourism, *Annals of Tourism Research* 23:2 (1996), 349.
43 Cited in Victoria Winkler, *Forty Years of Regeneration in the Upper Afan Valley* (Ebbw Vale: Bevan Foundation, 2010), 18.
44 Jones and Flynn, Flogging a Dead Horse.
45 For a brief overview of the history of Big Pit, see Stephen Wanhill, Mines – A Tourist Attraction: Coal Mining in Industrial South Wales, *Journal of Travel Research* 39 (2000), 60–69.
46 See www.visitblaenavon.co.uk
47 *The Times*, 8 June 1999.
48 *The Times*, 17 November 1980.
49 Wanhill, Mines – A Tourist Attraction, 62.
50 *Wales Visitor Attractions Survey* (2015), www.gov.wales/docs/caecd/research/2016/160721-visitor-attractions-survey-2015-en.pdf.
51 https://museum.wales/visitor_figures/april2015-march2016/
52 Krishan Karol, *Tourist Attractions: Current Trends, 2006–2013* (2013), www.gov.wales/docs/caecd/research/2014/140225-visits-tourist-attractions-trands-2013.
53 *Wales Visitor Attraction Survey 2015*.
54 Wanhill, Mines – A Tourist Attraction.
55 Ceri Thompson, interview. See Bethan Coupland, Heritage and Memory: Oral History and Mining Heritage in Wales and Cornwall (Exeter PhD diss., University of Exeter 2012), 120.
56 Ceri Thompson, interview.

57 Bella Dicks, *Heritage, Place and Community*, 246. See also Bella Dicks, Heritage, Governance and Marketisation: A Case-Study from Wales, *Museum and Society* 1 (2003), 30–44.
58 Paul interview by Leighton S. James, 1 September 2016.
59 *Rhondda Heritage Park – Improving the Visitor Experience*. Rhondda Cynon Taff Country Borough Council Cabinet, 8 September 2016, www.rctcbe.gov.uk.EN/Council/CouncillorsCommitteesandMeetings/Meetings/Cabinet/2016/09/08/Reports/Agendaitem6RhonddaHeritageParkImprovingtheVisitorsExperience.pdf
60 In 2009 it was estimated that the overall economic impact of the museum was £4.93 million in terms of visitor spend and that it supported 140 full time jobs. See www.cadw.gov.wales/docs/cadw/publications/ValuingWelshHistoricEnvironment_EN.pdf [Accessed: 15 March 2017].
61 Jones and Flynn, Flogging a Dead Horse.
62 Huw, interview.
63 Thompson, interview.
64 Huw, interview.
65 Ibid.
66 Bella Dicks, Performing the Hidden Injuries of Class in Coal-Mining Heritage, *Sociology* 42 (2008), 450.
67 Welsh Tourist Board, *Survey of Visitors to Big Pit Mining Museum, Blaenafon* (Cardiff: Welsh Tourist Board, 1984).
68 See Richard Prentice, Stephen Witt and Claire Hamer, The Experience of Industrial Heritage: The Case of Black Gold, *Built Environment* 19:2 (1993), 137–146 and Dicks, *Heritage*, 206–207.
69 Survey of Visitors to Big Pit, September 2016.
70 Thompson, interview.
71 Survey of Visitors to Big Pit, September 2016.
72 Ibid.
73 Huw, interview.
74 Ibid.
75 Paul, interview.
76 Nikolas Coupland, Peter Garrett and Hywel Bishop, Wales Underground: Discursive Frames and Authenticities in Welsh Mining Heritage, in Adam Jaworski and Annette Pritchard (eds.), *Discourse, Communication and Tourism* (Clevedon: Channel View, 2005), Kindle edition. See also Coupland, 'Heritage and Memory', 153–159.
77 Paul, interview.
78 Coupland, Heritage and Memory, 178–179.
79 *Realising the Tourism Potential of the South Wales Valleys*, 9.
80 Thompson, interview. In the 2015 General Election UKIP won 14 per cent of the vote in Wales.
81 Ibid.
82 Thompson, interview.
83 Huw, interview.
84 Thompson, interview.
85 *South Wales Argus*, 17 March 2015.
86 Huw, interview.

2 Looking back

Representations of the industrial past in Asturias

Rubén Vega García

Located on the north coast of Spain and currently populated by just over one million inhabitants, Asturias has been one of the focuses of Spanish industrialization, after Catalonia and the Basque Country. Throughout the 20th century, Asturias has been a mining and industrial region. It is on this foundation that its economic prosperity and social structures, as well as the power of its labor movement were built. Coal, steel and other industries held sway over most of the employment and acted as locomotives of the regional economy. Moreover, miners' and metal-workers' significance for the regional identity was even greater given their social, political and cultural influence.

The decline of the Asturian industries has been a long-term process, but the hardest moments of dismantlement have taken place since the mid-1980s. In 1980, when industrial decline was already apparent but the traditional sectors had not yet been restructured, there were 32.030 Asturian miners and 42.177 metalworkers, representing 20 per cent of the total labor market of 370.061 people.[1]

Job losses and adjustments of industries caused intense social conflicts. At the same time, paradoxically, the weakening of the mentioned workers' position on the labor market was accompanied by a strengthening of their union's power, to which fell the management of the economic decline. To a significant extent, young people's educational opportunities and living standards were little affected by these developments. This is due largely to the negotiations and struggles carried out on the part of their parents (or even grandparents), over wages, pensions and public funds for economic recovery and social protection.

The labor and industrial past, which casts a long shadow over present generations, acts as a 'territory' of memory, a source of identity and an origin of collective traumas.[2] The cultural transformations have been fundamental and dramatic, but many traces of the past remain – and retain relevance for both generations, the one who lived it and the one who grew up in a different context but lives with the memory of it.

The fact that identities and references to industrial work and working culture remain testifies to the retained importance of these industries for social structures, even after these industries themselves have disappeared. The importance of these industries can therefore be verified by examining the ways in which they have been preserved in collective memory. Asturias has a long history and a strong identity. Some myths about its indomitable nature rests on historic episodes like the resistance against the Roman, Muslim and French conquerors. 20th-century workers' struggles, and particularly the 1934 revolutionary uprising, which have added to this self-perception in the consciousness of Asturian people and also in the external image they project of themselves to others.[3]

In the realm of cultural expression, the memory of the industry and work is kept alive. In collective imagination, it configures a rich, intangible heritage that acts as a source of inspiration for artistic creation in many different ways. For many of these artists, who are rooted in a social environment marked by the working culture, the experience of industrial decline becomes an explanatory key to their own artworks.

Growing up in the mining area or in a working-class neighborhood often becomes the reason they offer for the issues treated in their pieces of art and also their ideological positions as citizens. These two issues are in fact often closely linked. Frequently, this personal origin in the industrial social context is present in writers' texts, or the lyrics of songs. In this regard, workers' struggles play a role of fundamental reference in society.

While these lines were being written, an Asturian newspaper started a survey asking about which song (apart from the regional anthem) could best represent the feelings of Asturian people. A group of 30 musicians (singers of very different ages and genres, from opera to hip-hop, composers and directors) voted first for "Asturias", a song that is a proletarian chant. The second one, "Santa Bárbara Bendita", is the miners' hymn. Among the 20 songs proposed for voting, there are four mining songs, three more include a reference to the mines and three further songs have a vindictive aim, expressing demands rather than feelings of revenge, regarding past labor movements or the current social crisis. In a subsequent vote through the web, more than 46 per cent preferred "Asturias". It is not, of course, a rigorous test, but it shows the strength with which the old industrial era and working-class symbols still exert an influence over people and their self-perception.[4]

Industrialization and deindustrialization

From the 19th century onwards, Asturian economy proved to be poorly diversified as well as highly dependent on protection given by the State. Its population grew around coal mining and the steel industry at the core of the region and this frame gave shape to a society and underpinned many of its social and political organizations and social conflicts. At the same time, the image of Asturias remained closely tied to its condition as a working-class fortress, personified in the combativeness of the miners, who participated in a revolutionary uprising in 1934 and throughout the Francoist period became the reference for all opposition to the regime. This tradition of strong working-class movements came to fruition when traditional industries started to show symptoms of weakness to which the state reacted by purchasing those companies, which in time turned the state into the main entrepreneur in the region. One great state-owned company managed most of the coal mining industry through the creation of HUNOSA in 1967 and the same happened in 1973 with the merging of all private steel companies into the also state-owned ENSIDESA. This disappearance of all private entrepreneurs in both sectors is related to different causes in its origins: coal was no longer profitable since the state reduced its protection (subsidies and duties) in 1959 and mine owners solved their resulting problem of diminishing revenue by selling their pits to the State. However, in those years, 1967 and 1973 respectively, the steel industry was still on the rise, and the bankruptcy of these companies was not so much caused by crisis as by massive debt provoked through their investment plans. In both cases, that of the steel factories and that of the coal mines, the State acted as a lifeguard for private interests.[5]

Consequently, when the effects of the international crisis that began in 1973 became evident, employment in the state-owned industries surpassed figures of 50.000 workers, which was more than a third of all industrial employment and amounted to 12 per cent of the employment in the entire region, considering all sectors. As the impact of the crisis translated into companies going out of business and the destruction of jobs in the private sector, the presence of the state-owned companies, safeguarded from the harshness of the market, grew until the moment in which, with some delay, the government finally faced their major restructuring.

Direct involvement of the State as an entrepreneur in economic sectors with long-standing traditions of working-class movements means better conditions for those workers who lose their jobs, ranging from a majority that becomes simply unemployed and other sectors, such as textile or shipbuilding, which become the subject of restructuring plans including social measures such as compensations for job-losses, increases in unemployment coverage, voluntary contract terminations, early retirements, relocation in different companies etc. Nevertheless, the reach and coverage of these different measures will prove to be unequal, improving only due to workers' ability to exert pressure on the government. Organization of workers and their tradition of class struggle will become, at this point, determining factors. The ability shown by workers of certain companies and sectors to put their labor troubles in the avant-garde of all social mobilization and their social leadership whether local or even regional will widen the political dimension of the conflicts. It will also give working-class organizations a major role in the management of the industrial decline which was reinforced by the weakness of the business class and the public agencies that was evident in a few and weak company owners, regional public institutions with little prestige and power, as well as a lack of strategies for future projects.[6]

Roughly, troubles related to industrial decline in Asturias during the last quarter of the 20th century are typical of industrial regions dominated by ageing sectors (mining, steel, shipbuilding) which are no longer competitive. In the given case, this is exacerbated by the concurrent opening of the country to world markets and Spain's membership in the European Union. Social repercussions were delayed or softened in the short term by the presence of state-owned companies and the strength of labor unions, but in the long term they will be much stronger, although workers' resistance and social mobilization gave way to a serious attempt by the state to buy social peace via huge public funds for infrastructures, re-activation plans and unemployment benefits, the majority of them through the form of early retirements.[7] In perspective, the strength of the working-class movement did not prevent de-industrialization, but it ensured many public funds that softened immediate social effects. In exchange, the State avoided major social disruptions and managed to withdraw as an entrepreneur through the closure or privatization of the public industrial companies: just 1.407 employees remain today in HUNOSA, the only state-owned company still active in the region. Its definitive shut-down is scheduled for 2018. This date will most likely also see the disappearance of all coal mines still in operation, putting an end to a period of two centuries of mining activity.

The disappearance or the drastic reduction of the foundations of former prosperity, together with the spread of unemployment or underemployment among the youth, has given way to a phenomenon of cross-generational solidarity. Family structures have played a key role in this regard, facilitating processes of income distribution from elder generations (mining or factory workers and former workers) towards their children or even grandchildren, who managed to subsist with precarious jobs or even gained access to university degrees thanks to family aid. This way, the huge transfers from the State both to the workers who were directly affected by restructuring policies and indirectly to the territory have played an important part in preventing further deterioration of living conditions, which otherwise could have translated into increasing problems of marginalization and crime.[8]

The beginning of the 21st century has brought drastic changes in the scenario previously characterized by working-class and industrial identity: once the traditional sectors were reduced in size or disappeared entirely, the traditional working-class organizations were weakened and discredited. Work in this sector has become precarious employment. Compensations for restructuring of the labor market (public investment, European funds, social subsidies etc.) will not continue unlimited. The transmission of the cultural codes and experiences of the workers, the memory of their struggles, together with the legacy left by mines and factories, have entered a process of transformation and reassignment of meanings that is still open. A migratory flow commenced two decades ago and thousands of young people have seen themselves forced to leave the region year after year. This exodus introduces an additional difficulty into the preservation of this memory, although some of these young migrants, by looking to the past, adopt mechanisms to compensate the perceived feeling of a loss of roots. Quite often, the uprooting experience of emigration is compensated by a reinforcement use of and attachment to symbolic references (flag, music etc.) and testimonies or self-descriptions in which they consider themselves economic exiles.

Regional identity and industrial heritage

Mining and industrial activities have shaped a notable part of the identity of the social environment in which mining pits and factories were inserted. First of all, this has meant local identities marked by a specific economical basis: mining in those towns that grew around coal basins, steel in those towns that developed thanks to the factories, as well as other activities in smaller villages. From this mosaic emerged a working-class identity that relied upon the strength of the class unions and the transcendence of several episodes of struggle performed by workers.

This working-class component has been incorporated into the collective portrait of Asturian society. The image of the miners as a collective subject has been permanently attached to the image of the region itself, and, along with the idea of the left as the main political trend and rebellion as the most prominent attitude, the miners' prominence owes a lot to the leadership of the working-class movement throughout the 20th century.

Historian Francisco Erice refers to the "almost legendary tale" linked to the "archetypical image of the Red Asturias or the Revolutionary Asturias" and whose main characters are mostly miners.

> The History of the working class movement and social struggles in Asturias is plenty of resounding episodes with great power to project themselves as images and myths. From these real struggles has emerged a whole imagery, rhetoric and epic narration that has permeated the collective consciousness of all the Asturians, projecting itself beyond regional borders. Asturian working class is the focus of this narrative, but, above all, there are the miners, identified as its symbol, quintessence or militant avant-garde.[9]

However, the region had an old and strong identity which has merged – sometimes harmoniously, contradictorily at other times – with this new ingredient of the Red and Working-Class Asturias. The name of the territory comes from the populations which settled before the Roman conquest and, somehow, the region has preserved distinguishing features and a distinct identity over more than 2.000 years. Mines or factories are usually placed near megaliths, pre-Roman villages, Roman ruins or medieval churches. Over the course of two centuries (722–925) at the beginnings of the so-called Reconquest, there was an independent Asturian kingdom, and its local language ('Bable' or 'Asturian', which derives from Latin just as Castilian) is also millenary. In the epic of regional history, the resistance against the Roman conquest, the role of the region as initial focus of the Christian re-conquest after the Muslim invasion of the Iberian Peninsula and, less commonly, the uprising against Napoleon's army in 1808, are counted as widely popularized milestones. In fact, when Asturias gained political autonomy in the process of decentralization that accompanied the transition towards democracy, the two dates that were proposed as regional holidays were 25 May (uprising against French invaders in 1808) and 8 September (Battle of Covadonga against the Umayyads in 722). The debate was solved in favor of the second option.

Working-class epics have connected with that tale, since it provides rich episodes of struggle such as the 1934 proletarian revolution or the strikes that challenged the Francoist dictatorship. These situations are consistent with the idea of a rebel, fighting and untamed people as it is frequently expressed in popular speeches in the form of a never-conquered or subdued Asturias. This has also been sung in different songs, building bridges between the most recent time and the remote past on the basis of a conductive thread of constant defiance of superior forces and an interpretation that emphasizes the will to retain one's own identity. One of the most popular bands in the Asturian music scene of the last 40 years, Nuberu, still plays in its concerts "Dios te llibre de Castiella" (God save you from Castile), a 1980 song whose lyrics begin with references to the war against Rome, to continue with the beginnings of the re-conquest and a medieval revolt against the Crown of Castile, to end with the 1934 revolution and the post-war strikes. More recently, the bands Gomeru and Skama la Rede have used the same references in two different songs ("Dos sieglos de llucha" – Two centuries of fight – from 2005, and "Ye too mentira" – Everything's false – from 2010): the declaration of war against Napoleon and working-class struggles past and present, thereby linking episodes of a different nature and distant chronologies to appeal to the fighting spirit and the defensiveness of the Asturian identity, with its core elements of the language and a claim to independence. Nevertheless, these ideas are accepted to varying degrees among Asturians, mired in a long and unresolved debate on the status that the Asturian language should obtain. Although the claim to independence has not been advocated to great effect, pride of local history is kept alive, as it is explained in the sort of epic poetry represented by the two songs mentioned above. The same imagery can be found in a speech made in 1996 by the president of the Academy of the Asturian Language, an institution that lacks visible connections or even ideological affinity with the working-class movement:

> This people, who fought against Rome beyond the limit of its possibilities, who did not admit the Godes, who created a kingdom, their own kingdom, who created a General Council without any means but their own, who declared, alone and fearless, war on Napoleon, who made alone a revolution in 1934, who made the first post-war strikes.[10]

But, at the same time, the incorporation of the working-class struggle into this historical sequence is vitiated as it offers a specific political interpretation as well as an indubitable class component which are hard to assume for the most conservative sectors. The remembrance of the miners taking Oviedo (the capital of the region) by assault in the harsh combats of October 1934 and again during the Civil War, or strikes led by Communists during the dictatorship cannot be a source for consensus. On the contrary, they are part of the heritage of the political left and, in some way, of the labor unions, whose image has deteriorated along with the advance of de-industrialization. Anyway, the miners' power and their ability to fight has shaped their image into that of an archetype of the proletariat and their perception as a courageous collective, always ready to fight, has persisted through time. The mining strike of the summer of 2012 – perhaps the last great mobilization of a sector on the verge of disappearing – highlighted how easily the mechanisms of sympathy towards and admiration of miners could be re-animated.[11]

The degree to which people made mining a cornerstone of their self-perception and identify and the lack of alternatives capable of substituting it as a source of pride and collective identification allows us to understand how inhabitants of the mining basins still see themselves as part of a community tightly linked to coal mining, even when only a few of them in fact still work in the coal pits. The political facet of this identity, added to the work-related conflicts of the past, plays a part in the survival of these identity markers and it seems to be fully compatible with other ingredients of identity without apparent relationship between them: the stall of the Municipality of Langreo in the International Commercial Fair (Gijón, August 2016) offered as a characteristic trait and attraction for possible tourists and visitors a mix of nature, landscape, heritage, mining and . . . maquis. The partisans' fight in the mountains after the Civil War is presented there as a substantial part of a memory linked to the geographical framework in which it took place, and the mining activity to which most of the fighters were connected by means of employment, i.e. most fighters came from the mining workers' milieu.

Meanings are controversial and those who fought for or have created powerful organizations may be faced with opposition, inscribing a political facet into the realm of employment. But it shows, at the same time, troubles related to the traumatic consequences of the defeats suffered in the attempts to stop pit closures and deindustrialization. The conversion of old working spaces into museums holds a bitter taste for those who fought for their survival as factories and pits, and the future is frequently perceived as some kind of 'tabula rasa' of their past that aims to get rid of these buildings and premises in order to put the spaces at the service of hypothetical (but unfeasible) new investments. In contrast to this, others react by appreciating the touristic potential of industrial heritage, so they see the remnants as an economical asset. And others find in that heritage is an element of identity to be preserved regardless of its material value or its economical profit. Some collectives and clubs of former workers have emerged as especially active in recent years in the defense and valuation of the memory of industrial work.[12]

In the Asturian identity, the rural element has always remained as the essence of tradition. So, although in the industrial towns it was confronted with factories, in the coal basins it merged quite well with mining. The class component represented by industrial workers and miners has never had to compete with nationalism and its inter-classist view of society. Regional identity is strong, but it counts on a weak political tradition. Nationalism and regionalism have always been lightweight in political terms in Asturias, which sets it apart from the other two regions of long-standing industrialization (Catalonia and Basque Country) where nationalism emerged from the late 19th century as a will to self-government and as an identity contrasted to the Spanish one, merging all class differences in a collective aim of national construction and struggle for sovereignty.[13] None of this has happened in Asturias, whose bourgeoisie has been traditionally weak and with interests close to those of the Spanish State. Thus, it has always kept away from secessionist temptations. Neither did the feelings of identity among popular classes result in differentiated political expressions.

The myth of a People who have never been subdued by any conqueror is a source of pride and differentiated self-affirmation, but it has not driven Asturians to pro-independence feeling. The link between the Asturian and Spanish identities does not represent an open political conflict as it does in the Basque and Catalonian cases. In contrast to the Catalan and Basque cases, a twofold identity (Spanish and Asturian) combines without conflict, notwithstanding the strength of identification with Asturias. Only 7,7 per cent of Asturian inhabitants do not feel Asturian at all, and the same percentage puts their Spanish identity in the first place before their belonging to Asturias, whereas 58,3 per cent places both identities on the same level and 24,1 per cent feel they are mainly or exclusively Asturians.[14]

On the other hand, industrialization attracted migratory streams of workers from other Spanish regions. The fact that a significant part of the Asturian working class did have foreign origins has not impeded people's self-identification with the region, as long as integration is complete. The only exceptions were those who came to Avilés in the 1950s and 1960s to work in the steel industry, whose adaptation and integration has had a slower pace. The mining basins, destination of huge quotas of workers during the years of the Great War (1914–18) and again in the Spanish post-war years (1940s and 1950s) have remained one of the spaces where the Asturian language has been preserved more vividly than in other places, along with some traditions and habits as well as cultural expressions of traditional roots. The cohesive powers of mining work and shared experiences have contributed to the preservation of these roots, as work and experiences compose a history of pain and struggle which acts as a source of collective pride. Regarding this, mining offers an especially powerful bond with a strong identity component. And the way in which human and physical landscapes are related (and sometimes merged) with the rural and peasant elements strengthens the semiotic ability of the coal basins to condense the (self-)image of Asturias even when both mining and agriculture have been reduced to their minimum. As an external observer (the North American P. Zimmerman) states:

> At the end of the century, the combination of extensive deindustrialization and migration to the cities did little to alter the perception of Asturias as mainly inhabited only by the two extreme archetypes of industrial or mining workers and rural cowboys. This is reflected in the image Asturians give of themselves and in which those living outside the region receive (or perceive).[15]

Industrial decline came together with an effort to find alternative economical activities and sources for employment. Tourism – almost irrelevant in the heyday of mines and industry – has acquired an increasing importance. In 2015, the region received 6.775.000 visitors (only 14.6 per cent of them foreigners: mainly French, German and British) and directly or indirectly the sector provides 11 per cent of the employment: 40,724 jobs.[16] This fact has had consequences for the images that Asturians create of their own land and project outside. Given the fact that the local climate does not allow for attracting the typical visitors in search of sun and beaches, the tourism industry has looked for different attractions. The beauty of the natural environment became the most prominent asset and 30 years ago, the Asturian tourism brand adopted the motto "Asturias, Natural Paradise", which is not easily reconciled with the older image which is characterized by mining and industrial heritage. Along with nature and landscape, the rich historical heritage acts as another mark of identity. In this context of other rich and influential identity markers, the industrial and mining heritage has experienced difficulties in making its own niche in the scenario. The richness of the artistic and monumental acquis that left its footprints in Asturias from prehistory (Paleolithic cave paintings) to the Middle Ages (Pre-Romanesque architecture) overshadowed industrial heritage, making valuing it more difficult.

For the society in general, the transformation of old facilities and working spaces into museums or protected buildings has also brought with it bitter feelings of defeat. In a satirical way, the movie *Carne de gallina* (in English: Hen flesh, 2002) featured a character whose catchphrase insisted in building a "Museum of the mining holocaust" as a need to reflect the death of the Asturian mines. Each closed pit or factory emerged, in the eyes of many people, as silent accusations of the industrial dismantlement. The ruins translated into something physical in the state of mind of the region. And their restoration for visitors was not always welcome, but frequently misunderstood. The creation in 1994 of the Asturian Museum of Mining was preceded by polemic, and similar debates have taken place since then. The Museum of the Steel Industry, which opened in 2006, occupies the space of the old factory of La Felguera, but almost all of its original facilities had been already demolished 20 years before. Consciousness regarding mining and industrial remnants as a valuable heritage is recent and not free from contradictions and weaknesses. Even with these setbacks, the range of museums, pathways and interpretation centers continues to grow. Apart from the mining and steel museums which have been already named, we must mention among the most important ones the Railway Museum (opened to the public in 1998), the Samuño Valley Museum and the Arnao Coalmine Museum (both in 2013) as well as the visiting program to a real coal pit, Sotón Mine, which started in 2015.

Cultural expressions and artistic narratives

Throughout the 20th century, Asturias has developed an important cultural creation related to work and working class. Literature, painting and music have widely exposed this reality and have also reflected the struggles of the labor movement. The 1934 revolution itself is a section of cultural creation in its own right and the miners put themselves in a position of major players and were also put there by others.[17]

Far from reducing its presence, industrial decline has been accompanied by a strengthening of this subject in cultural and artistic creation. The beginning of the new century has produced a considerable amount of works inspired by the recent past or the loss of the foundations on which the life of previous generations rested.

Novels, poems, plays, fiction films and documentaries, songs, paintings, sculptures and installations shift from vindication to nostalgia, trying to preserve the past and searching for new meanings. Cultural creativity has become even more productive in this regard after the material foundations that once seemed solid had revealed their fragility. These expressions (songs, books, plays etc.) often act as markers of identity or are used as stimuli to achieve mobilization, preferably aimed at the new generations and increasingly covered by criticism against the current lack of reactions.

The search for past references often mixes workers' everyday life with effort, sacrifices and fight. Political views fit easily in that kind of approach, but the idea is so commonly accepted that it forms a part of the collective imagination of the Asturians (and many non-Asturians) and allows uses with both purely literary intention or even for commercial purposes. As a result, an openly political text could, as the lyrics of the song "Asturias", become a sort of parallel unofficial anthem, which is usually sung by or provokes thrilling reactions in people who do not necessarily share its message dedicated to the proletarian struggle. The song, born from a poem of an exiled writer (Pedro Garfias) and popularized by a famous Asturian singer (Víctor Manuel), asks the workers of the world to look at the Asturian silhouette, which was left twice "alone, in the middle of the Earth" after a revolutionary uprising and strong resistance against fascism. At the same time but to different effects, it is possible to use the image of a miner as a publicity stunt for the sale of Asturian products by a commercial firm such as Tierra Astur, specialized in food and regional products. The context in which that happened is significant: during the miners' strike in the summer of 2012, mass media and street advertisements of the company linked its food products to the image of a miner. With purely commercial purpose, the text referred to struggle, strength and pride associated to the image of a miner.

In other spheres like football, which are apparently unrelated (or even opposed) to the industrial history, we can also detect the strong presence of mining as a collective reference. During their most important match of the past years (May 2015), Real Oviedo's supporters unfolded a banner representing the players dressed as miners with a mine behind them and a slogan saying "after days of struggle and sacrifice, it's time to leave the hole", sharing the same idea about miners' attributes.[18]

When cultural creativity refers to the collective memory constructed of work, it is often understandable to a broad audience that shares the same representations. If they want to explain their motivations, the artists frequently just need to appeal to their roots in terms of childhood memories or social origins. The rock band Desakato (Disobedience) sings "Fríu de xineru" (in Asturian language: January Cold, 2011), devoted to their parents who had to wake up in the middle of winter nights and go to work on the morning shift, trying to ensure a better life for their children.[19] Writer Pablo Rodríguez Medina considers his father, a former miner and union militant, a hero, the mirror into which he likes to look. But this admiration includes a bitter feeling because the world his father once belonged to has disappeared: he played according to some rules (workers' pride and class consciousness) without understanding the rules had already changed.[20] His novel *Los taraos* (The idiots) tells a story of betrayed fighters. The hardcore group Escuela de Odio (Hate School) recently released a new album, significantly titled *We can only fight* (2015). Explaining the social and political content of their songs, they say: "We live in a workers' village and were born between strikes".[21] The film-maker Marcos Merino, director of a documentary about the miners' strike held in the summer of 2012, explains the aim of his work as "a reencounter with my past", back to his origins in a workers' neighborhood and to his working class roots, far from "the world of appearances and escapisms" he lived in for 20 years in Madrid. So he felt the need of showing his children a different world by looking to a present (probably for a last time: the documentary entitles *Remine, The last workers' movement*) that represents the past of several generations.[22]

Further, some issues or subjects in collective memory act as powerful markers that do not need such direct links to the people who refer to them. Mineworkers and their struggles reveal iconic potential, shared by many people outside the coal basins. For example, the young girls who make up the melodic group Filanda define themselves as "daughters of coal and barricades" in a song titled "Enraigonaes" (in Asturian language: Rooted), but they are not from a coal town. Rather they live in a steel town and probably they have never seen a barricade close up if we consider their age and the neighborhood in which they live. Even if steel factories have played a main role, similar to the mines, in the regional economy, and these girls are more probably daughters of steel and smoke, the metaphor they chose proves the preponderance of mining over any other reference.

Occasionally, labor conflicts also find support from artists who put their creativity to the service of propaganda. With very explicit messages, murals and songs acted as reinforcement in long-term struggles, giving support to the miners, shipyards and metalworkers. But more frequently working-class battles are incorporated into a wider narrative about the Asturian people, their past and their present. In a depressive context in which employment opportunities and mobilization capacity decrease at par, the reference of the industrial and mining heyday as a much better time becomes almost obvious. In fact, the collective memory of workers' struggles acts as a source of pride, basis for collective representations, links in a historical chain and arguments for criticism of the present.

Spanta la Xente, a young band that plays rock with a taste of folk, expresses an idea of Asturias based on that kind of roots. Especially their song "La mio Asturies" (My Asturias, 2015) opens with a critique of the present that leads to a definition of what Asturias is (or should be). This is completely marked by mining identity and workers' struggles. "My Asturias is the black, proletarian and miner, the one of the social struggle. Mine is the one that bleeds under the coal ground." The song describes the current Asturias mourning for the children who have to leave, pride of being a daughter of mining and standing tall in the face of adversity. "A coalfield of slagheaps, silicotic, retired. A graveyard of headframes that foghorns don't guard anymore in the mornings". But its inhabitants, as the example stresses, are not enslaved, have retained their dignity and are still ready to fight.

With a more acid attitude, the hip-hop singer Arma X uses the same references to the past in order to offer a deeply pessimistic view of the current situation. An industrial landscape of rusty headframes and abandoned factories serves as the backdrop of a ruin that is also social and moral: political corruption, trade unions' betrayal and people's loss of values, memory and identity, performing on a stage that is decorated to mirror a sense of defeat that has also done away with the will to fight along with images of drugs as instruments for numbing the youth. Almost obsessive in his lyrics after more than 10 years and four albums, the song "Zona Minada" (Mined Zone, 2008) is a good example of that criticism: a grey and brown Asturias, whose "headframes are witness today of yesterday's shines, drawing lines on wrinkles made of firedamp". Suffering those who buy, sell, steal and trick . . . "the pain of a betrayal is worse if it comes from your own litter". The young people strive in not believing what the past was, "mining gives way to the white powder business" and, without coal, the engine powering the country stalled while unions signed accords trying to "cover their own asses".

Often, memory is a key element of both collective identity and the ability to fight. Its loss becomes a source of concern. The rock band Dixebra turns their gaze to remembrance when they try to characterize the current situation in the song "Esto ye Asturies" (This is Asturias, 1997):

> These are not the times to sing epics/when I was a child many were told/ about a dignified people, armed to the teeth/who sold their souls for a handful of ideas. . . . I tried also to sing these heroic deeds/I also willed to die in those battles/I can't see anybody, I can't hear voices but the air. . . . This is Asturias . . . where the deads light the ways/of those who are hardly still alive.

As for music, a huge amount of songs composed in recent years deals with past labor, the industrial crisis and the social problems of the present, especially among young people. Several themes are repeated insistently: references to past struggles, the defeat of the labor movement, the indictment to the unions and political leaders, the loss of old values, unemployment, emigration and drugs. With the exception of pop, that barely addresses social problems, no genre is foreign to these issues. Especially critical are punk, hardcore and hip hop singers, but these issues can be found under many other styles.

Maybe the highest quality expression of this feeling can be found in a multimedia product: the video clip for the song "Patria sin Sol" (Sunless Homeland, 2004), which combines the song of the same title performed by the group Stoned Atmosphere with images by filmmaker Gonzaga G. Antuña. With hip-hop sound and a setting of industrial ruins, workers' houses and a cemetery, these young people (barely 20 years' old) express anger and a feeling of collapse of old values in the mining area, with an absence of jobs and plenty of drugs for youngsters who are no longer able to fight as their elders did.

Leaving aside the large number of songs referring to the industrial past, the rest of artistic expressions also often deal with this matter. Theatrical plays (either comedy, tragedy or satire), novels, poems, films and documentaries focusing on deindustrialization and the resulting current social crisis can be easily found. Only referring to theater, more than a dozen plays whose plot is related to the mine or mining areas have been brought to the Asturian stages in the past 10 years.

A radically pessimistic view of the future – closely linked to the loss of past prosperity – is offered in *Nenyure* (No place – Jorge Rivero, 2005), a short film featuring Mieres, capital of a mining area, as an uninhabited city turned into a dead landscape. A ghost town converted into a cemetery, resounding echoes of the miners who once worked and lived there show a futuristic dystopia of the Asturian coalfield. Other times, pessimism is softened by comedy. That is the case of *Carne de Gallina* (Hen flesh – Javier Maqua, 2002), a film whose plot is based on the critical importance of early retirements of former miners to sustain the living standards of the younger generations in a context of high unemployment. A family decides to hide the father's death and freeze him instead of burying him in order to continue receiving his pension, which is the only means of living for them all.

Similarly, in recent Asturian literature the industrial past and the memory of the workers' struggles cast a long shadow and influence how the present is perceived. Expressly or implicitly, the contrast between the prosperity linked to the mines and factories and the current decline never fails to appear, as well as the distance between the fighting capacity of previous generations and the impotence felt by young people today. A deep pessimism usually marks the stories that set the comparison between past and present. Nostalgia is the main feeling in the novel *Les ruines* (The Ruins, Xandru Fernández, 2004), describing the decline of a small town in the mining area. Similar pessimism is projected to the past in the novel *Los taraos* (The idiots, Pablo Rodríguez Medina, 2004), which narrates the gestation of a miners' strike bitterly ended. Also *Dejar las cosas en sus días* (Leave things in their own days, Laura Castañón, 2013) tells a story that runs through several generations during the 20th century, developed in an archetypical enclave of industrial paternalism, a sophisticated project of social control in the mining area trying to create what one researcher called "The dreamed worker"[23] (from the business point of view). The novel recreates that atmosphere and travels through the years of the Second Republic, the Civil War and Franco's dictatorship from the perspective of a woman who, many years later, embarks on a journey to the traumatic memory of her family, searching for information about victims of repression and political violence. Again and again, work, memory, rights and freedom appear linked, in the same form in which the memorial dedicated to the miners who died in mine accidents in the small town of Turón reflects every name beside a short text that reads: "In memory of those miners that underpinned the mines of this valley with their lives to safeguard to others, their freedom and their prosperity".

Recent events in labor movement find new chroniclers among filmmakers who look for the latest links in a long chain. Several documentaries have noticed workers' struggles in shipyards (Alejandro Zapico: *El Astillero* (The shipyard), 2007 and Ruth Arias: *Cándido y Morala, ni un paso atrás* (Cándido and Morala, no step back), 2007), automobile (Javier Bauluz: *Deslocalizados* – Offshored – 2013), metal construction (Lucinda Torre: *Resistencia* – Resistance – 2006) and mining (Marcos M. Merino: *Remine*, 2014). The description of the current social reality also looks to the industrial past and the effects of deindustrialization:

Prejubilandia (Land of early retired people, Jaime Santos and Vanessa Castaño, 2009) shows the problems of the early retired workers as living proof of the defeat of the labor movement and the loss of the economic network. *Lluvina* (Xuan Luis Ruiz, 2002) mixes testimonies and fiction contrasting the nostalgia for the lost values that once gave meaning to the life of elders and contrasts this with the pain caused by younger persons' need to migrate in order to find work – always with the landscape of the coalfield as an essential part of a story that integrates industrial vestiges, the natural environment and the people who have given life and sense to this land and now have to powerlessly witness the disappearance of that world. The aim of *Remine* is not so different: a documentary that chronicles the last great miner's strike of 2012, providing an anthropological look at the miners as human archetype and a bitter aftertaste of defeat and weaknesses or inconsistencies in their organizations. All are approached from the intention of recording a world that is disappearing for the children to know their own past. This is exactly the reason the director provides:

> the film meant a reunion with a past closer to my working life nature rather than the life of appearances and vital escapism that had begun to dominate myself after 20 years living in Madrid. It was necessary to show my children another world.[24]

Urban environment, industrial ruins and natural landscape are usually part of every documentary, fiction film and musical video clip depicting Asturias. Even though the stories are not related to an industrial past, these elements seem to be part of a collective identity and often function as emotional references. Headframes serve as especially powerful iconic symbols. Industrial spaces and their ruin are a recurrent topic in painting and photography to the extent that it becomes impossible to list and difficult to select from the amount of artworks.

Filling the absences

The emptiness caused by closures of mines and factories also becomes a symbolic absence that some artists try to fill with works of remembrance and the creation of virtual spaces to replace those that have disappeared. Industrial areas serve as settings for the location of works, evoking the materials and the products of labor. All along the estuary of Avilés, beside the harbor and the steel factory facilities, a series of sculptures compose the so-called "Steel Route". The shapes they take and the materials of which they are made are direct reminiscences of the products of the metallurgical industry. In Gijón, rusty metal has been used to mark the territory where once a steel factory was located: the "Tower of Remembrance", erected in a park in a suburb of the city where the disappeared Fábrica de Moreda lasted for a hundred years. And in Mieres, located in front of the current university campus, on a ground that once was part of a mine, all the miners killed in accidents there are remembered by a sculpture of a male torso inside which burns an eternal flame. The same university campus is described in the dystopian film *Nenyure* (already mentioned above) as a funerary monument: the mine became a mass grave where the echoes of the voices of the miners who once worked underground still resound and a giant pantheon of concrete, steel, glass and cement has been built instead, exactly on the spot where the miners used to face the police.

The desire to preserve the memory of spaces, facilities and workers also inspires conceptual artists in projects that refer to the absence. Avelino Sala has created several pictorial and multimedia series and led several exhibitions focusing on missing factories. The Museum of Fine Arts of Asturias held the exhibition *Darkness at Noon* (2014) which consisted of paintings depicting characteristic elements of closed factories. Each piece's title was the name of the company and its closing year.[25] The disappearance and the consequential impression of absence create an emptiness that artists try to fill. In Gijon, taking the place of a former substandard housing quarter, a large group of artists have initiated an exhibition space and given life to an exhibition and creation space called *No Site* (2015). Their purpose was to combine art, heritage and collective memory in the same place that the poorest working people had inhabited. According to their definition, it was "an exercise in collective research of relations between the given territory, identity and belonging to a place" and a "use of uninhabited spaces as an alternative for the construction of a collective memory, a practical exercise in cultural empowerment". The program included exhibitions of photography, painting, sculpture, audiovisual, industrial arts, conferences and a barter shop.[26]

Multimedia installations also create spaces linked to mining and industrial memory. In Laboral City of Culture, an exhibition titled *Menhir* (2015) evokes traces of the past, interactively combining an atmosphere of lights, sounds, images and tactile sensations. In their words: the coal pieces act as conductors of sound and tactile stimuli and also connect the landscape to social, economic and ecological aspects.[27]

Trying to rescue the legacy of the mining and industrial heritage in symbiosis with nature, the architects Nacho Ruiz and Sara Lopez have experimented with a multimedia product called "Learning from the Basins" (2014).[28] Its object of attention is the coexistence of natural, rural, industrial and urban landscapes, with no defined boundaries between them:

> Together, the basins are perceived as a magma of opposing but intermixed identities. This has led to the emergence of deeply heterodox building models that have inscribed in their genetic code the conflict on which they stand. It is a matter of hybrid architectures, mutant artifacts, which, despite the invisibility that gives them their inevitable marginal condition today are able to offer very interesting architectural lessons. The study aims to test new areas of opportunity in contemporary architectural thought and reconvert the conventional image that the coal basins have, a traditionally reviled place which, examined from an unprejudiced look, forms a unique environment in European urban structure.[29]

While these lines were being written, the experimental theater group La Xata la Rifa started a long-term project titled "Industrial Music", a work in progress based on interactive road shows that will tour old railway stations bringing to mind the crisis and the difficulties resulting therefrom.[30] And simultaneously, the artist Fran Meana unveiled "Archaeologies of Future", whose designs are inspired by hydroelectric plants designed by the painter, sculptor and architect Vaquero Palacios in the 1950s and 1960s. The installation is "an expanded file, a time capsule, which takes visitors to an indeterminate point in time" composed of reliefs, animation films and texts that "appear as remnants of an obsolete energy model inviting visitors to analyze and reflect the links between work, industrial technology, nature and society".[31]

Conceptual artists usually do not need to insert any text, and, if they do so, they prefer Spanish and English. Many writers, however, and singers do not express their literature and music in Spanish. Rather, they use the Asturian language, which has no legal recognition as an official language the way that Basque, Catalan or Galician have. The insistence of the creators on using a minority and not legally recognized language is striking for two reasons: because it is new compared to the traditional use of Spanish by the Asturian labor movement[32] and also because it is much more present in these issues of industrial past and workers' memory than in others. The Asturian language has traditionally been used to address issues related to the rural and peasant world. Only in recent years have the generations that lived through the decline started to use the Asturian language when dealing with mining, the industrial past and the present deindustrialization. It is difficult to say why, but there seems to be a willingness to strengthen one's identity by combining the threatened identity of the old working class with similarly threatened local roots.

Representations focused on the industrial past and work-related memory are abundant and occupy an important place in the Asturian cultural production. Their meaning points directly to the need to reword the traumatic memory of the recent past. Much of the reactions that appeal to the industrial past are the result of the perception that this specific collective memory itself and its associated identity are threatened. Artistic creation largely revolves around recreation and redefinition of the past. It is linked to fights, the epics and values that are considered threatened or lost. But what is clear in terms of cultural creation must not necessarily be the case for Asturian society as a whole. The process is ongoing and presents vague constructions of memory that do not allow for final conclusions. We lack, in fact, research in this regard that would be able to shed light on the importance that the heritage of the industrial age can acquire for the identity of the Asturians. The heritage of mining and industry faces both negligence by authorities and a lack of resources. Among the affected populations, contradictory reactions combine, oscillating from rejection (as a symbol of defeat or due to a general perceived necessity to break with the past) to preservation as a core element of identity. The Asturian identity has other strong elements to be built on: nature and history provide powerful foundations that are less controversial than workers' memory or vernacular language. The perceived past of industry and labor has not been constitutive in its origin and neither is essential to its survival. It adds to (and to some extent enters into conflict with) existing elements. But, on the other hand, it has often coalesced with language and music, allowing for the construction of bridges to the younger generations.

Figure 2.1 Graffiti Tenneco Strike (2014), street art supporting the workers' resistance to a plant closure in Gijón.

Figure 2.2 Tower of Remembrance (Francisco Fresno, 2000), placed on the site of a former steel factory in Gijón.

Figure 2.3 The ruins (Xandru Fernández, 2004), a novel about the social and moral effects of deindustrialization in an unnamed village of the Asturian coalfields.

Figure 2.4 Grieska (Fight, 1990), album by Dixebra, the most senior rock band in Asturian language, showing industrial and working-class roots in Avilés.

Figure 2.5 Nenyure: a memorial to the miners (foreground) and a University campus (background) located at the former facilities of a coal pit in Mieres. The site is described as a funerary monument by the dystopic film Nenyure (2005).

Figure 2.6 Map of Asturias

Notes

1 Source: SADEI (Sociedad Asturiana de Estudios Económicos e Industriales).
2 Although it was originally created to describe extreme experiences (e.g. the holocaust, slavery etc.), the concept of cultural trauma can be useful for collective uncertainties linked to industrial decline, as well. It does not refer to "the result of a group experiencing pain". It is the result of this acute discomfort entering into the core of the collectivity's sense of its own identity. "Collective actors 'decide' to represent social pain as a fundamental threat to their sense of who they are, where they came from, and where they want to go" Jeffrey C. Alexander, *Trauma: A Social Theory* (Cambridge: Polity Press, 2012), 15. However, it is important to take into account that "the appeal to psychoanalytic concepts such as melancholia and mourning, acting out and working through, adds a necessary dimension to economic, social and political analyses but does not constitute a substitute for them" Dominique LaCapra, *Writing History, Writing Trauma* (Baltimore: John Hopkins University, 2001).
3 Francisco Erice, Entre el mito y la memoria histórica: las huelgas de 1962 y la tradición épica de la Asturias roja, in Rubén Vega (ed.), *Las huelgas de 1962 en Asturias* (Gijón: Trea, 2002), 413–436.
4 *El Comercio*, February 5th 2017.
5 Juan A. Vázquez, La minería del carbón (1940–1967). Expansión y crisis and Oscar Fleites, Expansión y ordenación siderúrgica, both in *Historia de la economía asturiana* (Oviedo: Prensa Ibérica, 1994), 561–576 and 593–608.
6 Rubén Vega, *Crisis industrial y conflicto social. Gijón 1976–1996* (Gijón: Trea, 1998).
7 The Asturian de-industrialization process and policies applied to face the problem have been studied, coinciding with the most critical moments, by Holm-Detlev Köhler (dir.), *Asturias: el declive de una región industrial* (Gijón: Trea, 1996) and Manuel Castells (dir.), *Estrategias para la reindustrialización de Asturias* (Madrid: Civitas, 1994).
8 Asturias has finished 2016 with the second lowest crime rate in Spain according to Police statistics. *La Nueva España*, January 14th 2017.
9 Francisco Erice, Hay una lumbre en Asturias . . . Notas sobre la imagen, el mito y la épica del movimiento obrero asturiano en el franquismo, in Rubén Vega (coord.), *El movimiento obrero en Asturias durante el franquismo 1937–1977* (Oviedo: KRK, 2013), 585.

10 In *Lletres Asturianes*, 62, 1997 (171).
11 Rubén Vega, España: la última gran huelga de mineros, in Salvador Aguilar (ed.), *Anuario de conflictos 2012* (Barcelona: Observatori del Conflicte Social, 2013), 831–854.
12 In Mieres, some members of Santa Bárbara, a former miners' association, have restored several heritage sites (two mine entrances, a Protestant cemetery) and in Gijón some ex shipyard workers promoted a memory recovery project focused on disappeared factories. Both have organized exhibitions and talks and created a digital photo archive. More information in www.asociacionsantabarbara.com/actividades/ and www.territorio museo.com/noticias/show/784-gijon-oeste-una-memoria-industrial-la-iniciativa-de-los-barrios-por-salvar-su-historia.
13 Xosé Manuel Núñez Seixas, *Nacionalismos en la España Contemporánea (siglos XIX y XX)*, (Barcelona: Hipotesi, 1999) and Juan Díez Medrano, *Divided Nations: Class, Politics and Nationalism in the Basque Country and Catalonia* (Ithaca, NY: Cornell University Press, 1995).
14 Francisco José Llera Ramo and Pablo San Martín Antuña, *II Estudio Sociolingüístico de Asturias 2002* (Oviedo: Academia Asturiana de la Llingua, 2003), 65.
15 Patrick W. Zimmerman, *Faer Asturies. La política llingüística y la construcción frustrada del nacionalismu asturianu (1974–1999)* (Oviedo: Trabe, 2012), 29.
16 Facultad de Comercio, Turismo y Ciencias Sociales Jovellanos, *El Turismo en Asturias en 2015* (Gijón: Sistema de Información Turística de Asturias, 2016), 58 and 66.
17 Benigno Delmiro, *La voz en el pozo. El trabajo en las minas y su presencia en la literatura* (Madrid: Akal, 1993); *Literatura y minas en la España de los siglos XIX y XX* (Gijón: Trea, 2004); El movimiento obrero asturiano en la literatura de posguerra, in Rubén Vega (coord.), *El movimiento obrero asturiano durante el franquismo* (Oviedo: KRK, 2013); La huelga del 62 en la literatura, in Rubén Vega (coord.), *Las huelgas de 1962 en Asturias* (Gijón: Trea, 2002). Albino Suárez, *Los poetas y la mina* (Pola de Laviana: 1995). Xana, *El son nos cantares de la revolución d'Ochobre de 1934* (Oviedo: Fonoastur, 1998). Francisco Zapico, *Evaristo Valle y Mariano Moré. Dos pintores ante la mina* (Gijón: Museo Evaristo Valle, 2007); *Hay una luz en Asturias . . . La güelga de 1962* (Oviedo: Fundación Juan Muñiz Zapico, 2002). Diego Díaz, El movimiento obrero asturiano en las artes visuales y la música: ausencias y presencias durante el franquismo y la transición, in Rubén Vega (coord.), *El movimiento obrero asturiano durante el franquismo* (Oviedo: KRK, 2013).
18 *La Nueva España*, May 24th 2015.
19 www.entreacordes.com/entrevista_desakato
20 Juan Luis Ruiz, *Lluvina* (Oviedo: Filmoteca de Asturias, 2002), 34–35.
21 *La Nueva España*, October 25th 2015.
22 Marcos M. Merino, *Remine. El ultimo movimiento obrero*, (Asturias: Freews, 2014) booklet accompanying the CD edition of the film.
23 José Sierra Álvarez, *El obrero soñado. Ensayo sobre el paternalismo industrial (Asturias, 1860–1917)* (Madrid: Siglo XXI, 1990).
24 Marcos M. Merino, *Remine. El ultimo movimiento obrero*, (Asturias: Freews, 2014) booklet accompanying the CD edition of the film.
25 A catalog of the exhibition has been published: Avelino Sala, *Darkness at Noon* (Oviedo: Museo de Bellas Artes de Asturias, 2014).
26 https://juventudgijon.wordpress.com/2015/06/05/no-sitio-arte-patrimonio-y-memoria-colectiva-en-la-ciudadela-de-capua/.
27 http://www.laboralcentrodearte.org/es/exposiciones/menhir
28 Sara López Arraiza and Nacho Ruiz Allén, *Aprendiendo de las cuencas. Hacia una puesta en valor del Paisaje Cultural de las Cuencas Mineras Asturianas / Learning from las cuencas: Towards Highlighting the Cultural Landscape of the Asturian Coalfields* (Asturias, 2014).
29 Ibid., 12.

30 *El Comercio*, May 13th 2016. *La Voz de Asturias*, October 12th 2016.
31 http://www.laboralcentrodearte.org/es/exposiciones/arqueologias-del-futuro
32 Rafael Rodríguez Valdés, *Llingua asturiana y movimientu obreru, 1899–1937* (Gijón: Ateneo Obrero, 2004).

Bibliography

Castells, Manuel (dir.), *Estrategias para la reindustrialización de Asturias* (Madrid: Civitas, 1994).
Caulton, Tim. 2006. *Hands-On Exhibitions: Managing Interactive Museums and Science Centres*. (London: Taylor and Francis).
Coupland, Bethan. 2012. *Heritage and Memory: Oral History and Mining Heritage in Wales and Cornwall*. (PhD diss., Exeter: University of Exeter).
Coupland, Nikolas Peter Garrett and Hywel Bishop. 2005. Wales Underground: Discursive Frames and Authenticities in Welsh Mining Heritage, in Adam Jaworski and Annette Pritchard, Eds. *Discourse, Communication and Tourism*. (Clevedon: Channel View, 1994–222).
Coupland, Nikolas. Ed. 1990. *English in Wales: Diversity, Conflict and Change*. (Clevedon: Philadelphia).
Curtis, Ben. 2013. *The South Wales Mienrs, 1964–1985*. (Cardiff: Cardiff University Press).
Davis, Kath, 1996. Cleaning Up the Coal Face and Doing Out the Kitchen: The Interpretation of Work and Workers in Wales', in Gaynor Kavanagh Ed. *Making Histories in Museums*. (London: Leicester University Press, 1054–115).
Dicks, Bella. 2000. *Heritage, Place and Community*. (Cardiff: Cardiff University Press).
Dicks, Bella. 2003. Heritage, Governance and Marketisation: A Case-Study from Wales. *Museum and Society* 1: 30–44.
Dicks, Bella. 2008. Performing the Hidden Injuries of Class in Coal-Mining Heritage. *Sociology* 42 (3): 4364–452.
Delmiro, Benigno, El movimiento obrero asturiano en la literatura de posguerra, in Rubén Vega García (coord.), *El movimiento obrero asturiano durante el franquismo* (Oviedo: KRK, 2013).
Delmiro, Benigno, La huelga del 62 en la literatura, in Rubén Vega García (coord.), *Las huelgas de 1962 en Asturias* (Gijón: Trea, 2002).
Delmiro, Benigno, *La voz en el pozo. El trabajo en las minas y su presencia en la literatura* (Madrid: Akal, 1993).
Delmiro, Benigno, *Literatura y minas en la España de los siglos XIX y XX* (Gijón: Trea, 2004).
Díaz, Diego, El movimiento obrero asturiano en las artes visuales y la música: ausencias y presencias durante el franquismo y la transición, in Rubén Vega (coord.), *El movimiento obrero asturiano durante el franquismo* (Oviedo: KRK, 2013).
Díez Medrano, Juan, *Divided Nations: Class, Politics and Nationalism in the Basque Country and Catalonia* (Ithaca, NY: Cornell University Press, 1995).
Edwards J. Arwel and Joan Carles Lourdes. 1996. Mines and Quarries: Industrial Heritage Tourism, *Annals of Tourism Research* 23 (2): 3414–363.
Erice, Francisco, Entre el mito y la memoria histórica: las huelgas de 1962 y la tradición épica de la Asturias roja, in Rubén Vega (ed.), *Las huelgas de 1962 en Asturias* (Gijón: Trea, 2002).
Erice, Francisco, Hay una lumbre en Asturias . . . Notas sobre la imagen, el mito y la épica del movimiento obrero asturiano en el franquismo, in Rubén Vega (coord.), *El movimiento obrero en Asturias durante el franquismo 1937–1977* (Oviedo: KRK, 2013).

Facultad de Comercio, Turismo y Ciencias Sociales Jovellanos, *El Turismo en Asturias en 2015* (Gijón: Sistema de Información Turística de Asturias, 2016).
Fisk, Malcolm J. 1996. *Housing in the Rhondda, 1800–1940*. (Cardiff: Merton Priory Press Ltd).
Fleites, Oscar, Expansión y ordenación siderúrgica, in *Historia de la economía asturiana* (Oviedo: Prensa Ibérica, 1994).
Foden, Mike, Steve Fothergill and Tony Gore. Eds. 2014. *The State of the Coalfields: Economic and Social Conditions in the Former Mining Communities of England, Scotland and Wales*. (Sheffield: Centre for Regional Economic and Social Research Sheffield Hallam University).
Francis, Hywel and Dai Smith. 1998. *The Fed: A History of the South Wales Miners in the Twentieth Century*. (Cardiff: Cardiff University Press).
Hewison, Robert. 1987. *The Heritage Industry: Britain in a Climate of Decline*. (London: Methuen).
Jenkins, John Geraint. 1992. *Getting Yesterday Right: Interpreting the Heritage of Wales*. (Cardiff: University of Wales Press).
Johnes, Martin. 2013. *Wales since 1939*. (Manchester: MUP).
Jones, Andrew L. and Kathryn Flynn. 2011. Flogging a Dead Horse or Creating Cultural Capacity: The Development and Impact of Mines as Alternative Tourist Destinations: A Case Study of South Wales, in Michael V. Conlin and Lee Jolliffe, Eds. *Mining Heritage and Tourism: A Global Synthesis*. (London: Routledge,1314–143).
Jones, Philip N. 1969. *Colliery Settlement in the South Wales Coalfield, 1850–19126*. (Hull: University of Hull).
Jones, Thomas. 1942. *Leeks and Daffodils*. (Newtown: Welsh Outlook Press).
Köhler, Holm-Detlev (dir.), *Asturias: el declive de una región industrial* (Gijón: Trea, 1996).
Lewis, Russell. 1964. *Wealth for Wales*. (London: Conservative Political Centre).
Llera Ramo, Francisco José and San Martín Antuña, Pablo, *II Estudio Sociolingüístico de Asturias 2002* (Oviedo: Academia Asturiana de la Llingua, 2003).
López Arraiza, Sara and Ruiz Allén, Nacho, *Aprendiendo de las cuencas. Hacia una puesta en valor del Paisaje Cultural de las Cuencas Mineras Asturianas/Learning from las cuencas: Towards Highlighting the Cultural Landscape of the Asturian Coalfields* (Asturias, 2014).
Mason, Rhiannon. 2007. *Museums, Nations, Identities: Wales and its National Museums*. (Cardiff: University of Wales Press).
Minchinton, Walter Edward. Ed. 1969. *Industrial South Wales, 1750–1914: Essays in Welsh Economic History*. (London: Frank Cass).
Morgan, Prys. 1983. From a Date to a View: The Hunt for the Welsh Past in the Romantic Period', in Eric Hobsbawm and Terence Ranger . Eds. *The Invention of Tradition*. (Cambridge: CUP, 434–100).
Morgan, Prys. 1986. The Gwerin of Wales: Myth and Reality, in Ian Hume and W. T. R. Pryce, Eds. *The Welsh and Their Country*. (Llandysul: Gomer Press, 134–152).
Núñez Seixas, Xosé Manuel, *Nacionalismos en la España Contemporánea (siglos XIX y XX)* (Barcelona: Hipotesi, 1999).
Peate, Iowerth. 1948. *Folk Museums*. (Cardiff: University of Wales Press).
Peate, Iowerth. 1929. *Guide to the Collection of Welsh Bygones: A Descriptive Account of Old Fashioned Life in Wales*. (Cardiff: National Museum of Wales and University of Wales Press).
Price, Derrick. 1992. *Gazing at the Valleys: Representation and the Cultural Construction of South Wales*. (PhD University of Birmingham).

Prentice, Richard, Stephen Witt and Claire Hamer. 1993. *The Experience of Industrial Heritage: The Case of Black Gold*. (Built Environment 19 (2): 137–146).
Pryce, W. T. R. 2000. Language Zones, Demographic Changes, and the Welsh Culture Area 1800–1911, in Geraint H. Jenkins Eds. *The Welsh Language and Its Social Domains*. (Cardiff: University of Wales Press).
Rhondda Heritage Park – Improving the Visitor Experience. Rhondda Cynon Taff Country Borough Council Cabinet, 8 September 2016, www.rctcbe.gov.uk.EN/Council/Councillors CommitteesandMeetings/Meetings/Cabinet/2016/09/08/Reports/Agendaitem6Rhondda HeritageParkImprovingtheVisitorsExperience.pdf
Rodríguez Valdés, Rafael, *Llingua asturiana y movimientu obreru, 1899–1937* (Gijón: Ateneo Obrero, 2004).
Sala, Avelino, *Darkness at Noon* (Oviedo: Museo de Bellas Artes de Asturias, 2014).
Samuel, Raphael. 2012. *Theatres of Memory: Past and Present in Contemporary Culture*, 2nd ed. (London: Verso).
Sierra Álvarez, José, *El obrero soñado. Ensayo sobre el paternalismo industrial (Asturias, 1860–1917)* (Madrid: Siglo XXI, 1990).
Smith, Laurajane. 2006. *Uses of Heritage*. (London: Routledge).
Suárez, Albino, *Los poetas y la mina* (Pola de Laviana, 1995).
Vázquez, Juan A., Expansión y ordenación siderúrgica, in *Historia de la economía asturiana* (Oviedo: Prensa Ibérica, 1994).
Vázquez, Juan A., La minería del carbón (1940–1967). Expansión y crisis, in *Historia de la economía asturiana* (Oviedo: Prensa Ibérica, 1994).
Vega García, Rubén, *Crisis industrial y conflicto social. Gijón 1976–1996* (Gijón: Trea, 1998).
Vega García, Rubén, España: la última gran huelga de mineros, in Salvador Aguilar (ed.), *Anuario de conflictos 2012* (Barcelona: Observatori del Conflicte Social, 2013).
Wales Visitor Attractions Survey (2015), www.gov.wales/docs/caecd/research/2016/160721-visitor-attractions-survey-2015-en.pdf.
Wanhill, Stephen. 2000. *Mines – A Tourist Attraction: Coal Mining in Industrial South Wales*. (Journal of Travel Research 39: 60–69).
Ward, Alexandra. 2008. *Archaeology, Heritage and Identity: The Creation and Development of a National Museum in Wales* (Cardiff: PhD diss., University of Cardiff).
Williams, Chris. 1996. *Democratic Rhondda: Politics and Society, 1885–1951*. (Cardiff: Cardiff University Press).
Williams, Colin H. 1990. The Anglicisation of Wales, in Nikolas Coupland, Ed. *English in Wales: Diversity, Conflict and Change*. (Clevedon: Philadelphia, 19–47).
Williams, Gwyn. 1985. *When Was Wales?* (London: Penguin).
Winkler, Victoria. 2010. *Forty Years of Regeneration in the Upper Afan Valley*. (Ebbw Vale: Bevan Foundation).
Wright, Patrick. 2009.*On Living in an Old Country: The Nationalist Past in Contemporary Britain*, 2nd ed. Oxford: OUP. www.visitblaenavon.co.uk
Zapico, Francisco, *Evaristo Valle y Mariano Moré. Dos pintores ante la mina* (Gijón: Museo Evaristo Valle, 2007).
Zapico, Francisco, *Hay una luz en Asturias . . . La güelga de 1962* (Oviedo: Fundación Juan Muñiz Zapico, 2002).
Zimmerman, Patrick W., *Faer Asturies. La política llingüística y la construcción frustrada del nacionalismu asturianu (1974–1999)* (Oviedo: Trabe, 2012).

3 Regional identity and industrial heritage in the mining area of Nord-Pas-de-Calais

Marion Fontaine

In 2012, the former mining basin of Nord-Pas-de-Calais was added to the list of UNESCO World Heritage Sites. Officially classified under the rubric of "Cultural Landscapes",[1] the site includes 17 pitheads, 21 headgears and 51 slag heaps, as well as 124 additional buildings and locations ranging from housing projects and schools to places of worship – even a football stadium (Félix Bollaert Stadium, located in the western part of the basin in Lens). More broadly, the site showcases close to 4000 hectares of landscape, collectively attesting not only to the bygone culture of the mining community but also to the vibrant life of an area that continues to evolve (Figure 3.1).[2] Both visitors and local agents (developers; representatives from cultural institutions and local communities) perceive the UNESCO classification as a form of consecration, and as a sign of the major role that industrial heritage now plays on a regional scale.[3] The showcasing of a heritage related to the exploitation of mines – a heritage both material (cultural landscapes, headgears, housing estates) and intangible (working-class culture, oral tradition) – is presented at once as a form of recognition and recovered pride for populations that have been profoundly impacted by crisis, and as a primordial lever of growth through the development of tourism and cultural activities. Seen this way, the region's mining history appears as a resource for its future. Such a valorization is not, however, without paradox. While the industrial (and notably mining) past of the region is celebrated, it is still largely perceived as stigmatizing and burdensome. In the eyes of many observers, it is precisely this heritage and its associated handicaps (the under-qualification of workers; welfare dependency) that serve to explain the economic and social difficulties of the region (e.g., a high unemployment rate), as well as its political problems (in particular, the high polling numbers of the Front national, the French political party of the far right). In fact, in the eyes of many observers,[4] some features of this industrial past – the under-qualification and the lack of autonomy of the miners, the closure of the mining community – are seen as handicaps for the modernization of this area. These handicaps serve to explain the persistent economic and social difficulties of the region – especially the high unemployment rate – as well as its political problems: the great success of the "Front national", the French political party of the far right, in this ancient working-class region.

Figure 3.1 The Nord-Pas-de-Calais mining area in France in the time of the closure of the mines.

Credit: The slagheaps 11/19, the symbol of the Northern mining heritage (1975). Source: Fonds Phot'R, Collections Centre Historique Minier du Nord-Pas-de-Calais, Lewarde, France.

We see here that, in the former mining basin of the Nord, which once was the most important in France, the region's relationship with its mining past remains a major and complex issue, extending far beyond the narrower question of what is left of the mines following their disuse. Drawing upon previous studies – some at the level of other French mining basins,[5] and others at the European level[6] (Conlin and Jolliffe, 2010, Dicks, 200) – it is this very complexity that the current paper would like to explore. After revisiting, briefly, the history of the basin, and the importance of that history in defining the image of the region and the identity of its inhabitants, this paper will place special emphasis on the processes at work from the moment (in the years 1960–1970) when the mine ceased, little by little, to be a living reality. In particular, this study seeks to understand how we have gone from a lack of familiarity with mining heritage – or, indeed, an impulse to erase it entirely – to its progressive valorization, up to and including the recognition that the 2012 UNESCO classification represents. I will show, especially, that this transformation does not come from a sudden and miraculous awareness, but rather that it is inscribed in the evolution of public policy and region development, as well as in the transformation of the actors who make up the life of the basin. Finally, I will investigate the ambiguities and questions that are raised today by the deployment of the Nord's mining heritage, most notably in terms of identity for the inhabitants of the region. Foregrounding the case of the Nord basin, my overall aim is to capture the relationships (both continuous and discontinuous) that contemporary societies maintain with their mining heritage, and to ask what possible use and signification such heritage might have for us today.

The Nord mining basin, from pinnacle to crisis

In French eyes, the Nord mining basin has been the symbol of the mining world since the second half of the 19th century.[7] Nearly 120 kilometers in length, the basin traverses the two departments of Nord and Pas-de-Calais, and is centered around the cities of Valenciennes and Anzin in the Nord, and Lens and Béthune in the Pas-de-Calais. Private mining companies, granted coal excavation rights by the State, competed to attract (and especially to retain) workers, who at first came from the surrounding countryside but were quickly followed by workers who came from other European nations: Belgians, in the first instance, and then Poles, Italians and North Africans.[8] Much more than the local authorities, it was these companies who became the true masters of the land.[9] Not content with devastating the landscape by developing the infrastructure necessary for coal extraction (pitheads, headgears, slag heaps, railways and canals, factories for derivative products), they created housing around the mining sites, housing projects that would become so many small, privatized towns.[10] In a process similar to that which we observe elsewhere in northwest Europe[11] (the companies took over the entirety of the local population's needs. The social policies of mining paternalism thus covered housing, education, leisure activity, religion and healthcare, all sectors that were represented by the construction of new infrastructure (e.g., schools, stadiums, cooperatives, hospitals and churches).

On the eve of World War II, the Nord mining basin represented more than 60 per cent of national coal production. Certain emblematic events contributed to give the basin a specific status in the French imagination: the major mining strikes, for example, or the 1906 mining disaster of Courrières, which claimed 1099 victims and was the worst catastrophe of its kind in Europe.[12] These events fueled a collective imagination, which was also nourished by a variety of novels and artwork beginning with Émile Zola's famous *Germinal* (1885). These events and depictions helped sculpt an image of the Nord as the *Pays Noir* (the Black Country), with its slag heaps, headframes and pervasive coal dust. The figure of 'the miner' also appeared, presented at once as a martyr, a soldier and a hero of triumphant industrialization. If indeed this mythological elaboration of the coalfield insists on the ugliness of the landscape and the hardness of mining life, it also underscores its positive traits. The Nord is presented as a land of richness and production; the miners, as the vanguard of the working class. During the interwar period, this representation was particularly showcased by the Communist Party.[13] Hence, in 1949, the Communist writer André Stil described the coalfield as "the site of new combat," which inscribed "by its sharpest point, France's present. And in moving toward a future worthy of her, it is the miners who are carving the path."[14]

At the same time, this set of representations helped give the mining basin a stable and homogenous appearance, which in reality was far from the case. Mining may indeed have appeared as a monolithic industry in the western part of the basin, but such was not the case everywhere, and the steel industry was very active in the Valenciennes region. Further, while in some cases the mining industry did give rise to new villages structured entirely around coalmining (such as Avion and Sallaumines), in other cases (Lens, Béthune) the old city centers persisted and harbored populations that did not necessarily identify with the industry.[15] Finally, I might note that the mining landscapes,[16] presented *a posteriori* as immutable (the headgears, the slag heaps, etc.), have in actuality not ceased to evolve due to the evolution of techniques (the use of wood, then iron and finally reinforced concrete in building the headgears) and the destruction caused by the two World Wars. Thus, it is difficult to reduce the mining towns to the stereotype of the *corons*, or rows of miners' cottages, depicted in *Germinal*: rebuilt after World War I, they took the form of residential towns and "garden cities" before ceding to the prefabricated and detached (or semi-detached) houses built in the 1950s.[17]

In this world of constant motion, shaken by crisis and war and crosscut by migratory flows, the forms of identity claimed are themselves plural. Certainly the vocation of miner, which governed professional life as well as the social and familial, constitutes a very strong principal of belonging. Still, even this identification takes diverse forms. One might feel a sense of general affiliation with the mining world, but also (more concretely) with one's neighborhood, town, neighborly relations and local landmarks (the street, the pit, the church). Within the mining community, individuals also fall back upon their ethnic identities (French/migrant) or their political affiliations (Socialist/Communist/Catholic). The local labor movement, which won solid union and municipal positions (the majority of mining communities were administered by Socialist or Communist elected officials), established its own forms of membership. Faced with the mining companies' hegemony, their infrastructure and buildings, elected representatives and unions in turn constructed stadiums, town halls and cooperatives.[18] In Lens, the CGT union headquarters – built in 1911 and today classified as a historic monument – has long been the center of working-class life and the vector of a militant identity. Through its supporters, a football club such as the Racing Club of Lens, directed from the 1930s to the 1960s by a mining company, can well attest to this layering of identities. These supporters – in their movement, as in their distribution within the stadium – manifest their affiliation with their neighborhood and their city. Simultaneously, they support together a club that represents, in their eyes, a professional identity (the miners of the Lens company), but also an urban identity (the citizens of Lens, the capital of the coalfield).

All of the mining companies in the North were nationalized between 1944 and 1946.[19] Within the state-run company of the *Charbonnages de France* (CDF), they were consolidated into a single entity: the Nord-Pas-de-Calais National Coal Mines, or the *Houillères nationales du bassin Nord-Pas-de-Calais* (HBNPC). In this way, the State and its representatives became a major interlocutor to the workers' movement and the municipalities. If in the beginning nationalization was presented as synonymous with modernization and unification (moving beyond the rivalries between companies), these ambitions fizzled. In France, as in Great Britain, nationalization failed the workers, who felt mining paternalism continued under the leadership of the State; the different groups of the HBNPC recommenced the territorial outlines of the old mining companies and had little effect, in the first instance, on the practices and daily life within the mining community.

It was, in reality, the beginning of the recession that introduced the greatest upheaval. The French collieries, like their European counterparts,[20] entered a period of crisis starting in the mid-1950s; this period, interspersed with brief rebound phases, continued until the closing of the last mines (1990 in the Nord; 2003–2004 in Provence and Lorraine) and the disappearance of the *Charbonnages de France* in 2007. Beginning in the early 1950s, the first mine closures occurred in the Midi and in the western part of the Nord basin. The role of carbon in energy consummation continued to decline in favor of oil.

The French government adopted an initial plan to orchestrate the closing of the mines in 1959 ("plan Jeanneney"), followed by a second in 1968 ("plan Bettencourt"). In the "Houillères du Nord", production was reduced by half, with numerous pits closing even if extraction continued at first in certain concentrated and modernized units, for example, the 11/19 pit in Lens. Whereas the HBNPC had employed 131,000 miners in 1959, by 1974 the number had decreased to no more than 47,000. The closing of the mines resulted not only in job loss and areas of industrial wasteland, but also had a broader destabilizing impact on the urban fabric, education, public affairs and leisure.[21]

We therefore witness a fragmentation, slow but certain, of the mining communities, even if its effects on employment were not easily visible at first. In fact, it might be said that deindustrialization was not abundantly apparent until the 1970s: the miners were not laid off but displaced to the remaining pits, having no alternative but to seek work elsewhere or to go into early retirement. What is more, the State and the HBNPC multiplied the structures meant to facilitate the re-industrialization of the basin, including those pertaining to automobile manufacturing (the *Française de mécanique* in Douvrin; Renault in Douai; the building of a new steel-working complex on the coast in Dunkerque).

Naturally, observers in the early 1970s pointed to the handicaps left by the monolithic coalmining industry (qualification issues, service shortages), declaring that the Nord did not yet have the characteristics of a 'modern economy'; nevertheless, it seemed that the quest to attain such modernity (and to overcome the 'archaism' of the mining industry) was making progress. Yet the crisis brought about by the first oil shock, in 1973, put an end to this dynamic, breaking the momentum of the substitute industries and creating mass unemployment for the new generation, as well as opening a definitive gulf between the miners' children and the typical norms and forms of life in mining communities.[22]

In parallel, a clear change registered in the image of both the region and the mining basin.[23] Without doubt, the Nord basin and its miners were depicted quite somberly (the darkness of the landscape, the suffering that came with mining life). However, the negative aspects of this vision were counterbalanced by the positive:

the role of the basin in the industrial dynamic of France, the representation of miners as heroes of production and as the vanguard of the working class. However, in the 1960s–1970s, the predominant view was purely pessimistic, marked by the corresponding seal of misery. The Nord basin no longer appeared as an area of dwindling industry, synonymous with the difficulties typically associated with deindustrialization (unemployment, industrial wastelands), associated with deindustrialization in the case of the heavy industry areas:[24] closure of the industrial sites, destruction of jobs and unemployment, industrial wastelands. For many journalists, writers, or social scientists, the miner became the symbol of the 'old' working class, in opposition to 'modern' workers (operators at automated factories, workers in state-of-the-art industries). Depicted as the poor and the sick, discarded by new forms of consumer society, witnesses to an archaic way of life, the miner became a foil, as it were, for modernity as it was defined at the end of the 20th century.

Erasing the traces of mining exploitation (1960s–1980s)?

Up to the mid-1980s, public policy (economic policy, land development) was still shaped by the idea that a new phase of industrialization would solve all of these problems. No doubt these policies, undertaken by developers enamored with modernization, were undermined by the crisis of 1973–1974; yet their guiding principle remained, and even received fresh impetus by the arrival of the Socialist François Mitterrand to the head of the State in 1981. During his visit to the Nord mining basin in April 1983, the President of the Republic may have tolled the bell for any fleeting hopes of reviving the coal industry, but in exchange he promised an "industrial rebirth of the mining basin." This promise was solidified by the contract of the State-region plan adopted in 1984, which created structures such as the FIBM ("*Fonds d'industrialisation des bassins miniers*" – Industrialization Fund for the Coalfields).[25] This policy was founded upon the idea that revitalized industrial organization might emerge after mining activity had ceased. Around the same time, the president of the *Charbonnages de France* insisted on the fact that his own activity in mining areas should not be understood solely as a form of reparation, but as means of "positive action in business development and in the modernisation of the French industrial system."[26]

It is in this context, first and foremost, that the question of mining heritage arises. In the largest mining basins, and especially those located in the Nord, this heritage – a word mostly understood at the time in its strictest sense, as pertaining to a set of sites and property assets – was enormous: more than 1,200,000 homes, thousands of hectares occupied by surface installations and slag heaps, dozens of churches, hospitals, stadiums and more (Baudelle 1992, 831–945).

If this material heritage strengthened the HBNPC during the mining period, it was primarily seen as a weight or burden as soon as mining activity ceased.[27] Therefore, the managers of the HBNPC sought to avoid letting it weigh upon their balance sheets, which were already in deficit. Thus, the most profitable elements of mining heritage (land, in particular) must be sold after being razed; others, often in disrepair, were abandoned to the local authorities. Mining heritage was therefore seen quite negatively, and in keeping with this view, the remains of the mining industry were doomed to disappear: the pits were filled in, the pitheads and the slagheaps were destroyed, and the headframes dismantled. This destruction was justified for a number of reasons – economic, of course, but also environmental and technical (the mining infrastructure loomed large in the landscape and did damage to the surrounding groundwater and soil).

Given their strong State support, these policies were implemented with little discussion or negotiation, and even without paying much attention to the symbolic brutality of destroying whole swaths of land that, for decades, had structured the daily life of the mining community and served as its landmarks.[28] At the same time, such policies were a source of bitter conflict between actors with divergent interests: on the one hand, the nationalized companies eager for managerial efficiency and looking to limit their deficits; on the other, the local elected officials who found themselves assuming new responsibilities without the means to do so. These local representatives, grouped together within the "*Association des communes minières*" (Union of the mining municipalities), created in 1970, accused the companies of abandoning the basin after their hegemonic rule, while at the same time leaving local communities with the burden of managing housing and infrastructure, which were often in very poor condition.[29] This period was marked by recurring battles between the State-assisted HBNPC and the local authorities, particularly with regard to the management of mining housing.[30] The local representatives depicted themselves as the new protectors for the inhabitants against the HBNPC and claimed the right to manage the mining housing, while the HBNPC wanted to sell the houses to reduce the deficit of the enterprise. In this way, these representatives gained an increase in their legitimacy – as the defenders and the spokesmen of the ancient mining community – even if they obtained the management of the mining housing only in the 2000s.

However, such divisions did not prevent an implicit consensus on one point: in the eyes of most mayors and HBNPC managers, the material remains of the old industry occupied space and perpetuated the now pejorative image of the region as the *Pays Noir*, and therefore needed to be eliminated so that the basin could come into a new era. The mayors of the large mining towns, who found themselves once again immerged in immense difficulties, simultaneously gained in power (the mining companies had previously administrated most of city life on their own) and claimed to be themselves the developers of new cities. In Liévin, as in Lens, they dreamed of ridding their city of all traces of mining and replacing them with modern attributes: bypasses and motorways would eliminate the canals and railways, and the *corons* would give way to large complexes and new shopping centers.[31] Certainly, the nuance of such policies differed according to the political color of a given municipality: the Socialists had a more diverse electorate, and were the most eager to efface all traces of the mines, while the Communists (for whom miners formed the principal electoral base) sought primarily to defend the mines and the miners to the end.[32] In this period, it remained the case that mining heritage was a subject of almost universal indifference, and was (for different reasons) largely absent from the public forum.[33]

General as such indifference may have been, however, it was not absolute. Some major initiatives pertaining to mining heritage were unfurled during this period, beginning with the 1973 creation of the *Centre Historique Minier de Lewarde* (CHM, Historic Mining Centre), which would become the principal mining museum in the region and even in France.[34] Contrary to what can be observed in other cases, especially that of Lorraine in the same period,[35] the initiative is in no way the product of the local labor movement: the CGT union of Northern miners therefore places a strong emphasis on the fight against closing the mines, and on the defense of a mine that continues to 'live' on other terms, and does not view a project like the museum as anything other than a means of accepting the death of the mines. The union is even less enthusiastic about the paternalistic origins of the creation of the *Centre Historique Minier*: it was none other than the managers of the HBNPC who had decided to establish a place likely to host their archives, while at the same time proffering an idealized image of mining. Hence the museum was set up on the grounds of a small pit situated close to Douai, and concentrated all of the stereotypes of the ideal mine (the headgear, the buildings clustered around it), even if it was not actually representative of the complexity of mining landscapes (it is situated in the countryside, far from the mining villages) or of the later phases of exploitation. The museum opened its doors in 1984, and in 1990 reconstructed a visit 'to the bottom' to attract visitors (in reality, for obvious safety reasons, the journey had to take place in a tunnel recreated at surface level). The museum became very successful at the local and national level and tried to associate some local 'miners' (in fact often foremen) to give the guided tours. If the mining unionists were firstly very suspicious of this initiative, they became after more conciliatory and supported the *Centre Historique Minier*. Meanwhile, though the HBNPC managers maintained a lasting influence on the museum, they began to share its direction with representatives from the local authorities (especially the region Nord-Pas-de-Calais).[36]

In fact, the creation of the *Centre Historique Minier* was initially the work of several individuals – especially the Secretary General of the HBNPC, Alexis Destruys – anxious to preserve mining-related archives and memorabilia. Yet a shift occurred on a more general level starting in the late 1970s.[37] The reasons were both a transnational movement (the success of the industrial heritage in other European countries in the 1960s, like Great-Britain or Germany, was really starting to spread in France) and a national change: the heritage was no longer seen only a monumental and a national heritage and was valorized as the multiple and various heritages (local, professional, cultural, etc.) which made the identities of the inhabitants. The first French associations to fight for the recognition of industrial heritage emerged, such as CILAC (the *Comité de liaison et d'information sur l'archéologie industrielle*, Liaison and Information Committee for Industrial Archaeology) in 1979, which is made up of academics and local associations. After the 1981 arrival to power of the Socialist left, the interest in industrial heritage was reinforced. This interest was primarily seen from a scientific and technical perspective. Thus, the task of preserving and spreading the knowledge (and know-how) of the mining industry came first and foremost, once again in order to serve the objectives of the country's reindustrialization. As the representative of the Nord Prefecture explained early in the 1980s, it was precisely this potential role as a scientific and technological center that could justify supporting the State at the Historic Mining Center:

> Knowing that attitudes and social gravity can affect how receptive our youth are to the high-level technical training that is necessary for the future, and given the obstacles of economic conversion, the *"Centre de Culture Scientifique et Technique"* of Lewarde would appear to be an essential tool for raising awareness, and for inciting and animating the reindustrialisation and development of the mining basin of the Nord-Pas-de-Calais region.[38]

Here heritage is envisioned as a form of education, one of the levers that must be activated for the Nord to become once again a leading area of industry.

The turning point for mining heritage in the Nord basin (1990s–2010)

In the mid-1980s, however, the Nord basin's situation seemed bleaker than ever. Several government-commissioned reports cited persistent economic and social problems in the mining area, as well as the repulsive appearance of its landscapes of industrial wasteland.[39] The authors of these reports further estimated that it was no longer possible to believe the area's salvation would come from a new industrial phase. "The commercial function must prevail over the function of production," asserted the engineer Jean-Paul Lacaze, who cited as a model of conversion the Smurfs' Village, a newly operational amusement park close to the old steel-working city of Hayange, in Lorraine. For Lacaze, the management of the industrial wastelands needed to change: the old 'industrial' model should give way to the 'post-industrial,' which would be based on the rendering of services, the call to new technologies, and the creation of centers for research and innovation (though Lacaze did little specify what forms the new model would take).[40]

This type of analysis attests to a major change in outlook that, both nationally and locally, came to be integrated by the majority of political actors. This shift first became manifest in the depletion of grand ambitions and massive plans for reindustrialization under the stewardship of developers and government officials. Instead, local authorities – who had acquired a much more important role thanks to the decentralization laws of 1982–1983 – increasingly tended to wager on skilled activities (those generally termed 'post-industrial') and on services, especially those relating to culture. This transformation proffered an early explanation for the fresh interest in the traces and remains of the mining industry: if they could no longer serve a productive function, policymakers and planners believed they might instead be integrated into a general reorientation of the mining basin and, on a broader scale, in the Nord-Pas-de-Calais region. Moving forward, the dynamic of the former industrial region should lean heavily upon a tertiary economy (valorizing tourism and cultural events, among others), and mining heritage would serve this dynamic.

During the 1990s, this change was facilitated by a number of actions that confirmed a definitive transition into the after-mine period.[41] The last mines in the Nord, at Oignies, closed in 1990, and the HBNPC was officially dissolved in 1992. At the national level, the 1994 adoption of the *Pacte charbonnier* (Coal Pact) put an end to social plans and scheduled a showdown of the mines still in production, in Lorraine and Provence. During this period, the management of mining heritage – whether related to housing, surface installations or even slag heaps – was turned over little by little to the local authorities, who again found themselves the sole masters of the land now that the former mine operators had disappeared from the scene. Meanwhile, under the terms of a law adopted in 1999, the State was charged with the guaranty and management of any ongoing risk, including environmental risks such as subsidence and water pollution.[42] The end of coal came about slowly, spanning over three decades (the 1960s–1990s), and had several decisive consequences. First, it gradually smoothed over conflicts related to the recession: the HBNPC disappeared, the remaining activists of the labor movement refocused their efforts on cultural action (the CGT union of miners created its own association, *Mémoires et Cultures* [Memory and Culture], in 1998), and local management was normalized. Mining heritage, now less tied to political or social conflict, became more likely to engender compromise between nostalgia for an idealized past and the redeployment of elements of that past to help meet the needs of the present.

The emphasis on mining heritage thereafter was remarkable, and took various forms.[43] The first affected the rescue and conservation of a certain number of monumental or landscape elements, at the instigation of an increasing number of associative groups (whose actions were encouraged by State services and local authorities). In the Nord, their actions resulted in the classification of certain elements of mining heritage as historical monuments. In the decade from 1990–2000, this was the case for the Wallers-Arenberg facilities, for some of the facilities of the n°9/9bis pit in Oignies in the Nord, and for the headgear and two slag heaps of the 11/9 pit in Loos-en-Gohelle in the Pas-de-Calais, deemed "the largest in Europe." Simultaneously, emphasis was placed on redeploying the industrial lands for new purposes, whether touristic, cultural, or associated with projects lead by innovation centers, which focused on sustainable development, information and communications. This movement is clearly demonstrated by the emergence of the 11/19 site as one of the most emblematic in the basin. Its remarkable character, and its role as a landmark for the local population, made the site an early subject for projects aiming at once to recognize its heritage dimension and to assure its repurposing for other uses. Under the leadership of the municipality of Loos-en-Gohelle, the entirety of the site was thus revitalized, notably through the creation of a business park geared toward sustainable development (Ecopôle), along with the installation of an inter-communal association for artistic and cultural development (Culture Commune). The process reached its peak slightly later, in 2004, when the President of the Republic Jacques Chirac – at the request of local elected officials – chose an old pithead from Lens as the site for a new branch of the Louvre.[44]

In a broader sense investment in heritage initiatives during this period became a form of legitimation for the local authorities (municipalities, regional council), which were largely comprised of members of the Socialist Party (Rabier 2002, Sawicki 1997, 67–175). While they showed little interest – to put it mildly – for mining heritage during the 1970s–1980s, they grew increasingly attentive. The Socialist majority of the regional council in the Nord-Pas-de-Calais, along with its president, Daniel Percheron, frequently played the 'heritage card,' as demonstrated by their fervent support for the Louvre-Lens project. The creation of an *ad hoc* organization *Mineurs du Monde* (Miners of the World), in recent years was another example. The latter was charged with initiating major projects relating to mining culture and history (the digitization of archives; colloquia), though not without competition from older organizations, namely the *Centre Historique Minier*. There were many reasons for this reversal (Tornatore 2010, 27–38).[45] The emphasis on working culture was a means of reaffirming a political identity (battered as it might have been by crisis and transformations of socialism), but also represented the hope that voters would rally around elected representatives who were portrayed as the heirs of the local labor movement. These representatives, having abandoned all hope of a reindustrialization of the basin, saw the establishment of cultural activities as the sole means of regaining economic momentum.[46] Presenting mining identity solely in a positive light appears, ultimately, as a means of making the basin attractive once more in the eyes of investors and tourists. Forgetting the conflicts, the strikes and the ruptures within the mining community, these representatives presented the mining region of the Nord as a "melting pot," traditionally working class, likeable and open, in hopes of contributing to the revitalization of the region's image.

All of these elements were at stake in the candidacy of the Nord mining basin for UNESCO's list of Global Heritage Sites. The project was born in the early 2000s, at the initiative of numerous local institutions and local officials, in particular the mayor of Loos-en-Gohelle, the ecologist Jean-François Caron. The locally rooted Caron, who had succeeded his Socialist father as Mayor of Loos-en-Gohelle, endeavored from the start to showcase his town as a regeneration of the mining basin.[47] He was also very involved with the organizations responsible for imagining the urban, social, economic and environmental restructuring of the basin after its mining activity had ended: namely, the *Conférence permanente du basin minier* (Permanent conference for the mining basin, 1997–1998), followed by the *Mission Bassin Minier Nord-Pas-de-Calais* (Mission for the Nord-Pas-de-Calais basin), created in 2000. The application he launched in these conditions was far from aiming at a 'museumification' of the mining basin. To the contrary, the UNESCO classification was perceived as an additional dynamic factor, meant to accelerate the redevelopment and enhancement of sites by giving them a national and international reputation. The project quickly received active support from the local authorities, especially from the Nord-Pas-de-Calais region. It was also characterized by a desire to actively mobilize people, particularly through workshops and clubs like the Bassin Minier UNESCO clubs which sought to develop local mobilizations and to involve residents in the preservation and transmission of mining heritage and memory.[48] The emphasis on the past, and on the traces left by the coal industry, was thus presented as a way to develop new forms of participatory democracy and to make residents adhere to the new dynamic of the mining basin.

What identity for the former Nord basin?

From this perspective, the year 2012 takes on the appearance of a consecration. The mining basin received its UNESCO classification in July, and its inauguration took place with great fanfare at the Lens branch of the Louvre on December 4, 2012. In the eyes of its promoters, which dreamed of the model of the Guggenheim Museum in Bilbao, the Louvre Lens was the manifestation *par excellence* of the development that should thereafter structure the Nord basin: built on an old pithead, it combined futuristic architecture with references to mining heritage (as seen in the surrounding park, for example). Thus blending tradition and modernity, it would become a new center for the city of Lens, simultaneously attracting tourists and energizing commercial activities in Lens and the surrounding area. We might note, however, that four years after its opening, the museum was far from fulfilling all the hopes entrusted to it: it remained somewhat insulated, and did not have the desired effect of momentum on the local economy.[49]

We will observe, more broadly, that the present situation of the former Nord basin is far from simply hoisting the banner of a happy ending (the recognition of mining heritage after decades of destructive frenzy). The management of its mining past remains a work in progress, molded by ambiguities and contradictions. The increasing value of certain elements of its mining heritage does not preclude the persistent stigmatization of the mine as a weight and as a handicap. Even today, this stigmatization continues to be active in the minds of developers and local stakeholders in the Nord. The balance sheets and prospective work, like the official reports, all insist upon this point, much as they all insist upon the need to change, to modernize mentalities, and to erase the traces of the old mining culture (seen as one of the factors in the population's difficulties, as well as in sanitary and environmental problems).

In reality, the objective of modernizing and erasing the archaism of mining – already present in the 1970s–1980s – persists today. What has changed is the place that mining heritage is likely to occupy within this perspective. If the remains of the mines were first seen as obstacles to remove in order to 'operate' modernization in the basins, they were next perceived as elements capable of moving in the direction of modernization, as long as they could be transformed or in some way reframed. Doing so would primarily involve their integration into new proposals for services and cultural infrastructure, even if their original meaning might be deformed (for example, a slag heap transformed into an artificial ski slope, or a headgear preserved in the center of a commercial area), or if they would function more as pretext or accessory. Furthermore, the vision of the area's mining past presented by today's local elite is largely simplified and idealized. They sketch an image of a stable and peaceful mining community that lived according to the rhythm of coal production, and that was marked by a solidarity and understanding that transcended political and ethnic difference.

Behind the praise for mining heritage, there remains a markedly inconsistent relationship with the area's mining past: it is unrecognized by some and glorified by others, and alternately viewed with nostalgia and seen as an obstacle. This erratic relationship is apparent today in the identity and image associated with the mining basin and, more generally, with the Nord region.[50] To give an example: when the Racing Club of Lens, the old mining club, won the French football championship in 1998, the local and national press alike celebrated the victory. The club's supporters were presented as the inheritors of working-class values (solidarity, enthusiasm, courage, unity). The club itself appeared as the bearer of regional identity, exemplifying the same local popular culture – so eminently positive and likeable – that was portrayed so well in the box office success *Bienvenue chez les Ch'tis* (2008). However, an entirely different image appeared when, on April 21, 2002 – the eve of the first round of the presidential election – the far right received considerable support in the former mining basin, a phenomenon that has continued ever since. In the media coverage, the image of the Nord took on much more appalling traits: presented as an impoverished and under-educated region, it seemed to be the very incarnation of stagnation, unemployment, exclusion and the refusal of an open and globalized society. The former heroes of the working class were depicted as lost children and as the new stokers of the far right.

We could very well say that today's relationship with the mining past, and the weight of that past on the present, raises questions that are far from being resolved. Such an admission should not be read as a denial of the heritage process that has been undertaken in recent decades. While its role in economic recovery may be questionable, it has nevertheless helped to preserve landscapes, housing and infrastructure, recognizing the utility and beauty in each. More importantly, initiatives such as the "Bassin Minier UNESCO," which experienced great popular success, attested to a democratization and re-appropriation of the local mining past by the residents themselves, and to the desire to use that past in shoring up their sense of identity and pride. Stated differently, the recognition of mining heritage had helped to mend a continuity that had been broken by the hardships and brutality of crisis. From a contemporary standpoint, the region's mining past appears to be simultaneously under- and over-valued, and it seems clear that current problems stem largely from the question of what role that past should play going forward. On the one hand, the legacy of the mines can no longer possibly be the final word in defining the region and its inhabitants, given the profound changes that occurred in the 25 years (or more) since the mines closed. Today, the population of the Nord basin is quite diverse, mingling former miners and their descendants with those who have no ties to the industry, with both groups maintaining different relationships with the region's mining past (e.g., forgetfulness, indifference, reinvention). On the other hand, I can imagine putting that past to work in more coherent and fruitful ways, which in turn could help define the future of the Nord. In effect, the valorization of this heritage suffers from numerous local and institutional rivalries – those who oppose the *Centre Historique Minier de Lewarde* and the *Mineurs du monde* being the most flagrant examples – making it difficult to fully develop its potential. The lack of recognition for industrial and working-class culture in France, a country that has historically wished to remain rural, has proven an additional barrier. In fact, in France, since the 19th century, the national identity is thought of as a political identity – the French Revolution, the Republic – or as a result of a very old heritage (the old Christian France, the old countryside and the traditional values of the peasants): it's more difficult for the industrial history and for the workers, who were often migrant workers – to be included in this representation of the nation.[51] However, the present-day meaning and usages of mining heritage must be re-evaluated as well. Rather than putting forward an idealized image whose inaccessibility is bound to prove limiting, it might be helpful to highlight the whole movement of mining history, including its darker or more ambiguous aspects (for example, the rifts and in-fighting among the mining community). Moreover, we would benefit from trying to understand which elements of this history might be re-employed – not as mere decoration, but as lived experience that could help serve the needs of the present. Thus, at a time when we frequently speak of environmental issues and sustainable development, the relationships that former mining communities sustained with nature – notably through community gardens – could serve as a source of inspiration in designing new neighborhoods. Between denial and idealization, the true challenge lies in mending the chain of time, and in showing that mining experience can still be a dynamic element – locally, regionally and beyond.

Clearly, the case of the Nord basin presents a certain number of specificities, and it deserves to weigh against other situations. At the least, future study might help to nuance the idea of a progressive and linear imposition of the concept of industrial heritage – a concept that has received growing attention, though only amid profound changes to both its context and its uses. Initially perceived as a burden, or seen only from a scientific and technical point of view, this heritage was later integrated (as an ensemble of images and *lieux de mémoire*) into projects aiming to build a post-industrial society. There is no value judgment to bear on such a process, but it should at least be taken into account, if only because it sheds light upon well-known contradictions in the management of industrial heritage – especially with regard to the reuse of slag heaps or other sites, whose new functions generally erase their original significations. Further, this movement underscores the interest in proposing a 'true' history of industrial heritage, which could help illuminate both the political and the imaginary (particularly with respect to the construction of dualities such as industrial/post-industrial, archaism/modernity), as well as more general issues, including the image that western societies born of industrialization now have of themselves.

Notes

1 L'Unesco distingue les terrils et les cités du bassin minier du Nord, *Le Monde*, 1 July 2012.
2 See the internet site for the management of the UNESCO label: www.bassinminier-patrimoinemondial.org.

3 Hélène Mélin, Le patrimoine minier du bassin Nord-Pas-de-Calais : un outil de dynamisation territoriale, in Jean-Claude Daumas (ed.), *La mémoire de l'industrie, de l'usine au patrimoine*, Besançon, Presses universitaires de Franche-Comté, 2006, pp. 237–254.
4 Mission Bassin Minier Nord-Pas-de-Calais, *Le Livre Blanc. Acte II. Cent propositions pour accompagner la mutation du Bassin minier*, décembre 2013.
5 Octave Debary, *La fin du Creusot ou l'art d'accommoder les restes*, Paris, Editions du CTHS, 2002. Hélène Mélin, *La construction d'un patrimoine industriel dans le Nord-Pas-de-Calais. Du travail de mémoire au développement local*, Ph.D, Lille, USTL, 2002. Jean-Louis Tornatore (ed.), *L'invention de la Lorraine industrielle. Quêtes de reconnaissance, politiques de la mémoire*, Paris, Riveneuse Editions, 2010.
6 Michael Conlin, Lee Jolliffe, *Mining Heritage and Tourism: A Global Synthesis*, London, Routledge, 2010. Bela Dicks, *Heritage, Place and Community*, Cardiff, University of Wales Press, 2000.
7 Diana Cooper-Richet, *Le peuple de la nuit. Mines et mineurs en France, XIXe-XXe siècle*, Paris, Perrin, 2002.
8 Marion Fontaine, Football, Migration, and Coal Mining in Northern France, *International Review of Social History*, October 2015, pp. 1–21.
9 Marcel Gillet, *Les charbonnages du Nord de la France au XIXe siècle*, Paris and La Haye, Mouton et Ecoles Pratiques des Hautes Etudes, 1973.
10 Olivier Kourchid, Annie Kuhnmunch, *Mines et cités minières du Nord et du Pas-de-Calais. Photographies aériennes de 1920 à nos jours*, Lille, Presses Universitaires de Lille, 1990. Yves Le Maner, *Du coron à la cité. Un siècle d'habitat minier dans le Nord-Pas-de-Calais, 1850–1950*, Lewarde, Centre Historique Minier de Lewarde, 1995.
11 Joël Michel, *Le mouvement ouvrier chez les mineurs d'Europe occidentale (Grande-Bretagne, Belgique, Allemagne, France): étude comparative des années 1880–1914*, Ph.D.Lyon, Université de Lyon II, 1987.
12 André Dubuc (ed.), *10 mars 1906. La catastrophe de Courrières . Et après?* Lewarde, Editions du Centre Historique Minier, 2007.
13 Marc Lazar, Le mineur de fond: un exemple de l'identité communiste, *Revue Française de Sciences politiques*, avril 1985, pp. 190–205.
14 André Stil, *Le mot "mineur", camarades*, Paris, Bibliothèque française, 1949, p. 28.
15 Claude Dubar, Gérard Gayot, Jacques Hédoux, Sociabilité et changement social à Sallaumines et à Noyelles-sous-Lens, *Revue du Nord*, April–June, pp. 365–371.
16 André Dubuc (ed.), *Les paysages de la mine, un patrimoine contesté?*, Lewarde, Éditions Centre Historique Minier du Nord-Pas-de-Calais, 2009.
17 Yves Le Maner, *Du coron à la cité. Un siècle d'habitat minier dans le Nord-Pas-de-Calais, 1850–1950*, Lewarde, Centre Historique Minier de Lewarde, 1995.
18 Isabelle Sentis, *Un aspect méconnu de la culture ouvrière, les châteaux construits par/pour les mineurs dans l'Europe du Nord-Ouest*, Master's thesis, Lille, Université de Lille III, 1996.
19 Rolande Trempé, Les charbonnages, un cas social, in dans Claire Andrieu, Lucette Le Van, Antoine Prost, (eds.), *Les Nationalisations de la Libération. De l'utopie au compromis*, Paris, Presses de la FNSP, 1982, pp. 294–309.
20 René Leboutte, *Vie et mort des bassins industriels en Europe, 1750–2000*, Paris, L'Harmattan, 1997. Nicolas Verschueren, *Fermer les mines en construisant l'Europe. Une histoire sociale de l'intégration européenne*, Bruxelles, Peter Lang, 2014.
21 Marion Fontaine, *Le Racing Club de Lens et les "Gueules noires". Essai d'histoire sociale*, Paris, Les Indes Savantes, 2010, pp. 197–219. Jean-François Eck, Peter Freidemann, Karl Lauschke (eds.), *La reconversion des bassins charbonniers. Une comparaison interrégionale entre la Ruhr et le Nord-Pas-de-Calais*, Lille, Université Charles de Gaulle – Lille III – Revue du Nord, 2006.
22 Olivier Schwartz, *Le monde privé des ouvriers. Hommes et femmes du Nord*, Paris, PUF, 1990.

23 Marion Fontaine, *Fin d'un monde ouvrier, Liévin, 1974*, Paris, Editions de l'EHESS, 2014, pp. 52–76.
24 Steven High, *Industrial sunset. The Making of North America's Rust Belt 1969–1984*, Toronto, University of Toronto Press, 2003.
25 Archives Nationales du Monde du Travail (ANMT), 1994 014 449, Ré-industrialisation dans le Nord (1983–1984).
26 ANMT, 1994 014 246, CDF à l'heure des choix, 1 June 1984.
27 Television report, Les friches industrielles des Houillères, 29 November 1971. The French National Institute for audio-visual archives (INA) associated itself with the region Nord-Pas-de-Calais to publish online the most part of the television reports devoted to the Nord coalfield. These reportages are a very important resource for the contemporary history of the basin. They can be consulted on the web site, Mémoires de mines, http://fresques.ina.fr/memoires-de-mines. The reportages mentioned here come from this web site.
28 Peter Goin, Elisabeth Raymond, Living in Anthracite: Mining Landscape and Sense of Place in Wyoming Valley, *Public Historians*, n°23, 2001, 29–43.
29 Interview with André Delelis, mayor of Lens (1966–1998), 8 January 1999; interview with Jean-Pierre Kucheida, mayor of Liévin (1981–2013), 18 January 2013.
30 Fabien Desage, *La "bataille des corons". Le contrôle du logement minier, enjeu politique majeur de l'après-charbon dans l'ancien bassin du Nord-Pas-de-Calais*, Master's thesis, Lille, Université de Lille II, 1999.
31 Television report, Les futures réalisations communales de Liévin après la fermeture des mines, 19 October 1974.
32 Dubar, Gayot, Hédoux 1982, pp. 399–436.
33 Hélène Melin, Olivier Kourchid, Mobilisations et mémoires du travail dans une grande région industrielle, *Le Mouvement Social*, n°199, 2002, p. 42.
34 Fabien Desage, *Le Centre historique minier de Lewarde. Ressorts et enjeux d'un "lieu de mémoire" en bassin minier*, Master's thesis, Institut d'études politiques de Lille, Université de Lille II, 1998.
35 Jean-Louis Tornatore 2010.
36 Desage 1998, pp. 25–33.
37 Louis Bergeron, L'âge industriel, in Pierre Nora (ed.), *Les lieux de mémoire. Les France*, Paris, Gallimard, 1992, pp. 373–397.
38 Note from the Prefecture mentioned *in* Desage 1998, 66.
39 Jean-Paul Lacaze, *Les grandes friches industrielles*, DATAR/ Ministère de l'Équipement, du logement et de l'aménagement du territoire, La Documentation française, 1985.
40 Ibid., p. 19.
41 Jean-Claude Rabier (ed.), *La remonte: le bassin minier du Pas-de-Calais entre passé et avenir*, Villeneuve d'Ascq, Presses Universitaires du Septentrion, 2002.
42 Kourchid and Mélin 2002, p. 42.
43 Ibid., pp. 42–49.
44 Television report, Le Louvre-Lens, c'est quoi ? L'historique du projet, 4 December 2004.
45 Tornatore 2010, pp. 27–38.
46 Daniel Percheron, Le Louvre à Lens, *Le Journal de l'Ecole de Paris*, n°78, July–August 2009, p. 29.
47 A Loos-en-Gohelle, la transition verte au pays des gueules noires, *Le Monde*, 23 July 2015, www.lemonde.fr/societe/visuel/2015/07/23/a-loos-en-gohelle-la-transition-verte-au-pays-des-gueules-noires_4692549_3224.html.
48 Television report, Le bassin minier du Nord-Pas-de-Calais candidat à l'Unesco, 1 February 2010.
49 Jean-Michel Tobelem, Le Louvre-Lens n'aura pas "l'effet Bilbao" escompté, *Le Monde*, 21 August 2016.
50 Fontaine 2010, pp. 237–259.

51 See for example, Fernand Braudel, *L'identité de la France*, Paris, Arthaud, 1986. For a critical approach of this definition of the French identity, see Gerard Noiriel, *Le creuset français: histoire de l'immigration XIXe–XXe siècle*, Paris, Seuil, 1988, pp. 22–28.

Bibliography

Baudelle, Guy, *Le système spatial de la Mine: l'exemple du bassin houiller du Nord-Pas-de-Calais*, Paris, Université de Paris I, 1992, 2 vol.

Bergeron, Louis, L'âge industriel, in Pierre Nora (ed.), *Les lieux de mémoire. Les France*, Paris, Gallimard, 1992.

Conlin, Michael, Lee Jolliffe, *Mining Heritage and Tourism: A Global Synthesis*, London, Routledge, 2010.

Cooper-Richet, Diana, *Le peuple de la nuit. Mines et mineurs en France, XIXe–XXe siècle*, Paris, Perrin, 2002.

Debary, Octave, *La fin du Creusot ou l'art d'accommoder les restes*, Paris, Editions du CTHS, 2002.

Desage, Fabien, *Le Centre historique minier de Lewarde. Ressorts et enjeux d'un "lieu de mémoire" en bassin minier*, Lille, Institut d'études politiques de Lille, 1998.

Desage, Fabien, *La "bataille des corons". Le contrôle du logement minier, enjeu politique majeur de l'après-charbon dans l'ancien bassin du Nord-Pas-de-Calais*, Lille, Université de Lille II, 1999.

Dicks, Marcel Bela, *Heritage, Place and Community*, Cardiff, University of Wales Press, 2000.

Dubar, Claude, Gérard Gayot, Jacques Hédoux, Sociabilité et changement social à Sallaumines et à Noyelles-sous-Lens, *Revue du Nord*, n°253, avril–juin 1982, pp. 365–463.

Dubuc, André (ed.), *10 mars 1906. La catastrophe de Courrières . . . Et après?* Lewarde, Editions du Centre Historique Minier, 2007.

Dubuc, André (ed.), *Les paysages de la mine, un patrimoine contesté?*, Lewarde, Éditions Centre Historique Minier du Nord-Pas-de-Calais, 2009.

Eck, Jean-François, Peter Freidemann, Karl Lauschke (eds.), *La reconversion des bassins charbonniers. Une comparaison interrégionale entre la Ruhr et le Nord-Pas-de-Calais, Revue du Nord*, Hors-Série, coll. Histoire, n°21, 2006, Université Charles de Gaulle – Lille III, 2006.

Fontaine, Marion, *Le Racing Club de Lens et les "Gueules noires". Essai d'histoire sociale*, Paris, Les Indes Savantes, 2010.

Fontaine, Marion, *Fin d'un monde ouvrier, Liévin, 1974*, Paris, Editions de l'EHESS, 2014.

Fontaine, Marion, Football, Migration, and Coal Mining in Northern France, *International Review of Social History*, October 2015, pp. 1–21.

Gillet, Marcel, *Les charbonnages du Nord de la France au XIXe siècle*. Paris and La Haye, Mouton et Ecoles Pratiques des Hautes Etudes, 1973.

Goun, Peter, Elisabeth Raymond, Living in Anthracite. Mining Landscape and Sense of Place in Wyoming Valley, *Public Historians*, n°23, 2001, pp. 29–43.

Kourchid, Olivier, Annie Kuhnmunch, *Mines et cités minières du Nord et du Pas-de-Calais. Photographies aériennes de 1920 à nos jours*, Lille, Presses Universitaires de Lille, 1990.

Lazar, Marc, Le mineur de fond: un exemple de l'identité communiste, *Revue Française de Sciences politiques*, avril 1985, pp. 190–205.

Leboutte, René, *Vie et mort des bassins industriels en Europe, 1750–2000*, Paris, L'Harmattan, 1997.

Le Maner, Yves, *Du coron à la cité. Un siècle d'habitat minier dans le Nord-Pas-de-Calais, 1850–1950*, Lewarde, Centre Historique Minier de Lewarde, 1995.

Mélin, Hélène, *La construction d'un patrimoine industriel dans le Nord-Pas-de-Calais. Du travail de mémoire au développement local*, thèse de doctorat de sociologie, Lille, USTL, 2002.

Mélin, Hélène, Le patrimoine minier du bassin Nord-Pas-de-Calais: un outil de dynamisation territoriale, in Jean-Claude Daumas (ed.), *La mémoire de l'industrie, de l'usine au patrimoine*, Besançon, Presses universitaires de Franche-Comté, 2006, pp. 237–254.

Melin, Hélène, Olivier Kourchid, Mobilisations et mémoires du travail dans une grande région industrielle, *Le Mouvement Social*, n°199, 2002, pp. 37–59.

Michel, Joël, *Le mouvement ouvrier chez les mineurs d'Europe occidentale (Grande-Bretagne, Belgique, Allemagne, France): étude comparative des années 1880–1914*, Lyon, Université de Lyon II, 1987, 6 vol., 2800p.

Rabier, Jean-Claude (ed.), *La remonte: le bassin minier du Pas-de-Calais entre passé et avenir*, Villeneuve d'Ascq, Presses Universitaires du Septentrion, 2002.

Sawicki, Frédéric, *Les réseaux du Parti socialiste. Sociologie d'un milieu partisan*, Paris, Belin, 1997.

Schwartz, Olivier, *Le monde privé des ouvriers. Hommes et femmes du Nord*, Paris, PUF, 1990.

Sentis, Isabelle, *Un aspect méconnu de la culture ouvrière, les châteaux construits par/pour les mineurs dans l'Europe du Nord-Ouest*, Lille, Université de Lille III, 1996, 2 vol.

Tornatore, Jean-Louis (ed.), *L'invention de la Lorraine industrielle. Quêtes de reconnaissance, politiques de la mémoire*, Paris, Riveneuse Editions, 2010.

Trempé, Rolande, Les charbonnages, un cas social, in dans Claire Andrieu, Lucette Le Van, Antoine Prost (eds.), *Les Nationalisations de la Libération. De l'utopie au compromis*, Paris, Presses de la FNSP, 1982, pp. 294–309.

Verschueren, Nicolas, *Fermer les mines en construisant l'Europe. Une histoire sociale de l'intégration européenne*, Bruxelles, Peter Lang, 2014.

4 A post-industrial mindscape? The mainstreaming and touristification of industrial heritage in the Ruhr

Stefan Berger, Jana Golombek and Christian Wicke

Introduction

Public history and identity construction enjoy a symbiotic relationship, in industrial heritage as in other areas of public history. This chapter focuses on the representations of regional identity throughout the Ruhr region's ongoing transition to a postindustrial landscape and asks to what extent industrial heritage plays a crucial role in shaping that identity.[1] After giving a brief survey of the region's industrialization and de-industrialization, the chapter will discuss the role of industrial heritage in the construction of regional identity in the Ruhr and introduce the origins and development of industrial heritage as well as its main promoters. Subsequently the mainstreaming of industrial heritage in the Ruhr from the 1990s onwards is analyzed, and the chapter will conclude with some observations on the increasing touristification of industrial heritage in the Ruhr. It is interesting to note that, unlike most other regions in Germany, the genesis of the Ruhr is not to be found in pre-modern geopolitics but in the industrial production of coal and steel, which led to the urbanization of the region in the 19th century.[2] Thus, effectively the region came into existence through industrialization. The concept of the Ruhr as a distinct region emerged much later during the interwar period.[3] In the course of its deindustrialization during the second half of the 20th century and the early 21st century, industrial heritage came to occupy an essential role in the limited identity repertoire of the Ruhr. In fact, it is hard to think of any other urban region in the world in which industrial heritage has taken on such a significant role in public representation of the region during massive processes of de-industrialization.

Industrialization and de-industrialization

Germany, at least in comparison to Britain, industrialized relatively late. In the second half of the 18th century some important coal mines and some steelworks were established in the Ruhr region. However, it was only in the late 19th century that the Ruhr was fundamentally transformed from a rural region to a heavily urbanized region that would become Germany's and one of continental Europe's economic heartlands. Around 1900 villages developed rapidly into large towns

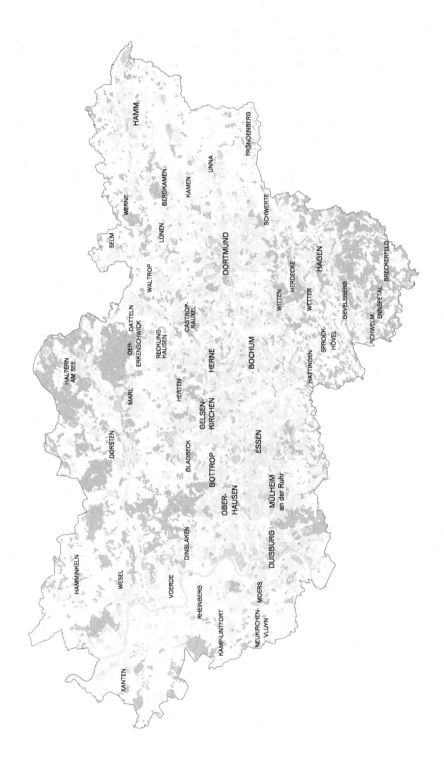

and cities. Both the coal and steel industries were booming, attracting hundreds of thousands of migrants from various German and non-German regions of Europe. The migration of Polish speakers was particularly numerous. The urbanization of the Ruhr cities followed a different trajectory than that of 'normal' cities. Christa Reicher speaks of "Ruhrbanity": it is hard to see one city center in the Ruhr. Rather the towns and cities of the Ruhr all have their own center which gives the region a marked polycentrism.[4] The Ruhr region comprises parts of the Rhineland and of Westphalia. It has its own regional association, the Regionalverband Ruhr (RVR) that goes back, under different names, to 1920.[5] The region was hit badly by the economic crises of the interwar period, but its fortunes revived under the Nazis' program of re-armament that was dependent on heavy industry. Having turned into heaps of rubble during the bombing war of the Second World War, the region was rebuilt and became one of the motors of German and West European recovery after the Second World War.

The coal crisis of 1957/58 is often seen as the vanishing point of the history of de-industrialization of the Ruhr. In the 1960s tens of thousands of miners in the Ruhr lost their jobs, as the crisis turned into a structural crisis and mine after mine closed. The international steel crisis started in the 1970s and led to the closure of many blast furnaces that had shaped the landscape and culture of the Ruhr. Over the course of six decades, and in the case of the coal industry, involving massive state subsidies, coal and steel became progressively less important to the economic make-up of the region. Today, the remaining steel industry is largely located in Duisburg along the Rhine River, and the last coal mine will shut in 2018. The massive structural change that the region witnessed involved an active engagement on behalf of the national and federal state (of North Rhine-Westphalia), the cities, towns and communities of the Ruhr, the mining and steel trade unions and major employers, such as the Ruhrkohle AG (RAG, est. 1968), and Thyssen-Krupp. It was the result of what has been described as Rhenish capitalism.[6] This structural change posed a challenge to the identity of the region, rooted as it was in heavy industry, and it also begged the question what to do with the remnants of that industrial past. As it happened, the confluence of those two challenges produced, as we shall see in the next sections, one of the strongest landscapes of industrial heritage in the world.

Industrial heritage and the construction of regional identity

Industrial heritage has become the main vehicle of the region's identity, because the Ruhr could not turn anywhere else. Unlike other regions of heavy industry that had also medieval or early modern or non-industrial aspects to their history, the Ruhr's identity repertoire was too limited. The remnants of the industrial past have been transformed through the leisure opportunities they now offer to many generations of inhabitants of the Ruhr, through their contribution to the touristification of the region and through the emergence of an 'industrial nature' (*Industrienatur*) that is part and parcel of a greening of the Ruhr that is highly valued by its inhabitants.[7] Added to this, the industrial remains of the past stand for the "ethos of the region" – a mentality of its inhabitants that is allegedly characterized by its "lack of arrogance, elegance and delusions of grandeur," the "repulsion of every attempt at exclusivity".[8] The roots of this mental world can be traced back to a "basic attitude of the deepest embarrassment" which had much to do with the negative image of the Ruhr as dirty and ugly.[9] Overcoming those negative stereotypes has always been a goal of local and regional authorities in the Ruhr. With the emergence of industrial heritage since the beginning of the 1970s a tool has been found with which to achieve those aims whilst retaining the allegedly attractive features of the Ruhr mentality.

Industrial heritage was 'discovered' in the Federal Republic during the 1960s, with artists, scholars and engaged citizens' initiatives taking a prominent role in preserving some of the iconic landmarks of the industrial landscape of the Ruhr.[10] With more than 3500 protected industrial monuments,[11] the German state of North Rhine-Westphalia (NRW) nowadays presents itself as situated between medieval and modern relics: "When you hear North Rhine-Westphalia, you think of Cologne Cathedral, a major landmark in Germany. And of the 'cathedrals of industry' such as Zollverein, a colliery turned World Heritage site."[12] Next to Essen's Zollverein, the 'mental skyline' of the Ruhr consists of dozens and dozens of industrial heritage sites, most prominently the tall blast furnaces at Duisburg Landschaftspark (a former Thyssen steel foundry), the Gasometer (a massive gas tank in Oberhausen), the Tetraeder in Bottrop (a walkable sculpture in the form of a tetrahedron on top of a very large slag heap next to a coal mine), the water tower in Bochum's Westpark (the site of a historic steel casting plant) and the U-Tower of a former brewery building in Dortmund. The industrial past has become the key feature in the public representation and perception of the Ruhr. Educational and cultural institutions that came in with de-industrialization, in particular the regions' universities, have contributed to this construction of an industrial past at the heart of the region's identity alongside a whole range of other actors, who shall be examined at somewhat greater depth in the next section. They were helped by an ongoing public history boom that affected many other parts of heritage.[13]

The origins and development of industrial heritage in the Ruhr and its main promoters

Despite the fact that from 1907 the *Deutsche Werkbund* had already intensively dealt with questions of industrial design, the art historian Tilmann Buddensieg is often considered as the creator of the very German term, *Industriekultur*, industrial culture that is often used synonymously with the English 'industrial heritage'.[14] While Buddensieg, in his work from 1979, primarily focused on business culture and aesthetic form, the cultural scientist Hermann Glaser, in the 1980s, extended the concept of *Industriekultur* by including the historical lifeworld of industrial modernity.[15] These efforts were linked to the research of historians of everyday life, such as Lutz Niethammer, who sought to explore the people and their 'ordinary', everyday experiences. The founding director of the Ruhr Museum, Ulrich

78 *Stefan Berger et al.*

Borsdorf, tried conceptually and practically to unite monument conservation with the everyday historical culture (*Geschichtskultur*). Borsdorf eventually materialized this conception through redesigning the Ruhr Museum, which opened at Zollverein in 2008.[16] Publications, such as *Leben vor Ort* by Franz-Josef Brüggemeier from 1983 and the *Hochlarmarker Lesebuch* from 1981, were part of this recognition of the everyday dimension of industrial heritage, which predominantly centered on miners and their families.[17]

German engineers have expressed enthusiasm for technological progress since the early 20th century, when new kinds of monuments were established in recognition of the rapid industrial rise of the country. The industrial archaeology movement that had started in the United Kingdom in the 1950s was closely observed by German historians of technology, such as Wolfhard Weber at Ruhr University Bochum and conservationists, who put their weight behind the preservation of industrial heritage.[18] Added to the enthusiasm of engineers came the belated recognition of industrial buildings as art. In 1969 the machine hall of the coalmine Zeche Zollern II/IV in Dortmund was protected as an industrial monument, not the least because art historians and architects had drawn attention to the artistic value of the art nouveau building by Bruno Möhring. Not only art historians, but artists themselves began to discover industrial heritage. Hilla and Bernd Becher, for example, who were then based in Dusseldorf, began photographing industrial objects in the Ruhr from the 1960s onwards.[19] Their exhibitions aimed primarily at the public realization of the aesthetic qualities of industrial buildings.[20] Such perspectives aligned themselves to an ideological and aesthetic

Figure 4.1 Zeche Zollern machine hall before preservation, 1969.
Source: LWL-Industriemuseum/Archiv

Figure 4.2 Zeche Zollern machine hall after restoration, 2016.
Source: LWL-Industriemuseum/Martin Holtappels

climate change in the 1960s that transcended Western European societies. Student protests and the emergence of the New Left both were driven by – and at the same time produced – a Marxist historical culture that took the industrial past seriously. Being left-wing became fashionable among the younger generations, and untold histories from below found a greater audience.[21] Artists, industrial heritage curators and industrial archeologists were mainly interested in objects, but the discovery of industrial heritage in the 1960s was also the discovery of the human beings, that is specifically the workers who had been working with these objects. Their culture, their lifeworld and their way of life were then revived and became part and parcel of alternative accounts of the past.[22] This new historical culture,[23] which articulated a new awareness of the industrial past in the public, flourished in the Ruhr and paved the ground for the success of industrial heritage.

A good example of an industrial heritage initiative from below was the initiative for the preservation of the Eisenheim workers' quarter in Oberhausen in the 1970s. Founded in 1848, this historic workers' settlement was to be demolished in the early 1970s. Some of its inhabitants signaled their resistance to this plan, and were supported by a project group lead by Roland Günter, a preservationist from Westphalia. When Eisenheim came under heritage protection in 1972, the long struggle for the historically sensitive modernization and maintenance of Eisenheim had been successful. Today, Eisenheim is a flagship for the official representation of industrial heritage in NRW and is part of the route of industrial heritage that connects dozens of industrial heritage sites across the Ruhr.[24] Eisenheim was a paradigmatic case, which was followed by various other initiatives across the Ruhr.[25] It represented the newly emerging trend for democratic historical culture, which combined academic research and the preservation of industrial heritage objects.

Another fascinating example for industrial heritage action from below is Zeche Carl. In 1977, the priest Willi Overbeck, looking for a place for a youth center in his neighborhood, organized a group of architects, heritage conservators and social workers to prevent the demolition of this mining complex. Zeche Carl subsequently developed into an important cultural center for Essen with a vibrant program for a great diversity of social groups.

Initiatives from below like these resulted in a rethinking of industrial heritage from above. Subsequent governments of North Rhine Westphalia, the communities in the Ruhr, the main coal and steel industrialists in the region, and the trade unions all became champions of industrial heritage. For the Social Democratic governments of NRW of the 1970s, industrial heritage not only legitimized the discovery of 'the ordinary people', but also served the purpose of democratizing the society's historical culture. In 1970, the state government announced the "North-Rhine Westphalia Program 1975" aiming at the preservation of technological-historical buildings, including shaft buildings, towers and machine halls.

In 1979, as part of an action program for the Ruhr, the Social Democratic government in NRW set aside public money to buy industrial properties. The effect of this decision on the development of the Ruhr landscape, both from environmental as well as cultural perspectives, can hardly be overestimated. A year later, in 1980, the NRW parliament adopted the State Heritage Preservation Law (*Landesdenkmalschutzgesetz*), which for the first time explicitly protected objects associated with industrial heritage.[26] From 1980 onwards the NRW Ministry for City Planning also became responsible for the protection of industrial heritage in the Ruhr cities incorporating many iconic objects into the cities' landscape.[27] Industrial heritage was now also positively accentuated by publicity campaigns of the RVR (including its predecessor organizations) that stressed the positive features of industrial heritage, for example in its 1985 campaign *Das Ruhrgebiet: Ein starkes Stück Deutschland* (The Ruhr: A Strong Piece of Germany).

The strong political and administrative support for the development of industrial heritage sites led to the creation of new monuments and the opening of new museums. In 1969 an archive and a research department became part of the time-honored German Mining Museum in Bochum. In 1973 the museum acquired a historical landmark when a massive pithead frame from a closed mine in Dortmund was shifted and re-erected on top of the museum complex, which was not located on an actual mining heritage site but on the site of the former Bochum slaughterhouse in 1930. The care of industrial heritage subsequently moved more and more into the center of the museum's activities, which would soon find further allies in its quest to promote the Ruhr for its industrial heritage.

In 1979, for example, the Westphalian Industrial Museum with a number of decentralized sites, also comprising important mining complexes, such as Zeche Zollern, was founded.[28] In 1984 its counterpart, the Rhenish Industrial Museum, was established in a former zinc factory in Oberhausen.[29] Industrial history was being presented at authentic sites. Museums have been, and continue to be, of key importance for the creation and promotion of industrial heritage in the Ruhr, as well as magnet for tourists which have been coming into the Ruhr in increasing numbers over recent years.

Another important actor in the recent history of the Ruhr's industrial heritage has been the Ruhrkohle AG, which was established in 1968 as the largest coal-mining corporation in Germany in order to master the coal crisis. For many years the RAG had been opposed to the industrial heritage movement, usually petitioning for the complete demolition of former mining complexes. The rehabilitated areas were, in the company's view, more useful as commercial parks and for creating new workplaces as well as residential neighborhoods.[30] The Federal Mining Law (*Bundesberggesetz*) from 1980 explicitly allowed companies to knock down existing buildings on closed mines. In view of the fact that the maintenance of industrial heritage sites involves not only technical difficulties but also horrendous costs, the RAG was only willing to make concessions in exceptional cases, where the Monument Offices were campaigning strongly for the realization of their interests. The vigorous documentation of industrial heritage objects by curators like Walter Buschmann was vital in this regard.[31] One should not forget that even today's UNESCO world heritage site, Zollverein, would have been largely demolished without the actions of the industrial heritage movement in opposition to the RAG management at the time.[32]

However, following the long process of change in thinking the region from the 1970s, the RAG also eventually turned into an important proponent of industrial heritage conservation, even if their commitment continued to be dependent on commercial interests.[33] From 1990 onwards, the RAG Montan Immobilien subsidiary of RAG has emerged as an internationally leading company for the historically sensitive conversion of mining sites. The moving of RAG Montan Immobilien to the Zollverein heritage site also signaled the commitment of the company to industrial heritage.[34]

The agency of the *Stiftung Industriedenkmalpflege und Geschichtkultur* (Foundation for Industrial Heritage Protection and Historical Culture), which has maintained close relations with the RAG, must not be ignored when it comes to the enshrining of industrial heritage as part of the broader regional historical culture. Following the National Trust model in Great Britain, the *Stiftung* was founded in the late 1980s, in order to take properties and buildings of various industries under its wings. The seat of the Foundation at one of its most iconic sites, the Hansa Coking Plant,[35] which came under heritage protection in 1998 and presents itself as a "huge walk-in sculpture",[36] is further proof of the commitment of the Foundation to industrial heritage as is its leading role in the ongoing attempts to extend world heritage status from Zollverein to other parts of the Ruhr.

Mainstreaming industrial heritage in the Ruhr

By the end of the 20th century, industrial heritage sites had become important interactive emblems of the cities in the Ruhr, forums of regional historical culture, venues for a diversity of public and private events, and international centers for encounters with a foreign past. One of the most significant events in the history of industrial heritage in the Ruhr was the International Building Exhibition (IBA) Emscher Park.[37] Between 1989 and 1999 the IBA aimed at the revitalization of the northern part of the Ruhr, which has been socioeconomically the weakest part of the region. Predominantly within this so-called Emscher zone, the IBA unleashed an overwhelming industrial heritage program. This ten-year project stretched across a large area of the Ruhr, from Duisburg in the east to Hamm in the west, and from Recklinghausen in the north to Bochum in the south, an area through which the river Emscher flows. The Emscher had become a by-word for industrial pollution and was not cleaned up and 're-naturized' (*renaturiert*).[38] The IBA's vision combined the regeneration of environment, economy and society. Environmental protection and industrial heritage protection formed an alliance. The damages of the industrialization were to be eliminated and a structural action program for the future viability of the region introduced. The industrial buildings were regarded as part of the regional culture. The charismatic manager of the IBA Emscher Park, Karl Ganser, used his budget of 5 billion deutschmarks to realize 120 city and landscape planning projects in 17 Ruhr municipalities.[39]

The IBA lead to a greater visualization and popularization of industrial heritage.[40] The lighthouse projects of the IBA comprised the gas tank in Oberhausen, the preservation of a Duisburg steel works, the Science Park in Gelsenkirchen and Zollverein Shaft 12 in Essen. One of the earlier art exhibitions at the Gasometer, titled *Feuer und Flamme* told the story of energy, for example, attracted half a million visitors. The Duisburg Landschaftspark, with its 200 hectares of the former Meiderich smelter, has not only become a refuge for birds and plants, but has also become a magnet for people from the region and abroad: its climbing walls, diving basin and stages for music and drama have attracted a broad range of social groups. In the meantime, Zollverein has become the central showpiece of the Ruhr as an UNESCO world heritage site.

Many industrial heritage places in the Ruhr were explicitly connected to issues of regional identity by those in charge of the IBA. The light installations, for example, contributed to an aesthetic exaltation of industrial heritage and therefore promoted the acceptance of industrial heritage among the regional population.[41] This grand public staging of industrial heritage has since been closely connected to regional image campaigns and the marketing of the Ruhr as a postindustrial space in search of revitalization. Moreover, it offered tourists from outside a coherent image of the Ruhr.[42] It is not for nothing that since 1999 large brown signs along the highways of the Ruhr have advertised the central industrial heritage objects.[43] Moreover, the IBA Emscher Park brought industrial heritage further into the focus of city planners.[44]

In 2001 Zollverein became a UNESCO world heritage site. This meant that wide-reaching heritage protection of the complex, including the cokery, was finally realized – which many had previously believed to be impossible.[45] NRW's state conservator, Günter Borchers, had already referred to Zollverein's potential as a heritage site before its closure in 1986. In 1985 the Minister for State and City Planning, Christoph Zöpel and the NRW Monument Office intervened in the decision by the RAG and the Essen council to demolish the complex. In 1986 Zollverein came under heritage protection. The state development agency of NRW, together with the NRW property fund, bought the area and recruited a working group for the future use of the heritage site. In 1988, the year before the beginning of the IBA, the decision was taken to develop it as a cultural site and the Zollverein Foundation, as well as a Zollverein development agency, came into being.

In 2010 the Ruhr (with the city of Essen as its representative) was European Capital of Culture.[46] Even though the majority of the related projects were not directly related to the industrial past, it was impossible to overlook the representation of the region's industrial heritage and associated regional identity. The symbolically powerful opening of the cultural capital year at the UNESCO world heritage site Zollverein lit a bright beacon of hope for the region and its industrial legacy. The regional history museum of the Ruhr, located at Zollverein, is explicitly not an industrial museum, but its emphasis on industrial heritage shows how important the remains of the industrial past are for the official representation of the region today.[47]

The mainstreaming of industrial heritage was also the beginning of a stronger touristification of the Ruhr. Eventization of the past has become a global phenomenon and expression of the western thrill-seeking societies.[48] There are different ways in which "social memory is externalized through the intensification of commodification and medialization", how "legislators and experts decontextualize memories pertinent to specific identities" and different "processes through which the past is simultaneously erased and (re)produced by the heritage industry."[49]

The Industrial Heritage Route, "the probably most ambitious project of industrial tourism", plays a decisive role in structuring the leisure space of the Ruhr by functioning as the "backbone of the touristy exploitation and marketing of the Ruhr region".[50] The "touristy valorization of this industrial landscape" has become "an important aspect" of industrial heritage.[51] Therefore, several private limited companies dealing with marketing the industrial heritage have come into being: the Projekt Ruhr GmbH as successor of the IBA, responsible for executing a follow-up masterplan for selected tourist sites, the Kultur Ruhr GmbH for developing cultural offers relevant for the tourism industry, like for example the cultural festival titled RuhrTriennale[52] and the Ruhrgebiet Tourismus GmbH as operational basis for the marketing of the region.[53] All of these efforts found their culmination in the successful application to become European Cultural Capital in 2010. Its motto "Wandel durch Kultur – Kultur durch Wandel" (change through culture – culture through change) signaled the close interrelationship between culture, heritage and structural change. The accompanying marketing campaign sought to brand the Ruhr with its slogan: "*Ruhr – vom Mythos zur Marke*"[54] (Ruhr – from the myth to the brand). At the heart of the ongoing touristification of the Ruhr stood the IBA in the 1990s: "With the industrial heritage trail the IBA has revaluated and developed the industrial heritage into a regional image bearer, a symbol of identification, a tourist attraction."[55]

Recent trends and debates

The fact that industrial heritage has been so comprehensively successful across the region, and is supported by all important regional actors, has much to do with the socially acceptable and consensual end to mining in the region. Many exponents of industrial heritage in the Ruhr have presented this region as a model for other deindustrializing regions.[56] There are a number of travel guides on industrial heritage in the Ruhr and a whole body of literature that reinforces the unbelievable success story of industrial heritage in this region.[57] The image of industrial heritage, from the ugly duckling to a secular shrine of modernity, has changed dramatically in the Ruhr.[58] The leisure culture in the Ruhr has been increasingly connected to industrial heritage. The preservation of industrial heritage in the Ruhr over the last decades has increasingly turned into a cultural event: Industrial heritage sites serve as parks, observation decks, landmarks, playgrounds, spaces for art installations and performances, museums, event venues, theatre and music halls, and dance clubs. Every summer art festivals like ExtraSchicht and today's world-renowned Ruhrtriennale, an annual festival which has used industrial heritage sites to stage outstanding international art projects,[59] attract hundreds of thousands of tourists to Germany's "Rust Belt". Former rail tracks between the 're-naturized' production sites have been turned into cycle paths and slag heaps have been greened for hikers.[60] Preservationists, in particular, have been critical of this development, as it seemed to them to change, sometimes beyond recognition, the places of industrial heritage.[61]

But overall, the huge success story of industrial heritage in the Ruhr can only be explained with reference to the simple fact that the Ruhr could only anchor its regional identity in industrial heritage. Other industrial regions in the world, such as the Spanish region of Asturias, with a greater diversity of historical narratives that could be publicly utilized for processes of identity construction, do not have to revert to a monocultural identity repertoire like the Ruhr. The representation of the history of the Ruhr, with its comparably insignificant network of preindustrial memory places along the Hellweg, is not able to sidestep the powerful industrial narrative. It appears like an existential need for the regional identity of the Ruhr to remember the industrial past. Yet industrial heritage in the Ruhr is not without its opponents. Thus, for example, a former high-ranking conservative politician, Laurenz Meyer, criticized the regional focus on the industrial past as too backward looking and described industrial heritage sites as 'ruins'.[62]

Criticism of the Ruhr's industrial heritage often highlights its tendency to provide the region with a static regional identity and to prevent the Ruhr's structural change and mental realignment to a post-industrial age. Some academics have warned of a paralyzing industrial antiquarianism. Others have pointed to a history of the Ruhr that is much older than the industrial age.[63] The recent death of Karl Albrecht, Germany's richest man and the founder of the Aldi discount supermarket chain, also reminded the people in the Ruhr that their economy was not exclusively based on heavy coal and steel industries and that their economic history has possibly been more diverse than the industrial heritage boom has been able to represent.[64] The industrial heritage conservators, however, find the view absurd that monuments would impair economic development: after all, the economically very successful state of Bavaria would never contest the legitimacy of the many palaces and castles for reasons of economic sustainability.[65] The advocates of industrial heritage, like Delf Slotta, prefer to argue that industrial heritage provides a foundation for sites of future successful economic development.[66] The social scientist Stefan Goch also has analyzed the profound identity construction through industrial heritage in the Ruhr in a positive light.[67]

Following Jörn Rüsen's work, one cannot overlook the centrality of industrial heritage in the historical culture of the Ruhr. This historical culture is closely connected to questions of sense-making, self-understanding and representation. In other words, industrial heritage opens horizons of meaning for (post-) industrial regions. Rüsen pointed to a problem in this process:

> when the conditions of life cannot remain the same as in the past, a society's ability to change depends on the extent to which it is able to source power from its historical memory for the transformation of these conditions. The Ruhr region is a good example for the fact that structural change can be consciously designed and accomplished through the servicing of memory.[68]

At the same time, however, there is the danger that "historical conditions and the actual life-nexus of the people in the Ruhr vanish into the beautiful appearance of aesthetically constructed relics. . . . The shadow of the aesthetic splendor is a de-historicized past."[69] This accusation is directed against the growing relation between industrial heritage and the contemporary entertainment culture. The form of 'histotainment,' as realized with the alpine center (with a sled run, high rope course and indoor ski slope) at the Prosper mine in Bottrop, next to the Tetraeder, and in many ways also with the CentrO next to the Gasometer, does not invite people to critically rethink the industrial past.

Notes

1 Parts of this article are based on Stefan Berger, Industriekultur und Strukturwandel in Deutschen Bergbauregionen nach 1945, in *Geschichte des deutschen Bergbaus. Vol 4: Rohstoffgewinnung im Strukturwandel: Der deutsche Bergbau im 20. Jahrhundert*, ed. Dieter Ziegler (Münster: Aschendorff Verlag, 2013), pp. 571–601. Other parts have been published in Portuguese: Stefan Berger and Christian Wicke, Um imaginário pós-industrial? A popularização do patrimônio industrial no Ruhr e a representação de sua identidade regional, *Estudos Históricos* 54 (2014): 231–254.
2 For fragments of a general history of the Ruhr region, see Klaus Tenfelde and Thomas Urban, *Das Ruhrgebiet. Ein historisches Lesebuch, Vol. 1 & 2* (Essen: Klartext Verlag, 2010).
3 Writers such as Hans Spethmann and Wilhelm Brepohl were influential in making the Ruhrgebiet a distinct industrial region through their writings. See for example, Hans Spethmann, *Das Ruhrgebiet im Wechselspiel von Land und Leuten, Wirtschaft, Technik und Politik*, 2 Volumes (Berlin: Reimer Hobbing, 1933); on Wilhelm Brepohl, see Stefan Goch, Wege und Abwege der Sozialwissenschaft: Wilhelm Brepohls

industrielle Volkskunde, *Mitteilungsblatt des Instituts für soziale Bewegungen* 26 (2001): 139–176.
4   Christa Reicher, Klaus R. Kunzmann, Jan Polívka, Frank Roost, Yasemin Utku and Michael Wegene, *Schichten einer Region. Kartenstücke zur räumlichen Struktur des Ruhrgebiets* (Berlin: Jovis Verlag, 2011).
5   See Metropole Ruhr, Regionalverband Ruhr, accessed September 5, 2014, www.rvr-online.de.
6   Stefan Goch, *Eine Region im Kampf mit dem Strukturwandel. Bewältigung von Strukturwandel and Strukturpolitik im Ruhrgebiet* (Essen: Klartext Verlag, 2002); Michael Farrenkopf, Die kokereitechnische Entwicklung in der Bundesrepublik Deutschland, in *Braunkohleveredelung im Niederlausitzer Revier: 50 Jahre Schwarze Pumpe*, ed. Günter Bayerl (Münster: Waxmann, 2009).
7   See Das Selbst(i) und das Ruhrgebiet, TU Dortmund, accessed December 5, 2016, www.selbsti.ruhr/.
8   Rolf Lindner, Das Ethos der Region, *Zeitschrift für Volkskunde* 89 (1993): 188.
9   Ibid., p. 175.
10 For the example of a former Thyssen steel mill in Duisburg, see Sarah Hemmings and Martin Kagel, Memory Gardens: Aesthetic Education and Political Emancipation in the "Landschaftspark Duisburg-Nord", *German Studies Review* 33:2 (2010): 243–261.
11 See MBWSV, Ministerium für Verkehr des Landes Nordrhein-Westfalen, accessed September 5, 2014, www.mbwsv.nrw.de/stadtentwicklung/baukultur/industriekultur.
12 See Wir in NRW. Das Landesportal, Die Landesregierung Nordrhein-Westfalen, accessed July 30, 2014, www.nrw.de/en/north-rhine-westphalia/state-and-people; (On the regional identity of the state of North-Rhine Westphalia, see: Christoph Cornelißen, Historische Identitätsbildung im Bindestrichland Nordrhein-Westfalen, *Schriften der Stiftung Bibliothek des Ruhrgebiets* (Essen: Klartext Verlag, 2008).
13 See for example, Stefan Berger, Chris Lorenz and Billie Melman (eds.), *Popularizing National Pasts: 1800 to the Present* (New York: Routledge, 2012); Stefan Berger, Linas Eriksonas and Andrew Mycock (eds.), *Narrating the Nation: Representations in History, Media and the Arts* (New York and Oxford: Berghahn Books, 2008); Karin Tilmans, Frank van Vree and Jay Winter, *Performing the Past: Memory, History and Identity in Modern Europe* (Chicago: University of Chicago Press, 2010); Barbara Korte and Syvia Paletschek: *Popular History Now and Then, International Perspectives* (Bielefeld: Transcript Verlag, 2012).
14 Tilmann Buddensieg and Henning Rogge, *Industriekultur. Peter Behrens und die AEG 1907–1914* (Berlin: Gebrüder Mann, 1979). It should be noted that both terms, the German 'Industriekultur' and the English 'industrial heritage' are often used very loosely and without great attention to define what is meant by it. Here in this article we examine physical remains of the industrial age and their preservation as well as re-use and structural transformation and adaptation to various forms of re-use.
15 Hermann Glaser, Industriekultur. Der anthropologische Aspekt, *Forum Industriedenkmalpflege und Geschichtskultur* 1 (2000): 10–14; Hermann Glaser, *Maschinenwelt und Alltagsleben. Industriekultur in Deutschland vom Biedermeier bis zur Weimarer Republik* (Frankfurt a.M.: Büchergilde Gutenberg, 1981).
16 Ulrich Borsdorf, Industriekultur und Geschichte, *Forum Industriedenkmalpflege und Geschichtskultur* 1 (2000): 16–19; see also Ruhrmuseum, accessed September 5, 2014, www.ruhrmuseum.de.
17 Franz-Josef Brüggemeier, *Leben vor Ort. Ruhrbergleute und Ruhrbergbau 1889–1919* (München: C. H. Beck, 1983); Hochlarmarker Lesebuch, *Kohle war nicht alles. 100 Jahre Ruhrgebietsgeschichte. Bergarbeiter und ihre Frauen aus Recklinghausen-Hochlarmark haben in Zusammenarbeit mit dem kommunalen Stadtkulturreferat ihre Geschichte aufgeschrieben* (Oberhausen, Asso, 1981).
18 Wolfhard Weber, Von der "Industriearchäologie" über das "industrielle Erbe" zur "Industriekultur", in *Technik-Geschichte. Historische Beiträge und neuere Ansätze*, ed. Ulrich Troitsch and Gabriele Wohlauf (Frankfurt a.M.: Suhrkamp Verlag, 1980).

A post-industrial mindscape? 87

19 Bernd Becher and Hilla Becher, *Anonyme Skulpturen* (Düsseldorf: Lempertz, 1970).
20 Susanne Lange, *Bernd und Hilla Becher: Life and Work* (Boston: The MIT Press, 2007).
21 Sven Reichert, *Authentizität und Gemeinschaft. Linksalternatives Leben in den siebziger und frühen achtziger Jahren* (Berlin: Suhrkamp, 2014).
22 On the German tradition of national historiography, see Stefan Berger, *The Search for Normality: National Identity and Historical Consciousness in Germany since 1800* (Oxford and New York: Berghahn Books, 1997); for the history of social history, see: Jürgen Kocka, *Sozialgeschichte in Deutschland seit 1945. Aufstieg, Krise und Perspektiven* (Bonn: Freidrich Ebert-Stiftung, 2002); for the social history of the miners in the Ruhr, see Klaus Tenfelde, *Sozialgeschichte der Bergarbeiterschaft an der Ruhr im 19. Jahrhundert* (Bonn: Dietz Verlag, 1977); for history of everyday life, see Alf Lüdke, *Alltagsgeschichte* (Frankfurt and New York: Campus, 1989); for oral history, see: Lutz Niethammer, *Lebenserfahrung und kollektives Gedächtnis. Die Praxis des Oral History.* (Frankfurt a.M.: Suhrkamp, 1980).
23 Historical culture (Geschichtskultur) here refers particularly to Jörn Rüsen's work; see Jörn Rüsen, Was ist Geschichtskultur? Überlegungen zu einer neuen Art, über Geschichte nachzudenken, in *Historische Faszination. Geschichtskultur heute*, ed. Jörn Rüsen, Theo Grütter and Klaus Füßmann (Köln et al.: Böhlau, 1994), pp. 3–26. For historical culture in the Ruhr, see Klaus Tenfelde, Geschichtskultur im Ruhrgebiet, *Gewerkschaftliche Monatshefte* 47 (1996): 240–253.
24 See Rout Industriekultur, Metropoleruhr, accessed September 5, 2014, www.route-industriekultur.de/.
25 See Christian Wicke, Urban Movement a la Ruhr? The Initiatives for the Preservation of Workers' Settlements in the 1970s, in *Cities Contested: Urban Politics, Heritage, and Social Movements in Italy and West Germany in the 1970s*, ed. Martin Baumeister et al. (Frankfurt: Campus, 2017), pp. 347–371.
26 Alexander Kierdorf and Uta Hassler, *Denkmale des Industriezeitalters. Von der Geschichte des Umgangs mit Industriekultur* (Tübigen: Wasmuth Verlag, 2000).
27 For the connection between future design and industrial heritage in the Ruhr, see Heiner Dürr and Jürgen Gramke, *Erneuerung des Ruhrgebiets. Regionales Erbe und Gestaltung für die Zukunft* (Paderborn: Schöningh, 1993).
28 LWL-Industriemuseum, LWL, accessed September 5, 2014, www.lwl.org/LWL/Kultur/wim/portal.
29 Holger Schmenk, *Von der Altlast zur Industriekultur. Der Strukturwandel im Ruhrgebiet am Beispiel der Zinkfabrik Altenberg* (Bottrop: Henselowsky und Boschmann, 2009); today LVR-Industriemuseum, see: Zinkfabrik Altenberg, LVR-Industriemuseum Altenberg, accessed September 5, 2014, www.industriemuseum.lvr.de/de/oberhausen/oberhausen.html.
30 See, for example, Norbert Huse, *Unbequeme Baudenkmale. Entsorgen? Schützen? Pflegen?* (München: C. H. Beck, 1997).
31 Walter Buschmann, Zechenanlagen in Essen, *Denkmalpflege im Rheinland* 2:1 (1985): 12–17; Walter Buschmann, Denkmäler des Aachener Steinkohlenreviers, *Denkmalpflege im Rheinland* 9:4 (1992): 97–107; Walter Buschmann, *Zechen und Kokereien im rheinischen Steinkohlebergbau* (Berlin: Gebrüder Mann, 1998).
32 Walter Buschmann, Wie Zollverein ein Denkmal wurde, *Forum Industriedenkmalpflege und Geschichtskultur* 1 (2002): 31–36; It is interesting to note that the German miners' union (*IG Bergbau*) sided with the managers of the coal industries against industrial heritage preservation, perceiving industrial heritage as the gravedigger of their profession. The union was instead foremost interested in the maintenance of working mines and employment providing workplaces, and thus observed the transition from mining to industrial heritage with suspicion. Despite this, many managers, engineers and workers in the Ruhr area were enthusiastic about the conservation of industrial artefacts and their traditions. Thus, the united hostility between unions and mining companies towards industrial heritage was of a strategic nature. This

relationship is certainly worth some further exploration but would go beyond the scope of this article.
33 Karl Kleineberg, Stillegen – was dann? Ansätze der Ruhrkohle AG, in *Das Denkmal als Altlast? Auf dem Weg in die Reparaturgesellschaft*, ed. Martin Hölscher (Munich: Lipp Verlag, 1996), pp. 64–69.
34 Hans-Peter Noll, Der Bergbau geht – die Fläche bleibt. Folgenutzungen ehemaliger Bargbaustandorde, *Bergbau* 11 (2009): 491–496; Hans-Peter Noll, Brachflächenentwicklung – ein Beitrag zur Nachhaltigkeit, *Glückauf* 145 (2009): 467.
35 Karl Ganser, Zehn Jahre Industriedenkmalpflege und Geschichtskultur – was war vorher und was kommt danach?, *Forum Industriedenkmalpflege und Geschichtskultur* 1 (2005): 13–15; Ursula Mehrfeld, 14 Standorte und mehr: zur zehnjährigen Arbeit der Stiftung Industriedenkmalpflege und Geschichtskultur, *Forum Industriedenkmalpflege und Geschichtskultur* 1 (2005): 16–19; Ursula Mehrfeld, Industriedenkmale – schützen, erhalten, nutzen, in *Industriedenkmale im Ruhrgebiet*, ed. Reinhold Budde et al. (Hamburg: Ellert & Richter, 2009), pp. 50–73.
36 Kokerei Hansa, Die Industriedenkmal Stiftung, accessed September 5, 2014, www.industriedenkmal-stiftung.de/docs/472991885334_de.php.
37 Internationale Bauausstellung Emscher Park, Ministerium für Städtebau und Wohnen, Kultur und Sport des Landes Nordrhein-Westfalen, accessed September 5, 2014, www.iba.nrw.de/main.htm.
38 Florian Matzner et al., *Emscherkunst. 2010. Eine Insel für die Kunst* (Berlin: Hantje Cantz, 2010).
39 Reicher et al., *Schichten einer Region*; Thomas Urban, *Visionen für das Ruhrgebiet. IBA Emscher Park. Konzepte – Projekte – Dokumentation* (Essen: Klartext Verlag, 2008); Manfred Sack, *Siebzig Kilometer Hoffnung. Die IBA Emscher Park – Erneuerung eines Industriegebiets* (Stuttgart: deutsche verlagsanstalt, 1999); Heiderose Kilper, *Die Internationale Bauausstellung Emscher Park. Eine Studie zur Steuerungsproblematik komplexer Erneuerungsprozesse in einer alten Industrieregion* (Leverkusen: Springer, 1999); Karl Ganser and Andrea Höber, Raum für Zukunft: die internationale Bauausstellung Emscher, in *Reform und Rhein und Ruhr: Nordrhein-Wesfalens Weg ins 21 Jahrhundert*, ed. Karsten Rudolph et al. (Bonn: Dietz, 2000), pp. 66–74; on tourism see also Rotraut Hücherig, *Tourismus im Ruhrgebiet – der Beitrag der Internationalen Bauausstellung Emscher Park* (Trier: Selbstverlag der Geographischen Gesellschaft Trier, 1992).
40 Achim Prossek, Visuelle Regionsproduktion. Ruhrgebiet im Blick, *Räume. Zeitschrift für Kulturwissenschaften* 2 (2008): 65–75.
41 Thomas Sievert, Denkmal und künstlerische Verfremdung, in *Mythos und Moderne im Ruhrgebiet*, ed. Andrea Höber and Karl Ganser (Essen: Klartext Verlag, 1999).
42 For these image strategies, see Jakob F. Dittmar, Inszenierte Industrie in der postindustriellen Stadt. Vom Umgang mit stillgelegten Industrieanlagen (PhD diss., Bochum: Ruhr-Universität Bochum, 2002).
43 For the relationship between tourism and industrial heritage, see Jürgen Schwark, *Tourismus und Industriekultur. Vermarktung von Technik und Arbeit* (Berlin: Erich Schmidt Verlag, 2004).
44 Christa Reicher, Industriekultur – gespeicherte Erinnerung und kulturelles Potential, in *Entwicklungsfaktor Kultur. Studien zum kulturellen und ökonomischen Potential der europäischen Stadt*, ed. Gudrun Quenzel (Bielefeld: Transcript Verlag, 2009), pp. 141–163.
45 Buschmann, Wie Zollverein ein Denkmal wurde; Angela Schwarz, *Industriekultur, Image, Identität. Die Zeche Zollverein und der Wandel in den Köpfen* (Essen: Klartext Verlag, 2008).
46 European Capital Ruhr, RUHR 20100 GmbH, accessed September 5, 2014, http://archiv.ruhr2010.de/en/home.html.
47 For a comparison of industrial museums in Germany, see Katja Röckner, *Ausgestellte Arbeit. Industriemuseen und ihr Umgang mit dem wirtschaftlichen Strukturwandel* (Stuttgart: Steiner Verlag, 2009).

48 Sharon Zukin, *Landscapes of Power: From Detroit to Disney World* (Berkeley et al.: University of California Press, 1991), 253.
49 Tim Edensor, *Industrial Ruins, Space, Aesthetics and Materiality* (New York: Berg, 2005), p. 126.
50 Transl. by the authors; Wolfgang Ebert, Strategien und Konzepte für eine nachhaltige Entwicklung des Tourismus zu Zielen der Industriekultur, in *Tourismus und Industriekultur. Vermarktung von Technik und Arbeit*, ed. Jürgen Schwank (Berlin: Erich Schmidt Verlag, 2004), p. 25.
51 Transl. by the authors; Ebert, "Strategien und Konzepte," p. 26.
52 Achim Prossek, Zwischen Kitsch und Kathedralen: die Ruhrtriennale und das Ruhrgebiet, in *Themenorte*, ed. Michael Flitner and Julia Lossau (Münster: LIT, 2005).
53 Ebert, Strategien und Konzepte, p. 27f.
54 Julia Frohne, Katharina Langsch, Fritz Pleitgen and Oliver Scheytt, *RUHR. Vom Mythos zur Marke. Marketing und PR für die Kulturhauptstadt Europas RUHR.2010* (Essen: Klartext Verlag, 2010).
55 Transl. by the authors; Kai Boldt and Martina Gelhar, *Das Ruhrgebiet. Landschaft – Industrie – Kultur* (Darmstadt: Primus, 2008), 75. For a critical discussion of the touristification of the industrial heritage movement in the Ruhr, see also Christian Wicke, Stefan Berger and Jana Golombek, Burdens of Eternity? Heritage, Identity and the "Great Transition" in the Ruhr special issue of *The Public Historian* (guest edited by the same authors) titled *Deindustrialization, Heritage, and Representations of Identity* (forthcoming, November 2017).
56 Ralf Ebert, Renaissance of Former Coal Mines: Learning from the Ruhr? in *On the Surface: The Heritage of Mines and Mining*, ed. Margaret L. Faul (Leeds: Metropolitan University, 2011).
57 One of many examples is Delia Bösch, *Ruhrgebiet. Entdeckungsreise Industriekultur* (Essen: Klartext Verlag, 2005); and also Walter Buschmann, *Koks – Gas – Kohlechemie. Geschichte und gegenständliche Überlieferung der Kohleveredelung* (Essen: Klartext Verlag, 1993).
58 See Hartwig Suhrbier, Weg vom Aschenputtel-Image. Zur veränderten Wahrnehmung von Bauten der Industrie- und Sozialgeschichte im Ruhrgebiet, in *Die Entdeckung des Ruhrgebiets. Das Ruhrgebiet in Nordrhein-Westfalen 1946–1996*, ed. Jan-Pieter Barbian and Ludger Heid (Essen: Klartext Verlag, 1997), pp. 246–258; Hermann Sturm, *Industriearchitektur als Kathedrale der Arbeit. Geschichte und Gegenwart eines Mythos* (Essen: Klartext Verlag, 2007).
59 Ruhrtriiienale, Kultur Ruhr GmbH, accessed September 5, 2014, www.ruhrtriennale.de.
60 Hillary Angelo, More than Exception: Categories and the Problem of "Nature" in the Ruhr, *Moving the Social* 50 (2013): 7–24.
61 Axel Föhl, The Palace of Projects oder was ist Industriekultur im Revier? *FORUM* 2 (2001): 49–54; Heinrich Grütter, Bausteine der Geschichte – die Route der Industriekultur, *Industriegeschichte und kulturelles Erbe* 1 (2004).
62 Man denkt doch, hier kann man nur Ruinen besichtigen, Bildzeitung, accessed September 5, 2014, www.bild.de/regional/ruhrgebiet/politiker/man-denkt-doch-hier-kann-man-nur-ruinen-besichtigen-37014162.bild.html.
63 Ulrich Heinemann, Industriekultur: vom Nutzen und Nachteil für das Ruhrgebiet, *Forum Industriedenkmalpflege und Geschichtskultur* 1 (2003): 56–58; Heinz Schrumpf and Rüdiger Budde, *Gibt es noch ein Ruhrgebiet? Wissenschaftliche Untersuchungen* (Essen: Rheinisches-Westfälisches Institut für Wirtschaftsforschung, 2001); Thomas Parent, Industriekultur ist mehr/Industriekultur und mehr. Überlegungen zur aktuellen Diskussion um Profil und ‚Identität' des Ruhrreviers, *Forum Industriedenkmalpflege und Geschichtskultur* 1 (2001): 27–31; Karl Rohe, Regionalkultur, regionale Identität und Regionalismus im Ruhrgebiet: empirische Sachverhalte und theoretische Überlegungen, in *Industriegesellschaft und Regionalkultur. Untersuchungen für Europa*, ed. Wolfgang Lipp (Köln: Carl Heymanns: 1984), pp. 123–153.

64 See Die Ursprünge von Aldi: Gut 100 Jahre Famileinunternehmen Albrecht, Ruhr-Nachrichten, accessed September 5, 2014, www.ruhrnachrichten.de/nachrichten/wirtschaft/aktuelles_berichte/Die-Urspruenge-von-Aldi-Gut-100-Jahre-Familienunternehmen-Albrecht;art318,2429554.

65 Many thanks to Walter Buschmann for this suggestion.

66 Delf Slotta, Das industrielle Erbe als Chance für Wirtschaft und Kultur, in *Bergmannskalender*, ed. Deutsche Steinkohle AG (Saarbrücken, 2001), p. 48.

67 Stefan Goch, Der Ruhrgebietler – Überlegungen zur Entstehung und Entwicklung des regionalen Bewußtseins im Ruhrgebiet, *Westfälische Forschungen* 47 (1997): 585–620.

68 Transl. by the authors; Jörn Rüsen, Industriedenkmale und Geschichtskultur im Ruhrgebiet, *Industriedenkmalpflege und Geschichtskultur* 2 (1998): 4.

69 Ibid., 4.

Bibliography

Becher, Bernd, and Hilla Becher, *Anonyme Skulpturen* (Düsseldorf: Lempertz, 1970).

Berger, Stefan, *The Search for Normality: National Identity and Historical Consciousness in Germany since 1800* (Oxford and New York: Berghahn Books, 1997).

Berger, Stefan, Industriekultur und Strukturwandel in Deutschen Bergbauregionen nach 1945, in *Geschichte des deutschen Bergbaus. Vol 4: Rohstoffgewinnung im Strukturwandel: Der deutsche Bergbau im 20. Jahrhundert*, ed. Dieter Ziegler (Münster: Aschendorff Verlag, 2013), pp. 571–601.

Berger, Stefan, Chris Lorenz, and Billie Melman (eds.), *Popularizing National Pasts: 1800 to the Present* (New York: Routledge, 2012).

Berger, Stefan, and Christian Wicke, Um imaginário pós-industrial? A popularização do patrimônio industrial no Ruhr e a representação de sua identidade regional, *Estudos Históricos* 54 (2014): 231–254.

Berger, Stefan, Linas Eriksonas, and Andrew Mycock (eds.), Narrating the Nation: Representations in History, Media and the Arts (New York and Oxford: Berghahn Books, 2008).

Berger, Stefan, Christian Wicke, and Jana Golombek, Burdens of Eternity? Heritage, Identity and the "Great Transition" in the Ruhr special issue of *The Public Historian* (guest edited by the same authors) titled *Deindustrialization, Heritage, and Representations of Identity* (November 2017, Vol. 39, No. 4).

Bild, Man denkt doch, hier kann man nur Ruinen besichtigen, accessed September 5, 2014, www.bild.de/regional/ruhrgebiet/politiker/man-denkt-doch-hier-kann-man-nur-ruinen-besichtigen-37014162.bild.html.

Boldt, Kai, and Martina Gelhar, *Das Ruhrgebiet. Landschaft – Industrie – Kultur* (Darmstadt: Primus, 2008), p. 75.

Borsdorf, Ulrich, Industriekultur und Geschichte, *Forum Industriedenkmalpflege und Geschichtskultur* 1 (2000): 16–19.

Bösch, Delia, *Ruhrgebiet. Entdeckungsreise Industriekultur* (Essen: Klartext Verlag, 2005).

Brüggemeier, Franz-Josef, *Leben vor Ort. Ruhrbergleute und Ruhrbergbau 1889–1919* (München: C. H. Beck, 1983).

Buddensieg, Tilman, and Henning Rogge, *Industriekultur. Peter Behrens und die AEG 1907–1914* (Berlin: Gebrüder Mann, 1979).

Buschmann, Walter, Denkmäler des Aachener Steinkohlenreviers, *Denkmalpflege im Rheinland* 9:4 (1992): 97–107.

Buschmann, Walter, *Koks – Gas – Kohlechemie. Geschichte und gegenständliche Überlieferung der Kohleveredelung* (Essen: Klartext Verlag, 1993).

Buschmann, Walter, Wie Zollverein ein Denkmal wurde, *Forum Industriedenkmalpflege und Geschichtskultur* 1 (2002): 31–36.
Buschmann, Walter, Zechenanlagen in Essen, *Denkmalpflege im Rheinland* 2:1 (1985): 12–17.
Buschmann, Walter, *Zechen und Kokereien im rheinischen Steinkohlebergbau* (Berlin: Gebrüder Mann, 1998).
Cornelißen, Christoph, Historische Identitätsbildung im Bindestrichland Nordrhein-Westfalen, in *Schriften der Stiftung Bibliothek des Ruhrgebiets* (Essen: Klartext Verlag, 2008).
Dittmar, Jakob F., Inszenierte Industrie in der postindustriellen Stadt. Vom Umgang mit stillgelegten Industrieanlagen (PhD diss., Bochum: Ruhr-Universität Bochum, 2002).
Dürr, Heiner, and Jürgen Gramke, *Erneuerung des Ruhrgebiets. Regionales Erbe und Gestaltung für die Zukunft* (Paderborn: Schöningh, 1993).
Ebert, Ralf, Renaissance of Former Coal Mines: Learning from the Ruhr? in *On the Surface: the Heritage of Mines and Mining*, ed. Margaret L. Faul (Leeds: Metropolitan University, 2011).
Ebert, Wolfgang, Strategien und Konzepte für eine nachhaltige Entwicklung des Tourismus zu Zielen der Industriekultur, in *Tourismus und Industriekultur. Vermarktung von Technik und Arbeit*, ed. Jürgen Schwank (Berlin: Erich Schmidt Verlag, 2004).
Edensor, Tim, *Industrial Ruins, Space, Aesthetics and Materiality* (New York: Berg, 2005).
Farrenkopf, Michael, Die kokereitechnische Entwicklung in der Bundesrepublik Deutschland, in *Braunkohleveredelung im Niederlausitzer Revier: 50 Jahre Schwarze Pumpe*, ed. Günter Bayerl (Münster: Waxmann, 2009).
Föhl, Axel, The Palace of Projects oder was ist Industriekultur im Revier? *FORUM* 2 (2001): 49–54.
Frohne, Julia, Katharina Langsch, Fritz Pleitgen, and Oliver Scheytt, *RUHR. Vom Mythos zur Marke. Marketing und PR für die Kulturhauptstadt Europas RUHR.2010* (Essen: Klartext Verlag, 2010).
Ganser, Karl, Zehn Jahre Industriedenkmalpflege und Geschichtskultur – was war vorher und was kommt danach? *Forum Industriedenkmalpflege und Geschichtskultur* 1 (2005): 13–15.
Ganser, Karl, and Andrea Höber, Raum für Zukunft: die internationale Bauausstellung Emscher, in *Reform und Rhein und Ruhr: Nordrhein-Wesfalens Weg ins 21 Jahrhundert*, ed. Karsten Rudolph. (Bonn: Dietz, 2000), pp. 66–74.
Glaser, Hermann, Industriekultur. Der anthropologische Aspekt, *Forum Industriedenkmalpflege und Geschichtskultur* 1 (2000): 10–14.
Glaser, Hermann, *Maschinenwelt und Alltagsleben. Industriekultur in Deutschland vom Biedermeier bis zur Weimarer Republik* (Frankfurt a.M.: Büchergilde Gutenberg, 1981).
Goch, Stefan, Der Ruhrgebietler – Überlegungen zur Entstehung und Entwicklung des regionalen Bewußtseins im Ruhrgebiet, *Westfälische Forschungen* 47 (1997): 585–620.
Goch, Stefan, *Eine Region im Kampf mit dem Strukturwandel. Bewältigung von Strukturwandel and Strukturpolitik im Ruhrgebiet* (Essen: Klartext Verlag, 2002).
Goch, Stefan, Wege und Abwege der Sozialwissenschaft: Wilhelm Brepohls industrielle Volkskunde, *Mitteilungsblatt des Instituts für soziale Bewegungen* 26 (2001): 139–176.
Grütter, Heinrich, Bausteine der Geschichte – die Route der Industriekultur, *Industriegeschichte und kulturelles Erbe* 1 (2004).
Heinemann, Ulrich, Industriekultur: vom Nutzen und Nachteil für das Ruhrgebiet, *Forum Industriedenkmalpflege und Geschichtskultur* 1 (2003): 56–58.
Hemmings, Sarah, and Martin Kagel, Memory Gardens: Aesthetic Education and Political Emancipation in the "Landschaftspark Duisburg-Nord", *German Studies Review* 33:2 (2010): 243–261.

Hochlarmarker Lesebuch, *Kohle war nicht alles. 100 Jahre Ruhrgebietsgeschichte. Bergarbeiter und ihre Frauen aus Recklinghausen-Hochlarmark haben in Zusammenarbeit mit dem kommunalen Stadtkulturreferat ihre Geschichte aufgeschrieben* (Oberhausen: Asso, 1981).

Hücherig, Rotraut, *Tourismus im Ruhrgebiet – der Beitrag der Internationalen Bauaustellung Emscher Park* (Trier: Selbstverlag der Geographischen Gesellschaft Trier, 1992).

Huse, Norbert, *Unbequeme Baudenkmale. Entsorgen? Schützen? Pflegen?* (München: C. H. Beck, 1997).

Kierdorf, Alexander, and Uta Hassler, *Denkmale des Industriezeitalters. Von der Geschichte des Umgangs mit Industriekultur* (Tübigen: Wasmuth Verlag, 2000).

Kilper, Heiderose, *Die Internationale Bauaustellung Emscher Park. Eine Studie zur Steuerungsproblematik komplexer Erneuerungsprozesse in einer alten Industrieregion* (Leverkusen: Springer, 1999).

Kleineberg, Karl, Stillegen – was dann? Ansätze der Ruhrkohle AG, in *Das Denkmal als Altlast? Auf dem Weg in die Reparaturgesellschaft*, ed. Martin Hölscher (Munich: Lipp Verlag, 1996), pp. 64–69.

Kocka, Jürgen, *Sozialgeschichte in Deutschland seit 1945. Aufstieg, Krise und Perspektiven* (Bonn: Friedrich Ebert-Stiftung, 2002).

Korte, Barbara, and Sylvia Paletschek, *Popular History Now and Then, International Perspectives* (Bielefeld: Transcript Verlag, 2012).

Lange, Susanne, *Bernd und Hilla Becher. Life and Work* (Boston: The MIT Press, 2007).

Lindner, Rolf, Das Ethos der Region, *Zeitschrift für Volkskunde* 89 (1993): 188.

Lüdke, Alf, *Alltagsgeschichte* (Frankfurt and New York: Campus, 1989).

Matzner, Florian, Karl-Heinz Petzinka, and Jochen Stemplewski, *Emscherkunst. 2010. Eine Insel für die Kunst* (Berlin: Hatje Cantz, 2010).

Mehrfeld, Ursula, 14 Standorte und mehr: zur zehnjährigen Arbeit der Stiftung Industriedenkmalpflege und Geschichtskultur, *Forum Industriedenkmalpflege und Geschichtskultur* 1 (2005): 16–19.

Mehrfeld, Ursula, Industriedenkmale – schützen, erhalten, nutzen, in *Industriedenkmale im Ruhrgebiet*, ed. Reinhold Budde et al. (Hamburg: Ellert & Richter, 2009), pp. 50–73.

Niethammer, Lutz, *Lebenserfahrung und kollektives Gedächtnis. Die Praxis des Oral History*. (Frankfurt a. M.: Suhrkamp, 1980).

Noll, Hans-Peter, Brachflächenentwicklung – ein Beitrag zur Nachhaltigkeit, *Glückauf* 145 (2009): 467.

Noll, Hans-Peter, Der Bergbau geht – die Fläche bleibt. Folgenutzungen ehemaliger Bargbaustandorde, *Bergbau* 11 (2009): 491–496.

Parent, Thomas, Industriekultur ist mehr/Industriekultur und mehr. Überlegungen zur aktuellen Diskussion um Profil und ‚Identität' des Ruhrreviers, *Forum Industriedenkmalpflege und Geschichtskultur* 1 (2001): 27–31.

Prossek, Achim, Visuelle Regionsproduktion. Ruhrgebiet im Blick, *Räume. Zeitschrift für Kulturwissenschaften* 2 (2008): 65–75.

Prossek, Achim, Zwischen Kitsch und Kathedralen: die Ruhrtriennale und das Ruhrgebiet, in *Themenorte*, ed. Michael Flitner and Julia Lossau (Münster: LIT, 2005).

Reicher, Christa, Industriekultur – gespeicherte Erinnerung und kulturelles Potential, in *Entwicklungsfaktor Kultur. Studien zum kulturellen und ökonomischen Potential der europäischen Stadt*, ed. Gudrun Quenzel (Bielefeld: Transcript Verlag, 2009): 141–163.

Reicher, Christa, Klaus R. Kunzmann, Jan Polívka, Frank Roost, Yasemin Utku and Michael Wegene, *Schichten einer Region. Kartenstücke zur räumlichen Struktur des Ruhrgebiets* (Berlin: Jovis Verlag, 2011).

Reichert, Sven, *Authentizität und Gemeinschaft. Linksalternatives Leben in den siebziger und frühen achtziger Jahren* (Berlin: Suhrkamp, 2014).
Röckner, Katja, *Ausgestellte Arbeit. Industriemuseen und ihr Umgang mit dem wirtschaftlichen Strukturwandel* (Stuttgart: Steiner Verlag, 2009).
Rohe, Karl, Regionalkultur, regionale Identität und Regionalismus im Ruhrgebiet: empirische Sachverhalte und theoretische Überlegungen, in *Industriegesellschaft und Regionalkultur. Untersuchungen für Europa*, ed. Wolfgang Lipp (Köln: Carl Heymanns, 1984), pp. 123–153.
Ruhr-Nachrichten, Die Ursprünge von Aldi: Gut 100 Jahre Famileinunternehmen Albrecht, accessed September 5, 2014, www.ruhrnachrichten.de/nachrichten/wirtschaft/aktuelles_berichte/Die-Urspruenge-von-Aldi-Gut-100-Jahre-Familienunternehmen-Albrecht;art318,2429554.
Rüsen, Jörn, Industriedenkmale und Geschichtskultur im Ruhrgebiet, *Industriedenkmalpflege und Geschichtskultur* 2 (1998).
Rüsen, Jörn, Was ist Geschichtskultur? Überlegungen zu einer neuen Art, über Geschichte nachzudenken, in *Historische Faszination. Geschichtskultur heute*, ed. Jörn Rüsen, Theo Grütter, and Klaus Füßmann (Köln et al.: Böhlau, 1994), pp. 3–26.
Sack, Manfred, *Siebzig Kilometer Hoffnung. Die IBA Emscher Park – Erneuerung eines Industriegebiets* (Stuttgart: Deutsche Verlagsanstalt, 1999).
Schmenk, Holger, *Von der Altlast zur Industriekultur. Der Strukturwandel im Ruhrgebiet am Beispiel der Zinkfabrik Altenberg* (Bottrop: Henselowsky und Boschmann, 2009).
Schrumpf, Heinz, and Rüdiger Budde, *Gibt es noch ein Ruhrgebiet? Wissenschaftliche Untersuchungen* (Essen: Rheinisches-Westfälisches Institut für Wissenschaftsforschung, 2001).
Schwark, Jürgen, *Tourismus und Industriekultur. Vermarktung von Technik und Arbeit* (Berlin: Erich Schmidt Verlag, 2004).
Schwarz, Angela, *Industriekultur, Image, Identität. Die Zeche Zollverein und der Wandel in den Köpfen* (Essen: Klartext Verlag, 2008).
Sievert, Thomas, Denkmal und künstlerische Verfremdung, in *Mythos und Moderne im Ruhrgebiet*, ed. Andrea Höber and Karl Ganser (Essen: Klartext Verlag, 1999).
Slotta, Delf, Das industrielle Erbe als Chance für Wirtschaft und Kultur, in *Bergmannskalender*, ed. Deutsche Steinkohle AG(Saarbrücken, 2001).
Spethmann, Hans, *Das Ruhrgebiet im Wechselspiel von Land und Leuten, Wirtschaft, Technik und Politik*, 2 Volumes (Berlin: Reimer Hobbing, 1933).
Sturm, Hermann, *Industriearchitektur als Kathedrale der Arbeit. Geschichte und Gegenwart eines Mythos* (Essen: Klartext Verlag, 2007).
Suhrbier, Hartwig, Weg vom Aschenputtel-Image. Zur veränderten Wahrnehmung von Bauten der Industrie- und Sozialgeschichte im Ruhrgebiet, in *Die Entdeckung des Ruhrgebiets. Das Ruhrgebiet in Nordrhein-Westfalen 1946–1996*, ed. Jan-Pieter Barbian and Ludger Heid (Essen: Klartext Verlag, 1997), pp. 246–258.
Tenfelde, Klaus, Geschichtskultur im Ruhrgebiet, *Gewerkschaftliche Monatshefte* 47 (1996): 240–253.
Tenfelde, Klaus, *Sozialgeschichte der Bergarbeiterschaft an der Ruhr im 19. Jahrhundert* (Bonn: Dietz Verlag, 1977).
Tenfelde, Klaus, and Thomas Urban, *Das Ruhrgebiet. Ein historisches Lesebuch, Vol 1 & 2* (Essen: Klartext Verlag, 2010).
Tilmans, Karin, Frank van Vree, and Jay Winter, *Performing the Past: Memory, History and Identity in Modern Europe* (Chicago: University of Chicago Press, 2010).
Urban, Thomas, *Visionen für das Ruhrgebiet. IBA Emscher Park. Konzepte – Projekte – Dokumentation* (Essen: Klartext Verlag, 2008).

Weber, Wolfhard, Von der "Industriearchäologie" über das "industrielle Erbe" zur "Industriekultur", in *Technik-Geschichte. Historische Beiträge und neuere Ansätze*, ed. Ulrich Troitsch and Gabriele Wohlauf (Frankfurt a.M.: Suhrkamp Verlag, 1980).

Wicke, Christian, Urban Movement a la Ruhr? The Initiatives for the Preservation of Workers' Settlements in the 1970s, in *Cities Contested: Urban Politics, Heritage, and Social Movements in Italy and West Germany in the 1970s*, ed. Martin Baumeister, Brono Bonomo and Dieter Schott (Frankfurt: Campus, 2017), pp. 347–371.

Zukin, Sharon, *Landscapes of Power. From Detroit to Disney World* (Berkeley et al.: University of California Press, 1991).

5 Contested heritage and regional identity in the Borsod Industrial Area in Hungary

Györgyi Németh

Introduction

The Borsod Industrial Area was a major heavy industrial region in Northern Hungary in the 19th and 20th centuries. Owing to its substantial brown coal and iron ore deposits, numerous coal mines were opened and two large iron and steel making complexes established over time, transforming the landscape tremendously. Urbanization also accelerated due to extensive industrialization. Besides the great number of workers' settlements erected in the vicinity of the mines and factories, two towns, Miskolc and Ózd were emerging as leading centers of iron and steel making (see Figure 5.1). In order to emphasize the significance of the region in the country's economy, it was labelled as the 'Hungarian Ruhr' between the two world wars, turning into the emblem of forced heavy industrialization in the state Socialist period. Following deindustrialization, however, the similarities between the two regions were completely disregarded. In the 'Hungarian Ruhr', no large-scale regional regeneration program, such as the *Internationale Bauausstellung Emscher Park*, has been developed capitalizing on its rich industrial heritage. As a result, the material culture of coal mining and iron making has been demolished or is desperately decaying; only little could be preserved. There can be no doubt that the complexity of recent historical developments, including the sudden change of the political system in the 1990s and subsequent extensive privatization, amongst others, is responsible for generally not considering the vestiges of heavy industry as valuable cultural heritage representing the regional identity. This chapter aims to investigate the current distressing state of heavy industrial heritage in relation to the region's industrial identity, which came to be faltering over the past three decades.

History of industrialization and urban development in the Borsod Industrial Area

Early industrialization started in the region at the end of the 18th century. Based on local natural resources, such as iron ore, wood and water power, the first charcoal blast furnace was erected in the Bükk Mountains, on the Diósgyőr Crown Estates at Ómassa, now part of Miskolc. The second, still surviving charcoal blast furnace was built nearby, at present-day Újmassa, in the 1810s.[1]

Modern industrialization, however, unfolded only from the last decades of the 19th century, due to the advantageous political and economic conditions created by the Austro-Hungarian Compromise. Reorganizing the lands of the House of Habsburg as a real union in 1867, the agreement reestablished the sovereignty of the Kingdom of Hungary within the framework of the Austro-Hungarian Monarchy. The autonomous Hungarian government placed railway infrastructure development in the center of its economic policy.[2] As a consequence, a state-owned modern ironworks was set up in Northern Hungary to provide rails, fixtures and fittings for railway construction. Located on a vacant territory between Miskolc and Diósgyőr, the plant was rapidly assembled and put in operation in the vicinity of the freshly-opened coal mines as early as the 1870s. From the 1860s onwards, satisfying the growing demand for railway materials was also the prominent aim of the private company, comprising noble landowners, aristocrats, as well as financiers, which had founded an iron-making factory at Ózd a few years earlier. As a late beneficiary of early modern iron making in neighboring Gömör County, the company successfully took advantage of the increasing business opportunities and developed into a considerable enterprise by the end of the century. The Rimamurány-Salgótarján Ironworks Company Ltd. (Rimamurány-Salgótarjáni Vasmű Rt.), frequently referred to as the Rima Steel Corporation or only 'Rima', established further iron and steel making premises at present Borsodnádasd, as well as at Salgótarján in adjacent Nógrád County, besides constantly expanding and improving the Ózd site. Brown coal was transported to the ironworks from the numerous mines opened by the company in the surroundings of Ózd, for example, at Bánszállás, Somsály and Farkaslyuk, while the bulk of iron ore was extracted in the Gömör mines, also owned by the corporation.[3] The third major heavy industrial enterprise in the region, the Borsod Mining Corporation (Borsodi Bányatársulat) was established in 1880 to supply primarily the Witkowitz Mining and Iron Corporation, the largest iron and steel works of the Austro-Hungarian Monarchy, with iron ore from the vast deposits newly discovered at Rudabánya.[4]

Parallel with the construction of a multitude of production facilities, several workers' settlements were erected adjoining the mines and factory sites in order to secure the necessary workforce otherwise locally not available. They accommodated miners and workers with great expertise and of multinational origin who migrated here from various parts of the Austro-Hungarian Monarchy, attracted by the favorable working and living circumstances. Providing a wide range of public services, the settlements gradually transformed into the homes of new communities characterized by a specific social structure, which was essentially different from the traditional social patterns of their environs. This evolution had a variety of outcomes, concerning also the process of urbanization. The State Ironworks, for example, aimed at gaining administrative independence for its large workers' housing estate adjacent to the factory site and its mining settlement at nearby Pereces, both subordinated to the municipality of Diósgyőr, referring to the substantially higher urban development of their residential area, amongst others. Although repeated several times, their initiative was finally not implemented mainly due to the contrary financial interests of Diósgyőr.[5] In Ózd, the former village in the neighborhood of the factory almost disappeared, and the multiplying colonies were evolving over time into a company town with the iron and steel making plant at the center.[6]

In 1913, 96 per cent of the total iron and steel production in the Kingdom of Hungary was produced by the Rimamurány-Salgótarján Ironworks Company and the State Ironworks together with the Austro-Hungarian Railway Company, the third large iron-making firm of the country, whose plants were situated in the south-east, in Krassó-Szörény County.[7] Succeeding the First World War, however, Hungarian iron industry suffered a serious decline having been deprived of diverse assets, like iron-making plants, iron ore mines and iron markets, in consequence of the Treaty of Trianon. Despite severe losses, the two iron-making complexes in Northern Hungary managed to survive, and after the Great Depression they became massively developed. By and large, however substantial the Borsod Industrial Area's contribution was to the economic achievements of Hungary, the country as a late-comer was lagging behind the industrialized countries, and remained slightly dominated by agriculture until the middle of the 20th century.[8]

Following Communist takeover in 1948, the significance of the Borsod Industrial Area increased immensely, and the region was considered to be the leading force of Hungary's economic development throughout the state Socialist period. This was due to the new economic policy of accelerated industrialization, with a main focus on heavy industries, devised in the Soviet Union and prevailing throughout the Eastern Bloc. In order to enhance the economic and political strength of the country – a smoke-screen for military purposes – Hungary was to be converted into a "land of iron and steel", quoting the frequently cited words of Ernő Gerő, a prominent Hungarian Communist leader. In the 1950s and 1960s, almost 90 per cent of the total industrial investment was devoted to heavy industries, entirely nationalized and administered according to centralized state plans. The Borsod Industrial Area became particularly developed due to the numerous coal mines and the two metallurgical complexes located on its territory. Subsequent to the commencement of large-scale reconstructions, the official denomination of the State Ironworks was altered to Lenin Metallurgical Works (Lenin Kohászati Művek), as industrialization was also an ideological requirement, being the central objective of the state Socialist system.[9] In 1965, at the height of ferrous metallurgical investments, 82 per cent of the total regional industrial workforce, 99.846 people worked in heavy industries in the region.[10] However, extensive development neglecting technological improvements remained characteristic even in the 1970s, while tendencies were opposite in the developed western countries. Likewise on Soviet initiatives, heavy industries were further expanded in the region by the establishment of various new plants, such as the chemical works at present Kazincbarcika and Tiszaújváros, the power stations erected at Berente and Tiszapalkonya, as well as the iron ore processing plants at Rudabánya and Sajókeresztúr. Owing to the huge investments, dedicated in high proportion to the Borsod Industrial Area, industry finally developed into the biggest sector of

Hungarian economy, while its backwardness kept increasing over the years due to the permanent supremacy of coal mining and traditional iron making, which came to decline globally in the meantime.[11]

Accelerated industrialization brought about major changes also in regional urban development. Next to both chemical works, on the outskirts of neighboring villages, modern workers' settlements were constructed, called 'Socialist cities'. Besides furnishing workers who originated from different social layers and locations with permanent accommodation locally, they were designated to function as melting pots. Planned in accordance with Stalinist principles, these ideal workers' cities were to provide inspiring spaces for the emergence of a new type of human and a new society, completely deprived of earlier social and national traits. Communist ideology was also represented by the very name of present Tiszaújváros since the former Socialist city was once called Leninváros (Lenin Town). In spite of its historical past, Ózd as a great beneficiary of the new economic policy of rapid industrialization came to be considered a Socialist city as well, acquiring the 'steel city' label simultaneously due to Communist propaganda.[12] Miskolc, which was developed into the second largest town of Hungary being merged with several neighboring communities, including Diósgyőr and Pereces, was also frequently mentioned as a Socialist city by high-standing central and regional Communist officials.[13] Primarily due to the intense expansion of the Lenin Metallurgical Works, as well as that of the Diósgyőr Machine Tool Factory (Diósgyőri Gépgyár), separated from the steel mill, its population nearly doubled, rising from 108.900 in 1947 to 211.390 at its peak in 1984.[14] Designated to be the flagship of forced heavy industrialization as the center of the Borsod Industrial Area, its prestige was further raised by the establishment of the Technical University of Heavy Industry, with its plot gradually evolving into a completely new quarter of the city. Emphasizing its crucial role in the advancement of the new economic policy, the university was initially bearing the name of the then General Secretary of the Communist Party, the Stalinist Mátyás Rákosi. In consequence of the territorial growth, the traditional urban structure of Miskolc was absolutely altered. Besides, the large housing estates built for the new working-class inhabitants transformed fundamentally its historical townscape.[15]

Deindustrialization in regional historical context

Although deep coal mining started to decline as early as the 1960s, deindustrialization became the distinctive feature of economic development only in the 1990s in Hungary. The main specificities of the process were its rapidity compared to similar movements in the developed western countries, as well as its crucial connection with the change of the political system. Unexpectedly, in 1989 and 1990, Hungary, accompanied by other Eastern Bloc countries, turned from a dictatorship based on state socialism to parliamentary democracy, replacing a centrally planned economy with a market economy at the same time. As a consequence, an economic crisis was quickly evolving, aggravated by the impacts of foreign policy reorientation. Owing to the disintegration of the Soviet Union and the successive end of Comecon (Council for Mutual Economic Assistance), Hungary was suddenly deprived of its customary markets and raw material resources, while aspiring to access the European Union also required breaking new grounds to answer adequately the emerging economic challenges. Privatization of state-owned properties became a key element of economic transformation and contributed substantially to the reduction of the incredibly high amount of state debt by increasing the incomes of the budget. However, its first phase known as spontaneous privatization went on fully uncontrolled, whereas the whole process was definitely not free of errors, with the shadow of corruption still lying over it.[16]

Not surprisingly, the Borsod Industrial Area was hit especially hard by the economic crisis as well as subsequent deindustrialization. In particular, the two metallurgical complexes in Ózd and Miskolc-Diósgyőr were struggling heavily with long-standing difficulties in the changing environment of the transitional period. This was due to the fundamental problems of state Socialist economy, such as the low productivity and high energy consumption of Hungarian industry based on obsolete technology. As a result, manufacturing was feasible only at a loss, while the demand for traditional iron and steel products was steadily declining in consequence of the termination of the Cold War era. Despite the enormous sum of state support and an endless row of attempts made mostly by foreign entrepreneurs to profitably operate them following privatization, the plants eventually were not modernized and came to be liquidated, gradually finishing production.[17] Postponed recently, the latest project for the establishment of a cutting-edge steel mill on the Diósgyőr factory site is an excellent representative of the slow process.[18] Downward development of the iron and steel making plants coincided with the accelerating closure of deep coal mines and power stations in the region, also following numerous fruitless efforts made by the central government for their successful privatization.[19] Privatization strategies, on the contrary, were rewarding in the case of the chemical works at Tiszaújváros and Kazincbarcika, currently owned and efficiently operated due to the introduction of modern technology by a Hungary-based multinational and a Chinese company, respectively.[20]

As coal mining and iron making provided workplaces for the majority of the regional labor force throughout decades, their decline brought about a variety of dramatic social effects, still prevailing in the area. The most important of them is unemployment, which kept rising constantly since the beginning of the 1990s and amounted to a staggering 22 per cent by 2012.[21] Job scarcity accompanied by the low living standards quickly increased migration, thereby considerably reducing the number of the inhabitants in the region. In addition, an ageing and less educated population has been left behind because principally better educated and younger people are moving away. At the same time, a growing number of Roma people are moving into the houses abandoned by their earlier residents in the one-time mining settlements and workers' housing estates, who completely lack work opportunities, belonging to a multiply disadvantaged social group. The town of Ózd is the most afflicted by the extremely unfavorable developments. It lost nearly 30 per cent of its inhabitants by 2012, while the unemployment rate was also approaching 30 per cent, substantially surpassing the national and even the regional average. With its population decreasing by 21 per cent to 166.823 in 2011, migration is likewise a challenge for Miskolc despite successfully attracting novel business enterprises in the city.[22] There can be no doubt that the region is still unable to cope with the diversity of economic and social problems, including the impacts of deindustrialization, which originate in the regime change almost three decades ago. On the list recently published by the European Commission on the competitiveness of European regions, the region of Northern Hungary, comprising the Borsod Industrial Area, was ranked 231st out of 263, sliding 13 places further down compared to its position in 2013.[23]

Development of regional identity

Providing a solid overview on the development of regional identity in the Borsod Industrial Area is rather difficult due to the absence of specific studies on the topic. Beyond question, the area emerged rapidly as an integrated region in Borsod County subsequent to the onset of modern industrialization, and was highly appreciated for its expanding heavy industries. Stretching for 125 km along the Sajó Valley, the industrial area was even identified as the 'Hungarian Ruhr' by the distinguished Hungarian writer, Zsigmond Móricz, in the most influential literary journal of Hungary in 1930.[24] The denomination also appeared in a prestigious volume dedicated to the presentation of the County of Borsod in 1939. One of the main authors of the book, published in the remarkable series comprising the sociographic survey of each Hungarian county, wrote the following:

> Here, in the basin of the Hungarian Ruhr, blessed with treasures, function the two largest ironworks of our country. . . . Even the Ruhr District [in Germany] could boast of these ironworks endowed with a multitude of chimneys, workers' settlements, thousands of workers, and outstanding welfare institutions. Here, on a smaller scale, they give a specific character to a whole area. . . . The values of the Hungarian Ruhr should be looked upon with pride and pleasure by every Hungarian. . . . Given that one of the greatest values of Hungary can be found on its own territory, the County of Borsod takes particular pride and pleasure in this jewel.[25]

Owing to the distinct perception of the region, the area-based members of the Hungarian Mining and Metallurgical Society (Országos Magyar Bányászati és Kohászati Egyesület) founded the regional section of the national association as early as 1897, manifesting clearly their regional identity.[26] However, regional identity definitely merged with the professional as well as the corporate identity of miners and iron workers according to available data. Miners and metallurgical laborers were primarily devoted to their work, developing strong affection for and adherence to their companies, private or state-owned, due to prevailing paternalism. In addition, their new communities, created throughout the years from various groups of multinational origin at the companies' housing estates, were distinguished with strong cohesion, high self-esteem and a peculiar mentality.

Nevertheless, because of the high proportion of rural dwellers in the workforce, there was a substantial divide developing between the identity of miners and iron workers living in the colonies and that of their companions commuting daily from rural dwellings to their workplaces. For commuters, industrial work and loyalty to the company was not a priority, being fundamentally attached to agriculture and their village communities.[27] Besides the deep imprint of heavy industries, regional identity included other features as well. Miskolc, for example, defined itself before World War Two as a commercial town famous for its wine cellars on the Avas Hill and its 19th-century theatre building.[28] However, while promoting the city's unique properties in the newly initiated tourist publication of the municipality, the mayor in his preface as well as the authors of the booklet highlighted also the attractivity of the heavy industrial sites in the region, which was presented as the 'hinterland' of Miskolc:

> We dedicate the following pages to the Hungarian Ruhr District, which is not only a major component of heavy industries but also a significant tourist attraction.[29]

Having seized power at the end of the 1940s, the Communist Party increased the appreciation of the Borsod Industrial Area further according to its economic, political and ideological aims. Owing to the Party's various measures and persistent propaganda, the industrial identity of the region considerably strengthened. Particularly, the coal miners identified with the industrial area, sustaining a weekly titled *Borsodi Bányász* (Borsod Miners) between 1952 and 1990, as well as sports clubs and cultural associations with the same denomination.[30] Reorganized in the 1950s, the regional section of the Hungarian Mining and Metallurgical Society continued to reinforce regional identity, which characterized a growing number of people as a result of extensive industrialization. The identity of earlier agricultural communities was substantially transformed in the region, for example, in the vicinity of Ózd at Arló and Hódoscsépány, due to the rising number of workers commuting daily from rural settlements to the large heavy industrial establishments.[31] Similarly, united with Diósgyőr and dominated by heavy industries as the center of the Borsod Industrial Area, major features of the traditional identity of Miskolc were obliterated or became de-emphasized by the central and local authorities. Regional identity, however, merged with professional identity, and came to be determined by the emerging new identity of miners and iron workers, who were assigned a fundamental role and privileged status by the Communists, emulating the Soviet model. They were expected to legitimate the dominance of the Party which was ruling in the name of the working class, functioning as the driving force in the fulfillment of the economic plans as well as in the transformation of their class. However, while embracing the Communist ideas, the identity of miners and iron workers was actually based on pretensions owing to the obvious discrepancy between propaganda and everyday experience. Nevertheless, despite fake achievements in Socialist competitions or false entries in the Socialist work brigades' diaries, miners and iron workers remained fascinated by the ideas and were addicted to their jobs and workplaces as well as their communities, frequently preserving the traditions of their ancestors.[32] Still, their attitude regarding the contrast between the ideologically based slogans and the real world was changing radically throughout the years. Due to extensive political violence and ideological pressure as well as their worsening labor and living conditions, the workers of the two iron and steel making plants in Miskolc-Diósgyőr and Ózd were the first to organize and demonstrate in the 1956 revolution. They were also accompanied by miners, for example, from Ormosbánya.[33] Following the revolution, their attitude came to be influenced by emerging new factors: first, by the conciliatory policy of the Communist Party; and second, by the measures taken to improve the circumstances of miners and iron workers, raising them far above working class average regarding wages and benefits. In consequence, their militancy transformed into informal shop-floor bargaining and a sort of acquiescence during the 1960s and 1970s. At last, in the 1980s, they acknowledged with disenchantment and resignation that Communist ideas were rapidly losing significance, permitting the dynamic rise of completely opposing economic and social developments. This was exacerbated by the fact that the Socialist state was apparently no longer capable of improving their standard of living.[34]

Following the change of the political system, the high appreciation of the Borsod Industrial Area was disappearing fast from national consciousness, to be quickly replaced by a strong aversion stemming from the unfavorable developments in the region. A dismal picture of the industrial area was widely spread by the documentaries of the prominent film director, Tamás Almási, and the photobook of Imre Benkő, which were raising public attention to the economic and social consequences of the dramatic decline of heavy industries, particularly in Ózd and its surroundings.[35] Struggling with the deteriorating image of the region, the professional identity of miners and iron workers was also utterly shaken, deprived of its foundations by the rapid regime change as well as the subsequent economic crisis. Identified by their previous social role, miners and iron workers became discredited for legitimating the rule of the Communist Party; in addition, they were compelled to face unemployment due to the accelerating closure of mines and the elongated decline of the iron and steel making complexes. Losing a job was frequently considered by them as a personal failure, therefore feelings of shame were superseding their former pride. Moreover, for the members of workers' dynasties, the efforts of their ancestors also seemed to be rendered futile by the termination of production and the liquidation of workplaces. "The factory has no meaning for us any more", was worded by a former worker of the iron ore processing plant at Rudabánya, expressing the general feelings of redundant workforce in the area.[36] Their disappointment increased further on account of privatization, miners and iron workers oftentimes blaming the management for following personal economic and financial interests rather than taking efficient measures to rescue the production units. Confronted with the constant deterioration of their standard of living due to unemployment or diminishing wages against the rapid fortune-making of their superiors, they became disillusioned by market economy as well. As a result, seemingly forgetting the inadequacies and pretensions of state socialism, they were inclined to remember it with nostalgia, longing for values like security in everyday existence and a fairly egalitarian social system.[37] However, there are remarkable internal differences within the Borsod Industrial Area, primarily at the official level, such as city governance, regarding identification with the region's industrial past. While at Ózd, iron making is at least occasionally taken into consideration by the local government as the defining element of the settlement's identity, Miskolc is struggling hard to completely dispose of its 'steel city' label, considered to be a stigma by its municipality. Contrasting forces do exist: a group of the younger generation in search of identity, comprising mostly Miskolc-born intellectuals, attributes an increasingly positive value to the industrial past of the city. Nevertheless, in the majority of former mining settlements, for example, at Somsály, Bánszállás and Farkaslyuk, community identity lacks any attachment to industry due to a complete exchange of inhabitants.[38]

History of industrial heritage in the region

Substantial interest towards the material remains of heavy industrial production in the region was first manifested in the middle of the 20th century. As early as 1952, the charcoal blast furnace erected at Újmassa in the first half of the 19th century was reconstructed and declared a legally protected national monument. The 18th-century administration building and store house of the ironworks were also given statutory protection, locating the newly founded Central Foundry Museum (Központi Kohászati Múzeum) within its walls.[39] Further museums were created at Ózd and Rudabánya in the 1960s and 1970s in order to present the history of the Ózd iron and steel works as well as the relics of ore and mineral mining, respectively.[40] Most of the highly valuable museum library of the Schemnitz Mining Academy, set up in the neighboring region in 1735 as one of the oldest institutions of technological higher education in the world, was also transported to its legal successor, the newly established university in Miskolc and opened for the public in this period.[41] The last museum of the state Socialist era in this line was initiated in 1983 at Borsodnádasd focusing on the history of the local sheet rolling mill, under the curatorship of the author of this paper.

In the 1990s, however, in the age of rapidly expanding deindustrialization, the preservation of heavy industrial vestiges was absolutely not taken into consideration. The demolishing of industrial buildings, structures and equipment was running parallel with the termination of production in the facilities. Following its destruction, the spectacular row of chimney stacks at the Ózd ironworks site, formerly the principal landmark of the town, turned into the symbol of industrial heritage quickly disappearing from the landscape of the region. In addition, the industrial museums established in the previous decades were also threatened by closure, endangering their collections.[42]

Public attention was first driven to the economic and cultural values of the obsolete remains of heavy industries in the Borsod Industrial Area at a major international conference in 1999, focusing particularly on the heavy industrial region. Organized by the University of Miskolc and TICCIH Hungary under the auspices of The International Committee for the Conservation of the Industrial Heritage (TICCIH), the conference was also supported by the Hungarian Mining and Metallurgical Society, the Hungarian Historical Association and ICOMOS Hungary.[43] Definitely a breakthrough in industrial heritage preservation in Hungary, following the conference nine buildings of the Miskolc-Diósgyőr iron and steel works, from the 19th and 20th centuries, became legally protected in 2001 in appreciation of the plant's architectural and industrial history values.[44] Regrettably, the temporary statutory protection expired in two years due to the lack of appropriate reuse. Apart from a workshop partially transformed into an indoor climbing gym, the other eight factory buildings have been in serious decay ever since despite recent protection provided by local authorities (see Figure 5.2).[45] In 2005, further industrial buildings were declared national monuments at the coal-mining settlement of Pereces, now part of Miskolc, as well as in Ózd.[46] By now, five of the eight protected buildings of the former Ózd iron and steel works have been reconstructed and reused, namely, the officers' casino, the foremen's and workers' reading society building (see Figure 5.3), the factory school, the rolling mill and the power plant, while the remaining three, the fire-clay factory, the office building and the public bath, are still in need of feasible ideas and financial resources for regeneration.[47] At Pereces, the protected industrial buildings and structures are all completely neglected, deteriorating apace together with the residential area of the one-time mining settlement.[48]

The same tendency of promising initiatives mostly ending, at least, in partial failure is noticeable also in the development of industrial museums. As regards the museums endangered in the region, they were finally able to survive; nevertheless, their collections still lack substantial improvement, and are presented in permanent exhibitions created several decades ago.[49] The long-dedicated project of establishing a regional coal-mining museum based on a variety of valuable mining relics collected for decades was also ill-fated. Being unable to acquire an independent institutional status, it was united in 2006 with the ore and mineral mining museum at Rudabánya, which became shortly downgraded to the level of a local museum.[50]

Initiated in the first decade of the 21st century by regional development authorities and supported by the Phare Cross-border Cooperation Programme of the European Commission, the projects intending to facilitate the preservation of heavy industrial remains through the establishment of industrial heritage trails were not successful either. Despite designed on the pattern of the highly attractive industrial heritage route implemented in the Ruhr, *Die Route der Industriekultur*, and embracing outstanding, though mostly decaying, examples of heavy industrial heritage in the region of Northern Hungary and in adjacent Slovakia, the tourist routes are still not functioning.[51]

In spite of the above rather unfavorable developments, the preservation of the quickly decreasing remnants of coal mining and iron making may get new impetus due to a multitude of projects accomplished recently. Aiming to raise public awareness to the values of industrial heritage in Miskolc, the projects promoted various activities such as guided visits to the factory sites in Miskolc-Diósgyőr, organization of cultural events in the same place and interactive programs for schoolchildren. In addition, interviews were made with the inhabitants of Pereces and the Miskolc-Diósgyőr ironworks' colony, books and diverse publications issued and exhibitions installed based on the researches, as well as meetings organized with the participants of the projects for a wide audience, inviting also experts and authorities.[52] As regards the material remains of industrial heritage, due to the 3D models available on a designated website in consequence of the projects, numerous buildings in the Miskolc-Diósgyőr iron and steel works and at its workers' housing estate have been already preserved virtually.[53] However, these endeavors have proved to be insufficient so far to promote their preservation and revitalization also in real life despite the ten-year time span of the programs.

Interaction of regional identity and industrial heritage in the Borsod Industrial Area

Studying the production of industrial heritage sites in the Borsod Industrial Area, there can be no doubt that there are substantial differences among the initiatives regarding motivation and intention. Proposals for the preservation of the charcoal blast furnace at Újmassa were originally made by prominent technology professionals referring to its historical values. However, reconstruction was finally accomplished in order to facilitate the implementation of the main objectives of Communist ideology, such as the public support of accelerated heavy industrialization and the creation of a new worker identity, based on the development of technology. On Communist Party demand, retrofitting was to be financed by the Diósgyőr ironworks whose official denomination had just been changed to Lenin Metallurgical Works. Its management was taking an active part in organization and provided advice in technical matters. Iron workers were to contribute a large amount of voluntary labor to reconstruction, turning the blast furnace site into a memorial as well as an arena of high priority for ceremonies and festivals organized by the ironworks.[54] Despite having been designed as an instrument for political propaganda, the reconstructed blast furnace was emerging over the years as a widely cherished monument, pertaining to the image of Miskolc beyond any doubt, and highly appreciated by iron workers for expressing their professional and regional identity.

Similarly, the establishment of the industrial museums at Miskolc, Ózd and Rudabánya was also originating in Communist ideology since the unique statute enacted in 1954 to arrange for the conservation of technical relics emphasized their significance for the community of Hungarians as valuable evidence of technological development.[55] Construction and maintenance of the museums, including financing, were the responsibility of the large state-owned mining and metallurgical complexes located in the region. In addition, museum work, such as collection and presentation, was generally advanced by a member of the management, who became personally dedicated to the history and traditions of his profession.[56] Although expected to support the museums with volunteer work, and to visit them regularly with their Socialist brigades on Communist Party directives, miners and iron workers were genuinely enthusiastic about the museums for assisting them to take pride in their professional communities as well as in their workplaces.

Subsequent to the rapid regime change, the state Socialist system of ideologically based industrial heritage preservation abruptly collapsed. This was indicated first by the fact that the industrial museums were completely deprived of financial resources parallel with the emerging decline of the region's mining and metallurgical complexes. The Central Foundry Museum, for instance, was even offered for sale as part of the Miskolc-Diósgyőr ironworks' liquidation process. However, owing to the joint efforts of technology professionals and cultural heritage experts, the museums came to be supported by central and local authorities, or freshly established public foundations, eventually being capable of continuing activities.[57]

Although former proponents kept making initiatives for the preservation of the regional heavy industrial heritage, their propositions were henceforth rooted in the traditional appreciation of the industrial past instead of implementing Communist ideology. For example, small groups of the disintegrating plants' former management created industrial history associations and launched novel festivities, such as the Fazola Festival at Újmassa, remembering Henrik and Frigyes Fazola, the founders of the charcoal blast furnace (see Figure 5.4). Nevertheless, they failed to focus substantial attention on the preservation of modern-age buildings and structures of heavy industrial production.[58] Protecting late nineteenth- and 20th-century industrial heritage was initiated by emerging new actors, namely a Miskolc-born historian and an architect originating in Ózd. They were followed by North-East Passage (Észak-Keleti Átjáró Egyesület), the cultural and academic association of young professionals mostly educated at the University of Miskolc. Raising public awareness of the region's industrial history, the members of the association promoted the preservation of the material remains of mining and iron making with diverse methods, which recently earned them a Europa Nostra Prize.[59] In contrast, former miners and iron workers were almost entirely missing from the advocates of heavy industrial heritage in the region.[60]

Preservation initiatives were supported by local authorities rather reluctantly, or were completely dismissed. The municipality of Ózd, while preventing the accomplishment of the ground-breaking scheme of the National Office of Cultural Heritage for heritage-based urban renewal at the beginning of the 21st century, was ready to endorse the recent investment program of the central government.[61] As a result, mostly due to the lobbying of an Ózd-born MP, two legally protected buildings were reconstructed and culturally reused, creating innovative tourist attractions on the former ironworks' site in the framework of the MaNDA project.[62] Still, despite including industrial heritage tourism in future urban development plans, the local authorities aim to demolish an emblematic workshop due to the lack of financial resources for its maintenance.[63] On the contrary, heavy industrial heritage was completely disregarded compiling the previous as well as the latest integrated urban development strategy of Miskolc.[64] Having placed culture in the focus as the major force determining the current identity and image of the city, the municipality launched over the years a series of cultural events, such as the Bartók Plus Operafestival and the Jameson Cinefest.[65] In addition, the medieval castle in Diósgyőr, reconstructed with considerable state support in the recent past, was turned into a gorgeous tourist site, as a proud symbol of the whole city.[66] Without doubt, the strikingly small number of valuable industrial heritage sites preserved in the Borsod Industrial Area with the majority of them having being demolished bears witness to the region's faltering industrial identity.

Conclusion

Having been the most significant heavy industrial region of Hungary for over 100 years, the Borsod Industrial Area possessed a highly valuable industrial heritage in the 1990s, vanishing fast from the regional landscape by now. This is clearly attributable to the fundamental connection of deindustrialization with regime change and privatization. In consequence of the multiple events, regional identity firmly based on the area's heavy industrial assets was absolutely shaken. Coal mining and iron making were the pride of the region from the onset of modern industrialization, their appreciation being substantially increased in the state Socialist period due to the accelerated development of heavy industries, the central objective of the political system. At the end of the 20th century, however, coal mining and iron making abruptly turned into an economic as well as an ideological burden, and a source of scandals owing to privatization. In addition, the professional identity of miners and iron workers, merged with their regional identity, came to be also significantly disturbed, since they were compelled to face the consequences of deindustrialization while getting discredited for legitimating the rule of the Communist Party. As a result, the industrial identity of the region faltered, the vestiges of heavy industries scarcely considered to be valuable cultural heritage. Most strikingly, Miskolc, the former flagship of accelerated heavy industrialization, is struggling especially hard to dispose of its 'steel city' label, as well as its late 19th- and 20th-century industrial heritage. Although mining and iron-making sites were presented by the municipality as major tourist attractions in 1936, currently modern heavy industrial heritage is completely missing from the urban development strategy, culture and medieval heritage having been placed in the focus as the main forces determining the present identity and image of the city. At Ózd, local authorities are occasionally willing to support industrial heritage preservation, the history as well as the cultural resources of the community depending exclusively on iron and steel making. Nevertheless, there are still proponents, such as the civic associations established by the former heavy industrial plants' retired management as well as that of young intellectuals originating in the region, who make various initiatives to preserve the industrial identity of the region. Despite their substantial efforts, regional identity keeps faltering and the scarcity of preserved industrial heritage reflects the multitude of negative connotations regarding the recent industrial history of the region.

Figure 5.1 Map of the Borsod Industrial Area stretching for 125 km along the Sajó Valley in Northern Hungary.

Copyright: Paulus

Figure 5.2 Temporary protection having expired, the building of the power plant is deteriorating in the former iron and steel works in Miskolc.

Photo: Györgyi Németh

Figure 5.3 The reconstructed reading society building of the former iron and steel works at Ózd.

Photo: Györgyi Németh

Figure 5.4 Participants of the first Fazola Festival initiated in 2008 at the charcoal blast furnace in Miskolc-Újmassa.

Notes

1 Gusztáv Heckenast, *A magyarországi vaskohászat története a feudalizmus korában: A XIII. század közepétől a XVIII. század végéig* (Budapest, 1991), 247–9.
2 László Katus, Transport revolution and economic growth in Hungary, in John Komlos (ed.), *Economic development in the Habsburg Monarchy in the nineteenth century: Essays*, East European Monographs (Boulder, 1983), 183–204.
3 László Katus, *Hungary in the dual monarchy, 1867–1914*, East European Monographs (Boulder, 2008), 188, 198–9, 243–64; Károly Jenei, Az alapítás előzményei, in Tibor Iván Berend (ed.), *Az Ózdi Kohászati Üzemek története* (Budapest, 1980), 43–87; Ákos Koroknai, Az óriásvállalat kibontakozása, 1881–1900, in Berend (ed.), *Az Ózdi Kohászati Üzemek története*, 103–49.
4 Endre Pantó, A 75 éves nagyüzemű vasércbányászat, 1880–1955, in Endre Pantó, Gábor Pantó, Tibor Podányi and Károly Moser (eds.), *Rudabánya ércbányászata* (Budapest, 1957), 104–5, 114.
5 *A diósgyőri m. kir. vas- és aczélgyár története, 1765–1910* (Miskolc, 1910), 30–1.
6 Györgyi Csontos and Tibor Vass, *Ózdi munkáskolóniák: gyári lakótelepek és lakásbelsők története a századfordulótól az ezredfordulóig* (Pomáz, 2001); Péter Nagy, *A Rima vonzásában: az ózdi helyi és gyári társadalom a késő dualizmustól az államosításig* (Budapest, 2016), 134–57.
7 Katus, *Hungary in the dual monarchy, 1867–1914*, 247–8.
8 Tamás Csató, Industrial development, in Tibor Iván Berend and Tamás Csató, *One-and-a-half centuries of semi-successful modernization, 1848–1989*, Vol. 1., East European Monographs (Boulder, 2001), 195–211; László Réti R., Fegyverkezési konjunktúra, 1933–1938, in Tibor Iván Berend (ed.), *Az Ózdi Kohászati Üzemek története*, 242–6.
9 Tibor Iván Berend, Rapid industrialization with obsolete technology, in Berend and Csató, *One-and-a-half centuries of semi-successful modernization, 1848–1989*, 323–30.
10 József Kóródi, A szocialista ipar és közlekedés fejlődése, in Gáborné Varga (ed.), *Borsod-Abaúj-Zemplén megye története és legújabb kori adattára* (Miskolc, 1970), 307.
11 József Kóródi, *A Borsodi Iparvidék* (Budapest, 1959), 137–8, 146–7, 202–4, 214–16; Tibor Iván Berend, Rapid industrialization with obsolete technology, in Berend and Csató, *One-and-a-half centuries of semi-successful modernization, 1848–1989*, 330–9.
12 Pál Germuska, Between theory and practice: Planning socialist cities in Hungary, in Mikael Hård and Thomas J. Misa (eds.), *Urban machinery: Inside European cities* (Cambridge, MA and London, England, 2008), 233–55.
13 Pál Germuska, Tradíció nélkül. A magyarországi városok önképe, 1949–1989, in Zsombor Bódy, Monika Mátay and Árpád Tóth (eds.), *A mesterség iskolája: tanulmányok Bácskai Vera 70. születésnapjára* (Budapest, 2000), 479.
14 Központi Statisztikai Hivatal, *Magyarország közigazgatási helységnévtára 1947. évre* (Budapest, 1947), 76; Központi Statisztikai Hivatal, *A Magyar Népköztársaság Helységnévtára, 1985* (Budapest, 1985), 300.
15 Béla Horváth, A miskolci városkép változása, *Herman Ottó Múzeum Évkönyve*, 11 (1972), 189–218.
16 Ignác Romsics, *From dictatorship to democracy: The birth of the third Hungarian republic, 1988–2001*, East European Monographs (Boulder, 2007), 321–33.
17 János Sziklavári, László Kiss, János Jung and István Sélei, *A diósgyőri acélgyártás története a folytacélgyártás bevezetésétől napjainkig* (Miskolc, 2004), 149–77.
18 *Mégsem lesz acélgyártás Diósgyőrben?* www.eszakonline.hu/miskolc/56Cez-toertent/27637-kifarol-a-kormuűanyzat-a-diosgyri-acelmbl/ (accessed 17 Jan. 2017); *Miskolci acélmű: csak pr-kampány volt*, http://eszon.hu/miskolc/56-ez-toertent/27662-miskolci-acelm-csak-pr-kampany-volt/ (accessed 17 Jan. 2017).

19 Imre Schmotzer, Árpád Majtényi and Endre Vadász, Volt egyszer egy... Borsodi Szénbányák, *Bányászati és Kohászati Lapok: Bányászat*, 138/3 (2005), 16–22.
20 *TVK 60: The history of Tiszai Vegyi Kombinát (Tisza Chemical Works) from 1953 to 2013*, https://mol.hu/images/pdf/About_MOL/petrochemical_business/about_tvk/history/TVK%2060_History.pdf/ (accessed 17 Jan. 2017); BorsodChem, *History: We've come a long way.* www.borsodchem-group.com/About-us/History.aspx/ (accessed 17 Jan. 2017).
21 *Ennyi munkanélküli van Borsodban*, www.profession.hu/cikk/20131004/ennyi-munkanelkuli-van-borsodban/3461/ (accessed 17 Jan. 2017).
22 Központi Statisztikai Hivatal, *A Magyar Népköztársaság Helységnévtára, 1985* (Budapest, 1985); Központi Statisztikai Hivatal, *Magyarország közigazgatási helynévkönyve, 2012. január 1* (Budapest, 2012); Központi Statisztikai Hivatal, *2011. évi népszámlálás. 3. Területi adatok. 3.5. Borsod-Abaúj-Zemplén megye* (Miskolc, 2013), 10–1, 21–3, www.ksh.hu/docs/hun/xftp/idoszaki/nepsz2011/nepsz_03_05_2011.pdf/ (accessed 17 Jan. 2017); Péter Alabán, "Siktából" az utcára. Ipari munkások az ózdi kistérség törésvonalain, *Korall*, 49 (2012), 88–92.
23 European Commission, *European regional competitiveness index, Hungary: Észak-Magyarország*, http://ec.europa.eu/regional_policy/en/information/maps/regional_competitiveness#2/ (accessed 17 Jan. 2017); Fruzsina Elöd, *Minden régiónk csúszik lefelé a lejtőn*, http://index.hu/gazdasag/2017/03/01/versenykepesseg_2016_eu_magyarorszag// (accessed 17 Jan. 2017).
24 Zsigmond Móricz, Mai napok: Miskolc, *Nyugat*, 22 (1930), http://epa.oszk.hu/00000/00022/nyugat.htm/ (accessed 17 May 2017).
25 Rezső Péchy-Horváth, Borsod, a magyar Ruhr, in Antal Csíkvári (ed.), *Borsod vármegye: Borsod, Gömör és Kishont k. e. e. vármegyék*, Vármegyei Szociográfiák V (Budapest, 1939), 52, 56. Translation by the author.
26 Jegyzőkönyv felvétetett 1897. évi június 29-én Rozsnyón az "Országos Magyar Bányászati és Kohászati Egyesület" Borsod-Gömör osztályának alakulási gyűléséről, *Az Országos Magyar Bányászati és Kohászati Egyesület Közlései. A "Bányászati és Kohászati Lapok" melléklapja*, 9 (1897), 56–7. Quoted by Lajos Mendly, Emlékek a borsod-gömöri bányászat múltjából, *Bányászattörténeti Közlemények*, 4 (2007), 32–6.
27 See, for example, Ákos Koroknai, Alfréd Lehoczky and Zoltán Sárközi, A gyár társadalma, in Berend (ed.), *Az Ózdi Kohászati Üzemek története*, 150–7; András Mándy, Szociális és társadalmi viszonyok, in István Benke and Viktor Reményi (eds.), *A magyar bányászat évezredes története*, Vol. 2 (Budapest, 1996), 48–9; Nagy, *A Rima vonzásában*, 271–8.
28 Lajos Marjalaki Kiss, Az Avas, in Csíkvári (ed.), *Borsod vármegye*, 12–4; Rezső Péchy-Horváth, Színművészet Miskolcon, in Csíkvári (ed.), *Borsod vármegye*, 34–5.
29 Sámuel Fazekas (ed.), *Miskolci kirakat* (Miskolc, 1936). Translation by the author.
30 Zsuzsanna Márkus, A Borsodi Bányász című hetilap, *Bányászattörténeti Közlemények*, 13 (2012), 60–4.
31 Kóródi, *A Borsodi Iparvidék*, 245; Alabán, "Siktából" az utcára, 86–7.
32 Michael Burawoy, Ideology as reality: The Lenin Steel Works, in Michael Burawoy and János Lukács, *The radiant past: Ideology and reality in Hungary's road to capitalism* (Chicago and London, 1992), 81–142; Mark Pittaway, Introduction: Workers and socialist states in postwar central and Eastern Europe, *International Labor and Working-Class History*, 68/Fall (2005), 1–8.
33 Mark Pittaway, The revolution and industrial workers: The disintegration and reconstruction of socialism, 1953–1958, *Hungarian Studies Review*, 34/1–2 (2007), 115–54; Attila Szakolczai, Tömegmozgalmak Miskolcon, 1956. október 25–26, in Zsuzsanna Kőrösi, Éva Standeisky and János Rainer M. (eds.), *Évkönyv VIII* (Budapest, 2000), 303–22; ead., Borsod – Abaúj – Zemplén megye, in Attila Szakolczai and László Á. Varga (eds.), *A vidék forradalma, 1956*, Vol. 1 (Budapest, 2003), 148–68.

34 Tibor Valuch, Changes in the structure and lifestyle of the Hungarian society in the second half of the 20th century, in Gábor Gyáni, György Kövér and Tibor Valuch (eds.), *Social history of Hungary from the reform era to the end of the twentieth century*, East European Monographs (Boulder, 2004), 603–10.
35 See the series of the documentaries titled *Ezredvégi krónika*, produced by Tamás Almási between 1987 and 1998, www.youtube.com/watch?v=h-QUW_AE4V8/ (accessed 10 Febr. 2017); Imre Benkő, *Acélváros: Steel town, 1987–1995: Fotóesszé: Photo essay* (Budapest, 1996).
36 József R. Nagy, "The factory has no meaning for us any more . . ." Similarities and differences in the identity coming from the industrial environment in the case of workers from Rudabánya and Diósgyőr, in Györgyi Németh (ed.), *Growth, decline and recovery: Heavy industrial regions in transition* (Budapest and Miskolc, 2007), 261–9.
37 Eszter Bartha, Ez a piacgazdaság minket a padlóra küldött. Munkásság és munkástudat a mai Magyarországon, *Replika*, 83/2 (2013), 61–76; ead., Forgotten histories: Workers and the new capitalism in East Germany and Hungary, in John W. Boyer and Berthold Molden (eds.), *EUtROPEs: The paradox of European empire* (Chicago, 2014), 309–23; István Murányi, A munkások lokális identitásának jellemzői Borsodnádasdon, *Korall*, 49 (2012), 112–13.
38 Péter Alabán, A vidék válságai: az ipari válságzóna jelenségeinek összefüggései a rendszerváltozás után az észak-borsodi bányásztelepülések példáján, *Korall*, 54 (2013), 125–33.
39 László Kiss, Gyula Kiszely and Pál Vajda, *Magyarország ipari műemlékei. Industrial monuments in Hungary* (Budapest, 1982), 62–7.
40 László Kiss and Gyula Kiszely, *Magyarország műszaki múzeumai* (Budapest, 1982), 73–80, 126–30.
41 László Zsámboki, *Die Schemnitzer Gedenkbibliothek von Miskolc in Ungarn* (Miskolc, 1978).
42 Györgyi Németh, The Miskolc-Diósgyőr Ironworks: How to go on? *Patrimoine de l'industrie. Industrial Patrimony*, 1/1 (1999), 41–5; ead., A Borsodi Iparvidék ipari öröksége, *Műemlékvédelem*, 43/4 (1999), 192–8.
43 Györgyi Németh (ed.), *Growth, decline and recovery: Heavy industrial regions in transition* (Budapest and Miskolc, 2007).
44 Ead., A diósgyőri vasgyár műemléki védelme, *Műemlékvédelem*, 45/2 (2001), 84–7.
45 Miskolc Megyei Jogú Város Önkormányzat 39/2009. (XII. 2.) rendelete az épített környezet értékeinek helyi védelméről (egységes szerkezetben a módosításáról szóló 2/2013. (II.19) és 4/2017. (II.21.) önkormányzati rendelettel) www.miskolc.hu/sites/default/files/dokumentumok/csatolmanyok/39_2009_e.pdf/ (accessed 11 Mar. 2017).
46 A nemzeti kulturális örökség miniszterének 25/2005. (IX. 16.) NKÖM rendelete egyes ingatlanok műemlékké, valamint műemléki jelentőségű területté nyilvánításáról, illetőleg műemléki védettségének megszüntetéséről. *Magyar Közlöny*, 124 (16 Sept. 2005), 6645–6, www.kozlonyok.hu/nkonline/MKPDF/2005/MK124.pdf/ (accessed 10 Febr. 2017).
47 See, for example, Mihály Rudolf, *Ózdi műemlék – Olvasó Egyleti Székház – felújítása*, http://epiteszforum.hu/ozdi-muemlek-olvaso-egyleti-szekhaz-felujitasa/ (accessed 9 Febr. 2017); Anett Mizsei, *Kiszínezett barna zóna: az ózdi projekt*, http://epiteszforum.hu/kiszinezett-barna-zona-az-ozdi-projekt/ (accessed 9 Febr. 2017).
48 *Elhagyatva Miskolcon: a perecesi bányaépületek*, http://miskolcadhatott.blog.hu/2015/03/05/elhagyatva_miskolcon_a_perecesi_banyaepuletek/ (accessed 10 Febr. 2017).
49 *Kohászati Múzeum*, http://kohmuz.t-online.hu/kohaszati_muzeum.htm/ (accessed 10 Febr. 2017); *Az Ózdi Muzeális Gyűjtemény bemutatása*, www.ozdimuzeum.hu/content.php?cid=cont_550c2882d7f724.22361398/ (accessed 10 Febr. 2017).
50 *Rudabánya város honlapja. Bányászattörténeti Múzeum*, www.rudabanya.hu/hu/muzeum.html/ (accessed 10 Febr. 2017).

51 Györgyi Németh, *Útikalauz a bányászat és kohászat emlékeihez Észak-Magyarországon és Szlovákiában. Guide to the monuments of mining and metallurgy in North-Hungary and Slovakia* (Miskolc, 2001).
52 See, for example, *Műszakváltás 2*, http://atjarokhe.hu/2010/06/muszakvaltas-2// (accessed 28 Jan. 2017); *Tündérkert Perecesen*, http://atjarokhe.hu/olvasnivalok/tunderkert-perecesen-2// (accessed 28 Jan. 2017); *Borsod 2050: Kézen fogni a fiatalokat*, www.boon.hu/borsod-2050-kezen-fogni-a-fiatalokat/2222579/ (accessed 28 Jan. 2017).
53 Zoltán Bereczki, *A diósgyőri gyár és kolóniája: a gyár modellje*, www.vasgyar.hu/nyitooldal/3d/gyar/ (accessed 28 Jan. 2017); ead., *A diósgyőri gyár és kolóniája: a kolónia modellje*, www.vasgyar.hu/nyitooldal/3d/kolonia/ (accessed 28 Jan. 2017).
54 Aladár Schleicher, Az 1813. évben épült és 1952-ben újjáépített újmassai nagyolvasztó, *A Magyar Tudományos Akadémia Műszaki Tudományok Osztályának Közleményei*, 12/1–4 (1954), 403–11. The management commissioned an academic volume on the ironworks' history also in this period. See Gyula Kiszely, Diósgyőr vaskohászatának történetéből, *Kohászati Lapok*, 8 Aug. 1954, p. 338.
55 A Népköztársaság Elnöki Tanácsának 4/1954. (II. 24.) törvényerejű rendelete a műszaki emlékek védelméről. *Magyar Közlöny*, 12 (24 Febr. 1954), 72–3.
56 In Rudabánya, for instance, a head of division at the iron ore mine finally changed profession and became the director of the newly established museum, following his more than a decade-long effort to improve the collection of ore and mineral mining artefacts. Gyula Viktor, *Murvay László élete és munkássága: 1918–1984, Érc- és Ásványbányászati Múzeumi Füzetek 15* (Rudabánya, 1985).
57 Katalin Lengyel Kiss, The Foundry Museum established in the former Ganz Foundry has been serving the public for 35 years, in Németh (ed.), *Growth, decline and recovery: Heavy industrial regions in transition*, 353–5.
58 *Ipartörténeti értékmentés*, www.boon.hu/ipartorteneti-ertekmentes/1874092/ (accessed 10 Febr. 2017); *IX. Fazola Fesztivál keretében ipartörténeti konferencia*, http://tab.mta.hu/miskolci-teruleti-bizottsag/esemenyek/ix/ (accessed 10 Febr. 2017).
59 *Észak-Keleti Átjáró Egyesület*, http://atjarokhe.hu/english/ (accessed 10 Febr. 2017); *Passage: From a rusty city to a new Miskolc*, www.europeanheritageawards.eu/winners/passage-rusty-city-new-miskolc/ (accessed 10 Febr. 2017).
60 Alabán, "Siktából" az utcára, 82–103.
61 Ágnes Kristóf and Piroska Váczi, *Ózd örökség alapú városrehabilitációjának előkészítése*, http://epiteszforum.hu/kris-agnes-dr-vaczi-piroska-ozd-orokseg-alapu-varosrehabilitaciojanak-elokeszitese/ (accessed 10 Jan. 2017).
62 *Digitális archívum és filmsúdió lett az ózdi gyárból*, www.boon.hu/digitalis-archivum-es-filmstudio-lett-az-ozdi-gyarbol/3099651/ (accessed 10 Jan. 2017); Máté Pálos, Digitális élménypark Ózdon: vakító vásznak, *Magyar Narancs*, 29/7 (2017), 30–2.
63 ITS2014 Konzorcium, *Ózd város integrált településfejlesztési stratégiája*, pp. 16–7, http://ozd.hu/content/cont_575e73f4e57191.23649128/ozd_integralt_telepulesfejlesztesi_strategia.pdf/ (accessed 10 Febr. 2017); Györgyi Csontos, *Nyílt levél az ózdi acélműi csarnokért*, http://epiteszforum.hu/nyilt-level-az-ozdi-acelmui-csarnokert/ (accessed 10 Febr. 2017).
64 Katalin Bana et als., *Miskolc megyei jogú város 2007–2013 közötti időszakra vonatkozó városfejlesztési stratégiája*, pp. 197–8, 203–4, www.miskolc.hu/sites/default/files/dokumentumok/csatolmanyok/varosfejlesztesiprogram.pdf/ (accessed 10 Febr. 2017); *Miskolc megyei jogú város integrált településfejlesztési stratégiája*, pp. 44–5, www.miskolcvaros2020.hu/sites/default/files/dokumentumok/miskolc_its.pdf/ (accessed 10 Febr. 2017).
65 *Bartók Plus Operafestival*, http://operafesztival.hu/index.php/en// (accessed 10 Febr. 2017); *Jameson CineFest*, www.cinefest.hu/eng/nyito_eng.html/ (accessed 10 Febr. 2017).
66 *Castle of Diósgyőr*, http://diosgyorivar.hu/en (accessed 10 Febr. 2017).

Bibliography

IX. Fazola Fesztivál keretében ipartörténeti konferencia, http://tab.mta.hu/miskolci-teruleti-bizottsag/esemenyek/ix/ (accessed 10 Febr. 2017).
Alabán, Péter, "Siktából" az utcára. Ipari munkások az ózdi kistérség törésvonalain, *Korall*, 49 (2012), 82–105.
Alabán, Péter, A vidék válságai: az ipari válságzóna jelenségeinek összefüggései a rendszerváltozás után az észak-borsodi bányásztelepülések példáján, *Korall*, 54 (2013), 118–40.
Almási, Tamás, *Ezredvégi krónika*, www.youtube.com/watch?v=h-QUW_AE4V8/ (accessed 10 Febr. 2017).
Bana, Katalin et al., *Miskolc megyei jogú város 2007–2013 közötti időszakra vonatkozó városfejlesztési stratégiája*, www.miskolc.hu/sites/default/files/dokumentumok/csatolmanyok/varosfejlesztesiprogram.pdf/ (accessed 10 Febr. 2017).
Bartha, Eszter, "Ez a piacgazdaság minket a padlóra küldött." Munkásság és munkástudat a mai Magyarországon, *Replika*, 83/2 (2013), 61–76.
Bartha, Eszter, Forgotten histories: Workers and the new capitalism in East Germany and Hungary, in John W. Boyer and Berthold Molden (eds.), *EUtROPEs: The paradox of European empire* (Chicago, 2014), 309–34.
Bartók Plus Operafestival, http://operafesztival.hu/index.php/en// (accessed 10 Febr. 2017).
Benkő, Imre, *Acélváros: Steel town, 1987–1995: Fotóesszé: Photo essay* (Budapest, 1996).
Bereczki, Zoltán, *A diósgyőri gyár és kolóniája: a gyár modellje*, www.vasgyar.hu/nyitooldal/3d/gyar/ (accessed 28 Jan. 2017).
Bereczki, Zoltán, *A diósgyőri gyár és kolóniája: a kolónia modellje*, www.vasgyar.hu/nyitooldal/3d/kolonia/ (accessed 28 Jan. 2017).
Berend, Tibor Iván, Rapid industrialization with obsolete technology, in Tibor Iván Berend and Tamás Csató, *One-and-a-half centuries of semi-successful modernization, 1848–1989*, Vol. 1., East European Monographs (Boulder, 2001), 323–44.
Borsod 2050: Kézen fogni a fiatalokat, www.boon.hu/borsod-2050-kezen-fogni-a-fiatalokat/2222579/ (accessed 28 Jan. 2017).
BorsodChem, History: We've come a long way, www.borsodchem-group.com/About-us/History.aspx/ (accessed 17 Jan. 2017).
Burawoy, Michael, Ideology as reality: The Lenin Steel Works, in Michael Burawoy and János Lukács, *The radiant past: Ideology and reality in Hungary's road to capitalism* (Chicago and London, 1992), 81–142.
Csató, Tamás, Industrial development, in Tibor Iván Berend and Tamás Csató, *One-and-a-half centuries of semi-successful modernization, 1848–1989*, Vol. 1., East European Monographs (Boulder, 2001), 195–211.
Csontos, Györgyi and Tibor Vass, *Ózdi munkáskolóniák: gyári lakótelepek és lakásbelsők története a századfordulótól az ezredfordulóig* (Pomáz, 2001).
Csontos, Györgyi, *Nyílt levél az ózdi acélműi csarnokért*, http://epiteszforum.hu/nyilt-level-az-ozdi-acelmui-csarnokert/ (accessed 10 Febr. 2017).
Digitális archívum és filmsúdió lett az ózdi gyárból, www.boon.hu/digitalis-archivum-es-filmstudio-lett-az-ozdi-gyarbol/3099651/ (accessed 10 Jan. 2017).
A diósgyőri m. kir. vas- és aczélgyár története, 1765–1910 (Miskolc, 1910).
Elhagyatva Miskolcon: a perecesi bányaépületek, http://miskolcadhatott.blog.hu/2015/03/05/elhagyatva_miskolcon_a_perecesi_banyaepuletek/ (accessed 10 Febr. 2017).
Előd, Fruzsina, *Minden régiónk csúszik lefelé a lejtőn*, http://index.hu/gazdasag/2017/03/01/versenykepesseg_2016_eu_magyarorszag// (accessed 17 Jan. 2017).

Ennyi munkanélküli van Borsodban, www.profession.hu/cikk/20131004/ennyi-munkanelkuli-van-borsodban/3461/ (accessed 17 Jan. 2017).

Észak-Keleti Átjáró Egyesület, http://atjarokhe.hu/english/ (accessed 10 Febr. 2017).

European Commission, *European regional competitiveness index, Hungary: Észak-Magyarország*, http://ec.europa.eu/regional_policy/en/information/maps/regional_competitiveness#2/ (accessed 17 Jan. 2017).

Fazekas, Sámuel (ed.), *Miskolci kirakat* (Miskolc, 1936).

Germuska, Pál, Tradíció nélkül. A magyarországi városok önképe, 1949–1989, in Zsombor Bódy, Monika Mátay and Árpád Tóth (eds.), *A mesterség iskolája: tanulmányok Bácskai Vera 70. születésnapjára* (Budapest, 2000), 479–99.

Germuska, Pál, Between Theory and Practice: Planning Socialist Cities in Hungary, in Mikael Hård and Thomas J. Misa (eds.), *Urban machinery: Inside European cities* (Cambridge, MA and London, England, 2008), 233–55.

Heckenast, Gusztáv, *A magyarországi vaskohászat története a feudalizmus korában: A XIII. század közepétől a XVIII. század végéig* (Budapest, 1991).

Horváth, Béla, A miskolci városkép változása, *Herman Ottó Múzeum Évkönyve*, 11 (1972), 189–218.

Ipartörténeti értékmentés, www.boon.hu/ipartorteneti-ertekmentes/1874092/ (accessed 10 Febr. 2017).

ITS2014 Konzorcium, *Ózd város integrált településfejlesztési stratégiája*, http://ozd.hu/content/cont_575e73f4e57191.23649128/ozd_integralt_telepulesfejlesztesi_strategia.pdf/ (accessed 10 Febr. 2017).

Jameson CineFest, www.cinefest.hu/eng/nyito_eng.html/ (accessed 10 Febr. 2017).

Jegyzőkönyv felvétetett 1897. évi június 29-én Rozsnyón az "Országos Magyar Bányászati és Kohászati Egyesület" Borsod-Gömör osztályának alakulási gyűléséről, *Az Országos Magyar Bányászati és Kohászati Egyesület Közlései. A "Bányászati és Kohászati Lapok" melléklapja*, 9 (1897), 56–7.

Jenei, Károly, Az alapítás előzményei, in Tibor Iván Berend (ed.), *Az Ózdi Kohászati Üzemek története* (Budapest, 1980), 43–51.

Katus, László, Transport revolution and economic growth in Hungary, in John Komlos (ed.), *Economic development in the Habsburg Monarchy in the nineteenth century: Essays*, East European Monographs (Boulder, 1983), 183–204.

Katus, László, *Hungary in the dual monarchy, 1867–1914*, East European Monographs (Boulder, 2008).

Kiss, László and Gyula Kiszely, *Magyarország műszaki múzeumai* (Budapest, 1982).

Kiss, László, Gyula Kiszely and Pál Vajda, *Magyarország ipari műemlékei. Industrial monuments in Hungary* (Budapest, 1982).

Kiszely, Gyula, Diósgyőr vaskohászatának történetéből, *Kohászati Lapok*, 8 Aug. 1954, p. 338.

Kohászati Múzeum, http://kohmuz.t-online.hu/kohaszati_muzeum.htm/ (accessed 10 Febr. 2017).

Kóródi, József, *A Borsodi Iparvidék* (Budapest, 1959).

Kóródi, József, A szocialista ipar és közlekedés fejlődése, in Gáborné Varga (ed.), *Borsod-Abaúj-Zemplén megye története és legújabb kori adattára* (Miskolc, 1970), 303–23.

Koroknai, Ákos, Az óriásvállalat kibontakozása, 1881–1900, in Tibor Iván Berend (ed.), *Az Ózdi Kohászati Üzemek története* (Budapest, 1980), 103–30.

Koroknai, Ákos, Alfréd Lehoczky and Zoltán Sárközi, A gyár társadalma, in Tibor Iván Berend (ed.), *Az Ózdi Kohászati Üzemek története* (Budapest, 1980), 150–85.

Központi Statisztikai Hivatal, *Magyarország közigazgatási helységnévtára 1947. évre* (Budapest, 1947).

Központi Statisztikai Hivatal, *A Magyar Népköztársaság Helységnévtára, 1985* (Budapest, 1985).

Központi Statisztikai Hivatal, *Magyarország közigazgatási helynévkönyve, 2012. január 1* (Budapest, 2012).

Központi Statisztikai Hivatal, *2011. évi népszámlálás. 3. Területi adatok. 3.5. Borsod-Abaúj-Zemplén megye* (Miskolc, 2013), www.ksh.hu/docs/hun/xftp/idoszaki/nepsz2011/nepsz_03_05_2011.pdf/ (accessed 17 Jan. 2017).

Kristóf, Ágnes and Piroska Váczi, *Ózd örökség alapú városrehabilitációjának előkészítése*, http://epiteszforum.hu/kristof-agnes-dr-vaczi-piroska-ozd-orokseg-alapu-varosrehabilitaciojanak-elokeszitese/ (accessed 10 Jan. 2017).

Lengyel Kiss, Katalin, The Foundry Museum established in the former Ganz Foundry has been serving the public for 35 years, in Györgyi Németh (ed.), *Growth, decline and recovery: Heavy industrial regions in transition* (Budapest and Miskolc, 2007), 351–6.

Mándy, András, Szociális és társadalmi viszonyok, in István Benke and Viktor Reményi (eds.), *A magyar bányászat évezredes története*, Vol. 2. (Budapest, 1996), 48–56.

Marjalaki Kiss, Lajos, Az Avas, in Antal Csíkvári (ed.), *Borsod vármegye: Borsod, Gömör és Kishont k. e. e. vármegyék*, Vármegyei Szociográfiák V. (Budapest, 1939), 12–4.

Márkus, Zsuzsanna, A Borsodi Bányász című hetilap, *Bányászattörténeti Közlemények*, 13 (2012), 60–4.

Mégsem lesz acélgyártás Diósgyőrben? www.eszakonline.hu/miskolc/56Cez-toertent/27637-kifarol-a-kormuűanyzat-a-diosgyri-acelmbl/ (accessed 17 Jan. 2017).

Mendly, Lajos, Emlékek a borsod-gömöri bányászat múltjából, *Bányászattörténeti Közlemények*, 4 (2007), 25–36.

Miskolc megyei jogú város integrált településfejlesztési stratégiája, www.miskolcvaros2020.hu/sites/default/files/dokumentumok/miskolc_its.pdf/ (accessed 10 Febr. 2017).

Miskolc Megyei Jogú Város Önkormányzat 39/2009. (XII. 2.) rendelete az épített környezet értékeinek helyi védelméről (egységes szerkezetben a módosításáról szóló 2/2013. (II.19) és 4/2017. (II.21.) önkormányzati rendelettel), www.miskolc.hu/sites/default/files/dokumentumok/csatolmanyok/39_2009_e.pdf/ (accessed 11 Mar. 2017).

Miskolci acélmű: csak pr-kampány volt, http://eszon.hu/miskolc/56-ez-toertent/27662-miskolci-acelm-csak-pr-kampany-volt/ (accessed 17 Jan. 2017).

Mizsei, Anett, *Kiszínezett barna zóna: az ózdi projekt*, http://epiteszforum.hu/kiszinezett-barna-zona-az-ozdi-projekt/ (accessed 9 Febr. 2017).

Móricz, Zsigmond, Mai napok: Miskolc, *Nyugat*, 22 (1930), http://epa.oszk.hu/00000/00022/nyugat.htm/ (accessed 17 May 2017).

Murányi, István, A munkások lokális identitásának jellemzői Borsodnádasdon, *Korall*, 49 (2012), 106–27.

Műszakváltás 2, http://atjarokhe.hu/2010/06/muszakvaltas-2// (accessed 28 Jan. 2017).

Nagy, Péter, *A Rima vonzásában: az ózdi helyi és gyári társadalom a késő dualizmustól az államosításig* (Budapest, 2016).

Németh, Györgyi, The Miskolc-Diósgyőr Ironworks: How to go on? *Patrimoine de l'industrie. Industrial Patrimony*, 1/1 (1999), 41–5.

Németh, Györgyi, A Borsodi Iparvidék ipari öröksége, *Műemlékvédelem*, 43/4 (1999), 192–8.

Németh, Györgyi, A diósgyőri vasgyár műemléki védelme, *Műemlékvédelem*, 45/2 (2001), 84–7.

Németh, Györgyi, *Útikalauz a bányászat és kohászat emlékeihez Észak-Magyarországon és Szlovákiában. Guide to the monuments of mining and metallurgy in North-Hungary and Slovakia* (Miskolc, 2001).

Németh, Györgyi (ed.), *Growth, decline and recovery: Heavy industrial regions in transition* (Budapest and Miskolc, 2007).
Az Ózdi Muzeális Gyűjtemény bemutatása, www.ozdimuzeum.hu/content.php?cid=cont_5 50c2882d7f724.22361398/ (accessed 10 Febr. 2017).
A nemzeti kulturális örökség miniszterének 25/2005. (IX. 16.) NKÖM rendelete egyes ingatlanok műemlékké, valamint műemléki jelentőségű területté nyilvánításáról, illetőleg műemléki védettségének megszüntetéséről. *Magyar Közlöny*, 124 (16 Sept. 2005), 6645–6, www.kozlonyok.hu/nkonline/MKPDF/2005/MK124.pdf/ (accessed 10 Febr. 2017).
A Népköztársaság Elnöki Tanácsának 4/1954. (II. 24.) törvényerejű rendelete a műszaki emlékek védelméről. *Magyar Közlöny*, 12 (24 Febr. 1954), 72–3.
Pálos, Máté, Digitális élménypark Ózdon: vakító vásznak, *Magyar Narancs*, 29/7 (2017), 30–2.
Pantó, Endre, A 75 éves nagyüzemű vasércbányászat, 1880–1955, in Endre Pantó, Gábor Pantó, Tibor Podányi and Károly Moser (eds.), *Rudabánya ércbányászata* (Budapest, 1957), 102–221.
Péchy-Horváth, Rezső, Borsod, a magyar Ruhr, in Antal Csíkvári (ed.), *Borsod vármegye: Borsod, Gömör és Kishont k. e. e. vármegyék*, Vármegyei Szociográfiák V (Budapest, 1939), 52–6.
Péchy-Horváth, Rezső, Színművészet Miskolcon, in Antal Csíkvári (ed.), *Borsod vármegye: Borsod, Gömör és Kishont k. e. e. vármegyék*, Vármegyei Szociográfiák V (Budapest, 1939), 34–5.
Pittaway, Mark, Introduction: Workers and socialist states in postwar central and Eastern Europe, *International Labor and Working-Class History*, 68/Fall (2005), 1–8.
Pittaway, Mark, The revolution and industrial workers: The disintegration and reconstruction of socialism, 1953–1958, *Hungarian Studies Review*, 34/1–2 (2007), 115–54.
R. Nagy, József, "The factory has no meaning for us any more. . . " Similarities and differences in the identity coming from the industrial environment in the case of workers from Rudabánya and Diósgyőr, in Györgyi Németh (ed.), *Growth, decline and recovery: Heavy industrial regions in transition* (Budapest and Miskolc, 2007), 261–9.
Réti R., László, Fegyverkezési konjunktúra (1933–1938), in Tibor Iván Berend (ed.), *Az Ózdi Kohászati Üzemek története* (Budapest, 1980), 242–53.
Romsics, Ignác, *From dictatorship to democracy: The birth of the third Hungarian republic, 1988–2001*, East European Monographs (Boulder, 2007).
Rudabánya város honlapja. Bányászattörténeti Múzeum, www.rudabanya.hu/hu/muzeum. html/ (accessed 10 Febr. 2017).
Rudolf, Mihály, *Ózdi műemlék – Olvasó Egyleti Székház – felújítása*, http://epiteszforum. hu/ozdi-muemlek-olvaso-egyleti-szekhaz-felujitasa/ (accessed 9 Febr. 2017).
Schleicher, Aladár, Az 1813. évben épült és 1952-ben újjáépített újmassai nagyolvasztó, *A Magyar Tudományos Akadémia Műszaki Tudományok Osztályának Közleményei*, 12/1–4 (1954), 403–11.
Schmotzer, Imre, Árpád Majtényi and Endre Vadász, Volt egyszer egy . . . . . . Borsodi Szénbányák [At one time . . . . . there were Borsod Coal Mines], *Bányászati és Kohászati Lapok: Bányászat*, 138/3 (2005), 16–22.
Szakolczai, Attila, Tömegmozgalmak Miskolcon, 1956. október 25–26, in Zsuzsanna Kőrösi, Éva Standeisky and János Rainer M. (eds.), *Évkönyv VIII* (Budapest, 2000), 303–22.
Szakolczai, Attila, Borsod – Abaúj – Zemplén megye, in Attila Szakolczai and László Á. Varga (eds.), *A vidék forradalma, 1956*, Vol. 1 (Budapest, 2003), 148–68.
Sziklavári, János, László Kiss, János Jung and István Sélei, *A diósgyőri acélgyártás története a folytacélgyártás bevezetésétől napjainkig* (Miskolc, 2004).

Tündérkert Perecesen, http://atjarokhe.hu/olvasnivalok/tunderkert-perecesen-2// (accessed 28 Jan. 2017).

TVK 60: The history of Tiszai Vegyi Kombinát (Tisza Chemical Works) from 1953 to 2013, https://mol.hu/images/pdf/About_MOL/petrochemical_business/about_tvk/history/TVK%2060_History.pdf/ (accessed 17 Jan. 2017).

Valuch, Tibor, Changes in the structure and lifestyle of the Hungarian society in the second half of the 20th century, in Gábor Gyáni, György Kövér and Tibor Valuch (eds.), *Social history of Hungary from the reform era to the end of the twentieth century*, East European Monographs (Boulder, 2004), 511–671.

Viktor, Gyula, *Murvay László élete és munkássága: 1918–1984, Érc- és Ásványbányászati Múzeumi Füzetek 15* (Rudabánya, 1985).

Zsámboki, László, *Die Schemnitzer Gedenkbibliothek von Miskolc in Ungarn* (Miskolc, 1978).

6 Identity and mining heritage in Romania's Jiu Valley coal region
Commodification, alienation, renaissance

David A. Kideckel

The decline of coal heritage: commodification, dark heritage and fragmented identity

Coal mining and working-class culture are threatened in Romania's Jiu Valley. Since the mid-19th century the Valley had been a premier coal-producing region and its miners and coal industry (*minerit*) storied in Romanian socialism's rise and fall. Jiu Valley identity developed alongside mining, and most people in the region have family members directly implicated in mining. However, with socialism's end, economic restructuring and Romanian EU integration, much of the *minerit's* physical plant has been eliminated or slated for demolition. This coincides with decreased concern for preserving mining heritage. Town halls or state agencies fail to conserve or inventory technology, architecture and artistic representations. Statues, mosaics, paraphernalia fade into the background. Some older buildings are preserved, but removed from general use. Other sites, some from the 19th century, degrade from inattention.[1]

Heritage is context, cause and casualty of Valley transformation. Broken buildings, abandoned sites and rusting metal illustrate heritage as casualty. But understanding the decline of heritage as context and partial cause of regional transformation must be contextualized by consideration of regional identity. Three aspects of the heritage-identity relationship are pertinent. Thus, heritage decline is hastened by distrust between regional business and political leaders, on one hand, and working people, on the other, spurred by differential conceptions of resource and value growing from the commodification and treatment of mine heritage in postsocialism. Second, heritage decline is enabled by peoples' failure to lay bare and overcome the Valley's dark heritage,[2] especially related to the 1990s *mineriade*, miner violent invasions of Bucharest in service to heirs of Communist control. Third, the fractures of commodification and dark heritage ramify due to weak regional identity and atomization of small group identities, growing from emigration, expanded service industries and widespread Internet use.

To explore the significance of commodification, dark heritage and identity fragmentation I first examine heritage theoretically, in diverse ethnographic contexts. Subsequently, I trace the actual trajectory of *minerit* development, expansion and decline, beginning with the 1840s industrialization of Valley coal production.

Rapid growth of the region's coal industry and ancillary services made the Valley one of the more densely populated urban zones in Romania.[3] However, over time, identities were transformed from those roughly unified around labor to today's fragmented conditions. This process flowered after a Valley-wide miner's strike in 1977, and then literally exploded with 1990s' *mineriade* and ensuing mass unemployment.

Subsequently, I analyze structural factors and processes behind the decline of regional industrial and mining heritage. The *minerit's* end has largely resulted from post-Socialist economic change, intense commodification and marketization of Valley industry, coal trade globalization and the 2010 European Commission's decision to close inefficient mines. These changes encourage destruction or inattention to most heritage elements and diversion of others away from general access. Weak efforts on behalf of heritage are worsened by the general passivity of the Romanian state in classifying and protecting heritage resources.

If commodification and fragmented lives threaten heritage, actions to use heritage as focal points for group identities might reverse the course of decline. Thus, I close with a discussion of some challenges to heritage decline and identity fragmentation, including on-going, though equivocal, work to preserve the Petrila mine. I consider the activities of some people and groups whose work, both in local communities and at the level of the state, returns heritage to the community. They thus transform heritage use while reversing working people's alienation. Whether these activities will grow beyond restricted beginnings or enable greater degrees of fit between Valley identity and Valley mining heritage remains an open question.

Perspectives on heritage, identity and politics

I understand heritage as processual. That is, heritage is more shaped by and influencing social and political processes, practices, performance and identity relationships than as characterized as objects or places.[4] Social and political groups engage heritage over control of value, meaning and identity, and through them resources, history and power.[5] Struggles over heritage are often key to define the past of contested communities and control of places on which those heritage resources sit.[6] Political contests throughout society are waged over the power to define the meaning, representations and practices of the past, to name and categorize heritage elements, to control access to heritage places, and valorize that control. Heritage is invented to further that control[7] and mobilized in performance after political objectives.[8] As Franquesa notes "the prerogative of ultimately sanctioning what is heritage is held by the state . . . guarded by experts holding a hegemonic objectifying discourse . . . influenced by views of dominant groups."[9]

Contests over heritage are intensive as these resources are laden with meaning, useful for power, typically commodified or marketed,[10] and of potential value as capital and symbolic capital. Thus in the Argentinian Chaco, Gaston Gordillo shows how use and control of rubble is the focus of both state seeking to consolidate control through myth, and community challenging that control through ritual practice.[11] In the Bangkok Pom Mahakan neighborhood, planners, speculators and bureaucrats policies "oppose interests of locals and . . . (seek to) subjugate residents' lives to impersonal imperatives masquerading as 'improvement' and 'development'."[12] In Mexico private sector intervention used national cultural heritage laws to transform sites such as remarkable Mayan Chichen Itza, into monumental and profitable heritage.[13]

For the Jiu Valley, degradation of the mines and mining heritage is shaped first by crude commodification. This developed coincidental to the fall of socialism in 1989, and gathered speed and breadth since the beginning of the new century. As restructuring and privatization replaced Socialist institutions, much of the region's industrial plant, and heritage along with that, was physically destroyed. Destruction was both from above and below. Those whom I call 'magnates,' powerful business-political leaders, some from outside Romania, bought, demolished and sold as scrap whole Socialist industrial complexes. They paid little attention to community needs, or the historical and cultural values represented by industrial sites. Meanwhile heritage was undermined from below by those termed locally as 'magnets' who, operating in organized networks or individually, scavenge the random metal remaining in the wake of industrial destruction.[14] By virtue of such mass destruction, Jiu Valley conditions destroy the content of heritage and block its use by the region's many groups. This contrasts with the Argentinian, Thai and Mexican examples above, where heritage is a touchstone in struggles for identity, human rights and even access to life's essentials.

But heritage has few defenders in the Jiu Valley. The region's leaders are compelled by position and interest to valorize *minerit* institutions, whether closed or open mines or other heritage elements, by articulating them with markets and international institutions. Meanwhile miners, pensioners, and their family members are alienated from the industry and their history by the intense decline of the *minerit.* They become angry, overly nostalgic, and narrowly focused on dwindling occupations and barely cognizant of their heritage in decline. "Ruins," as Gordillo suggests, are places where "space, history, decay, and memory coalesce."[15] The actual and planned obliteration of mining spaces is thus an active attempt to obliterate memory in service to market, a process thus far abetted by regional identity conceptions and practices.

Like heritage, identity is not a condition, but a process. Events, historical pressures, and individual and group responses to one another form the context of malleable identities. Identity is expressed by different group norms, models of reality, and understandings of self and other.[16] In this, people's affinities and interests, and the nature and intensity of their expression wax and wane in response to changing circumstances. Identity is scalable and fractal.[17] Larger groups, their commitments and symbols, potentially branch to ever-smaller micro-identities. Whether or not larger group identities are able to motivate common action depends on their strength in satisfying or threatening individual and small group interest.

In the Jiu Valley, then, regional labor and mining identity is expressed variously; in media presentations of regional development or of the position of the region in Romanian history (such as discussions of the *mineriade* – the miner invasions of

Bucharest in the 1990s), in the existence of institutions based on regional identity such as the Jiu Valley Mining Museum, in general conversation and daily life. Most people within the region have a general sense of the Valley as a geographic and historic entity organized around the mining industry and the region remains an active force in many lives; the miner whose job depends on the regional-based Complexul Energetic Hunedoara (CEH), entrepreneurs with properties across the Valley; sportsmen who visit regional peaks, parks and trails; women with children, students, seniors, coming and going in the dozens of maxi-taxis plying the region. However, given the region's and industry's recent history, most individuals express a waning positive identity with industry and coal mining and thus fail to be motivated toward actions related to industrial heritage. In particular, after 1989, the region as coal zone became a place structured to produce social convulsion,[18] with strikes, mine closings, mass unemployment and other struggles percolating into regional identities, producing negative associations no matter the group from which one derives. The role of the Jiu Valley miners and their union in the violence of the *mineriade* especially is a constant echo in regional memories.[19] This dark history and its failure to be accounted for publicly in the region[20] contribute to polarization of attitudes toward mining, by extension mine heritage, and to the continued hyperbolic perception of the region in Romanian civil society discourse. Common regional discourses vary from discussion of unemployment to how the Jiu Valley political system was destroyed by SOVROM domination, or how the Valley fails to develop its tourist potentials (viewed exclusively as rural and mountain oriented). Even positive views of the region that emphasize the extraordinary natural beauty of the mountains that ring the Valley or the availability of a well-trained work force (the result of the efforts of the mining industry), are often coupled with negative qualifiers, such as complaint of the region's treatment by the Romanian state and international institutions, and the failure of investment.[21]

Alongside elites' market-oriented views, contradictory attitudes about mining and mine heritage are ubiquitous. Pensioners, current and former miners, and their families vociferously support the industry, which they see as the 'soul' of the Valley.[22] They claim that Valley mines have coal deposits to last one hundred years. They express anger about the current state of the *minerit*, are nostalgic about the secure employment of the Socialist past, but have only passing recognition or concern about preservation of that past and its meaning and significance for other than mineral extraction. To them, mine remains are less sites of history than testimony to decades of lies and decisions of outsiders. Others in the region see the *minerit* as anachronistic, wasteful, polluting and used throughout Valley history for political control. Some, like a former mine electrician and now a university professor, suggest they "look forward with joy to the day where grass grows where the mines stood" (Alin Rus, Personal Communication). Middle-class service employees and independent business people say that the region needs to go beyond mining as its comparative economic advantage lies in agriculture and tourism. To them the miners' unions are corrupt, the coal company mismanaged, and the region better off to move to a more ecologically friendly future. Thus no group rallies round mining heritage. Formation, growth, and decline of the *minerit* and Jiu Valley industrial heritage, and their relation to regional identity and politics are considered next.

Development of Jiu Valley coal mining, mining heritage and regional identity

Coal's dominance in the Jiu Valley dates to the mid-1840s, when Habsburg[23] entrepreneurs opened the first mines as private mine ownership was legalized.[24] Industrial coal production, railway expansion, and demographic and cultural change went hand-in-hand in the *minerit's* formative decades.[25] Investment societies controlling mine concessions dug the first shafts (*puțuri*), and constructed halls, galleries and processing areas. Between 1892 and 1900 production grew 12 times, and number of workers from 250 to 1500.[26]

Most regional coal deposits were plotted and opened by the early 20th century, but regional identity remained incipient. People's worlds were defined more by place of origin than labor. The new industry attracted a multicultural population from across the Empire: Romanians, Hungarians, Czechs, Poles, Slovaks, Szeklers, Ruthenians, Italians, Germans, of diverse religious identity, including Roman and Uniate Catholics, Orthodox Christians and Jews.[27] The mine companies built workers' housing complexes (*colonie*) on the rail lines to supply their labor force, while foremen and managers had housing on the fairer side of the tracks. Workforce diversity and outlawing of labor syndicalism restricted labor unity but home life was rich and the *colonie* zones of intense sociality and commerce.[28] As mining expanded, the Valley population more than doubled from 1870 (12,671) to 1900 (28,711).[29] Schools, libraries, cinemas, and newspapers enriched cultural life and helped craft an identity of an urbane and cosmopolitan region. Ethnic associations sponsored bands, theatre groups and religious institutions. The region's industrial identity was attested to by Petroșani's hosting the Congress of the Hungarian Mining and Metallurgical Industry, a major international industrial exposition, in 1903.[30]

The flowering of a regional mining identity came on the heels of World War I. Then, annexation of Transylvania (of which the Valley is part) to Greater Romania, and a fluctuating population, fueled by industrial bust and boom and strong labor syndicalism spurred industrial identities. The period leading to the Great Depression was marked by labor unrest, like the General Strike of 1920[31] or the strike of August 1929, when 22 miners died.[32] Statuary in Lupeni town and the ceremonial cross in the mine courtyard attest to the 1929 violence, as does a monument in the Vulcan cemetery. The dynamism and development of a mining identity is reflected in the many period *minerit* buildings remaining in the region. These include the Cazinoul Muncitoresc (Workers' Club) in Petroșani's Lower Colony that is today an upscale restaurant,[33] the Cazinoul Funcționarilor (the Mine Functionaries' Club), today the main building of Petroșani's I.D. Sârbu Theatre,[34] the Cazinoul Muncitoresc in Vulcan,[35] now the privately-leased IMAX Club entertainment complex, and the Miners' Cultural Palace in Lupeni, built in 1924 (currently being refurbished by Lupeni town authorities).

With socialism, the party-state consolidated control and expanded production in the *minerit*, brought the miners to heel, and generated major cultural and identity transformation. Three phases characterize the *minerit* over Socialist years: external (SOVROM) control (1945–56), intense expansion and growth (1956–77), and flux and agitation following the strike of 1977. Each period left their mark on the industry, on the built environment, on conceptualization of labor and on regional identity. Under the SOVROMs, Soviet-Romanian institutions charged to expand coal production for development and for Romanian reparations to the USSR, new housing complexes were built for workers and for SOVROM personnel, like the 'Dimitrov' neighborhood in Petroşani (named after the Bulgarian Socialist leader), with distinctive Soviet-style tiled roofs and high-ceilinged apartments.[36] Iconography also changed, with Communist attempts to craft a left working-class identity. Notable is the large brick Hammer and Sickle, dated 1948, with Romanian Workers' Party (PMR) initials, visible on a retaining wall in the Jiu defile, linking Transylvania and Oltenia, and now site of a new hydroelectric plant in the making.

After Stalin's death Romania gained hegemony over coal production and the Jiu Valley workforce. In 1956 the consolidated mining company, Combinatul Carbonifer Valea Jiului (The Jiu Valley Carbon Combine) took over the mines. Institutions like URUMP, producing tools and fittings for the mining industry, the SALVAMIN mine safety organization, or INSEMEX, devoted to explosives research, were further developed. New neighborhoods to house the working population were built, including the 'New Center' complex in Petroşani and 'Dallas' in Vulcan, whose lack of amenities caused it to be jokingly named after the American TV series flaunting luxury and power. The so-called "cult of labor" (*cultul muncii*),[37] and labor's depiction via Socialist realist sculptures, monuments, and mosaics contributed to differentiating miners from others and embellished a sub-culture that celebrated male labor and relegated women to domestic spheres.[38] Statuary from the period includes that of the miner hewn roughly from stone in Petroşani's Municipal Park, or the paired miners in Uricani. Sport was critical, so each mine sponsored soccer teams and others, like Aninoasă's champion archery teams.[39]

Change ensued after August 1977 when 35,000 miners struck the mines,[40] protesting state demands for increased production, increased retirement age and elimination of pension subsidies for the injured.[41] The strike ended only after Ceauşescu was forced to the Valley and offered concessions. Soon after, to dilute miner power, the regime flooded the region with new workers from poor areas like Moldavia or army and prison populations. To keep labor peace, the state further subsidized coal production with relatively high miners' salaries and benefits. The industry was highly inefficient, costing 16 dollars for each dollar of production.[42] Until the regime fell, the *minerit*'s decline was camouflaged by new construction initiatives, like the Câmpul lui Neag surface mine, begun in 1979, and the Valea de Braz mine in 1986. After the strike, fissures developed in miner identity, distinguishing newcomers and earlier residents. The rural arrivistes, with large families and rough ways, were judged of low culture, evidenced by conditions in new neighborhoods like 'the Rose' in Lupeni or the 'Airport' in Petroşani. By

1989, the Jiu Valley miners had become compromised by the regime, internally stratified, and unified only tentatively around privileges and union, but perched on the edge of an abyss.

The 1990s brought major change. Fearing loss of status and privilege, and led on by Miron Cozma, their demagogic union president, the miners 'invaded' Bucharest three times in 1990 and 1991 on behalf of Ceaușescu's successor, Ioan Iliescu. But the violence against persons and property defamed them and hastened *minerit* reform.[43,44] There was slight growth in population through most of the decade, rising from roughly 169,000 in 1990 to 171,000 in 1997.[45] But structural reform and mass layoffs (*disponibilizare*), begun in 1997[46] and post-EU accession increased labor migration to Western Europe, and contributed to a steady exodus of people. By 2011 only 140,000 residents remained, and authorities prefigured a decline to 100,000,[47] the approximate population today (2016).

Population decline and *minerit* decline go hand-in-hand. By 1999 three mines had closed (Câmpul lui Neag, Valea de Braz, Dâljă), and another (Aninoasă) put on notice. Dressing halls and food services were privatized, and other functions outsourced to new "tick (i.e. parasitical) firms" further fracturing common interests, if not identities.[48] Industries like Viscoze textiles in Lupeni, most of the GEROM tool complex in Petroșani, or the Uricani coal preparation facility were privatized and scrapped. All the changes split miner ranks. *Mineriade* repercussions brought on distrust, while differential employment status created hierarchies, limited miner agency and shaped interpretation of the past.[49]

Disaggregating *minerit*, heritage, politics and identity

Structural forces have now aligned to force the imminent end of coal mining in the Jiu Valley. Romania's post-Socialist integration into global networks, changing concern for global climate and energetic efficiency, and especially Romania's EU 2007 integration has presaged the *minerit's* undoing. Jiu Valley coal production is highly disadvantaged in Romania's newly privatized power distribution network due to its folded and gaseous coal seams, outmoded technologies and high costs of production. Thus, the *minerit* has suffered constant annual losses and need for extensive state subsidization made worse by corruption and mismanagement.[50] International markets offer coal at better quality and price. Romania's EU accession was the *coup de grâce* for Valley coal production. Chapter Fourteen of the *acquis comunitaire* specifies integrating Europe's energy market, eliminating production inefficiencies, limiting fossil fuel use and expanding renewable energy.[51] An EC decision[52] required the phased closing of all Valley mines. Contradicting EU cultural heritage policy,[53] the scope, pace and likely results of this legislation threaten to not only end mining, but to obscure forever the industry's 175-year history, regional working-class culture and related heritage. The 'ecologized' land remaining after razing the mines will be deeded to the towns for other ends and owners. Those 'on the in' are likely to profit. But the potential loss for knowledge of the region's past, of symbols for regional identity, if not heritage-related commerce, is astounding.

Three of seven remaining mines (Paroşeni, Petrila and Uricani) are to be immediately put on a path to being closed, razed and 'ecologized' by 2018. But this blundering process has contributed to a rise of activism and new identity relationships. The closure process is run by the National Society for the Closing of Jiu Valley Mines (*Societatea Naţională de Închideri Mine din Valea Jiului*, or SNIMVJ), born from the EC decision. Petrila, the Valley's oldest mine,[54] is the first to close. SNIMVJ planned this for October 2015, but their work was stayed. A petition to the county branch of the Ministry of Culture to protect seven mine structures as heritage sites was ultimately granted by the Ministry. The Plus-Minus Association, an NGO of artists, architects, and students from Petrila, Bucharest, and elsewhere, motivated by aesthetic, historical, or identity interests, spent a year preparing the petition. This included an end-run around the Petrila mayor, who refused to sign necessary documents. The activists faced general regional disinterest in industrial heritage as well as resistance from the SNIMVJ, which claimed assistance would continue only if it fulfilled EC criteria.[55] Echoing a neoliberal mantra of limiting state institutions to unleash growth, an SNIMVJ official stated "once all of Petrila is razed, the land can be used for anything, for gardens, workshops, business incubators, housing" (Aurel Anghel, personal communication). Challenging this, local activists said SNIMVJ was a tool of outsiders and deaf to local concerns.[56] Thus, the issue of Petrila's preservation produced a heritage-focused coalition and sharpened attitudes toward closure. Still, such concerns do not yet motivate others.

Heritage at the closing mines is clearly threatened, but heritage at operational mines is also at risk. The Complexul Energetic Hunedoara (CEH), heir of the National Thermal Coal Company (CNH),[57] integrates the Paroşeni and Mintea[58] thermoelectric complexes, and functioning Lonea, Livezeni, Lupeni and Vulcan mines. Those mines are to close by 2020, but union protests compelled an agreement delaying that until 2024.[59] Absorbed with staving off the inevitable, three mine directors I spoke with planned no inventories, analyses, or conservation of objects. Excluding on-site technologies and buildings, each mine contains important documents, and other heritage elements. Some have religious significance, like crosses commemorating accidents or icons of Saint Barbara, the miners' patron saint. Trophy cases with commemorative lamps, plates, plaques and pins go largely unremarked by management or labor. The last CEH directors salvaged some prize objects from obliterated mines, like marble bas-reliefs from Dâljă, now displayed in the CEH lobby, but much of value was lost.

Romanian state and institutional culture contribute to the problematic of mining heritage. Until recently, heritage designation was mainly granted sites pertaining to faith, the Romanian nation, and historic and prehistoric pasts. Industrial and mining heritage registered at the Hunedoara county branch of the Ministry of Culture only listed the Petroşani Mining Museum and diverse architectural examples, but nothing production or labor-related. The stay of demolition granted Petrila is a happy exception. State processes to delimit and protect heritage are complicated and weak.[60] Mayors can influence the process, but claim few resources, and often have questionable commitment or unrealistic approaches. Petroşani's mayor discussed an initiative to develop the local Mining Museum into a regional attraction. However, the Museum is staffed by an aging lady serving as director, custodian, cashier, secretary and docent. She claimed a team from the county Ministry of Culture reviewed the space months ago, but nothing came of this. The last Aninoasă mayor wanted to build an underground mining museum and attracted preliminary funding from the World Bank, but the project ended due to high costs, complexity and safety.

As some mining heritage is lost, other properties are diverted from general use and separated from industrial history by commodification under guise of development. Entrepreneurs, politicians and technocrats spearhead these projects. They gain control of some classic buildings from the early *minerit*, and convert them for other uses. The former Petroșani workers' club (Cazinoul Muncitoresc) is now a luxurious restaurant-banquet hall. As the building is registered with the county Ministry of Culture, permission is required for refurbishment. But this was not a problem since a former member of the Petroșani town council holds the restaurant lease. Similarly, a former Vulcan mine director has a 20-year lease on the old Mine Worker's club from the local miner's union. With loans, he turned the deteriorating building into a facility for young adults with clubroom, dance floor, paintball court, and regular and VIP bars. This is a fine facility, and such distraction is needed. However, the reconstructed site offers little connection to mining heritage or identity. Other industrial sites are repurposed for niche production in lumber and scrap metal, as warehouses, or other commercial activity, like Aninoasă's machine shop where second-hand clothes from Germany are sorted. Some people have important collections of heritage objects, like the 7,000 plus items displayed by a local restauranteur, or old *minerit* photographs held by a mine dispatcher. But these are largely inaccessible, non-systematized, and are not used or presented in ways that articulate them with regional identity.

Heritage 'decline' adversely affects labor's political response by limiting symbolic repertoires, obscuring common history, restricting local initiative, and narrowing affect across groups. For example, at union protests in September 2015, speeches proclaimed support for CEH and for continued use of coal due to insecurity of renewable energy resources. However, the crowd was silent about SNIMVJ destruction of their sister mines, and few symbols and heritage references were visible. Even ritualized singing of the miner's hymn, usually loud and boastful at every meeting, strike, or celebration related to mining, was barely audible. The power of the miners' complaint was reduced by its thin connection to heritage, to families and communities, to region and history. Marchers of miners and the unemployed in the late 1990s and early 2000s contrasted greatly. These bristled with heritage elements including icons, tools, uniforms, helmets, banners, music and song, as well as effigies and funerary images. But today the region's workers and union representatives seem too consumed with threats to employment to devote much attention to heritage. A regional journalist opined, "People protest because of losing workplaces. They aren't conscious about their patrimony's value" (Marian Boboc, Personal Communication).

Heritage in the future

As mining declines, the Valley's industrial heritage future will likely be defined by decreased integrity of sites, declining community visibility, and weakening of its identity and political qualities. Still some have begun to challenge these trends by campaigns to protect regional heritage, to inform others of heritage's importance, and develop heritage programs to serve community purposes. These efforts will be successful if they can replace commodified heritage with institutions valorized by community creation and use. For example, journalist, artist and activist, Ion Barbu, crosses media boundaries in projects based on regional traditions. Barbu's projects bring together diverse people to boost regional spirit through transformation of heritage into living practices. He was the leading force behind Start-Up Petrila[61] that began life refurbishing the home of Petrila writer, I. D. Sârbu, transformed the old mine pump house (Stația de Pompe) into a community center, and then linked with the Plus-Minus Foundation that organized the Petrila petition. Each project sought to incorporate ideas and efforts of students, miners, housewives. For example the pump house was renamed *Stația de Pompe-Dieu* ("God's Pumping Station," a play on the name of the famed Paris museum), and turned into a community center with theatre, salons, games, film and music presentations. Journalists Marian Boboc and Gheorghe Oltean of the Jiu Valley Daily News (*Ziarul Văii Jiului*) chronicle and critique heritage's history and decline. Boboc's monographs concern architectural achievements of the *minerit's* past while explicitly calling out the commodification heritage by lauding that past. In a series of articles, Olteanu exposed destruction of the regional industrial past by scrap iron thieves, the so-called 'magnets.'[62]

Beyond this nucleus, few work to develop regional heritage. People are put off by distrust in relationships beyond immediate circles, and heritage is not articulated with everyday concerns like housing, work place, or community. Institutions that integrate local life, like the University of Petroșani or the Chamber of Commerce, could facilitate heritage conservation but take a pass. Pensioners, too, could be a huge force for development and use of heritage in political ways, although they are either angry about decline in the *minerit* or not particularly attuned to contemporary issues. Whoever is to act, industrial and mining heritage can play key roles defining the region's future through education, interpretation and entertainment. Above all, heritage can motivate and underlay regional social change if defined and valorized for diverse and inclusive groups. Miners, former miners and sympathizers ought to raise heritage issues regularly to connect regional history to the politics of the everyday.

With few exceptions, heritage critical issues – definition, preservation, control, performance and purpose[63] – are elided in Valley debates. Citizens misunderstand industrial heritage, or think it superfluous. Authorities give heritage short shrift in regional transformation. Heritage objects are commandeered by private interest. Hesitancy to deal with dark heritage keeps people wary of each other, contributing to fragmentary identity. But challenging these conditions through heritage action could rebuild an effective politics, if not common identity. Working-class culture and industrial heritage should be embellished as a Valley 'brand.' Heritage must

Identity and mining heritage in Romania 129

connect to issues of daily life like housing, food and recreation. Facing forward, heritage must not only portray the past, but define a common Valley future.

Notes

1 'Heritage' is defined formally by state policy, but in this paper 'heritage' concerns resources, objects and sites both formally recognized or with historic value without formal recognition. Thanks to Vali Fulger and University of Petroșani students for assisting with a survey for this project.
2 Soyez, Dietrich. 2009. Europeanizing Industrial Heritage in Europe: Addressing Its Transboundary and Dark Sides. *Geographische Zeitschrift* 97(1): 43–55.
3 Iancu, Florentina-Cristina. 2007. The Economic, Social, Demographic and Environmental Effects of the Economic Reorganization within Petrosani Depression. *Geography*. University of Craiova, 10: 127–35. http://analegeo.ro/wp-content/uploads/2010/07/Articolul-13-Iancu-Cristina.pdf. p. 130–1. Accessed 12–15-15.
4 Lisa Breglia. 2006. *Monumental Ambivalence: The Politics of Heritage*. Austin, TX: University of Texas Press.
5 Catherine M. Cameron. 2000. Emergent Industrial Heritage: The Politics of Selection. *Museum Anthropology* 23(3): 58–73. Bella Dicks. 2008. Performing the Hidden Injuries of Class in Coal-Mining Heritage. *Sociology* 42(3): 436–52. Jaume Franquesa. 2013. On Keeping and Selling: The Political Economy of Heritage Making in Contemporary Spain. *Current Anthropology* 54(3): 346–69.
6 Chiara DeCesari. 2010. Creative Heritage: Palestinian Heritage NGOs and Defiant Arts of Government. *American Anthropologist* 112(4): 625–37.
7 Eric J. Hobsbawm, and Terence R. Ranger, Eds. 1983. *The Invention of Tradition*. Cambridge: Cambridge University Press.
8 Laurajane Smith. 2006. *Uses of Heritage*. London: Routledge. Tilly, Charles. 2008. *Contentious Performances*. Cambridge: Cambridge University Press.
9 Jaume Franquesa. 2013. On Keeping and Selling: The Political Economy of Heritage Making in Contemporary Spain. *Current Anthropology* 54(3): 346–69. p. 348.
10 Catherine M. Cameron. 2008. The Marketing of Heritage: From the Western World to the Global Stage. *City & Society* 20(2): 160–8.
11 Gaston Gordillo. 2014. *Rubble: The Afterlife of Destruction*. Durham: Duke. p. 14.
12 Michael Herzfeld. 2010. Engagement, Gentrification, and the Neoliberal Hijacking of History. *Current Anthropology* 51(S2): S259–67. p. S260.
13 Lisa Breglia. 2006. *Monumental Ambivalence: The Politics of Heritage*. Austin, TX: University of Texas Press, p. 6.
14 Liviu Chelcea. 2015. Postindustrial Ecologies: Industrial Rubble, Nature, and the Limits of Representation. In *Parcours Anthropologiques: Ethnographies du changement et de l'attachement*, Bianca Botea and Sarah Rojon, Eds. http://pa.revues.org/448, p. 4, Accessed 1–31-16.
15 Gaston Gordillo. 2014. *Rubble: The Afterlife of Destruction*. Durham: Duke. p. 2.
16 Rawi Abdelal and Yoshiko M. Herrera, Alastair Iain Johnston, and Rose McDermott. 2006. Identity as a Variable. *Perspectives on Politics* 4(4): 695–711, pp. 696–7.
17 Susan Gal and Gail Kligman. 2000. *The Politics of Gender after Socialism: A Comparative-Historical Essay*. Princeton: Princeton University Press.
18 Ioan Valentin Fulger. 2007. *Valea Jiului după 1989, Spațiu Generator de Convulsii Sociale*. Petroșani: Focus.
19 Matei Martin, Ed. 2015. Dosar Dilema: Mineriada din iunie '90. *Dilema Veche* 12(592): 18–24.
20 Alin Rus. 2007. *Mineriadele-între manipulare politică și solidaritate muncitorească*. Bucharest: Curtea Veche.

21 In an April 2015 survey, 76.9 per cent of respondents (N = 615/800) indicated that the Jiu Valley has been presented very poorly or poorly in Romanian media.
22 Some 74 per cent of respondents (N = 593/800) approved of Communist-led industrialization of the Jiu Valley, because of the jobs it provided.
23 The border between Habsburg territory and Oltenia ran south of Vulcan.
24 Mircea Baron. 1998. *Cărbune și societate în Valea Jiului: Perioada interbelică.* Petroșani: Editura Universitas, pp. 64–5.
25 Mircea Baron and Oana Dobre-Baron. 2009. The Emergence of the Jiu Valley Coal Basin (Romania): A Consequence of the Industrial Revolution. *Annals of the University of Petrosani, Economics Department.* University of Petrosani, Romania, 9(3): 53–80.
26 Mircea Baron. 1998. *Cărbune și societate în Valea Jiului: Perioada interbelică.* Petroșani: Editura Universitas, p. 69, Adrian-Bogdan Bădău. 2014. The Miner Industry from Jiu Valley – Environmental and Social Influences. In *Annals the "Constantin Brâncuși" University of Târgu Jiu.* Economy Series, Special Issue 2014-Information Society and Sustainable Development, p. 103–6.
27 This multicultural identity was celebrated throughout regional history and cited as a key reason why people resisted ethnic and national claims of German National Socialism and latter-day Romanian Communism. See Kideckel, David A. 2007. Metaphors of America: Labor, Global Integration, and Transylvanian Identities. *Hungarian Studies* 1–2: 111–34.
28 Of four *colonie*, the Ministry of Culture has only recognized Petroșani's lower colony.
29 Mircea Baron. 1998. *Cărbune și societate în Valea Jiului: Perioada interbelică.* Petroșani: Editura Universitas, p. 46.
30 Mircea Baron. 1998. *Cărbune și societate în Valea Jiului: Perioada interbelică.* Petroșani: Editura Universitas, p. 356.
31 Mircea Baron. 1998. *Cărbune și societate în Valea Jiului: Perioada interbelică.* Petroșani: Editura Universitas, p. 273, Margareta Toth-Gaspar. 1964. Condițiile de Munca și Viața ale Minerilor din Valea Jiului și Luptele lor Greviste pînă la Sfârșitul Secolului al XIX-lea. *Acta Musei Napocensis*, 255–85, cited in Jack R. Friedman 2003. *Ambiguous Transitions and Abjected Selves: Betrayal, Enlightenment, and Globalization in Romania's Jiu Valley.* Ph.D Dissertation. University of North Carolina-Chapel Hill, Department of Cultural Anthropology.
32 Ion Oprea. 1970. *Istoria Românilor.* Bucharest: Editura Didactică și Pedagogică, Țic, Nicolae. 1977. *Roșu pe Alb.* Craiova: Publisher Unknown.
33 Marian Boboc. 2012. *Casinoul Muncitoresc din Colonia de Jos a Petroșaniului.* Craiova: Corso de la George Enescu la A.R.L.U.S. Ed. Autograf MJM.
34 Marian Boboc. 2014. *Palatul Cultural (Teatrul Minier)Lupeni.* Craiova: Ed. Autograf MJM.
35 Marian Boboc. 2007. *Vulcanul din inima noastră – O incursiune prin antebelicul și interbelicul Vulcanului.* Deva: Ed. Corvin.
36 Carol Gigi Nicolau. 2015. *Roșu Adânc de Valea Jiului.* Petroșani: Focus, pp. 26–7.
37 Valeriu Bârgău. 1984. Oamenii Subpămîntului. In *Planeta Cărbunului*, Gligor Hașa, Ed. București: Editura Eminescu, pp. 115–70.
38 For Jiu Valley gender identity, see David A Kideckel. 2004. Miners and Wives in Romania's Jiu Valley: Perspectives on Post-Socialist Class, Gender, and Social Change. *Identities: Global Studies in Culture and Power* 11(1): 39–63. See also Alin Rus. 2003. *Valea Jiului: O Capacană Istorică.* Târgu Jiu: Realitatea Românească.
39 Local mines still sponsor five Valley football teams.
40 Matinal. 1997. *După 20 de Ani sau Lupeni '77- Lupeni '97.* Petroșani: Imprimeria Grapho Tipex.
41 Rus, ibid. Ion Velica and Carol Schreter. 1993. *Călătorie prin Vârstele Văii Jiului: Istoria în date a Văii Jiului.* Deva: Editura Destin.
42 World Bank. 2004. *The Jiu Valley: A Multi-Dimensional Assessment.* Washington: World Bank, p. 6.
43 Dan Perjovschi. 1999. Mineri buni, mineri rai. *Revista 22* 3: 1–3.

Identity and mining heritage in Romania 131

44 Most Romanians reviled the miners for these actions, but some others supported them, and children even played '*minerii și scuterii*' (miners and motor-scooterists), like 'cops and robbers,' the former heroes, the latter villains.
45 Felicia Andrioni, Mariana Anghel and Lavinia Elisabeta Popp. 2014. Jiu Valley's Demographic Dimensions at the Intersection of Socio-Economic Transformations. *University of Petroșani Proceedings of the Socio-Human Sciences* 10(1): 660–5.
46 Government of Romania. 1997. Ordonanța Nr. 22/1997 Privind unele măsuri de protecție ce se acordă personalului din industria minieră și din activitățile de prospecțiuni și explorări geologice.
47 Corneliu Bran. 2011. Recent încheiatul recensământ arată că Valea Jiului a ajuns la limita sutei de mii de locuitori! *Ziarul Vaii Jiului*, 10–11–2011. www.zvj.ro/articole-376-Recent+incheiatul+recens++mant+arat+++c++++Valea+Jiului+a+ajuns+la+limita+sutei+de+mii+de+locuitori.html. Accessed 2–23–16.
48 Magdalena Crăciun, Maria Grecu and Razvan Stan. 2002. *Lumea Vaii. Unitatea minei, diversitatea minerilor*. Bucharest: Paideia.
49 Maria Voichita Grecu. 2014. "We Remained the Foam of the Trade": The Impact of Restructurings on Jiu Valley Miners, 1997–2013: "A Crisis without Precedence?" *Travail et emploi* 137: 123–38, David A. Kideckel, 2008. *Getting By in Postsocialist Romania: Labor, the Body and Working Class Culture*. Bloomington, IN: Indiana University Press, David A. Kideckel, 2011. The End of Politics in Romania's Jiu Valley: Global Normalization and the Reproduction of Inequality. In *Emerging Inequalities in Europe: Poverty and Transnational Migration*, Deema Kaneff and Frances Pine, Eds. London: Anthem Press, pp. 125–43.
50 Jiu Valley coal cost 107 lei/gcal, imported coal 48 lei/gcal. Societate Națională de Închideri Mine Valea Jiului. 2012. *Mineritul în Valea Jiului – Repere Istorice*. www.snimvj.ro/istoric.aspx. Accessed 10–20–15.
51 Luciana Ghica. 2006. *România și Uniunea Europeană: O istorie cronologică*. București: Meronia, pp. 71–2.
52 European Commission. 2010. Decizia Consilului din 10 decembrie 2010 privind ajutorul de stat pentru facilitarea închiderii minelor de carbune necompetitive. *Official Journal of the European Union* (Romania) 1(336): 24–9.
53 Nina Obuljen. 2004. Why We Need European Cultural Policies. *The Impact of EU Enlargement on Cultural Policies in Transition Countries*. Amsterdam: European Cultural Foundation. www.encatc.org/pages/uploads/media/2004_cpra_publication.pdf. Accessed 2–11–16.
54 Marian Boboc. 2009. *Mina Petrila: 150 de ani. Oameni, fapte, întâmplări*. Craiova: Ed. Autograf MJM.
55 The EU offers decreasing assistance funds until 2018. Most miners let go are close to their pension while some retraining is provided for programs in construction, transportation, etc.
56 Mihaiela Mihai. 2015. Incompetența politică, sancționată de profesioniști. Directorul de la Închideri, pus la punct de arhitecții care "simt zidurile clădirilor." *Gazeta de dimineața*, 21 October. http://gazetadedimineata.ro/actualitate/incompetenta-politica-sanctionata-de-profesionisti-directorul-de-la-inchideri-pus-la-punct-de-arhitectii-care-simt-zidurile-cladirilor/#.ViZCPtw0z9U.facebook. Accessed 10–21–15.
57 CNH's previous identity was as the *Regia Autonoma a Huilei din România*, the successor of the *Combinatul Minier Valea Jiului*, adopted after the 1977 strike.
58 Mintea is north of the Jiu Valley, near the county capital, Deva.
59 According to Cosmin Pam Matei. 2015. Cum a fost bagat mamutul CE Hunedoara in faliment. *Cotidianul*. www.cotidianul.ro/cum-a-fost-bagat-mamutul-ce-hunedoara-in-faliment-274439/January 14. Accessed 1–14–16, CEH's recent declaration of insolvency and steps toward bankruptcy may speed this.
60 Romanian industrial heritage is legally defined, including Government of Romania. 2008 a. Law No. 182 of 25 October 2000 on the Protection of National Cultural Heritage Mobile, Published in the Official Gazette No. 828 9 December 2008, and

Government of Romania. 2008 b. Law on the Legal, Technical and Industrial Heritage, Law No. 6/2008. Designation of Jiu Valley heritage sites is a function of the Hunedoara County Directory of the Ministry of Culture and Faiths. Only five of 48 registered sites relate to mining. See also Anda Becuţ. 2015. Heritage Policy and Management in Romania and Wider Benefits of Participating in the Ljubljana Process. In *Heritage for Development in Southeast Europe: New Visions and Perceptions of Heritage through the Ljubljana Process*, Gojko Rikalovic and Hristina Mikic, Eds. Brussels: Council of Europe, Chelcea, Liviu, Anda Becut and Bianca Balsan. 2012. Romania. In *Council of Europe/ ERICarts: Compendium of Cultural Policies and Trends in Europe*, 13th edition 2012. www.culturalpolicies.net. Accessed 2–7–16.

61 Ilinca Păun Constantinescu, Dragoş Dascălu and Cristina Sucală. 2017. An Activist Perspective on Petrila, A Romanian Mining City. *The Public Historian* 39 (4): 114–41.

62 Gheorghe Olteanu. 2013. Vulcan / Legendă cu fier vechi. *Ziarul Văii Jiului*. 10 August 2013. www.zvj.ro/articole-20811-Vulcan++Legend+++cu+fier+vechi.html. Accessed 10–21–15.

63 Andreea-Loreta Cercleux, Florentina-Cristina Merciu and George-Laurenţiu Merciu. 2012. Models of Technical and Industrial Heritage Re-Use in Romania. *Procedia Environmental Sciences* 14: 216–25.

Bibliography

Abdelal, Rawi, Yoshiko M. Herrera, Alastair Iain Johnston and Rose McDermott. 2006. Identity as a Variable. *Perspectives on Politics* 4(4): 695–711.

Andrioni, Felicia, Mariana Anghel and Lavinia Elisabeta Popp. 2014. Jiu Valley's Demographic Dimensions at the Intersection of Socio-Economic Transformations. *University of Petroşani Proceedings of the Socio-Human Sciences* 10(1): 660–5.

Bădău Adrian-Bogdan. 2014. The Miner Industry from Jiu Valley – Environmental and Social Influences. In *Annals of the "Constantin Brâncuşi" University of Târgu Jiu.* Economy Series, Special Issue 2014– Information Society and Sustainable Development, pp. 103–6.

Bârgău, Valeriu. 1984. Oamenii Subpământului. In *Planeta Cărbunului*, Gligor Haşa, Ed. Bucureşti: Editura Eminescu, pp. 115–70.

Baron, Mircea. 1998. *Cărbune şi societate în Valea Jiului: Perioada interbelică*. Petroşani: Editura Universitas.

Baron, Mircea and Oana Dobre-Baron. 2009. The Emergence of the Jiu Valley Coal Basin (Romania): A Consequence of the Industrial Revolution. *Annals of the University of Petrosani, Economics Department*. University of Petrosani, Romania, 9(3): 53–80.

Becuţ, Anda. 2015. Heritage Policy and Management in Romania and Wider Benefits of Participating in the Ljubljana Process. In *Heritage for Development in Southeast Europe: New Visions and Perceptions of Heritage through the Ljubljana Process*, Gojko Rikalovic and Hristina Mikic, Eds. Brussels: Council of Europe.

Boboc, Marian. 2007. *Vulcanul din inima noastră – O incursiune prin antebelicul şi interbelicul Vulcanului*. Deva: Ed. Corvin.

———. 2009. *Mina Petrila: 150 de ani. Oameni, fapte, întâmplări*. Craiova: Ed. Autograf MJM.

———. 2012. *Casinoul Muncitoresc din Colonia de Jos a Petroşaniului*. Craiova: Corso de la George Enescu la A.R.L.U.S. Ed. Autograf MJM.

———. 2014. *Palatul Cultural (Teatrul Minier)Lupeni*. Craiova: Ed. Autograf MJM.

Bran, Corneliu. 2011. Recent încheiatul recensământ arată că Valea Jiului a ajuns la limita sutei de mii de locuitori! *Ziarul Vaii Jiului*, 10–11–2011. www.zvj.ro/articole-376-Recent+

incheiatul+recens++mant+arat+++c++++Valea+Jiului+a+ajuns+la+limita+sutei+de+mii+de+locuitori.html. Accessed 2–23–16.
Breglia, Lisa. 2006. *Monumental Ambivalence: The Politics of Heritage*. Austin, TX: University of Texas Press.
Cameron, Catherine M. 2000. Emergent Industrial Heritage: The Politics of Selection. *Museum Anthropology* 23(3): 58–73.
———. 2008. The Marketing of Heritage: From the Western World to the Global Stage. *City & Society* 20(2): 160–8.
Cercleux, Andreea-Loreta, Florentina-Cristina Merciu and George-Laurenţiu Merciu. 2012. Models of Technical and Industrial Heritage Re-Use in Romania. *Procedia Environmental Sciences* 14: 216–25.
Chelcea, Liviu. 2015. Postindustrial Ecologies: Industrial Rubble, Nature, and the Limits of Representation. In *Parcours Anthropologiques: Ethnographies du changement et de l'attachement*, Bianca Botea and Sarah Rojon, Eds. http://pa.revues.org/448. Accessed 1–31–16.
Chelcea, Liviu, Anda Becut and Bianca Balsan. 2012. Romania. In *Council of Europe/ ERICarts: Compendium of Cultural Policies and Trends in Europe*, 13th edition 2012. www.culturalpolicies.net.
Constantinescu, Ilinca Păun, Dragoş Dascălu and Cristina Sucală. 2017. An Activist Perspective on Petrila, A Romanian Mining City. *The Public Historian* 39 (4): 114–41.
Crăciun, Magdalena, Maria Grecu and Razvan Stan. 2002. *Lumea Vaii. Unitatea minei, diversitatea minerilor*. Bucharest: Paideia.
DeCesari, Chiara. 2010. Creative Heritage: Palestinian Heritage NGOs and Defiant Arts of Government. *American Anthropologist* 112(4): 625–37.
Dicks, Bella. 2008. Performing the Hidden Injuries of Class in Coal-Mining Heritage. *Sociology* 42(3): 436–52.
Directia Judeteana pentru Cultura, Culte, si Patrimoniul Cultural National Hunedoara. 2014. www.hunedoara.djc.ro/Index.aspx. Accessed 10–17–15.
European Commission. 2010. Decizia Consilului din 10 decembrie 2010 privind ajutorul de stat pentru facilitarea închiderii minelor de carbune necompetitive. *Official Journal of the European Union* (Romania) 1(336): 24–9.
Franquesa, Jaume. 2013. On Keeping and Selling: The Political Economy of Heritage Making in Contemporary Spain. *Current Anthropology* 54(3): 346–69.
Friedman, Jack R. 2003. *Ambiguous Transitions and Abjected Selves: Betrayal, Enlightenment, and Globalization in Romania's Jiu Valley*. Ph.D Dissertation. University of North Carolina-Chapel Hill, Department of Cultural Anthropology.
Fulger, Ioan Valentin. 2007. *Valea Jiului după 1989, Spaţiu Generator de Convulsii Sociale*. Petroşani: Focus.
Gal, Susan and Gail Kligman. 2000. *The Politics of Gender after Socialism: A Comparative-Historical Essay*. Princeton: Princeton University Press.
Ghica, Luciana. 2006. *România şi Uniunea Europeană: O istorie cronologică*. Bucureşti: Meronia.
Gordillo, Gaston. 2014. *Rubble: The Afterlife of Destruction*. Durham: Duke.
Government of Romania. 1997. Ordonanţa Nr. 22/1997 Privind unele măsuri de protecţie ce se acordă personalului din industria minieră şi din activităţile de prospecţiuni şi explorări geologice. Monitorul Oficial No. 200, 20 august 1997.
———. 2008 a. Law No. 182 of 25 October 2000 (* Republished *) on the Protection of National Cultural Heritage Mobile *) Issued by the Parliament Published in the Official Gazette No. 828, 9 December 2008.

———. 2008 b. Law on the Legal, Technical and Industrial Heritage, Law No. 6/2008.
Grecu, Maria Voichita. 2014. "We Remained the Foam of the Trade": The Impact of Restructurings on Jiu Valley Miners, 1997–2013: "A Crisis without Precedence?" *Travail et emploi* 137: 123–38.
Herzfeld, Michael. 2010. Engagement, Gentrification, and the Neoliberal Hijacking of History. *Current Anthropology* 51(S2): S259–67.
Hobsbawm, Eric J. and Terrence R. Ranger, Eds. 1983. *The Invention of Tradition*. Cambridge: Cambridge University Press.
Iancu, Florentina-Cristina. 2007. The Economic, Social, Demographic and Environmental Effects of the Economic Reorganization within Petrosani Depression. *Geography*. University of Craiova, 10: 127–35. http://analegeo.ro/wp-content/uploads/2010/07/Articolul-13-Iancu-Cristina.pdf. Accessed 12–15–15.
Kideckel, David A. 2004. Miners and Wives in Romania's Jiu Valley: Perspectives on Post-Socialist Class, Gender, and Social Change. *Identities: Global Studies in Culture and Power* 11(1): 39–63.
———. 2008. *Getting By in Postsocialist Romania: Labor, the Body and Working Class Culture*. Bloomington, IN. Indiana University Press.
———. 2011. The End of Politics in Romania's Jiu Valley: Global Normalization and the Reproduction of Inequality. In *Emerging Inequalities in Europe: Poverty and Transnational Migration*, Deema Kaneff and Frances Pine, Eds. London: Anthem Press, pp. 125–43.
Martin, Matei, Ed. 2015. Dosar Dilema: Mineriada din iunie '90. *Dilema Veche* 12(592): 18–24.
Matei, Cosmin Pam. 2015. Cum a fost bagat mamutul CE Hunedoara in faliment. *Cotidianul*. www.cotidianul.ro/cum-a-fost-bagat-mamutul-ce-hunedoara-in-faliment-274439/ January14. Accessed 1–14–16.
Matinal. 1997. *După 20 de Ani sau Lupeni '77- Lupeni '97*. Petroşani: Imprimeria Grapho Tipex.
Mihai, Mihaiela. 2015. Incompetența politică, sancționată de profesioniști. Directorul de la Închideri, pus la punct de arhitecții care "simt zidurile clădirilor." *Gazeta de dimineața*, 21 October. http://gazetadedimineata.ro/actualitate/incompetenta-politica-sanctionata-de-profesionisti-directorul-de-la-inchideri-pus-la-punct-de-arhitectii-care-simt-zidurile-cladirilor/#.ViZCPtw0z9U.facebook. Accessed 10–21–15.
Nicolau, Carol Gigi. 2015. *Roşu Adânc de Valea Jiului*. Petroşani: Focus.
Obuljen, Nina. 2004. Why We Need European Cultural Policies. In *The Impact of EU Enlargement on Cultural Policies in Transition Countries*. Amsterdam: European Cultural Foundation. www.encatc.org/pages/uploads/media/2004_cpra_publication.pdf. Accessed 2–11–16.
Olteanu, Gheorghe. 2013. Vulcan/Legendă cu fier vechi. *Ziarul Văii Jiului*. 10 August 2013. www.zvj.ro/articole-20811-Vulcan+++Legend+++cu+fier+vechi.html. Accessed 10–21–15.
———. 2014. Nu contează, fier să fie. *Ziarul Văii Jiului*, 5 May 2014. www.zvj.ro/articole-25207-Vulcan++Nu+conteaz++++fier+s+++fie.html. Accessed 10–21–15.
Oprea, Ion. 1970. *Istoria Românilor*. Bucharest: Editura Didactică şi Pedagogică.
Perjovschi, Dan. 1999. Mineri buni, mineri rai. *Revista 22* 3: 1–3.
Rus, Alin. 2003. *Valea Jiului: O Capacană Istorică*. Târgu Jiu: Realitatea Românească.
———. 2007. *Mineriadele-între manipulare politică şi solidaritate muncitorească*. Bucharest: Curtea Veche.
Societate Naţională de Închideri Mine Valea Jiului. 2012. *Mineritul în Valea Jiului – Repere Istorice*. www.snimvj.ro/istoric.aspx. Accessed 10–20–15.

Soyez, Dietrich. 2009. Europeanizing Industrial Heritage in Europe: Addressing Its Transboundary and Dark Sides. *Geographische Zeitschrift* 97(1): 43–55.
Ţic, Nicolae. 1977. *Roşu pe Alb*. Craiova: Publisher Unknown.
Tilly, Charles. 2008. *Contentious Performances*. Cambridge: Cambridge University Press.
Toth-Gaspar, Margareta. 1964. Condiţiile de Munca şi Viaţa ale Minerilor din Valea Jiului şi Luptele lor Greviste pînă la Sfârşitul Secolului al XIX-lea. *Acta Musei Napocensis*, 255–85.
Velica, Ion and Carol Schreter. 1993. *Călătorie prin Vârstele Văii Jiului: Istoria în date a Văii Jiului*. Deva: Editura Destin.
World Bank. 2004. *The Jiu Valley: A Multi-Dimensional Assessment*. Washington: World Bank.

7 Regional identity in the making? Industrial heritage and regional identity in the coal region of Northern Kyūshū in Japan

Regine Mathias

The coal and steel area of Northern Kyūshū is one of the oldest industrial regions in Japan and a core area of the UNESCO World Heritage sites in Japan titled "Sites of Japan's Meiji Industrial Revolution". During the industrial revolution in Japan, which started in the middle of the 19th century, the tradition of coal mining in that region and the construction of the first modern Japanese steel plant there in 1901 turned Northern Kyūshū into one of the hubs of industrial development in the country and drew a large number of workers and their families into the area. New towns and settlements sprang up alongside older cities, which also experienced rapid population growth. Mining communities, mostly situated in rural areas or small towns, developed their own identities that were often based on feelings of seclusion and social discrimination as well as a sense of professional pride.

Like the German Ruhr region, Northern Kyūshū was deeply affected by the decline of the coal industry which started in the late 1950s, and the impact of the oil shocks of the 1970s and 1980s on steel production and affiliated industries. The ensuing de-industrialization led to various efforts to restructure existing industries and create new regional policies. In order to analyze these policies and their ties to the regional industrial heritage, this chapter focuses on three mining areas that represent different geographical and industrial settings: the coal mining region of Chikuhō, Japan's largest mine Miike near Ōmuta and Arao, and the coal mines of Nishi-Sonogi in the bay of Nagasaki.

The idea of preserving industrial heritage sites began to spread in Japan in the late 1970s, parallel to the foundation of the Japan Industrial Archaeology Society (JIAS; *Sangyō kōko gakkai*) in 1977. Even before that time there had been isolated attempts to preserve the local culture and memories of the coal mining industry in Northern Kyūshū, although few of these were successful, and many structures were destroyed before preservation measures could be initiated. Since the 1990s remnants of coal mines, blast furnaces, harbor structures, factories and other buildings have been put on the national preservation list, and in July 2015 several sites in Northern Kyūshū became part of a large network of UNESCO World Heritage sites centering on early industrialization in Japan.[1] This development seems to have had a strong impact on the re-evaluation of the mining heritage in Northern Kyūshū, and on its interaction with regional and local identity. While for a long time the coal industry and especially its decline was remembered as a dark episode of the past, recent indicators point to an increasing correlation between industrial heritage and regional and local identity. While there are a few studies on such an interaction for coal mining areas in Hokkaidō,[2] hardly any research has been done on the topic with regard to the older mining regions in Kyūshū.[3]

The history of industrialization and urban development in Japan

The industrial revolution in Japan started in the middle of the 19th century. The first phase between 1850 and 1870 could be called Japan's 'industrial apprenticeship'.[4] In 1850, Japan was still ruled by the Shogun, a military leader from the Tokugawa family, and about 250 feudal lords, who were in charge of their domains. Foreign relations and foreign trade were strictly controlled by the Shogun. Nevertheless, Western (technical) knowledge mostly in the form of books came into the country. These were translated and distributed all over Japan. This knowledge did not suffice to trigger full-scale industrialization, but it led to experiments with innovative foreign technology.[5]

With the onset of political modernization starting in 1868, in the wake of the so-called Meiji Restoration and subsequent reforms, the industrial revolution entered its second phase, which lasted until the end of the First World War. In 1920 the share of industrial production as a percentage of gross national product exceeded that of agricultural production for the first time, which means that Japan had become an industrialized nation, with shipyards, steel plants, arsenals, textile mills and many other industrial enterprises. Being a latecomer among the industrialized nations just like Germany, Japan's industrial policy during those years was driven by the desire to catch up with the so-called developed countries and avoid the fate of neighboring China. Industrialism therefore became an important part of her modern national identity very early on.

The boom after the First World War was followed by a period of slow growth and stagnation, until industrial production increased again in the 1930s not least boosted by the growing military demand, which peaked in 1943. The ensuing breakdown of the economy was overcome in the second half of the 1950s, when production exceeded the prewar level, and a period of high economic growth started. This lasted until the oil crisis in 1973. During this period growth once again centered on heavy industries like shipbuilding and steel as well as on the chemical industry. Four large industrial zones, which had developed around Tōkyō/Yokohama, Nagoya, Ōsaka/Kyōto and the industrial district in Northern Kyūshū[6] and comprised factories, shipyards and ports, became the hubs of economic and urban growth.

In the midst of this high growth period, the energy revolution occurred and energy supply switched from native coal to cheaper imported coal and to oil, setting off the decline of the coal mining industry in the late 1950s. After the oil shock in 1973, steel and other industries began to face problems, too, which led to measures aimed at adjustment and restructuring, and especially affected older industrial zones like Northern Kyūshū. But in contrast to the coal mining industry the decline of the steel industry was less steep and the consequences of de-industrialization for areas like Kitakyūshū were less severe. In the long run, however, the shift away from heavy industries to the so-called knowledge-intensive industries changed the industrial landscape in the old industrial zones, too. For example, in Kitakyūshū a large, abandoned industrial site was successfully transformed into the 'Space World' theme park, and the city re-invented itself as a 'green city', focusing on renewable energy and other ecological schemes.

The coal regions in Northern Kyūshū

Coal was found in various parts of Japan (see Figure 7.1) but the coal mines in Northern Kyūshū were the oldest in Japan and the backbone of Japan's early industrialization. The history of coal mining in this region dates back to the seventeenth and eighteenth centuries, when coal was extracted and used as house coal. However, it was only in the mid-19th century that coal became an important source of energy e.g. for salt production along the coast of the Inland Sea. After the opening of the country, coal mines supplied coal to steam ships and the newly built railways. It also became one of the three most important export goods together with silk and tea. Starting in the late 1880s the so-called *zaibatsu*, large industrial conglomerates like Mitsui and Mitsubishi, took over several mines from local entrepreneurs or the state and became major players in coal mining.[7]

Among the three mining areas to be investigated in this article, the coalfields of Chikuhō area are the most prominent. Situated in the Northern part of Fukuoka prefecture, the area covers more than 900 square kilometers in a valley cut in half by the Onga river. Just like the Ruhr area, to which it is often compared, the Chikuhō region is an artificial creation that had no common pre-coal history. In the early modern period the large coal deposits there extended over the territory of two feudal domains separated by a political border. After the abolishment of the domains in 1871, the political borders disappeared, but it can be assumed that the people living there kept their regional identity tied to the older political units for some time. In the 1880s, however, coal mining in the area gathered momentum, and in 1886 the mine owners in the region, heeding the advice of the administration of Fukuoka prefecture, joined forces in a union, eventually called Chikuhō sekitan kōgyō kumiai (The Chikuhō coal mines union). That is said to have been the birth of this new region, which was named Chikuhō.[8] The name was soon taken up by other organizations like, e.g. the company that was founded in 1889 to construct a new railway for the transport of the coal, and called Chikuhō kōgyō tetsudō (Chikuhō railway [company] to promote industrial development). The coal deposits there were among the largest in Japan, and the Chikuhō mines were the leading producers of coal in the country from the beginnings of the industrial revolution until the late 1950s, when its output of more than 13 million tons per year still accounted for more than 30 per cent of Japan's total production.[9] It was a rural mining district where large mines run by nation-wide operating corporations or the few remaining local entrepreneurs co-existed with smaller ones that were

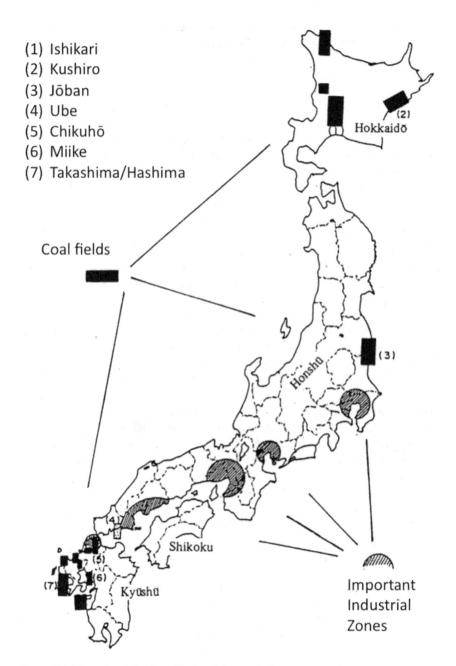

Figure 7.1 Map of coal fields and industrial zones in Japan.
Graph: R. Mathias

often worked for just a short time. The Chikuhō area was hardest hit by the mine closures during the so-called energy revolution, i.e. the switch from domestic coal to oil and import coal in the late 1950s and 1960s, and the last mines there shut down in 1973.[10]

The second region around the Miike coalfield extends across the southern part of Fukuoka prefecture and stretches into the neighboring Kumamoto prefecture. The Miike mine was the oldest, largest and most productive mine in Japan and had a very varied history. Its beginnings are said to go back to 1469. In the modern period Miike coal mine was taken over by the government in 1873, but sold to the Mitsui Corporation in 1889. It was one of the few coal mines in Kyūshū that used convict labour on a big scale until the 1930s. Later, miners from very different backgrounds, including immigrants, and forced laborers from Korea, Taiwan and China as well as POWs worked in Miike during the Second World War. After the war the Miike mine experienced a period of ups and downs, strikes and accidents. Although productivity greatly increased after 1960 and the output of coal reached a high with 6.5 million tons in 1969,[11] in the long run the mine could not reverse the severe consequences of the government's policy of rationalization and workforce cuts. Miike mine was finally closed in 1997, after having produced coal for 124 years.[12]

In the third mining region of Nishi Sonogi in Nagasaki prefecture most coal beds extend into the sea, so several mines were situated on small islands in Nagasaki Bay. Shafts were sunk under the sea and the coal was extracted from below the seabed in a costly and technically complicated procedure. Therefore, nearly all mines were opened and run by large enterprises, mostly by the Mitsubishi Corporation. Two of the most important mines were on the islands Takashima and Hashima, which were located 14 and 18 km southwest of Nagasaki port respectively. Just like the Miike mine, the Takashima mine ranked among Japan's largest mines with a long history, starting at the end of the 17th century. It was one of the first coal mines to be modernized in Japan during the 1860s, when the first vertical shaft in a Japanese coal mine was sunk in 1868 using Western technology.[13] The island, which originally housed only a small fishing community supplying the local market, was soon overwhelmed by an ever-growing number of miners and their families. Production peaked in 1965 with 1,272,400 tons,[14] but after a coal dust explosion in 1985 the Takashima mine was closed a year later.

The nearby Hashima mine started to extract coal in 1891. It was situated on an island, which originally consisted of only two large rocks. In order to install a mineshaft and accommodate workers on this small barren island Mitsubishi had to carry out large-scale land-fill projects and surround the newly created land by a high wall to protect it against the sea. The excellent quality of the coal extracted there from a depth of down to 1,000 m and primarily used for the steel works in Yawata seems to have been worth all these efforts. Although coal extraction reached an all-time high of 350,000 tons in 1972, the Hashima mine was shut down in 1974 due to geological and economic reasons.[15]

The decades between the 1880s and 1920 were a period of almost continuous growth for coal mining throughout Japan. Production increased significantly from the middle of the 1880s, when domestic demand, triggered by rapid industrial growth and the expansion of the railway networks, overtook exports as the main consumer of coal. Between 1893 and 1913, coal consumption rose from two million tons to 15 million tons.[16] The highpoint of this development was during the years of First World War, which saw an unprecedented boom in the Japanese economy and also in coal mining. In 1919 the total output of coal in Japan amounted to 31 million tons, of which 22 million tons or more than 70 per cent were produced in Fukuoka prefecture.[17]

As this increase in output was mostly achieved by expanding the labor force, mining and related industries in Northern Kyūshū attracted a large number of workers from all over Japan and neighboring Korea. Subsequently, mining villages rapidly developed into towns and larger cities. For example, in Tagawa county, where the Mitsui Corporation established Mitsui Mining in 1900, the population doubled from 75,359 in 1903 to 156,916 in 1921.[18] This increase was largely due to the immigration of coal miners and their families. Although figures are not completely reliable, it is clear that this group already accounted for one-third or even 40 per cent of the total population in 1917.[19] Other regions in the Chikuhō area experienced a similar development, and in the 1930s and 1940s the so-called three mining cities, Tagawa, Iizuka and Nōgata, emerged alongside other smaller towns in the region and changed the character of this once rural region.

Even more striking is the growth of the towns of Ōmuta in the southern part of Fukuoka prefecture, and neighboring Arao in the adjoining Kumamoto prefecture. Starting as a small coal mining community, which was dependent on the Miike coal mine, Ōmuta developed into an important industrial center. In 1908, a large port was opened to facilitate the shipping of raw materials and goods. Mitsui mining company and a growing number of often Mitsui-related small and medium companies created an ever-growing demand for workers, and the population grew from 121,000 in 1920 to 177,000 in 1940. After a short interruption during the last years of the Second World War, the population again started to grow and peaked in 1960, when more than 205,000 people lived in Ōmuta city, which made it second only to the steel city Yawata as an industrial center in the whole region.[20]

The coal mining region of Nishi-Sonogi in Nagasaki prefecture also experienced rapid growth. As the mines there were situated on small islands, space was extremely limited. This led to very special living conditions for the miners and their families. Whereas in the Chikuhō region miners were mostly accommodated in company owned barn-like 'long houses', i.e. rows of small, wooden, single-story flats that spread out over a large area, on the islands, especially on Hashima, Japan's first high-rise reinforced concrete buildings were built in 1916 to accommodate the rapidly growing workforce and their families. Hashima Island, which is only 480 meters long and 160 meters wide, had a population of more than 5,000 in 1960 and was the most densely populated place on earth at that time. Because of the closely packed three to five-story buildings and the aforementioned protective wall around the island, the silhouette of Hashima resembled a battleship

Figure 7.2 The island mine of Hashima in November 2016. With some of Japan's oldest high-rising ferroconcrete buildings and the wall around the island its silhouette resembles a battleship, which led to the nickname Gunkanjima (Battleship-island).

Photo: R. Mathias

and for this reason it became widely known as Gunkan-jima or Battleship Island (see Figure 7.2).[21]

In short, coal mining and related industries, including Japan's first integrated steel plant in Yawata, which was founded in 1901 north of Chikuhō area where the Onga river flows into the sea, had a great impact on shaping the industrial landscape of Northern Kyūshū, turning it from a region mainly relying on agriculture and fishing into one of the most highly industrialized areas of Japan.

Villages and counties (*gun*) grew into industrial towns and cities, but most of them especially in the Chikuhō region largely kept their traditional character and did not develop into centers of urbanism and modernity. In such a typical mining town traditional one- or two-story wooden houses and shops lined the narrow streets. Modern Western-style buildings were rare and often limited to official buildings like the town hall, the local Chamber of Industry and Commerce or in the 1930s the cinemas. Near the mines and factories that dominated the landscape with their winding towers, smokestacks and slag heaps, miners lived in large, sprawling settlements of company-owned houses, i.e. small wooden barracks built in long rows. With the exception of Hashima, multi-story concrete apartment houses were not constructed until the 1950s (see Figure 7.3).

The growing communities depended economically to a large degree or even exclusively on mining and related industries. Therefore, the rapid decline of coal mining since the late 1950s hit all three regions hard, but the consequences for the mining area of Chikuhō were especially severe and led to a feeling of being victimized – often combined with a negative attitude towards the mining industry and its relics.

Figure 7.3 Company housing of the Kaijima Ōnoura mine in Chikuhō. The long rows of barracks each housed several families, a typical mining landscape with slag heaps and smokestacks in the background. The text on top of the postcard reads (in translation): "One part of the company houses for miners of the second shaft of Kaibara Ōnoura mine, always cheerful and bright homes".

De-industrialization: decline of coal in Northern Kyūshū, challenges for the regions

During the decade after the end of the Second World War, when Japanese industries were struggling to recover from the damage of the war, coal and steel production were given priority in the government's national industrial policy and soon started to increase production. However, the upswing, additionally boosted by the Korean War in 1950/51, was largely due to the opening of small- and medium-sized mines and did not lead to sustained growth. The attempt of the government to restructure the mining sector by implementing the so-called scrap-and-build policy, led to the closure of small, inefficient mines and the introduction of new technologies as well as a drastic reduction of the labor force in order to raise productivity in the larger mines. A first rationalization law in 1955[22] started the so-called energy revolution in Japan, which in the course of a just few years reversed the 'coal-first' policy of the immediate post-war era to an 'oil-first' policy, thereby dealing the coal industry a fatal blow.[23]

The strong repercussions were felt in all mining areas in Japan, but Chikuhō region suffered most from the economic downturn and the ensuing population decline which unfolded at unprecedented speed. During the short-lived boom soon after the end of Second World War, mining communities in Chikuhō had once again started to flourish. The number of coal mines rose from 76 in 1946 to 265 in 1951, and production grew from 7 million tons to 14 million tons, which amounted to one-third of national production at that time.[24] The number of inhabitants also grew and peaked in 1958 at more than 900,000.[25] Thereafter the scrap-and-build policy hit the Chikuhō area especially hard, due to the large number of small, inefficient mines operating there, which were the first to be shut down following the introduction of rationalization measures. Starting at the end of the 1950s, mine closures rolled over the region "like an avalanche".[26] A comparison with the Sorachi mining region in Hokkaidō shows the differences in speed and steepness of the decline (see Figure 7.4).

Within less than ten years nearly all mines, except very few large ones, were shut down, and the number of coal miners in Chikuhō decreased between 1956 and 1959 by nearly 30,000.[27] The population in the Chikuhō area declined by 23 per cent between 1960 and 1965,[28] and local merchants and services suffered increasingly from the dwindling numbers of customers.

> Th[e] iconic Chikuho came to a destructive end in the late1950s. As mine after mine shut down, communities collapsed and the local economy plummeted to a level that left cities and villages teetering on the edge of survival. The Chikuho region thus came to be characterized by its high rate of welfare recipients.[29]

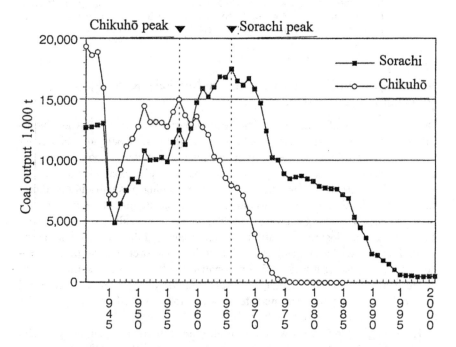

Figure 7.4 Decline of mining in Sorachi and Chikuhō.
Source: Adapted from Yoshioka, *Akarui tankō*, 2012.

Those who remained, many of them elderly or sick, had great difficulty finding new employment, and lived on unemployment insurance or had to rely on the newly created Law on Special Measures to Promote Coal mine Regions (*Santan chiiki shinkō rinji sochi hō*). This law was enacted by the central government in 1961 in response to the deteriorating situation in Chikuhō and other mining regions.[30] Chikuhō area became the poorhouse of Japan, with the country's highest per capita rate of people receiving benefits, and dire consequences like malnutrition in children.[31] An impressive testimony to this grim situation is a photo book by one of Japan's most famous photographers, Domon Ken, titled *Chikuhō no kodomotachi* (The Children of Chikuhō). Published in 1960, it made the sad fate of the Chikuhō region known throughout Japan and was instrumental in spreading a dark and gloomy image of mining regions, which also in turn had an impact on regional identity as will be shown later.[32]

The rationalization policy in the mines during the 1950s and 1960s resulted in increasingly sharp conflicts between companies and labor unions. In addition, a number of Socialist/leftist literary activists like Ueno Eishin, Tanigawa Gan and Morisaki Kazue moved to Chikuhō in the second half of the 1950s to support the struggle of the miners. Their group organized literary circles and published the journal *The Circle Village*,[33] and actively participated in one of the larger strikes in the region, the Taishō mine struggle in 1960.[34] Ueno and Morisaki later published extensively on Chikuhō and the miners' fate, thereby raising public awareness of the situation there.

While strikes in Chikuhō were scattered and resistance therefore relatively weak, the strong labor unions at the Miike mine put up fierce resistance to the 'scrap-and-build' restructuring policy, which involved considerable workforce cutbacks. Especially in 1959/1960 protests, strikes and lockouts were staged which lasted for over a year. In the end the company prevailed, and during the following decade the workforce was halved from 14,000 to 7,000. This 'great Miike strike' (*sōgi*), which attracted nationwide support, has become a symbol not only for the fight against the decline in the mining industry, but also more generally for the struggle of workers in Japan against rationalization and work force reductions. As such it has been documented in great detail and became engraved in the history of Japan's labor movement.[35] In the Ōmuta region the ultimately unsuccessful strike, which had also led to the establishment of a second, more compliant union, seems to have left scars rather than becoming a legend. A documentary film maker, Kumagai Hiroko, who produced a film called *Echos from the Miike Mine* in 2006, relates how she encountered difficulties while interviewing former miners who were reluctant to "break the ingrained taboo of talking about the labour dispute".[36]

The final closure of the Miike mine in 1997 greatly affected Ōmuta and the surrounding region, where the population had already gradually declined after the great strike. In 1960 Ōmuta city had a population of more than 205,700. In 2000, after the closure of the Miike mine, the population of Ōmuta had dwindled to 138,000, and the downward trend continues to the present day.[37] All attempts by the city and the Mitsui Corporation to stop the decline by establishing new businesses could not reverse the tide. Suppliers went out of business, merchants and service providers lost their clients, department stores like Matsuya and Kurume Izutsuya closed after the turn of the millennium, and the economic situation of the city deteriorated further.

The closure of the Hashima mine in 1974 and the Takashima mine in 1986 had even more drastic consequences. The island of Hashima, which was owned by the Mitsubishi Corporation and served the sole purpose of producing coal, was completely abandoned. Its population of about 5,000 people was moved to other places on the mainland. The island itself with its high-rise reinforced concrete structures was left to the elements in an experiment to observe the long-term effects of the weather on the durability of this material.

The decline of coal and the process that led to the final closure of the Takashima mine in 1986 also resulted in a steep population decrease, leaving the island, which had had a population of nearly 21,000 in 1960, with less than 6,500 in 1985. In the years immediately after the closure in November 1986 the population further decreased to ca. 2,000 people, mostly fishermen, small shop owners and elderly miners.[38]

In general, former mining communities all over Japan dealt quite differently with the process of de-industrialization. Some turned to agriculture. Most of them tried to attract new industries or services and/or to promote tourism. For many local politicians the past was something to be forgotten the sooner the better in order to tackle the future.[39]

Mining communities in Northern Kyūshū also made great efforts to stem the tide and revitalize their economies, but on the whole it was difficult to find new investors, not least because of the remote locations of many mining sites. In the Chikuhō region only a few towns like Iizuka and Nōgata, which had good transport links to major centers like Fukuoka city or Kitakyūshū, were able to "shrug off the stigma of the associations with the coal industry and develop competitive local industries, generally service-sector orientated".[40] Most other towns and former mining communities were less successful.

The cities of Ōmuta and Arao and the surrounding region fared better, as they had a greater diversity of industries and a port, but in the long run they also lost out to the other industrial areas closer to the central regions of Ōsaka and Tōkyō. A comparative study of the two company towns Ōmuta and Flint (in Michigan) provides a very detailed report on the re-development projects that have been carried out in Ōmuta since the 1970s. According to the report, Ōmuta was at first quite successful in acquiring external funds for various planned projects, but internal disputes, problems with site selection and ownership, and local resistance delayed or prevented several important projects from being implemented. At the same time the lack of innovative approaches also undermined their competitiveness.[41] Therefore, urban re-development in Ōmuta ultimately failed at least until the turn of the millennium.

In the Nishi-Sonogi region in Nagasaki prefecture, Hashima Island remained closed to the public and was abandoned. On Takashima Island several plans to revitalize the economy through tourism, leisure facilities and other amenities carried out by the small shop owners association there also eventually failed.[42] Only recently some parts of the coast there have been transformed into an attractive swimming beach with white sand and palm trees and a campsite nearby. On the homepage advertising this new attraction it says that Takashima was once "famous for a coal mine established in 1869", but is now a "popular hangout for tourists and locals".[43]

To sum up, it can be said that de-industrialization in the mining areas of Northern Kyūshū had severe economic and social repercussions. Attempts by the national government and local officials and institutions to revitalize and redevelop the regions often implied turning away from coal mining. However, few were successful, and the regions continued to struggle with the consequences of the loss of their core industry.

History of regional identity

Any attempt to briefly describe the history of regional identity in the coal mining areas of Northern Kyūshū or Japan as a whole is fraught with difficulty. Conditions for the evolvement of a regional identity in the three regions dealt with here were quite different and have changed over time. In the case of Chikuhō an important question is when Chikuhō was actually perceived as a contiguous region rather than just a name for Japan's largest coal deposits. As there is no explicit study on the regional identity of Chikuhō, one has to use other ways to approach this topic. A survey of the titles of a wide range of publications (books, articles, movies, music) on Chikuhō since the 1890s shows that from the 1890s until 1945 the place name Chikuhō only appears in connection with words related to mining, technology or geology. It is only after the Second World War, starting in 1950, that we find the expressions "region/area of the Chikuhō coal fields" (Chikuhō *tanden chihō*), "Chikuhō region/area" (Chikuhō *chihō*) or "Chikuhō area/belt" (Chikuhō *chitai*) and "Chikuhō zone/area" (Chikuhō *chiku*), not only in connection with coal mining topics but also with new ones like labor or health conditions. In the 1960s the word *chiiki* (region, regional) is increasingly used in phrases like "Chikuhō regional society" (Chikuhō *chiiki shakai*). All this points to a growing perception of Chikuhō as a geographical and social unit. A study on the Chikuhō dialect, which appeared in 1968/9, suggesting that there is also linguistic coherence, and a book on *Folksongs of Chikuhō*, published in 1972, are even stronger indications of this perception. Starting in 1976 a series "Autobiography – Living in Chikuhō", presented individuals and groups from Chikuhō, not from certain towns or mines.[44] The list of examples could be continued to the present, but even this admittedly limited evidence shows that the concept of Chikuhō as a regional denomination survived the end of coal mining. It strongly suggests that after the war and especially in the 1960s Chikuhō had grown together and become an integrated region with which people could identify.

The abovementioned survey also reveals that this regional identity remained closely connected to coal mining and the life in coal mining communities, even after the complete closure of the mines. Nearly all titles until at least the middle of the 1990s are related to coal mining, its decline and the devastating economic and social consequences for the region. Thereafter topics become more diversified, including a growing number of publications on Chikuhō's industrial heritage as part of Japan's modernization. This means that regional identity took shape in a period when its main elements had a negative connotation for many people there.

These negative connotations reinforced an already existing negative image that miners and mining communities had had in Japan for long time. It had its roots in the early decades of industrialization, when mining was a dangerous industry with low pay, and the people working in the mines, many of them belonging to discriminated minorities like Koreans or *burakumin*,[45] were often poor and ignorant. Miners had a very low social status and were regarded as dirty and violent.[46] The famous writer Natsume Sōseki depicted miners in a novel published in 1908 as "a group of uniformly heartless brutes. Education was obviously not to be found among them. When I heard their outsized laughter, I thought to myself: animals. To me they were not human".[47] A few years later a Baroness Ishimoto Shizue, whose husband was working in the coal-mining districts of Northern Kyūshū from 1915 to 1917, described the life of miners under the heading: "Are miners human beings", and had difficulty in giving an affirmative answer.[48] Movies set in mining regions often showed brawls and violent fights between miners, and dwelled on their relationship with brutal labor bosses and *yakuza*-gangs.[49]

As Chikuhō was one of the oldest coal-mining areas in Japan, pre-modern working and living conditions prevailed in the small and medium mines there for a long time, thereby supporting the negative image as a dirty, poverty-stricken place with high rates of crime and violence.[50] Publications like the aforementioned photo book *Chikuhō no kodomotachi* (The Children of Chikuhō) or an extremely popular, award winning TV drama *Seishun no mon* (Gate of Youth) set in Chikuhō[51] were influential in spreading this dark and gloomy picture all over Japan and beyond. According to the activist and author Yoshioka Hirotaka, who is fighting for the preservation of mining heritage in Hokkaidō, the situation in Chikuhō had a strong impact on the dark image of mining and mining regions throughout Japan and greatly influenced the attitude of politicians and local leaders, who often strove to repress this dark aspect of regional identity in their efforts to revive former mining communities.[52]

Discrimination is another factor to be considered when trying to describe the history of regional identity, not only because many miners belonged to discriminated minorities, but also because of the frequent discrimination of all people living in mining communities. Mining communities often had little or no contact with other inhabitants, and there seems to have been deep distrust between the two population groups.[53] The reports on social segregation are corroborated by accounts like that of Idegawa Yasuko, who moved to Chikuhō area with her family and was told by her parents not to play with the 'strange' coalminers' children.[54]

General studies on identity formation have shown that discrimination or perceived discrimination can have a positive effect on the intensity of regional identification.[55] Even though there is little concrete proof, it seems plausible that the frequent discrimination against people from the mining communities might in turn have strengthened their identification with their communities. This assumption is supported by many stories by and about miners that stress the strong cohesion of their close-knit "rough, yet dense communities"[56] and the "legendary warmth"[57] which is said to have prevailed in the communities of the Chikuhō region, despite frequent quarrels and outbreaks of violence which are also described as typical.[58] This local identity with its positive elements must also have contributed to Chikuhō's regional identity.

Evidence on the extent to which inhabitants of Chikuhō de facto identified with their region remains sketchy. The fact that coal mines and agriculture existed side by side in the area, the large influx of migrant workers from all parts of Japan and, last but not least, the displacement of local mine owners by the large *zaibatsu* corporations like Mitsui and Mitsubishi, who took over many mines in the late 1880s and 1890s, all these partly conflicting factors surely left their mark on the evolving regional identity, but there can be no doubt that a regional identity developed in the post-war era.

The situation in the Ōmuta and Sonogi region, on the islands of Hashima and Takashima, is more difficult to grasp. Ōmuta was primarily a company town where the existence of most people depended directly or indirectly on the Mitsui Corporation, which not only owned the mines but also most of the factories and other facilities in the city. Therefore, an emerging regional or local identity would have had to compete against or merge with a corporate identity, which permeated the daily life of most people in the city and its surroundings. An article written in 2002 explicitly links a campaign to preserve the heritage of modernization sites in the area to an attempt to construct a regional identity,[59] but otherwise the term 'regional identity' is rarely mentioned specifically, even though there were NPO activities which pressed for that goal (see as follows).

Takashima and Hashima can also be regarded as company towns, albeit small ones. The slogan "One island – one town – one company"[60] characterizes their special situation under the dominance of the Mitsubishi Corporation. Here, too, corporate identity must have influenced any existing local identity. With regard to Hashima it is often said that due to the lack of space and privacy people there lived like a large family, especially after the war, when labor and living conditions greatly improved. The strong social cohesion is also mentioned in many stories of former inhabitants, who kept contact in a Hashima Association (Hashima-*kai*), after they had to leave the island.[61] But it is difficult to say whether this obviously strong sense of community contributed to a regional identity while people lived on the island.

History of industrial heritage in Japan and the coal mining areas

The first attempts to preserve 'industrial heritage' (*sangyō isan*) and the 'heritage of modernization' (*kindaika isan*) in Japan on a broader scale date back to 1970s. In 1977 the Japan Industrial Archaeology Society (JIAS, Sangyō kōko gakkai) was founded and became a very active member of TICCIH (International Committee for the Preservation of Industrial Heritage). Besides JIAS other organizations like the Architectural Institute of Japan (AIJ, *Nihon kensetsu gakkai*), the Committee on Historical Studies on Civil Engineering (JSCE, *Doboku gakkai dobokushi kenkyū iinkai*) and the Japan Society of Mechanical Engineers (JSME, Nihon kikai gakkai) were also involved in the study of various structures and monuments of Japan's period of modernization, which roughly corresponds to the 100 years between 1850 and 1950. In 1999 JIAS opened a database for industrial heritage sites.[62] Early efforts to preserve these 'modern' structures were often organized by local NPOs and bore fruit mostly on prefectural and municipal levels, whereas the impact on the national level was insignificant. This changed in the 1990s.

Starting in 1990 the government's Agency for Cultural Affairs (Bunka-*chō*) and various committees on the prefectural level began to carry out comprehensive investigations into the heritage of modernization (*kindaika isan*) under their administration. While the term *sangyō isan* is a direct translation of the English words 'industrial heritage', the term *kindaika isan* (heritage of modernization) preferred, e.g. by the Agency for Cultural Affairs and other official institutions, has a much broader meaning and includes industrial, military, public and living and business heritage. The heritage of modernization represents all aspects of Japan's comprehensive modernization after the opening of the country in 1854, including but not limited to industrialization. Both terms are sometimes combined as *kindaika sangyō isan* (heritage of industrial modernization).[63]

In 1993 the heritage of modernization structures became eligible under the national preservation scheme as "Important Cultural Properties" in the category "Buildings" (*kenchiku butsu*),[64] and in 1996 an amendment to the Cultural Property Law supplemented the existing two categories "Important Cultural Properties" and "National Treasures" with a third, the "Registered Cultural Properties", which applied to "items especially in need of preservation and utilisation".[65] This category had lower standards, and emphasized the voluntary protection of the properties by their owners, but offered them advice and support with their maintenance. In this form, it was a chance for many decaying industrial sites to be saved from the wrecking ball by obtaining national recognition, even though they did not (yet) qualify as "Important Cultural Properties". According to the homepage of the Agency of Cultural Affairs there were 9,643 items registered in this category in August 2014.[66]

These developments formed the legal framework within which a number of government campaigns as well as business and private activities were carried out that led to a rapid re-evaluation of industrial heritage throughout the country after the turn of the millennium. This change was mainly driven by government initiatives, led by the Ministry of Economy, Trade and Industry (METI) and the Ministry of Land, Infrastructure, Transport and Tourism (MLIT) to revitalize regions experiencing economic and population decline, programs for the promotion of tourism also from abroad, and emerging plans for a World Cultural Heritage application project that would include different sites in several regions.

Regional identity in the making? 151

First results included, e.g. a tourist guidebook *Kyūshū isan* (Kyushu Heritage) 1847–1955, which was published in 2005 and comprised 101 sites of industrial, military, public and living and business heritage[67] on the island, selected by a group of representatives from public institutions, private companies and NPOs. In 2007 and 2008 the Ministry of Economy, Trade and Industry (METI) recognized a total of 66 constellations as "Heritage of Industrial Modernization"[68] in anticipation of the planned World Heritage application. Industrial tourism (*sangyō kankō*), which combined visits to industrial heritage sites with those to active factories and workshops became a new trend in tourism. Thus, the re-evaluation of Japan's industrial heritage was closely linked to regional redevelopment and revitalization plans and strategies (*chiiki kasseika, machi-zukuri*), which were also designed to strengthen local initiatives. In its initial paragraph the first of the abovementioned reports by the METI stated the ministry's policy, stressing that

> it is very important in a region to link the knowledge about the past with the vital energy that is headed toward the future in order to promote the revitalisation of a region. Therein the process of industrial modernization from the 1850s to the 1950s (*bakumatsu kara Shōwa shoki made*) is of great relevance as a basis for present-day Japan as a Great Country of *monozukuri*[69] and for each region as the root of the present key industries. [. . .] we have assembled this group of heritage of industrial modernisation properties with the aim of strengthening the awareness of the value that these heritage of industrial modernisation properties possess, and to support the revitalisation of the regions, centring around the stories of industrial and regional history.[70]

The preparation of Japan's application to register a large World Heritage Property consisting of a series of 23 sites in 11 cities across eight prefectures, which were mostly concentrated in Northern Kyūshū and the adjacent Yamaguchi prefecture, had a strong impact on many of these developments while at the same time promoting the cause of the heritage of (industrial) modernization in Japan and especially in Kyūshū. The series of sites included proto-industrial and industrial sites: coal mines, shipyards and iron- and steel-producing locations, and combines areas of production, administration and housing with the aim of representing "the unique process of and response to, technology transfer from Western to Eastern Cultures, between 1850 and 1910"[71] which initiated and shaped the first industrialization in a non-Western country. The property was registered in 2015. There can be no doubt that this application and the preceding comprehensive preparations over many years, in so many places and on all political levels, greatly boosted the cause of industrial heritage in Japan.

For the coal mining regions in Northern Kyūshū these developments brought many changes. Among the areas considered to represent 'coal' in the concept underlying the application were the Ōmuta/Arao region, the Chikuhō region and the Sonogi region in Nagasaki (Takashima and Hashima). However, during the preparations for the Kyūshū-Yamaguchi World Heritage application, Chikuhō was dropped from the sites considered for the project for reasons not completely clear, but which included the poor physical conditions of the sites, lack of production-related sites at the Mitsui Tagawa site of the Ita shaft (though winding tower and smoke-stacks are both registered tangible cultural properties), and insufficient preservation of the last remnants of miners' housing.[72] The disappointment in Chikuhō, where in Tagawa, Nōgata and Iizuka a total of ca. 80 sites are registered as industrial and/or modernization heritage, was great and many could not understand why the cradle of Japan's coal mining industry would not be included in the application. But in 2011 Tagawa obtained its own World Heritage, when more than a thousand water color paintings as well as notebooks, diaries and other manuscripts of Yamamoto Sakubei (1892–1984), a former coal miner, were successfully submitted for registration with the UNESCO Memory of the World Program. Yamamoto's paintings and documents, in which he portrayed life and work in the Chikuhō mines in great detail, were the first Japanese item to be registered there.[73]

Among the coal mining regions dealt with here, Ōmuta and its neighboring city, Arao, have probably the largest number of coal-related industrial heritage sites remaining. Even though many structures were demolished since the 1960s, the relics of several mines, railways, port facilities and other buildings still exist. In the Ōmuta and Arao region the whole process of coal production, coal transport and coal export via the port can be observed at the various sites. When the Miike mine closed in 1997, the idea of cultural heritage was no longer a newcomer, but had already started to gain momentum. In the years following the closure of the mine, several sites were registered as important cultural properties or important historical sites. In some cases, however, like e.g. the preservation of the remains of the Manda mine, this happened only after local organizations put up resistance against plans to scrap the structures and persuaded the municipal government to buy the sites.[74] So when the selection committee of the World Heritage project toured the potential sites, the region around the Miike mine, especially the cities of Ōmuta and Arao, were able to present some attractive sites and in the end were successful in joining the application. Among the Ōmuta/Arao industrial heritage sites in the World Heritage project are parts of the Mitsui Miyanohara and Manda mines, the special railway system for transporting coal and other goods to and from the mine, built in 1891, and the port which was opened in 1908 as well as related facilities.

Nagasaki offers a broad range of industrial and modernization heritage sites to visitors. In addition, and in contrast to the Chikuhō and the Ōmuta/Arao regions, the city has an important pre-industrial history as a port, which was open to foreigners from the Netherlands and China during Japan's more than 200 years of seclusion. Thus, Nagasaki's industrial heritage is part of a larger historical context, which presumably also affects the degree of identification with its industrial heritage.

The coal mine on Takashima Island is closely related to this historical context. When Japan opened some of its ports in 1854, Nagasaki became a key port for steam ships to restock their coal supplies and also for coal exports. The coal mine on Takashima Island was developed with the support of the trading company Glover & Co and British technology. Under the supervision of British engineer Samuel John Morris, Takashima became the first mine in Japan to extract coal

Regional identity in the making? 153

from under the sea (43 m depth) by using a shaft, and the first to use a steam engine installed outside the pit in 1869 for hoisting. Steam was also used for drainage and ventilation. The early shaft was abandoned due to flooding in 1876, but the coal production technology used there spread to other mines in Japan. The pithead of the first shaft in Japan, the Hokkei Well shaft, was preserved and was designated a national historic site in 2014. Together with the Western-style residence of Thomas B. Glover in the center of Nagasaki city, it has been given World Heritage site status.

Hashima coal mine is probably the most famous island mine in Japan. When it closed in 1974 and everyone had to leave the island, Mitsubishi took down all landing facilities and prohibited people from entering the island. Most residential buildings and many production structures were left in place. After nearly three decades, Mitsubishi transferred the ownership of the island to the town of Takashima in 2001, and in 2005 all the former coal mining islands in Nagasaki bay became part of Nagasaki city. At the same time, the remaining production facilities on both islands were removed and except for the Hokkei Well shaft virtually no tangible 'industrial heritage' survived. This was quite different in 1987, when the author visited the island with a manager from Mitsubishi, who happened to have been born on Hashima. At that time many parts of the production facilities were still standing on both islands (see Figure 7.5). In the second decade of

Figure 7.5 In 1987, thirteen years after the complete closure of Hashima mine, relicts of the equipment were still left in place: a crane to load and unload ships, a dorr thickener as part of the coal dressing equipment and the relicts of the no. 2 winding tower (middle right). The building in the lower middle housed the flotation machine.

Photo: R. Mathias

the 21st century, with almost no traces of the former mining structures remaining (as shown by pictures on various websites), the full stories of these two heritage sites has to be reconstructed by photographs and the testimonies of former inhabitants who bear witness to the life and work there.

Industrial heritage and regional identity

There is no doubt that the coal mining industry has played the decisive role in shaping the economic and social environment of the communities in coal mining regions and dominated their daily life. But when mining came to an end, the communities had to develop strategies to survive. Due to the dark image of mining, towns and cities often tried to eliminate the stigma of the coal industry by erasing the past and its material witnesses and literally clear the ground for new businesses and institutions, which they hoped to attract. Yoshioka remarks that the slogan: "Let's eradicate the dark past of the mines"[75] was cited widely in former mining communities in Hokkaidō. Many younger local politicians there argued that "[b]ecause mining has a dark image, measures to preserve and make good use of the mining heritage will not be appreciated by the citizens",[76] a statement that Yoshioka and other supporters of preserving the heritage disputed. While the controversy about the mining heritage was conducted much more out in the open in Hokkaidō, Arima Manabu sees a similar attitude in Kyūshū, where "[c]oal became nothing but a memory the local people had to deny and forget as soon as they could".[77]

In Iizuka, one of the three coal cities in Chikuhō, the statue of a miner, which had been erected in front of the train station in 1954 as a symbol of the "bright future of the town", was taken down in 1996 and replaced by a steel monument composed of steel pipes and a large cogwheel, representing modern industries. According to a blog, it happened because "the statue was an inappropriate sight in present times".[78] The statue was re-erected later well away from the center of the city in a park near the Onga river, with a plaque on its pedestal telling the story of the Coal-digging Warrior (*sumi-horu senshi*) monument and its relocation, which was obviously not appreciated by everybody in the city. Another example of the difficulties in preserving the past is the Shime mine winding tower, one of the few Hammerhead winding towers in Japan, constructed in 1943. After the mine closure in 1964, the city council wanted to re-develop the site and negotiated with the owner. While most buildings were demolished, the winding tower survived, because the costs of tearing it down were too high. In 2002 the Japanese Society of Civil Engineers started a campaign for its preservation, joined by other academic societies and by a citizens' movement. It took the city council four years to abandon its original plan to dismantle the winding tower and eventually agree to the preservation of the site in 2006. At this time the national campaign for the World Heritage application was under way and had already led to a re-evaluation of mining heritage, which might well have influenced this decision. In 2007 the winding tower was registered as industrial heritage in the category "registered tangible cultural property", and became a famous landmark for Shime.[79] Since, however, most of the other mining facilities were gone by that time its value as industrial heritage is limited.

These examples show that official policies and company planning often seem to have worked against the emergence of a regional identity connected to the past. However, there were also concepts to preserve the memory of the former mining industry and/or community by collecting historical sources from the mining era or by establishing special museums or parks. Already in the 1970s a Research Centre for Historical Sources on Coal Mining was established at Kyūshū University in Fukuoka city in order to preserve documents and other sources that were on the verge of being destroyed during the wave of mine closures.

In the Chikuhō region Mitsui promoted the establishment of an industrial park and a museum in Tagawa on the grounds of the former Ita mine no.1 shaft, which opened in 1983. Coal museums or centers were also established in the cities of Nōgata and Kurate, the latter becoming the center of a network around the local historian Idegawa Yasuko who aims to present an alternative view on the history of Chikuhō, stressing the human side.[80] But at the same time the landmarks of the mining industry that had dominated the landscape for a century, i.e. winding towers, smokestacks and slag heaps, disappeared. As Arima remarks: "The idea of cultural heritage is a latecomer",[81] and for many industrial sites in the coal mining areas of Northern Kyūshū, which had been shut down in the 1960s and 1970s, it was too late.

However, as we have seen, the situation has gradually changed since the late 1990s and especially after the turn of the millennium. Industrial heritage is increasingly becoming an accepted part of the past, and a re-evaluation of the remaining sites has taken place in the last 15 years especially. A re-appraisal of coal mining in the context of the World Heritage application process triggered or further strengthened local and regional initiatives centering on the region's heritage of (industrial) modernization sites.

In 1996 the internationally known Japanese sculptor and photographer Kawamata Tadashi began a ten-year art project on Chikuhō. The Kawamata coal mine project in Tagawa comprised art events, a (Onga river) boat project and other performances in the region, seminars, lectures, photo exhibitions and movie screenings all over Japan, invitations to foreign artists and contacts to Korea. The project was documented in various publications and focused a great deal of external attention on Chikuhō, while in the region itself it had a mixed reception.[82]

After the turn of the millennium, the three former coal cities – Tagawa, Nōgata and Iizuka – started to re-discover their mining past and integrate it into their official web presentations, obviously catering for tourists. A brochure called "The story of the coal cities in Chikuhō", presented in the web in 2014 praises the Chikuhō mines as pillars of Japan's modernization. "Coal is the pride of our home region Chikuhō. [. . .] Let us be proud that we supported the modernisation of our country and let us relate [this story] to the younger generations".[83] In Tagawa the Tagawa City Coal Mining Historical Museum is at the center of many activities. Its exhibitions showcase the city's coal mining past. As custodian of the Yamamoto Sakubei Collection, it tries to establish relations to other mining museums worldwide in order to put the collection on the map and eventually arrange exhibitions elsewhere. City and Museum also try to raise public awareness by various popular activities promoting the local heritage as part of a regional identity. Publications include picture postcards with motives by Yamamoto Sakubei, and a comic about the Memory of Tagawa for children. As the birthplace of a famous coal miners' song, *Tankō bushi*, which became popular in Japan after the 1930s, Tagawa started in 2006 to celebrate the Tagawa Coal Mine Festival (also called *Tankō bushi matsuri*) in the Coal Memorial Park each November. The program is aimed at tourists and locals alike and can be seen as instrumental in raising awareness and relating the story of the city's industrial heritage. The program of the two-day festival includes *tankō bushi* singing and dancing, kids wrestling, a lottery, traditional folk art and a show by Tagatan, a newly created mascot. Tagatan is a mole in a hard hat, who tells the story of Tagawa's mining past and the Yamamoto Sakubei collection to the audience in Japanese and English.[84] The festival ends with the illumination of the heritage buildings and a firework display, something which is popular at other heritage sites, too. As is common in Japan, regional identity is also represented by special dishes and sweets, which in Tagawa and other former mining areas are related to mining in form, color and name and are bought as souvenirs, e.g. the typical miner's dish *horumon yaki*, a "slagheap curry" or cookies called "memory of coal pits" (see Figure 7.6).[85]

On the whole, there are a rapidly growing number of activities on the regional and local level in Chikuhō using industrial heritage sites or what is left of them to

Figure 7.6 Industrial Heritage Souvenirs. Cookies from Tagawa in Chikuhō in a box with pictures by Yamamoto Sakubei (World Memory Heritage; left) and from Hashima-Gunkanjima (right).

Photo: R. Mathias

distinguish themselves from other regions. As a result, coal mining is increasingly becoming a respectable part of regional identity, but the question is how sustainable this development will be.

For the Ōmuta and Arao region, the World Heritage selection committee that visited potential sites in 2009 had still stated in its report that even though there were important industrial heritage sites related to coal mining, they "were not yet sufficiently linked to a regional identity".[86] As we have seen, the policies of the municipal government and the Mitsui Corporation had not always been supportive in preserving industrial heritage. Many mining facilities, including the Yotsuyama winding tower that had become a landmark of the Miike mine, were torn down shortly before or after the closure. Resistance increasingly came from local groups, which campaigned for the preservation of the mining structures. One example is given by Nagayoshi Mamoru, a member of TICCIH, who was co-founder of a group in which

> some residents, a small number of other citizens and public servants recognised these facilities as part of the region's industrial heritage, but they were few in number at that time. City authorities, many companies and citizens consciously resigned [sic] to get rid of the coal mine.[87]

Participants in this movement felt that "the mining facilities are part of the industrial heritage and identity of the local community".[88] In 2001 they founded the NPO Omuta-Arao Coal Mining Fan Club whose members, numbering approximately 70 to 80 in 2003, actively campaigned for the preservation of industrial heritage sites and community revitalization. Even though this is just one small example and it is not clear how successful the group's efforts were, it nevertheless demonstrates that industrial heritage was increasingly regarded as part of a regional identity. Over the years and not least due to the World Heritage campaign, the municipal government also increased their activities in promoting the industrial heritage. The Coal Industry and Science Museum now coordinates many activities and events related to industrial heritage. In July 2016 there was a celebration to mark the first anniversary of the World Heritage registration at the Miyanohara mine site. One month later the arrival of historical coal trains at their final destination was also turned into a big event.

The situation on the islands of Takashima and Hashima is quite different. Most miners have left the islands, and before Mitsubishi handed both islands over to the city of Nagasaki, production structures were obviously scrapped. Relics directly related to coal mining are scarce, but as both sites represent certain stages in the development of coal mining, namely the first use of Western technology in the Takashima mine and the beginning of successful undersea mining in the Hashima mine, they are closely linked to the national modernization process.

The island of Hashima became a famous spot for so-called dark or ruin tourism in Japan (*haikyo*), and many photographers entered the island illegally. In 2004 a *Gunkan-jima mania* (Gunkanjima craze) started and various tourist agencies began to offer cruises around the island. People from Takashima also attempted to use the neighboring Hashima Island as a resource for tourism. A recent article about Hashima's World Heritage activities contains an interview with a small entrepreneur from Takashima who started an association of Gunkan-jima (Battleship Island) guides in 2004. Two years later he developed plans for tours around Hashima and designed a program which combined a cruise around the island with a virtual tour through the island by using a model of Hashima situated at a place on Takashima, which provided a good view of neighboring Hashima. Until the opening of Hashima for tourists, this was a very successful program, which also integrated local restaurants and other services.[89]

In 2009 Nagasaki city constructed a walkway around the decaying island and opened it for tourists. But visits are limited to guided tours. As there are no production facilities remaining and no museum to present the history of Hashima, the tour guides are very important in relating the story of Hashima to visitors.[90]

In 2001 a former inhabitant of Hashima, who had moved there when he was 12 and lived there for ca. six years, started a website campaigning to make Gunkan-jima a World Heritage site. In 2003 he founded a local association to promote this goal. But at first he found little support from local authorities and from former inhabitants of Hashima.[91] Not until 2006 did Nagasaki city join the Kyushu-Yamaguchi World Heritage application and was officially admitted to the list of sites in 2009.

Kimura concludes that it was the growing interest of people outside of Nagasaki prefecture in the island of Hashima, as well as the implication of national importance linked to the World Heritage application that changed the attitude of the local officials and former inhabitants of the island towards preserving the site.[92]

Summing up, while studies on the development of a regional identity, and the interaction between identity and industrial heritage are still rare as far as Northern Kyūshū is concerned, very recent trends, reflected in the self-representations of former mining communities and regions especially in the worldwide web indicate an increasing tendency to re-evaluate the industrial past and turn it into an asset. When mining declined, regions had tended to dissociate themselves from the former core industry rather than preserve its industrial heritage. At that stage this was at best preserved in coal museums or memorial parks, while the original sites perished. But in the 1990s and especially after the turn of the millennium, the preservation of sites linked to the heritage of (industrial) modernization became an important goal in national and local politics. In this context the preservation and utilization of heritage sites were consciously linked to the revitalization of certain regions and their identity. This development was no doubt accelerated by the preparations for the World Heritage application, which brought many local institutions and people into the game and promoted interest in the industrial heritage. It seems that by placing the heritage of Japan's early industrial development in the context of the national narrative of modernization, which was a dominant topic in Japan's modern historiography encompassing themes like industrialization, urbanization and political and social change, the campaign offered local and regional agents a new perspective on their industrial heritage sites. As this development has started only recently, it is still too early to predict whether the

Regional identity in the making? 159

re-appraisal of the coal-mining heritage will be a sustainable development, and to what extent it will inform regional identity.

Notes

1 See e.g. whc.unesco.org/en/list/1484; and www.japansmeijiindustrialrevolution.com/en (both accessed 22 November 2017).
2 See Bunsaku Aono, *Yubari shichō machi-okoshi funsen ki* [Report of the Desperate Fight of the Mayor of Yubari-city] (Kyōto: PHP Kenkyūsho, 1987); Suzanne Culter, *Managing Decline: Japan's Coal Industry Restructuring and Community Response* (Honolulu: University of Hawai'i Press, 1999); Hirotaka Yoshioka, *Akarui tankō* [Bright Mine] (Ōsaka: Sōgen-sha, 2012).
3 E.g. Mamoru Nagayoshi, Ōmuta, Arao ni okeru kindaika isan hozon ni muketeno shimin undō. Eko myujiumu, bunka kankō, chiiki aidentitī kōchiku e no kokoromi [A Citizens' Movement to Preserve the Heritage of Modernization in Ōmuta and Arao: Attempts to Construct an Eco-Museum, Culture Tourism and a Regional Identity], *Kyūshū Minzokugaku* 2 (2002), 61–70; Kimura Shisei, *Sangyō isan no kioku to hyōshō* [Memory and Representation of Industrial Heritage] (Kyōto: Kyōto daigaku gakujutsu shuppankai, 2014).
4 Erich Pauer, *Japans Industrielle Lehrzeit. Die Bedeutung des Flammofens in der wirtschaftlichen und technischen Entwicklung Japans für den Beginn der industriellen Revolution* [Japan's Industrial Apprenticeship: The Initiative Role of the Reverberatory Furnace in the Economic and Technological Development for the Beginning of the Industrial Revolution], 2 vols. (Bonn: Bonner Zeitschrift für Japanologie 4/1 and 4/2, 1983), here vol. 4/1, 3–6.
5 One example is the construction of 11 reverberatory furnaces, which were needed to cast large iron cannons in order to defend the coastline. Even though only a few of these foundries were actually successful, people taking part in these projects profited greatly from what they learned about raw materials, operational procedures and sequence of work. And the fact that some foundries actually did work successfully shows that the level of knowledge of technical procedures was already quite high (see Pauer, *Japan's Industrielle Lehrzeit*, passim). The last remaining reverberatory furnaces in Niirayama (Shizuoka prefecture) and Hagi (Yamaguchi prefecture) became World Heritage sites in 2015.
6 The names in Japanese are Keihin, Chūkyō, Hanshin and Kitakyūshū industrial zones.
7 For a more detailed description of the development of coal mining in Northern Kyūshū, see e.g. Regine Mathias, *Industrialisierung und Lohnarbeit. Der Kohlebergbau in Nord-Kyūshū und sein Einfluß auf die Herausbildung einer Lohnarbeiterschaft* [Industrialization and Wage Labor: Coal Mining in Northern Kyūshū and Its Influence on the Emergence of Wage Labor] (Wien: Beiträge zur Japanologie 15, 1978); Erich Pauer, ed., *Schwarzes Gold in Japan. Beiträge zur Geschichte der japanischen Steinkohlenindustrie* [Black Gold in Japan. Contributions to the History of the Coal Industry in Japan] (Marburg: Marburger Japan-Reihe 4, 1991); Matthew Allen, *Undermining the Japanese Miracle: Work and Conflict in a Coalmining Community* (Cambridge: Cambridge University Press, 1994).
8 The place name 'Chikuhō' itself combines two Chinese characters, which were borrowed from two traditional regional names. See Toshio Nagasue, *Chikuhō. Sekitan no chiiki shi* [Chikuhō: The Regional History of Coal] (Tōkyō: Nihon hōso shuppan kyōkai, 1973), 9.
9 Chikuhō sekitan kōgyō shi nenpyō hensan iinkai, ed., *Chikuhō sekitan kōgyō shi nenpyō* [Chronology of the History of Coal Mining in Chikuhō] (Fukuoka: Nishi Nihon bunka kyōkai, 1973), 580; Toshifumi Yada, *Sengo Nihon no sekitan sangyō* [The Coal Industry in Postwar Japan] (Tōkyō: Shinhyōron-sha, 1975), 76, table 2–20.

10 Nagasue, *Chikuhō*, 242.
11 Asahi Shinbun Miike sōgi [The Miike Strike], February 18, 1997, nishi bu, 29.
12 There are numerous publications on Miike. A short but comprehensive overview of the history of the mine is Yukihide Kōzuma, *Miike tankō shi* [The History of the Miike Mine] (Tōkyō: Kyōiku-sha, 1980).
13 Mitsubishi kōgyō semento k.k. Takashima tankō shi hensan iinkai, ed., *Takashima tankō shi* [The History of the Takashima Mine] (Tōkyō: Mitsubishi kōgyō semento k.k., 1989), 5–6; John McMaster, The Takashima Mine: British Capital and Japanese Industrialization, *Business History Review* 38, 3 (1963), 215–239.
14 Mitsubishi, *Takashima tankō shi*, 492.
15 Mitsubishi, *Takashima tankō shi*, 445, 492.
16 William W. Lockwood, *The Economic Development of Japan: Growth and Structural Change 1868–1938* (Princeton: Princeton University Press, 1954), 22.
17 Chikuhō sekitan kōgyō shi, *Nenpyō*, 298.
18 Tagawa-shi shi hensan iinkai, ed., *Tagawa-shi shi* [The History of Tagawa City], vol. 2 (Tagawa: Tagawa-shi yakusho, 1976), 265–266, tables 6, 7.
19 Tagawa-shi shi hensan iinkai, ed., *Tagawa-shi shi*, 267, table 8.
20 *Ōmuta-shi jinkō bijion* [Vision of the Population Development of Ōmuta City], www.city.omuta.lg.jp/common/UploadFileDsp.aspx?c_id=5&id=7896&sub_id=1&flid=20652 [5_7896_20652_up_UCG60DD3.pdf], (accessed Aug. 20, 2016), 1.
21 Keinosuke Gotoh and Doutoku Sakamoto, *Gunkanjima no isan. Fūka suru kindai Nihon no shōchō* [The Heritage of Gunkanjima: A Weathered Symbol of Modern Japan] (Nagasaki: Nagasaki shinbun-sha, 2010), passim (see Figure 7.2).
22 Coal Mining Special Measures (Sekitan kōgyō gōrika rinji setchi hō) see Richard J. Samuels, *The Business of the Japanese State: Energy Markets in Comparative and Historical Perspective* (Ithaca and London: Cornell University Press, 1987), 109.
23 For a detailed description of the energy revolution and its consequences, see Laura E. Hein, *Fuelling Growth: The Energy Revolution and Economic Policy in Postwar Japan* (Cambridge: Council on East Asian Studies, Harvard University, 1990); Culter, *Managing Decline*.
24 Nagasue, *Chikuhō*, 207
25 Chikuhō sekitan kōgyō shi, *Nenpyō*, 551.
26 Yoshihiro Ogino, Sengo Nihon no sekitan seisaku no tenkai katei to kaigai no yunyū, kaihatsu mondai [The Development of the Japanese Coal Policy and the Problems in Importing Coal and Developing Overseas Deposits after the War], in *Ajia no sekitan mondai to Nihon no sekitan seisan ni kansuru sōgōteki kentō*, unpublished report of the Kyūshū daigaku sekitan kenkyū shiryō sentaa (Fukuoka: Kyūshū University, 1999), 14.
27 Nagasue, *Chikuhō*, 225.
28 Nagasue, *Chikuhō*, 240.
29 Manabu Arima, Thoughts on Yamamoto Sakubei's Coalmine Paintings: Modernization That Disappeared and UNESCO Memory of the World, www.japanpolicyforum.jp/archives/culture/pt20111124141258.html (accessed Aug. 22, 2016).
30 Manabu Arima, Thoughts on Yamamoto Sakubei's Coalmine Paintings.
31 Nagasue, *Chikuhō*, 240; Benjamin Martin, Japanese Mining Labor: The Miike Strike, *Far Eastern Survey* 30, 2 (Feb. 1961), 26.
32 Ken Domon, *Shashin shū Chikuhō no kodomotachi* [Photo Collection: The Children of Chikuhō] (Tōkyō: Patoria shoten, 1960).
33 In Japanese: *Saakuru mura*, published 1958 to 1960. For the activities, see e.g. Mayumi Mizutamari, *'Sākuru mura' to Morisaki Kazue. Kōryū to rentai no bijion* [Circle Village and Morisaki Kazue: A Vision of Exchange and Solidarity] (Kyōto: Nakanishiya, 2013).
34 The Taishō mine struggle in Nakama-city occurred in 1960, when the mine tried to reduce the workforce. It was one of the larger strikes in Chikuhō and mobilized several unions and external supporters like Ueno Eishin. See also Naomasa Tanaka, *Taishō*

kōgyō shimatsu ki. Rō-shi tairitsu no higeki [Report on the Management of the Taishō Mining Corporation: The Tragedy of the Antagonism between Labor and Capital] (Fukuoka: Taishō kōgyō seisan jimusho, 1965).
35 There are numerous publications on the Great Strike, including personal reports of individual miners, reports and a collection of historical sources concerning the strike, published by Mitsui company, comprising more than 1.100 pages.
36 That is the English version of the film *Miike – owaranai yama no monogatari*, www.japantimes.co.jp/news/2011/08/14/national/history/film-mines-rich-seams-of-history/#.WLk3VRh_Wqg (accessed Mar. 3, 2017).
37 *Ōmuta-shi jinkō bijion*, 1.
38 Jun Nishihara, *Tankō chiiki shakai to tankō heizan ato no jinkō genshō purosesu* [The Society in a Mining Region and the Process of Demographic Decline after Mine Closure], in *Tankō heizan no shima kara mananda koto. Nagasaki-ken Takashima ni okeru gakusaiteki chiiki kenkyū no kokoromi* [What We Learned from an Island Where the Mine Was Shut Down: An Attempt of Interdisciplinary Regional Studies in Takashima, Nagasaki Prefecture], ed. Takashima machi chiiki hoken kenkyū kai (Nagasaki: Takashima machi, 1991), 86.
39 The most extreme turn from coal to a completely new endeavor was the founding of a "Hawaiian Center" in the former Joban mining area in Fukushima prefecture in Northern Honshū, with a famous dance group of local "Hawaiian girls". Later renamed "Spa Resort Hawaiians" the resort attracted more than 1.5 million visitors in peak years until it was affected by the triple catastrophe of the Tōhoku earthquake, tsunami and meltdown of the Fukushima nuclear reactor in March 2011.
40 Allen, *Undermining the Japanese Miracle*, 15.
41 Theodore J. Gilman, *No Miracles Here: Fighting Urban Decline in Japan and the United States,* (Albany: State University of New York Press, 2001), 47–56, especially 55–56.
42 It was obviously difficult to attract companies to Takashima, not least due to the remote geographical situation of the island, which caused high transportation costs to and from the island; see Yuji Yamamoto, Takashima tankō shakai ni miru "tankō bunka" to "inshu izonsei" ["Coal Culture" and "Alcohol Addiction" in the Takashima Coal-miners' Society], in Takashima machi, ed., *Tankō heizan no shima*, 23–24.
43 Nagasaki Official Visitor Guide, http://visit-nagasaki.com/spots/detail/659 (accessed Mar. 2, 2017).
44 This rather preliminary survey by the author is based on 1024 titles of publications on Chikuhō listed in the catalogue of Japan's National Library of Congress, covering the years 1892 to 2015.
45 *Burakumin* are an outcast group of Japanese origin, who faced (and still face) severe discrimination.
46 Mathias, *Industrialisierung und Lohnarbeit*, 200–204.
47 Sōseki Natsume, *The Miner*, English Translation by Jay Rubin (Stanford: Stanford University Press, 1988), 84.
48 Shidzue Ishimoto, *Facing Two Ways* (New York: Farrar and Rinehart, 1935), 167–169.
49 Masazumi Sakaki, Geki eiga ni tōjō suru tankō rōdō [Coal Mining Work as Represented in Narrative Films], *Energii shi kenkyū* 27 (2012), passim.
50 This is shown by the study of Allen, *Undermining the Japanese Miracle*, passim, who did field work there in the late 1980s and early 1990s and still encountered such stories.
51 *Seishun no mon* (Gate of Youth), based on a story by Itsuki Hiroyuki about a young man who was born and spent his youth in Chikuhō, later making a career in Tokyo. The novel was originally serialized in the weekly magazine *Shukan Gendai* in 1969–70. The same story was made into a movie twice, in 1975 and 1981, and inspired three separate television productions in 1976–77 (TBS), 1991 (TV Tokyo) and 2005 (TBS).
52 Yoshioka, *Akarui tankō*, 184–199.
53 Nagasue, *Chikuhō*, 13.

54 Interview in Allen, *Undermining the Japanese Miracle*, 51.
55 Kurt Mühler and Karl-Dieter Opp, Ursachen für die Identifikation von Bürgern mit ihrer Region und Wirkungen auf ihr individuelles Handeln [Causes for the Identification of Citizens with their Region and the Effects on their Individual Actions], Abschlußbericht Symposium "Regionale Identität" St. Marienthal, April 16–18. www.kulturregionen.org/2008-04_symposium.html (accessed Jun. 3, 2016), 10–11.
56 Arima, Thoughts on Yamamoto Sakubei's Coalmine Paintings, 3.
57 Allen, *Undermining the Japanese Miracle*, 29.
58 Allen, *Undermining the Japanese Miracle*, 106–123.
59 Nagayoshi, Ōmuta, Arao ni okeru kindaika isan hozon, passim.
60 Kōichi Miyairi, Tankō heizan to chiiki keizai, jichitai zaisei [Mine Closure and the Regional Economy and Local Finance Policy], in *Tankō heizan no shima*, ed. Takashima machi, 101.
61 Gotoh and Sakamoto, *Gunkanjima no isan*, 146–150.
62 Toshiyuki Morishima, Kindaika sangyō isan no hozon to katsuyō ni kansuru seisakuteki taiō no hikaku [Comparing Policy Responses for the Conservation and Utilization of the Heritage of Industrial Modernization], *E-journal GEO*, 9, no. 2 (2014), (accessed Febr. 14, 2016), 102.
63 Morishima, Kindaika sangyō isan no hozon, shows in detail the difference and often arbitrariness of contents construction concerning the three categories *sangyō isan*, *kindaika isan* and *kindaika sanygō isan*.
64 Ministry of Economy, Trade and Industry (METI), ed., *Sangyō isan wo katsuyō shita kōiki renkei oyobi tayōna shutai no renkei ni yoru chiiki kasseika hōsaku ni kansuru chōsa (Sangyō isan wo katsuka shita chiiki kasseika e no minkan katsuryoku donyū ni kansuru chōsa hōkokusho)* [Investigation Concerning Regional Revitalization Strategies by Regional Cooperation and Cooperation of Various Entities by Making Use of the Industrial Heritage: Report on the Investigation Concerning the Involvement of Private (Sector) Activities in the Regional Revitalization by Making Use of the Industrial Heritage], 2010, www.mlit.go.jp/common/000131035.pdf. (accessed Feb. 15, 2016), 2.
65 Agency of Cultural Affairs (Bunka-chō), ed., *Cultural Properties for the Future Generations*, (Tokyo, 2015), www.bunka.go.jp/tokei_hakusho_shuppan/shuppanbutsu/bunkazai-pamphlet/pdf/pamphlet_en_03_ver04.pdf) (accessed Aug. 14, 2016), 3.
66 Agency of Cultural Affairs (Bunka-chō), ed., *Cultural Properties*, 2.
67 Kōki Sunada et al., eds., *Kyūshū isan. Kin- gendai isan hen 101* [Kyushu Heritage 1847–1955. 101 Heritage Sites of Modern and Present Japan] (Fukuoka: Gen shobō, 2015).
68 Ministry of Economy, Trade and Industry (METI), ed., *Kindaika sangyō isan gun 33* [33 Heritage Constellations of Industrial Modernization], vols. 1 and 2, 2007 and 2008, www.meti.go.jp/policy/local_economy/nipponsaikoh/pdf/isangun.pdf (accessed Jan. 21, 2016).
69 *Monozukuri* is difficult to translate. It literally means "making or creating things". The term became popular in the late1990s, implicating a re-evaluation of the process of manufacturing goods. It implies a positive connotation of the "art, science and craft of making things" (Fujimoto Takahiro) or "having the spirit of producing excellent products and the ability to constantly improve a production system and – process," (JETRO).
70 Ministry of Economy, Trade and Industry (METI), ed., *Kindaika sangyō isan gun 33* [33 Heritage Constellations of Industrial Modernization], vol. 1, 2007, www.meti.go.jp/policy/local_economy/nipponsaikoh/pdf/isangun.pdf (accessed Jan. 21, 2016), 1.
71 An English description of the whole project can be found e.g. in Emergence of Industrial Japan: Kyushu, Yamaguchi (Application report Oct. 22, 2009) http://apjjf.org/data/4332-kyuyama.pdf (accessed Nov. 14, 2015) and on the official homepage of the World Heritage Property, www.japansmeijiindustrialrevolution.com/en/. The

ICOMOS evaluation report on this application is published in *ICOMOS Report for the World Heritage Committee, 39th ordinary* session, Bonn, June-July 2015, http://whc.unesco.org/archive/2015/whc15-39com-inf8B1-en.pdf (accessed. Dec. 17, 2015), 88–102.
72 Arima, Thoughts on Yamamoto Sakubei's Coalmine Paintings, 2–3.
73 Yamamoto Sakubei, *Chikuhō tankō emaki* [Picture Scroll of the Chikuhō Coal Mines] (Fukuoka: Ashi shobo, 1973).
74 Asahi Shinbun, *Kyū Manda kō, itten hozon e* [The Old Manda Mine Will be Preserved], Mar. 1, 1997.
75 *Tankō no kurai kakō o fusshoku suru*, Yoshioka, *Akarui tankō*, 184.
76 Yoshioka, *Akarui tankō*,185.
77 Arima, Thoughts on Yamamoto Sakubei's Coalmine Paintings, 3.
78 Nōgata-shi no kōfu zō (Blog) [The Statue of a Coal Miner in Nōgata City] http://hasiru.net/~maekawa/mine/nogata/nogata.html
79 Kyūshū sangyō kōkogakkai, ed., *Fukuoka no kindaika isan* [The Industrial Heritage of Fukuoka Prefecture] (Fukuoka: Genshobō, 2008), 114–122.
80 Allen, *Undermining the Japanese Miracle*, 38–45.
81 Arima, Thoughts on Yamamoto Sakubei's Coalmine Paintings, 4.
82 One publication in English is Tadashi Kawamata, *Coalmine Project, 1996–2006* (Tokyo: Meguro Museum of Art, 2009). It was published in association with Art Insatsu, Hokkaidō on the occasion of an exhibition titled *Tadashi Kawamata's Coal Mine Project: Its Development in Chikuho, Sorachi and Ruhr*.
83 Iizuka kankō kyōkai, ed., *Chikuhō tanto monogatari* [The Story of the Coal Cities in Chikuhō] (2014.10), www.kankou-iizuka.jp/public/chikuhotantomonogatari.pdf (accessed Feb. 25, 2017).
84 Tagatan has a fan club. His image is on bags, T-shirts and other merchandise. He not only acts on the stage during the coal-mine festival, but also visits homes for the elderly and other places. A special "Taga-Tango" song tells the story of the industrial heritage in Tagawa. See e.g. http://charazoo.com/TAGATAN.
85 These local specialities are listed in the internet *Tagawa City Guide Book* (Tagawa city office n.d.).
86 METI, *Sangyō isan wo katsuyō shita kōiki renkei*, 74.
87 The word "resigned" in the English text is not clear. The respective word in the Japanese version of the same text is *shikō*, which means to intend to, to aspire to. Mamoru Nagayoshi, NPO Activities towards Revitalisation and Heritage Preservation in the Miike Coal Mining Community, *6th International Mining History Congress in Japan 2003.9.26–29*, 2.
88 Nagayoshi, NPO Activities, 3.
89 Shisei Kimura, Sangyō isan no hyōshō to chiiki shakai no henyō [The Representation of Industrial Heritage and the Transformation of the Regional Society], *Shakaigaku hyōron* 60, 3 (2009): 425–426.
90 Kimura, Sangyō isan no hyōshō, 423.
91 Kimura, Sangyō isan no hyōshō, 423–425; see also Gotoh and Sakamoto, *Gunkanjima no isan*, passim.
92 Kimura, Sangyō isan no hyōshō, 424.

Bibliography

Agency of Cultural Affairs (Bunka-cho), ed., *Cultural Properties for the FutureGenerations* (Tokyo, 2015). www.bunka.go.jp/tokei_hakusho_shuppan/shuppanbutsu/bunkazai-pamphlet/pdf/pamphlet_en_03_ver04.pdf (accessed Aug. 14, 2016).
Allen, Matthew, *Undermining the Japanese Miracle: Work and Conflict in a Coalmining Community* (Cambridge: Cambridge University Press, 1994).

Aono Bunsaku, *Yubari shichō machi-okoshi funsen ki* [Report of the Desperate Fight of the Mayor of Yubari-city] (Kyōto: PHP Kenkyūsho, 1987).
Arima Manabu, Thoughts on Yamamoto Sakubei's Coalmine Paintings: Modernization That Disappeared and UNESCO Memory of the World, www.japanpolicyforum.jp/archives/culture/pt20111124141258.html (accessed Aug. 22, 2016); English translation of the Japanese article Yamamoto Sakubei tankōga wo megutte. Shōmetsu shita 'kindaika' to sekai kioku isan, *Chūō kōron* 9 (2011): 212–221.
Asahi Shinbun. Kyū Manda kō, itten hozon e [The Old Manda Mine Will be Preserved], Mar. 1, 1997.
———. Miike sōgi [The Miike Strike], Feb. 18, 1997, nishi bu, 29.
Chikuhō sekitan kōgyō shi nenpyō hensan iinkai, ed., *Chikuhō sekitan kōgyō shi nenpyō* [Chronology of the History of Coal Mining in Chikuhō] (Fukuoka: Nishi Nihon bunka kyōkai, 1973).
Culter, Suzanne, *Managing Decline: Japan's Coal Industry Restructuring and Community Response* (Honululu: University of Hawai'i Press, 1999).
Domon Ken, *Shashin shū Chikuhō no kodomotachi* [Photo Collection: The Children of Chikuhō] (Tōkyō: Patoria shoten, 1960).
Emergence of Industrial Japan: Kyushu, Yamaguchi (World Heritage Application Report Oct. 22, 2009) http://apjjf.org/data/4332-kyuyama.pdf (accessed Nov. 14, 2015).
Gilman, Theodore J., *No Miracles Here: Fighting Urban Decline in Japan and the United States* (Albany: State University of New York Press, 2001).
Gotoh Keinosuke; Sakamoto Doutoku, *Gunkanjima no isan. Fūka suru kindai Nihon no shōchō* [The Heritage of Gunkanjima: A Weathered Symbol of Modern Japan] (Nagasaki: Nagasaki shinbun-sha, 2010).
Hein, Laura E., *Fuelling Growth: The Energy Revolution and Economic Policy in Postwar Japan* (Cambridge: Council on East Asian Studies, Harvard University, 1990).
ICOMOS, ed., *ICOMOS Report for the World Heritage Committee, 39th Ordinary Session, Bonn, June–July 2015*, http://whc.unesco.org/archive/2015/whc15-39com-inf8B1-en.pdf (accessed Dec. 17, 2015), 88–102.
Iizuka kankō kyōkai, ed., *Chikuhō tanto monogatari* [The Story of the Coal Cities in Chikuhō] (2014.10), www.kankou-iizuka.jp/public/chikuhotantomonogatari.pdf (accessed Feb. 25, 2017).
Ishimoto Shidzue, *Facing Two Ways* (New York: Farrar and Rinehart, 1935).
Kawamata Tadashi, *Coalmine Project, 1996–2006* (Tokyo: Meguro Museum of Art, 2009).
Kimura Shisei, Sangyō isan no hyōshō to chiiki shakai no henyō [The Representation of Industrial Heritage and the Transformation of the Regional Society], *Shakaigaku hyōron* 60, 3 (2009): 415–432.
Kimura Shisei, *Sangyō isan no kioku to hyōshō* [Memory and Representation of Industrial Heritage] (Kyōto: Kyōto Daigaku Gakujutsu Shuppankai, 2014).
Kōzuma Yukihide, *Miike tankō shi* [The History of the Miike Mine] (Tōkyō: Kyōiku-sha, 1980).
Kyūshū sangyō kōkogakkai, ed., *Fukuoka no kindaika isan* [The Industrial Heritage of Fukuoka Prefecture] (Fukuoka: Genshobō, 2008).
Lockwood, William W., *The Economic Development of Japan: Growth and Structural Change, 1868–1938* (Princeton: Princeton University Press, 1968).
Martin, Benjamin, Japanese Mining Labor: The Miike Strike, *Far Eastern Survey* 30, 2 (Feb. 1961): 26–30.
Mathias, Regine, *Industrialisierung und Lohnarbeit. Der Kohlebergbau in Nord-Kyūshū und sein Einfluß auf die Herausbildung einer Lohnarbeiterschaft* [Industrialization and

Wage Labor: Coal Mining in Northern Kyūshū and Its Influence on the Emergence of Wage Labor] (Wien [Beiträge zur Japanologie 15], Institut für Japanologie, 1978).

McMaster, John, The Takashima Mine: British Capital and Japanese Industrialization, *Business History Review* 38, 3 (1963): 215–239.

Ministry of Economy, Trade and Industry (METI), ed., *Kindaika sangyō isan gun 33* [33 Heritage Constellations of Industrial Modernization], vols. 1 and 2, 2007 and 2008, www.meti.go.jp/policy/local_economy/nipponsaikoh/pdf/isangun.pdf (accessed Jan. 21, 2016).

Ministry of Economy, Trade and Industry (METI), ed., *Sangyō isan wo katsuyō shita kōiki renkei oyobi tayōna shutai no renkei ni yoru chiiki kasseika hōsaku ni kansuru chōsa (Sangyō isan wo katsuka shita chiiki kasseika e no minkan katsuryoku donyū ni kansuru chōsa hōkokusho)* [Investigation Concerning Regional Revitalization Strategies by Regional Cooperation and Cooperation of Various Entities by Making Use of the Industrial Heritage: Report on the Investigation Concerning the Involvement of Private (Sector) Activities in the Regional Revitalization by Making Use of the Industrial Heritage], 2010, www.mlit.go.jp/common/000131035.pdf (accessed Feb. 15, 2016).

Mitsubishi kōgyō semento k.k. Takashima tankō shi hensan iinkai, ed., *Takashima tankō shi* [The History of the Takashima Mine] (Tōkyō: Mitsubishi kōgyō semento k.k., 1989).

Miyairi Kōichi, Tankō heizan to chiiki keizai, jichitai zaisei [Mine Closure and the Regional Economy and Local Finance Policy], in *Tankō heizan no shima, Tankō heizan no shima kara mananda koto. Nagasaki-ken Takashima ni okeru gakusaiteki chiiki kenkyū no kokoromi* [What We Learned from an Island Where the Mine Was Shut Down: An Attempt of Interdisciplinary Regional Studies in Takashima, Nagasaki Prefecture], ed. Takashima machi chiiki hoken kenkyû kai (Nagasaki: Takashima machi, 1991), 101–138.

Mizutamari Mayumi, *'Sākuru mura' to Morisaki Kazue. Kōryū to rentai no bijion* [The Circle Village and Morisaki Kazue: A Vision of Exchange and Solidarity] (Kyōto: Nakanishiya, 2013).

Morishima Toshiyuki, Kindaika sangyō isan no hozon to katsuyō ni kansuru seisakuteki taiō no hikaku [Comparing Policy Responses for the Conservation and Utilization of the Heritage of Industrial Modernization], *E-Journal GEO* 9, 2 (2014), 102–117 (accessed Jan. 14, 2016).

Mühler, Kurt; Opp, Karl-Dieter, Ursachen für die Identifikation von Bürgern mit ihrer Region und Wirkungen auf ihr individuelles Handeln [Causes for the Identification of Citizens with Their Region and the Effects on Their Individual Actions], *Abschlußbericht Symposium "Regionale Identität" St. Marienthal 4.16–18*. www.kulturregionen.org/2008-04_symposium.html, (accessed Jun. 3, 2016).

Nagasaki Official Visitor Guide, http://visit-nagasaki.com/spots/detail/659 (accessed Feb. 3, 2017).

Nagasue Toshio, *Chikuhō. Sekitan no chiiki shi* (Chikuhō: The Regional History of Coal) (Tōkyō: Nihon hōsō shuppan kyōkai, 1973).

Nagayoshi Mamoru, NPO Activities towards Revitalisation and Heritage Preservation in the Miike Coal Mining Community, *Proceedings: The 6th International Mining History Congress in Japan 2003.9.26–29*, (Akabira, The 6th International Mining History Congress, 2003)286–289.

Nagayoshi Mamoru, Ōmuta, Arao ni okeru kindaika isan hozon ni mukete no shimin undō. Eko myujiumu, bunka kankō, chiiki aidentitī kōchiku e no kokoromi [A Citizens' Movement to Preserve the Heritage of Modernization in Ōmuta and Arao: Attempts to

Construct an Eco-Museum, Culture Tourism, and a Regional Identity], *Kyūshū Minzokugaku* 2 (2002), 61–70.
Natsume Sōseki, *The Miner*, English Translation by Jay Rubin (Stanford: Stanford University Press, 1988), Original published as *Kōfu* in 1908.
Nishihara Jun, Tankō chiiki shakai to tankō heizan ato no jinkō genshō purosesu [The Society in a Mining Region and the Process of Demographic Decline after Mine Closure], in *Tankō heizan no shima kara mananda koto. Nagasaki-ken Takashima ni okeru gakusaiteki chiiki kenkyū no kokoromi* [What We Learned from an Island Where the Mine Was Shut Down: An Attempt of Interdisciplinary Regional Studies in Takashima, Nagasaki Prefecture], ed. Takashima machi chiiki hoken kenkyû kai (Nagasaki: Takashima machi, 1991), 75–101.
Nōgata-shi no kōfu zō (Blog) [The Statue of a Coal Miner in Nōgata City], http://hasiru.net/~maekawa/mine/nogata/nogata.html (accessed Mar. 2, 2017).
Ogino Yoshihiro, Sengo Nihon no sekitan seisaku no tenkai katei to kaigai no yunyū, kaihatsu mondai [The Development of the Japanese Coal Policy and the Problems in Importing Coal and Developing Overseas Deposits after the War], in *Ajia no sekitan mondai to Nihon no sekitan seisan ni kansuru sōgōteki kentō*, ed. Sekitan kenkyū shiryō sentaa (Fukuoka: Sekitan kenkyū shiryō sentaa,1999), 4–37.
Ōmuta-shi jinkō bijion [Vision of the Population Development of Ōmuta City], www.city.omuta.lg.jp/common/UploadFileDsp.aspx?c_id=5&id=7896&sub_id=1&flid=20652 [5_7896_20652_up_UCG60DD3.pdf], (accessed Sept. 9, 2016).
Pauer, Erich, *Japans Industrielle Lehrzeit. Die Bedeutung des Flammofens in der wirtschaftlichen und technischen Entwicklung Japans für den Beginn der industriellen Revolution* [Japan's Industrial Apprenticeship: The Initiative Role of the Reverberatory Furnace in the Economic and Technological Development for the Beginning of the Industrial Revolution], 2 vols. (Bonn: Bonner Zeitschrift für Japanologie, 4/1 and 4/2, 1983).
Pauer, Erich, ed., *Schwarzes Gold in Japan. Beiträge zur Geschichte der japanischen Steinkohlenindustrie* [Black Gold in Japan: Contributions to the History of the Coal Industry in Japan] (Marburg: Marburger Japan-Reihe, 4, 1991).
Sakaki Masazumi (2012), Geki eiga ni tōjō suru tankō rōdō [Coal Mining Work as Represented in Narrative Films], *Energī shi kenkyū* 27 (2012): 41–48.
Samuels, Richard J., *The Business of the Japanese State: Energy Markets in Comparative and Historical Perspective* (Ithaca and London: Cornell University Press, 1987).
Sunada Kōki ed., *Kyūshū isan. Kin- gendai isan hen 101* [Kyūshū Heritage 1847–1955.101 Heritage Sites of Modern and Present Japan] (Fukuoka: Gen shobō, 2005).
Tagawa-shi shi hensan iinkai, ed., *Tagawa-shi shi* [The History of Tagawa City], vol. 2 (*chū kan*), (Tagawa: Tagawa-shi yakusho, 1976).
Takashima machi chiiki hoken kenkyû kai, ed., *Tankō heizan no shima kara mananda koto. Nagasaki-ken Takashima ni okeru gakusaiteki chiiki kenkyū no kokoromi* [What We Learned from an Island Where the Mine Was Shut Down: An Attempt of Interdisciplinary Regional Studies in Takashima, Nagasaki Prefecture] (Nagasaki: Takashima machi, 1991).
Tanaka Naomasa, *Taishō kōgyō shimatsu ki. Rō-shi tairitsu no higeki* [Report on the Taishō Mining Organization: The Tragedy of the Antagonism between Labor and Capital] (Fukuoka: Taishō kōgyō seisan jimusho, 1965).
Yada Toshifumi, *Sengo Nihon no sekitan sangyō* [The Coal Industry in Postwar Japan] (Tōkyō: Shinhyōron, 1975).
Yamamoto Sakubei, *Chikuhō tankō emaki* [Picture Scroll of the Chikuhō Coal Mines] (Fukuoka: Ashi shobo, 1973).

Yamamoto Yuji, Takashima tankō shakai ni miru "tankō bunka" to "inshu izonsei" izonsei' ["Mine Culture" and "Alcohol Addiction" in the Takashima Coal-Miners' Society], in *Tankō heizan no shima kara mananda koto. Nagasaki-ken Takashima ni okeru gakusaiteki chiiki kenkyū no kokoromi* [What We Learned from an Island Where the Mine Was Shut Down: An Attempt of Interdisciplinary Regional Studies in Takashima, Nagasaki prefecture], ed. Takashima machi chiiki hoken kenkyû kai (Nagasaki: Takashima machi, 1991), 19–74.

Yoshioka Hirotaka, *Akarui tankō* [Bright Mine] (Ōsaka: Sōgensha, 2012).

8 "There needs to be something there for people to remember"

Industrial heritage in Newcastle and the Hunter Valley, Australia

Erik Eklund

Newcastle is located on the east coast of Australia in the state of New South Wales (NSW). Coal mining began in the early 19th century, and from the 1850s encouraged the development of pit-top towns gathered around an increasingly busy river port. Coal mining shifted west into the Hunter Valley where there are still vast amounts of open pit coal production. Mining also encouraged industrial development in engineering, transport and, from 1915, iron and steel production. Deindustrialization in Newcastle dates from the mid-1970s and plant closures accelerated in the 1980s and 1990s as the steel works and other related manufacturing industries closed down.

Thereafter the region experienced a steady decline in mining and industrial activity, although coal mining in the Hunter Valley boomed again after 2001. The most important industrial site in New South Wales, the Broken Hill Propriety Ltd's (BHP) iron and steelworks in Newcastle, is now a barren and featureless scar on a remnant cultural landscape, while a determined heritage group with limited recognition and resources attempts to preserve the tangible and intangible heritage of that workplace, which produced steel from 1915 to 1999. As the steelworks example suggests, industrial heritage developed an uneasy and ambivalent relationship to regional identity. During the deindustrializing phase this ambivalence was only magnified. Some cultural projects and representations celebrated the region's industrial age and its legacies, while others sought to carve out a new post-industrial niche for the city that distanced regional identity from its industrial origins.[1] The return of large-scale coal mining was a further confounding factor. It was not clear whether Newcastle was a post-industrial city looking to remake its industrial age image, or a re-industrializing site that was returning to dependence on coal mining revenue and employment. We shall explore the relationship between industrial heritage and regional identity in this complicated environment. Suffice to say that the old industrial and manufacturing base was declining, like many regions in the west, yet unlike most others a dramatic return of mining added a new level of complexity to any assessment.

The situation in the region mirrors a wider state and federal policy environment in Australia where industrial heritage is only partially recognized and poorly represented. Settler societies appear to show quite a hostile orientation to the preserving the past, especially the industrial past. Industrial heritage maintains an uneasy even fraught place within what Laurajane Smith has called the "Authorized Heritage Discourse".[2] It is overlooked partly because, as Anna Storm has noted, the industrial past is "of a mundane character, and consist[s] of complicated, large-scale, polluted or otherwise devastated landscapes and built environments".[3] Furthermore, as a settler society founded in the context of enlightenment values of progress and improvement (including the moral redemption of its convict settlers), Australia has developed and continues to evince a powerful resistance to the past since the past is identified as a form of old world resistance to change. These enlightenment values have shaped a contemporary worldview that encourages there to be 'no past' and 'no heritage'.[4] This may be linked subconsciously to a similar colonial denial of frontier history and frontier violence.[5] All of these reasons and other local issues as well account for the fact that there has been only modest progress since 1991 when Peter Spearritt wrote that "Industrial heritage in Australia is usually thought of as a residual category".[6] This has been compounded in Newcastle by the major return of mining from 2001. Yet as we shall see below there are points of resistance and difference. To use John Bodnar's useful shorthand concepts, while 'official history' is less than amenable to industrial heritage, there are dissenting notions coming from 'vernacular' sources.[7]

This chapter initially surveys the history of industrialization and deindustrialization before exploring industrial heritage and regional identity in greater detail. The scope for the chapter is the city of Newcastle and the region of the Hunter Valley which lies in that city's hinterland. Newcastle is a coastal city 160 kilometers north of Sydney. The Hunter River reaches the sea at Newcastle; its passage through the Hunter Valley forms the spine of the region. For the most part, for reasons of space, my comments will focus on Newcastle, but it is clear that there were strong economic and political links between Newcastle and the Hunter Valley as the coal mining industry steadily progressed west from Newcastle to the Lower Hunter Valley and now is firmly located in the Upper Hunter Valley. Therefore the Hunter Valley should be included to some extent. The examples illustrated below are broadly indicative of key patterns but much work remains to be done in this field, so this analysis is one that requires further elaboration in the future.

The history of industrialization/urbanization

The British colonization of New South Wales began in 1788 when a fleet of convict ships landed at a place the colonizers called Botany Bay, and then later established a convict settlement north of there at Sydney Cove. While the British colonization of NSW was primarily motivated to rid Britain and Ireland of its excess convict population, there were secondary commercial motives and locating and perhaps profiteering from local natural resources was an interest from the very beginning. This meant that outcrops of coal seams located both north and south of Sydney began to attract official interest in the 1790s.[8]

The NSW Government took control of the coal resource in 1801 and used convict labor to extract it. This was both a form of penal punishment but also part of a move to make the convict settlement more economically viable.[9] From 1804 the site, named Coal River and only later Newcastle, became a place of convict labor in the coal mine and elsewhere in and around the settlement. It received convicts and free settlers who had re-offended usually from Sydney and who were transferred to Newcastle as a kind of hard-working banishment. By 1815 there were 1200 convicts working in Newcastle. This was both a form of penal punishment but also part of a move to make the convict settlement more economically viable.[10]

This period of unfree labor and government control of commercial operations was replaced by a nascent free market in the 1840s. The mines were transferred to private ownership, the last of the convict workforce was removed from Newcastle and new coal mines were developed in the immediate Newcastle area with more than a dozen opening in the 20 years to 1870. Coal mines required transport and engineering infrastructure serviced by engineering and small manufacturing works. These were soon joined by other industries taking advantage of the transport links and the supply of coal for fuel. By the end of the 19th century Newcastle and its surrounding suburbs had a population of 53,741, and an increasingly important industrial and manufacturing base.[11] New coal mines were developed further west of Newcastle and ultimately in the lower Hunter Valley as the Greta seam was discovered and developed by the late 1880s. The South Maitland coal seam, in the Lower Hunter Valley, became an important growth center for the new mines of the late 19th century at Aberdare, Abermaine and Pelaw Main.[12]

New larger industries were also establishing themselves in or near Newcastle. A base metals smelter, The Sulphide Corporation Pty Ltd, began producing on the shores of nearby Lake Macquarie from the late 1890s.[13] The railway wagon, carriage and engineering firm Goninans was founded in 1899, initially focusing on the coal industry, but soon diversifying into supplying the manufacturing industry, and the Government-owned railways.[14] The railways, public works and harbor employment, a State-owned dockyard from 1913, as well as significant public support for private industries also reveals the crucial role of Government in this industrial expansion and concentration.

One of the largest mining companies in Australian history was the Broken Hill Proprietary Ltd (or BHP), which took a decision to diversify away from mining to become an integrated iron and steel maker from 1915. The Newcastle site on the Hunter River was chosen since it was close to coal resources, possessed a good deep-water harbor and a readily available labor force. From 1915 to 1999 iron and steel were produced in Newcastle. The company, through joint ventures or wholly owned subsidiaries, established new manufacturing industries in the city, utilizing the products from the iron and steel works to fashion steel rails, sheet metal and other products for specialized markets.[15]

The BHP steelworks loomed large in the city's economic life and shaped outside perceptions of the town as a 'steel city'. The steelworks remained the largest Australian steel plant until 1955 (when it was overtaken by the steelworks at Port Kembla, another BHP-controlled entity). At the peak of its scale and production the Newcastle steel works employed some 12,000 workers in 1960, and continued to grow steadily until 1975. This kind of large single employer with a network of associated businesses had far-reaching impacts on the labor market. By 1966

Newcastle's population had grown to 327,503, which was also twice the size of its southern rival, Wollongong (at 178,100), and was by far the state's largest city outside of Sydney (2,539,627).[16]

The steelworks sits at the edge of the Hunter River, and was a large 125-hectare site that included plant, repair, transport and administrative buildings. It also included BHP subsidiary sites nearby. There were industries that utilized BHP products to manufacture specialist products. As the site and its associated industries developed from the early 1920s, an industrial suburb grew at nearby Mayfield. This area became the largest suburb in the Newcastle local government area. Its distinctive housing stock, three-bedroom workers' cottages, was constructed during the boom years at the steel works, and its busy main street reflected the economic impact of the wages paid to BHP employees.[17]

Mayfield represents a large evolved industrial landscape in Newcastle – a suburb of up to 10,000 which provided both numerous workplaces and jobs, as well as a dormitory zone that serviced the needs of this industrial community.[18] This was arguably the most important industrial cultural landscape in NSW and certainly one of the largest in Australia. The sheer size of the workforce meant that many hundreds of thousands of workers and their families had some meaningful direct connection to this place, while many in the region and throughout Australia knew the city as the 'steel city'.

The history of deindustrialization

The turn towards decline and closure of manufacturing industries will be a familiar story to those who have studied this process in other nations and regions of the western world. The initial cause for concern for western manufacturing arose in the late 1960s, and then the oil crisis of 1973–1974 accelerated some of these patterns. In Newcastle the first manifestation of these broader global patterns occurred in 1976 when the State Dockyard was threatened with closure, and 1500 workers, or 75 per cent of the workforce, were retrenched by the end of that year, with the Dockyard closing altogether in 1987.[19] There were less high profile but no less concerning developments across the labor market more generally. A rise of youth unemployment from 1975, and concerns about the future of young workers, became apparent.[20]

Across the region unemployment grew steadily from 1.7 per cent in 1970 to 5.7 per cent in 1981 and then peaked again during the recession of the early 1990s at 16.7 per cent in February 1993. The effect of this long-term economic crisis was a decline in Newcastle's population from 146,009 in 1971 to 129,490 in 1986.[21] This was capped by the 1997 announcement that BHP was to cease steelmaking in Newcastle by 1999. This decision alone was estimated to lead to the loss of 4500 jobs both directly and indirectly, and it came on the top of decades of minimal investment in the plant as management scaled back growth plans and became far more cost-conscious.[22] The steady decline in manufacturing from the 1970s had come on top of the erosion of coal mining jobs in the 1960s, and the consequent closure of the network of rail lines that connected them to the port of Newcastle.

The history of regional identity

Identity is very broad concept encompassing a sense of affiliation or self-identification. The discussions here must necessarily be brief, but I will suggest that common forms of public identities that formed were typical of regional mining and industrial areas. The region had its share of class conflicts and moments of crisis in industrial relations. In these periods, class identity and the sense of wage earners versus the masters was paramount. But there were also geographic affiliations, complex and somewhat unfinished as we shall see, but nonetheless present in varying forms in the region from the beginnings of white occupation.

We shall start with a discussion of the geographical affiliations and then move on to the more familiar class-based identities. As a small outpost north of Sydney, Newcastle had a sense of being at the margins of a larger place that usually made decisions that had profound effects on local life. Issues such as differential freight rates, which made the wool of the Hunter Valley cheaper to transport to Sydney as compared to the port of Newcastle, raised the ire of many in the city and its hinterland. In 1935 the Nicholas Royal Commission into possible new state boundaries within NSW reported that "People of Newcastle have for years complained that the administration of public departments is too much centred in Sydney". "There is", as the report noted "a sense of common grievance and common ambition uniting Newcastle with certain sections of the proposed northern area".[23]

Yet the city and its suburbs that developed from the 1850s and beyond was a collection of scattered pit top villages. In these coal mining towns identity was very much focused upon the town itself. If the town economy was built on the health of the mine, it was also a community that had its own social and industrial organization. The coalminers develop lodges based on each mine site while fraternal orders, retail co-operatives, banks, churches and many other organizations of civil society were based at the town or suburb level. Some of the larger mining towns even had their own newspapers, which were an important way for a local identity to be cultivated through the shared space of the newspapers columns, with its focus on local news and local society.[24]

These town-based regional identities were also encouraged by a form of local government which tended to have boundaries based on town boundaries. By 1901 Newcastle had 12 municipalities, many of which were centered on the city center or the suburban boundaries of the coal mining towns that had developed from the 1850s.

Yet there were forces that encouraged a long-term growth of a 'regional' sentiment. All of these areas whether they were centered around the Newcastle area, or the coal mining towns in the Hunter Valley such as Cessnock, Greta and Kurri Kurri shared a common concern with their treatment by Sydney-based politicians and administrators. Newcastle and Hunter Valley-based members of parliament sometimes had shared positions regardless of their political affiliation which supported better infrastructure or services for the region. And while there were small local newspapers, one newspaper came to dominate this market and that was increasingly *The Newcastle Herald and Miners' Advocate*, which was published from an office in Newcastle city from 1876. Significantly from *The Newcastle Herald* (as it eventually became known) was an amalgam of one Newcastle newspaper and another from the mining town of Wallsend, some 10 kilometers west of Newcastle. The slow and uneven process of creating a regional voice can be dated from this point with *The Newcastle Herald* becoming a vigorous advocate for the region.

But the boundaries of this advocacy did not extend to encompass the Hunter Valley to any great extent. Towns such as Maitland, which was an important rural service town at the base of the lower Hunter Valley, actually matured well before Newcastle and had developed its own institutions of civil society. Granted there were shared interests between the miners, the commercial interests in Newcastle and the farming and rural interests in the Hunter Valley (over the state of the Newcastle port or freight rates for example), but there were also significant economic and political differences between them as well.

These long-term forces for regional cohesion, as fragmented as they were, did gain some further traction from 1938 when the 11 small municipalities were merged with the Newcastle City Council to create the City of Greater Newcastle. This process was not simply a legislative change initiated from Sydney; it involved a long political campaign and the formation of the Greater Newcastle League in 1917 to advocate for the administrative reorganization.[25] Rapid suburbanization from the 1950s onwards slowly eroded the spatial and social boundaries between these old mining towns, helping to cement a larger spatial identification.

Such was the state of regional affiliation in Newcastle and the Hunter Valley. There was patchy development of some regional cohesion in the Newcastle area and there were some issues that tended to unite the river port with its hinterland. But many of the small mining towns were self-sufficient communities that had their own distinctive sense of place and identity.

The region was punctuated by moments of strain or crisis in class relations, mostly expressed in the form of industrial action which occasionally involved public disorder and the use of state force to suppress protest. These patterns will be familiar to many who have studied industrial regions. The coal miners unions were important trailblazers in this regard and also assisted other waterfront, transport and eventually manufacturing unions. Key moments of conflict included the increasing industrial tension in the late 1880s which culminated in the unsuccessful maritime strike of 1890; strikes and lockouts in the period before and just after the First World War, and then the 1929 coal mines lockout. During and after the Second World War, regular strikes were often somewhat more successful as labor gained slightly more bargaining power in conditions of near full employment. By this time however the coal miners were reducing in number and major mines in the lower Hunter Valley were beginning to close from the early 1960s. The focus of union action and employment shifted to the large industrial workplaces, the waterfront and the railways.[26]

What did transcend these class and spatial complexities were common public images of the city that had their origin in the convict period (1801 to 1847) and were further reinforced during the coal mining age (1847 to 1915) and again during the steel city period (1915 to 1999). These images tended to posit Newcastle as a working man's town with an authentic and roughly hewn edge.[27] Little matter that Newcastle had a vigorous cultural and artistic life (that was both working class and middle class) or even a large commercial and professional class who performed an important role in the city's political and industrial life. The presence of a large male workforce whether they be convicts, free miners or steel workers have profoundly shaped the sense of the city's image. One astute analysis from the 1990s argued that "The imagery of Newcastle retains the bias of male, blue-collar and Anglo-centric narratives, and significant silences with regard to women, non-Anglo and indigenous culture".[28]

The history of industrial heritage

As noted by the useful overview *Industrial Heritage Retooled*, "industrial heritage is a complex amalgam of places and people, practices and processes, which continues to defy explanation of its origins and astounds in its effects of its subsequent development and decay".[29] It includes the built heritage, but also the attitudes, skills, practices and cultures that arose from, and supported, the industrial age. It represents a reminder of how we got to where we are. The structures and work patterns of the industrial age underpinned a way of life, providing a sense of who we are and from where we have come. Industrial heritage was often a product of rapid industrialization and urban development associated with the industrial revolution of the early 1800s, including large-scale factories, integrated transport systems and urban environments that provided a workforce and a market for industrial age products.

Australia is a federal political system with responsibilities divided between different levels of Government. In the context of heritage management, to put it simply, the Commonwealth Government looks after National Heritage, the State Government takes responsibility for State heritage and local government looks after items of local significance, and is beholden to the laws and requirements of the two higher spheres. 'Industrial Heritage' is not specifically defined or codified in National Heritage legislation, but there are relevant references to national heritage of 'historic significance' coming from key themes such as 'mining and resource use', 'industrialization and manufacturing', 'transport and communication' and 'urban development'. All of these themes could provide ample scope for recognition of industrial heritage.[30] The Commonwealth enacted legislation for heritage protection from 1975 while the NSW passed *The Heritage Act* in 1977.

Despite the overall rather negative assessment offered here of the status of industrial heritage in Australia, and in particular in Newcastle and Hunter Valley, there are some bright spots. Mining heritage in particular has been well served through the efforts of various levels of government and the actions of engaged local communities. For example in 2014 the city of Broken Hill in far western New South Wales has been added to the National Heritage List highlighting its "dramatic desert landscape, its unique character and remarkable industrial and geological heritage."[31] The old copper mining region of Burra in South Australia was the scene of important international work with the town giving its name to the Burra Charter which defines the values which shape cultural significance. The gold mining city of Ballarat, which developed into an important regional center in Victoria, is a participant in the Historic Urban Landscape (HUL) initiative that is supported by UNESCO. HUL is a holistic approach to urban management that seeks to integrate tangible and intangible heritage with economic and social development.[32]

This is only a summary of selected projects; however, the significance here is that good outcomes for industrial heritage can be achieved in Australia, and this offers at least some cause for optimism in the Newcastle/Hunter Valley case. Perhaps there are possibilities that can be explored for development in this area that draw upon the successes in Australia and indeed elsewhere? There is no shortage of valuable items and associated cultural practices upon which to draw. The following section surveys only the major heritage assets in the region. I will focus here on Newcastle and make only passing references to the Hunter Valley.

Indigenous heritage and industrial heritage

Before doing so however in the context of a settler society where the growth of industry represented the effective occupation of Indigenous land and the removal of its people, we need to consider (even if only briefly) the relationship between Indigenous and Industrial Heritage. The region, like all regions throughout Australia, has a rich Aboriginal history and heritage. This heritage can be found uncovered in building sites, and in road and infrastructure projects, as material remains from hunter-gather societies including those of the Awakabal, who lived south of the Hunter River, and those of the Worimi who lived to the north and towards what later became Port Stephens. Aboriginal artefacts often take the form of stone tools and implements finely adapted to the local environment. These stone tools were used to interact with and transform the resources of the natural environment and so thus are a form or type of 'industrial heritage'.

It is significant that local usages of 'industrial heritage' usually do not include these items as part of that heritage. They are labelled 'Indigenous heritage'. That is especially significant, and understandable, because their origin in the first communities of Australia separates them uniquely from those of the settler communities that followed. Nonetheless, what is clearly a specialized form of industrial heritage is once again poorly recognized because of the predominance of other labels and descriptors for this material.

Using 'industrial heritage' for this Indigenous material also might emphasize links with subsequent settler economies that also utilized the resources of the environment but in less sustainable ways. The identification of Indigenous heritage as 'industrial heritage' is not a straightforward proposition and does present significant cultural and political issues for Indigenous groups and heritage specialists in Australia. The co-location of these items with the sites of European industrial heritage is particularly significant. The issue is to what extent should 'Indigenous heritage' be considered a part of 'industrial heritage' – a unique problem for settler societies such as Australia, New Zealand and Canada.[33]

Industrial heritage in Newcastle

With a focus on settler heritage then we can identify the moves towards conserving and protecting industrial heritage. Some of the surviving material industrial heritage from Newcastle and the Hunter Valley was a result not so much of careful planning and protection but rather the absence of a major economic boom which destroyed previous structures. Certainly there were periods in Newcastle's history where there were boom conditions and rapid industrial and urban growth. These did take their toll but the city center, for example, is surprisingly well preserved and includes some fine examples of late 19th- and early 20th-century industrial and commercial buildings such as the Civic Railways Workshops (1874–1886), and the Earp Gillam Bond Store, designed by Frederick Menckens and built in 1888.[34] Newcastle city center was not a major focus on urban redevelopment until the early 1990s, and then heritage protection legislation has at least stayed the hand of the demolishers on some occasions.

Coal River historic precinct

One important collection of convict-related industrial heritage deserves some attention. The precinct is a collection of interrelated sites associated with the birth of the city of Newcastle and its early colonial history of occupation, industry and work patterns from the late 1790s. It is named from an early colonial name for the area, which later became formally known as Newcastle, though the Coal River name persisted for some years. This area has been subject to much debate and contestation since it occupies a central location at the gateway of the city of Newcastle. It was placed on the State Heritage Register in 2003, and elements of the precinct are also separately listed on the State or National Heritage Registers. It is a cultural landscape that speaks to the foundation of the city and its period as an exemplar of colonization and industrial development through the use of unfree or convict labor. The precinct includes the site of the convict coal mines located beneath a prominent military fortification, Fort Scratchley (which dates from the 1880s), but are also honeycombed throughout the city center. The presence of coal was the main attraction for early colonial occupation which was permanent from 1804. There is also the site of Convict Lumberyard or Stockade, which is the region's first factory site, a place where coal, lime and tools were stored, as well as a place where convict workers labored on construction and repair jobs. After 1833 the usage changed to reflect changing patterns of convict labor and incarceration and the area became known as a stockade.

While key sites within the precinct are listed on the State Heritage Register and sites such as the Nobbys Lighthouse and Fort Scratchley are on the National Heritage Register, the *entire* precinct has been the subject of four unsuccessful attempts to secure National Heritage listing. This suggests a resistance to the concept of a 'heritage landscape', where individual sites come together to form a unique amalgam of inter-related heritage significance across a landscape. My colleague David Roberts and I have argued that the Coal River Precinct embodies a form of heritage that is not privileged within both the Australian and world heritage schemas. While noting the degradation of the surviving physical fabric at

Coal River, we also argued that the area embodies a series of transformations in regional and national history, from convict to free labor, from government controlled to private enterprise and from sole industry to a combined industry-leisure usages. "The Precinct", we argued,

> and many comparable Australian convict sites embody what we call a "heritage of adaptation", where what is evidenced is a history of transformation rather than preservation. The idea owes more to the subjective and nuanced notions of "living", "cultural", "intangible" and "inclusive heritage" which, internationally, have broadened the scope and definition of heritage, especially in the wake of UNESCO's Convention for the Safeguarding of the Intangible Cultural Heritage (2003).[35]

By emphasizing intact, isolated and disconnected convict sites, we are unwittingly isolating the convict period from contemporary Australia and offering a safe, sanitized view of a distant convict past.

Railway heritage

Connecting the sites of resource extraction with the harbor, and later, its industrial infrastructure, made the railway network a vital feature of the industrial infrastructure of the region. The first railways were private ones connecting the coal mines to the harbor. The rail line from Sydney was completed in 1889 but there was a line from Newcastle heading west to inland East Maitland in 1857 and connecting other upper Hunter towns in the following decades (Singleton in 1863, Muswellbrook 1869 and Scone 1871). The railways were initially developed to carry raw material or finished products, but later became public transport systems that were also very important to cater for the mass numbers of employees at large industrial workplaces such as the Newcastle steel works.

The New South Wales State Heritage Register records a number of sites of railway heritage throughout the region. One of the most important preserved sites is the Richmond Vale Railway Museum, south of Kurri Kurri. Many of these sites and landscapes blend into one another, or overlap across physical boundaries. Railway heritage traversed large amounts of land often located well way from major urban centers so there was a better chance that these items and infrastructure might survive.[36] The strong representation of railway heritage both in the Hunter and more broadly across the country is, curiously, mirrored in a strong academic literature on railway heritage.[37]

Any discussion of railway heritage cannot be divorced from the recent controversy of cutting the rail link which connects Newcastle to the rail line south to Sydney, west Mailand and north to the north coast of NSW. This plan dates back many decades in the minds of various state governments, local developers and the Property Council, who all viewed the railway along the lateral transverse of the city center as a 'barrier' between the city center and the harbor foreshore. This is a telling image of their overall approach to heritage and public transport per se. In the minds of those who resisted the proposal to cut the railway line, the closure was simply a way to gain access to valuable land in an area amenable for commercial and residential development. The alternative transport route (via a yet-to-be built light rail line) is both less convenient and slower than the existing rail line.

The debate was not so much about railway heritage as about who controlled the city for whose benefit. But nonetheless the blithe destruction of a functional transport network that includes working heritage items such as stations and associated transport heritage dating back to the 1870s again says much about the gulf between ideas for developing the city of Newcastle and the role (or lack thereof) for heritage in this process. The city's heritage infrastructure, even where it was functional and valued by the local community, was swept aside for a speculative property development venture where even the alternative transport route had not yet been designed let alone built. Another key example of industrial heritage, the steelworks and its associated residential and commercial landscape, will be discussed in greater detail as follows.

The relationship between regional identity and industrial heritage

Regional identity is fractured through complex urban systems and multiple layers of government. This means that spatial identification is loose and ever-changing, shifting from suburb to town to region. The absence of a strong regional governance structure has also inhibited the development of a regional identity.

Even with these caveats in mind, industrial heritage still maintains an uneasy place within the regional identity or regional identities of the Hunter. There is a profound ambivalence about the industrial age. It was widely celebrated and was at one stage a dominant regime in the 1940s and 1950s, but even the largest steelworks as the major employer was seen by some as an outsider – never an authentic part of Newcastle.[38] Deindustrialization unleashed once muted forces that expressed unease over the industrial and manufacturing base. From the 1970s onwards, new conceptions of Newcastle and the Hunter emphasized the need to diversify and transform its industrial base, which was indeed worryingly narrow. In 1971 28.8 per cent of the Hunter workforce was employed in manufacturing (compared to 23.2 per cent Australia-wide) and 4.7 per cent in mining (compared to 1.4 per cent Australia-wide).[39] In the process of deindustrialization, industrial heritage became equated with old thinking, a legacy that acted as a barrier that the region had to overcome. This shaped a profoundly ahistorical notion of transformation, which sought a radical break from the past rather than an adaptive and evolutionary building upon it. As Rofe noted, as deindustrialization proceeded, Newcastle increasingly became identified as a 'problem city', a development that was further reinforced by the Newcastle Earthquake of December 1989, where 13 people were killed in a tragic building collapse in the city center.[40] The earthquake appeared to reinforce a notion that Newcastle was a city of tragedy, that its fate was out of its hands and that it was inevitably in decline.

The industrial age is marked by a distinct break and shift towards downturn, decline and closure, yet the end point for this era is unclear and its power is such that it can re-emerge or persist perhaps beyond what might be expected. Coal

There needs to be something there 179

mining in fact made a decisive return to the regional economy from the early 2000s as the commodity boom proceeded apace and new open pit coal mines were developed in the Upper Hunter Valley. Like in the 19th and 20th centuries, this affected the transport sector, through hauling the coal to the harbor and loading the coal onto large ocean-going vessels. Newcastle harbor once again became one of the busiest coal ports in Australia moving 89 million tons of coal in 2007–2008, increasing to 154 million tons in 2013–2014.[41] The return of mining has reset the heritage clock, shifting the focus at least of government and business interests to production in old economy terms. The revival of mining has delayed the need for a serious consideration of a post-industrial economic restructuring, and this has adversely affected a consideration of heritage and heritage tourism as one part of the overall response to industrial decline.

This re-assertion of mining and production along with the continued challenges for finding new economic directions has influenced a strongly anti-heritage disposition, where the common immediate response to the idea of 'heritage protection', or 'heritage concerns' is an abrupt dismissal. This environment posits a simple dichotomy between development and heritage. Development means jobs and economic opportunity while heritage means delay, frustration and economic decline. Heritage is also cast as a minority middle-class cultural practice and this representation gains some traction in a city with a strong working-class heritage.

This situation in Newcastle and the Hunter Valley cannot be separated from a wider controversial issue in NSW politics. The relationships between the political elite (on both the Labor Party and Liberal Party sides) and key developers have been revealed in great detail in recent Independent Commission Against Corruption (ICAC) hearings from 2013 to 2015. It is difficult to make sense of this morass of allegations, controversies, conflicts of interest and obscure arrangements and deals, but it is clear that Newcastle and the Hunter region were important locations where these issues played out. What is also certain is that the return of mining and the great potential financial benefits that this entailed for some meant renewed pressure on heritage items. Some of the issues raised before the ICAC hearings and a Parliamentary Enquiry included fast-track approvals for major infrastructure projects, and one of the perceived barriers for approval was the heritage overlay on the BHP steelworks site.[42]

A highly politicized, potentially compromised development process, layered on top of a stale and ossified local debate represents undoubtedly the worst possible environment for any meaningful exchange of views and discussion around breaking down a simplistic dichotomy, perhaps more accurately a vast gulf, which exists between development and heritage. Yet the exploration of these two concepts and their progressive integration is at the very forefront of the latest developments in heritage studies and heritage management. The best work in this area shows how a positive integration of heritage management and local sustainable development actually leads to very good outcomes for both the heritage protection and for local economic growth.[43]

If this is not enough, industrial heritage has been placed under further pressure by the progressive sale of state or 'crown' owned assets such as transport infrastructure, superseded water and energy plants, port facilities, post offices and military installations. This process, common to many countries where a neo-liberal policy of state divestment has been pursued, has meant that industrial heritage assets have passed out of public ownership and now lack sufficient resources for maintenance let alone appropriate re-development and adaptive re-use. At times these assets have passed into the hands of local government which has far fewer resources to pursue effective strategies. There are numerous examples of this in Newcastle. Fort Scratchley, a large military installation at the entrance of Newcastle harbor had been present since the late 1880s, and had played a crucial role in the history of the city, including returning fire at Japanese submarines in 1942. In the late 1980s the Commonwealth Government passed the Fort over to the ownership and control of local government.[44] Likewise the Newcastle Post Office, a fine turn-of-century sandstone public building, passed from State Government to private hands in the 1980s. It has slowly deteriorated and its future is currently in doubt with proposals for a major modernist addition above the historic building attracting widespread concern from the heritage community.[45]

There were two principal sources of a vernacular or dissenting view of industrial heritage, which can challenge and disrupt an official focus on development, refashioning and above all removing tangible expressions of the industrial past from the regional landscape. The first, and arguably the strongest in the region, is from retired workers from particular industrial sites who wish to see their former workplaces preserved. Retired workers have an insider's view of the factory site, often knowing in great detail the intricacies of construction and production. At the same time, they naturally share a commitment to see their workplace as significant both locally and nationally. Workers wish to see their workplace as a place that made a difference. They have an investment in making sense of their working lives, particularly since they are often long-term workers who have gained a sense of themselves and their identity from lengthy employment. Likewise they wish to encourage others to see it in these terms too, and this can become activated when their former workplace is threatened with destruction.

The Newcastle Industrial Heritage Association, formed in 2000 by retired BHP workers, presented itself as a moderate group, siting above battles between heritage activists and developers.[46] It has achieved much in terms of accommodating the ongoing personal and community needs of retired workers (on a very small budget) but the strategy to pursue a 'moderate' policy on preserving tangible heritage has been a failure. The last of the BHP buildings were demolished in 2015. This form of vernacular heritage has gained good profile and standing, but the lack of a coherent industrial heritage strategy, and the power of opposing forces, were hurdles simply way too high for small volunteer groups. The title of this chapter – "there needs to be something there for people to remember" – is a quote from the Vice President of the Association, Aubrey Brooks.[47] The NIHA has ultimately been unable the stem the tide of the complete destruction of the old steelworks site even while organizing reunions of former steelworkers and the installation of a series of commemorative monuments.

The second source of vernacular or dissenting heritage comes from an amorphous group of heritage activists, local councilors, university academics and local professionals who see the industrial past as a key part of the historical and cultural legacy of the region's history. They see a part of themselves and all others reflected in these industrial landscapes and intuitively respond with a concern to protect and preserve that which is under threat. This is hardly a powerful group, but they have had some success in protecting particular sites and encouraging the region to embrace its historical and heritage legacies. Indeed many of the region's spectacular survival stories can be attributed to the commitment of these groups and individuals. In the case of the Coal River Heritage Precinct, it was this collection of activists, academics and community groups that was able to secure the State Heritage listing for the assemblage of early colonial sites in 2003 at Newcastle's harbor entrance.[48] Despite that achievement, efforts to elevate the equivalent area to the National Heritage List have been unsuccessful on four separate occasions.[49] The fact that one of Australia's premier colonial industrial sites cannot find recognition within the national heritage framework is highly significant, providing further evidence of the marginal status of industrial heritage.

For this second group, protection of industrial heritage is also bound up with protection of the urban and suburban fabric more generally. They wish to see a city and a region that has a human scale and focus, where planning decisions are based on social and cultural needs as well as solid and sustainable economic grounds. As a result of years of bitter experience, they are wary of development projects that are not so much about sustainable business, but about speculative investment in poor quality housing or infrastructure with little provision for open space, public transport and social amenity.

Other sites of resistance have been unofficial, often personal laments for the destruction of industrial heritage. One blogger and author, Mark Maclean from the suburban location of Hamilton North, maintained a chronicle of his regular walks along the open concrete drains of his suburb evincing a curious longing and deepening appreciation of the remnant industrial heritage in his locale. In one entry he hears demolition noises coming from the nearby Gasworks Tower, and raced down to check:

> It was like seeing the body of an elephant shot by poachers or an American dentist. Surely that tiny digger could not have caused that behemoth to fall? But it had. As we watched, the digger moved around the base of the collapsed tower. The digger made pneumatic huffing and puffing sounds as though it were a living beast gathering its breath for the next part of its work. It had a kind of grabbing or cutting claw which it sunk into the wall of the tower and our ears were assaulted with the hideous animal screech I'd been hearing.

Maclean's visceral response and his quiet sadness at the loss of the local landmark was of a kind experienced by residents in industrial suburbs throughout the western world:

> I felt a sadness for the loss of something that was ugly and utilitarian but a part of our industrial heritage and a landmark that we'll soon struggle to remember ever existed. Goodbye, old mate.[50]

By positioning the city as firstly a 'problem child' of industrialization and secondly as a harbinger of a new cosmopolitan future, city planners and property interests had reframed a sense of the city's future by demonizing its past. The destruction of its industrial heritage proceeded at a remarkable pace, virtually unchecked aside from the dissonant responses of workers, former workers and residents who had grown to see industrial places as a normal part of their everyday lives.[51]

Conclusion

There are sites in Newcastle and the Hunter Valley that do reflect the region's rich industrial past including its convict, mining, manufacturing and railway heritage. These sites however lack an integrated focus and tend to be seen, and to have been conserved, in isolation from the entire industrial heritage landscape. Tangible industrial heritage has fared very badly and steps to preserve this 'heritage' 'virtually', to re-create it using new technologies need to be approached with caution. Some efforts were made to record the intangible heritage of the BHP site with interviews of former workers in the late 1990s as closure approached.[52] But these appeared to emerge in the Hunter at the very time when tangible heritage was being demolished. The dominant presentation of the city's identity had little room for an appreciation of its industrial past, and certainly that history has not been integrated into new conceptions of the city and its future.

Settler societies have a strong ahistorical disposition, as evidenced by the energy and enthusiasm that comes with the destruction of the industrial past. This sense of denial of the past is similar to Australian cultural amnesia over frontier violence or the stolen generations. The renewed mining boom from 2001 has fatally compromised heritage efforts. Finally, at a formal or official level the idea of building on the industrial past has been avoided by Newcastle and Hunter Valley Councils, and state government policy makers. The region's public presentation, and arguably its 'identity' are now about lifestyle and urban living but without seeing the industrial past as a resource upon which that can be built. In the context of controversial and occasionally corrupt processes that are supposed to manage high profile development opportunities, the past is just another hurdle in the way of a last gasp opportunity for capital accumulation of a dying economic regime.

Notes

1 Kevin Dunn, Pauline McGuirk & Hilary Winchester, Place Making: The Social Construction of Newcastle, *Geographical Research*, October 1995, DOI: 10.1111/j.1467–8470.1995.tb00691.x & Mark Rofe, From "Problem City" to "Promise City": Gentrification and the Revitalisation of Newcastle, *Australian Geographical Studies*, Volume 42, Issue 2, June 2004, pp. 193–206.
2 Laurajane Smith, *The Uses of Heritage*, Routledge, London and New York, 2006, p. 29.
3 Anna Storm & Krister Olsson, The Pit: Landscape Scars as Potential Cultural Tools, *International Journal of Heritage Studies*, Volume 19, Issue 7, 2013, p. 693.
4 See John Gascoigne, *The Enlightenment and the Origins of Australia*, Cambridge University Press, New York, 2002. See especially page 171: "Utilitarianism suited a new society like European Australia, relatively uncluttered by the past. In their quest for

'the greatest good for the greatest number", the Utilitarians naturally valued the possibility of being able to construct new institutions from the ground up, *without the need to build around the relics of the past*" (my emphasis). There appears to be a strong synergy between this Australian manifestation and Jeffersonian democracy with its rejection of history and tradition.

5 Dirk Moses, *Genocide and Settler Society: Frontier Violence and Stolen Indigenous Children in Australian History*, Berghahn, New York, 2004 & Frances Peter-Little, Ann Curthoys & John Docker (eds), *Passionate Histories: Myth, Memory and Indigenous Australia*, ANU E Press, Canberra, 2010.

6 Peter Spearitt, Money, Taste and Industrial Heritage, *Australian Historical Studies*, Volume 23, Issue 96, 1991, p. 34. Similar concerns have been expressed over the fate of industrial heritage in the UK and Ireland. See Michael Nevell, Editorial – Industrial Heritage at Risk, *Industrial Archaeology Review*, Volume 33, Issue 2, November 2011, pp. 79–80. Another valuable and more recent survey is Lucy Taksa, Machines and Ghosts: Politics, Industrial Heritage and the History of Working Life at the Eveleigh Workshops, *Labour History*, Issue 85, November 2003, pp. 65–88.

7 On these concepts, see John Bodnar, *Remaking America: Public Memory, Commemoration, and Patriotism in the Twentieth Century*, Princeton University Press, Princeton, NJ, 1994, especially pp. 13–14. 'Official' industrial heritage is sourced from State and Local Government policies and plans, and is only partially realized in a policy environment where 'industrial heritage' is not a priority. 'Vernacular' history and heritage – that which originates from diverse groups and individuals, especially retired workers – has the power of contestation and rebellion on its side, but often lack a co-ordinated presence.

8 Alan Atkinson, *The Europeans in Australia: A History Volume One: The Beginning*, Oxford University Press, Melbourne, 1997; John W. Turner, *Coal Mining in Newcastle, 1801 to 1900*, Newcastle City Council, Newcastle, 1982 & Shortland, Jun., To J. Shortland, Sen. HMS Reliance, Sydney Cove, Port Jackson, Historical Records of New South Wales, Volume 3, pp. 481–482.

9 David Roberts & Lisa Ford, New South Wales Penal Settlements and the Transformation of Secondary Punishment in the Nineteenth-Century British Empire, *Journal of Colonialism and Colonial History*, Volume 15, Issue 3, http://dx.doi.org/10.1353/cch.2014.0038

10 Turner, *Coal Mining in Newcastle, 1801 to 1900*.

11 Census of NSW, 1901, Habitations, Table VII: The Population and Number of Inhabited Dwellings in Each Municipality in 1891 and 1901, http://hccda.anu.edu.au/pages/NSW-1901-census-02_481 [accessed 8 August 2016].

12 David Branagan, *Geology and Coal Mining in the Hunter Valley, 1791–1861*, Newcastle Public Library, Newcastle, NSW, 1972 & Gifford H. Eardley, *The Railways of the South Maitland Coalfields*, Australian Railway Historical Society, NSW Division, Sydney, 1969.

13 Erik Eklund, Managers, Workers, and Industrial Welfarism: Management Strategies at ER&S and the Sulphide Corporation, 1895–1929, *Australian Economic History Review*, Volume 37, Issue 2, July 1997, DOI: 10.1111/1467-8446.00010

14 L.E. Fredman, Goninan, Alfed (1865–1953) and Ralph Williams Goninan (1874–1948), Engineers, in John Ritchie (ed.), *Australian Dictionary of Biography*, Vol. 14, Melbourne University Press, Melbourne, 1996, pp. 291–292. Also available at www.adb.online.anu.edu.au/biogs/A140330b.htm [accessed 1 July 2016].

15 James Docherty, *Newcastle: The Making of an Australian city*, Allen & Unwin, Sydney, 1983, pp. 1–25 & Chris Wright, The Formative Years of Management Control at the Newcastle Steelworks, 1913–1924, *Labour History*, Issue 55, November 1988, pp. 55–70.

16 *Official Yearbook of the Commonwealth of Australia*, No.53, Commonwealth Bureau of Census and Statistics, Canberra, 1967, p. 175.

17 See Newcastle City-Wide Heritage Study, 1996–1997: Volume 3, Newcastle City Council, Newcastle, 1997, https://coalriver.files.wordpress.com/2008/02/1997-nhs-v3-images-m-w.pdf [accessed 1 August 2016].
18 On evolved industrial landscapes, see *Retooling Industrial Heritage*, Identifying industrial landscapes, p. 49: "Its significant distinguishing features are, however, still visible in material form (or present as buried archaeological remains) but may not be complete or may lack integrity".
19 The Bleak Future Facing Newcastle and its Hinterland, *Canberra Times*, 9 October 1976, p. 2.
20 For a useful State-wide summary, see John Wilkinson, Manufacturing and Services in New South Wales, *NSW Parliamentary Library Research Service*, Paper No. 3/07, www.parliament.nsw.gov.au/researchpapers/Documents/manufacturing-and-services-in-nsw/ManuFINALandINDEX.pdf [accessed 1 May 2016].
21 The 1971 and 1986 Census Returns for the Newcastle Statistical District, NSW, www.abs.gov.au/ausstats/abs@.nsf/ViewContent?readform&view=productsbyCatalogue&Action=Expand&Num=2.2 [accessed 11 May 2016].
22 Hunter Valley Research Foundation, *Diversification of the Hunter Economy Post-BHP*, Hunter Valley Research Foundation, Maryville (Newcastle), 2011, pp. 5–12.
23 Evidence of the Royal Commission of Inquiry as to the Areas in New South Wales Suitable for Self-Government as States in the Commonwealth of Australia: Also List of Exhibits, *New States Royal Commission*. (H.S. Nicholas), New South Wales, Parliament. Legislative Assembly, Alfred James Kent, Government Printer, Sydney, 1935. The problematic relationship to Sydney is a theme that recurs in Docherty's, *Newcastle*, pp. 2, 6 & 162.
24 These observations are based on a random sampling of the *Newcastle Herald*, especially in the period 1890 to 1930.
25 Greater Newcastle, *The Newcastle Herald and Miners Advocate*, 10 July 1917, p. 7.
26 See the relevant chapters in James Bennett, Nancy Cushing and Erik Eklund, *Radical Newcastle*, New South, Sydney, 2015.
27 See both Andrew Metcalfe, Mud and Steel: The imagination of Newcastle, *Labour History*, Issue. 64, May 1993, pp. 6–7 & Rofe, From "Problem City" to "Promise City", p. 195.
28 Dunn, McGuirk & Winchester, Place Making, p. 149.
29 James Douet (ed), *Industrial Heritage Retooled*, Carnegie Publishing, Lancaster, UK, 2013, p. 7.
30 Commonwealth Department of the Environment and Energy, National Heritage List Criteria, www.environment.gov.au/heritage/about/national/national-heritage-list-criteria [accessed 20 July 2017].
31 See City of Broken Hill National Heritage Listing, www.environment.gov.au/cgi-bin/ahdb/search.pl?mode=place_detail;place_id=105861 [accessed 20 July 2017].
32 UNESCO, Historic Urban Landscape Approach Explained, http://whc.unesco.org/en/news/1026/ [accessed 28 May 2015]. & 'Historic Urban Landscape Ballarat', www.hulballarat.org.au [accessed 28 May 2015].
33 Roy Jones & Christina Birdsall Jones, The Contestation of Heritage: The Colonizer and the Colonized in Australia, in Brian Graham and Peter Howard (eds.), *The Ashgate Research Companion to Heritage and Identity*, Ashgate Publishing Limited, New York, 2008, pp. 365–440.
34 See NSW State Heritage Register, Entry for the Civic Railway Workshops, www.environment.nsw.gov.au/heritageapp/ViewHeritageItemDetails.aspx?ID=5044977 & NSW State Heritage Register, Entry for Earp Gillam Bond Store, www.environment.nsw.gov.au/heritageapp/ViewHeritageItemDetails.aspx?ID=5044982 [accessed 10 August 2016]. Numerous other examples can be accessed through the NSW Heritage Database.

35 David Roberts & Erik Eklund, Australian Convict Sites and the Heritage of Adaptation: The Case of Newcastle's Coal River Heritage Precinct, *Australian Historical Studies*, Volume 43, Issue 3, 2012, pp. 363–380.
36 For the Richmond Vale Railway Museum website, see www.richmondvalerailwaymuseum.org/ [1 May 2016].
37 See for example Lucy Taksa, Machines and Ghosts: Politics, Industrial Heritage and the History of Working Life at the Eveleigh Workshops, *Labour History*, Issue 85, November 2003, pp. 65–88 & Bobbie Oliver, More Than Just Locomotives: Re-Discovering Working Lives at the Midland Railway Workshops, *Historic Environment*, Volume 21, Issue 2, 2008, pp. 20–24.
38 See Nancy Cushing, Remembering BHP: Memory and Industrial Heritage, *Workers' Online*, Issue No.13, 14 May 1999, http://workers.labor.net.au/13/c_historicalfeature_bhp.html [accessed 6 June 2015]. I am particularly indebted to Nancy Cushing for her insightful articles on Newcastle and heritage. See also her Revisiting "Living History: The City of Newcastle as a Museum", revised version of paper presented to Hunter Heritage Network Symposium, 30 September 2011, http://hunterheritagenetwork.org/wp-content/uploads/2011/10/nancy-cushing_paper_newcastle-as-a-museum-revisited1.pdf [accessed 1 June 2015].
39 Hunter Valley Research Foundation, *The Hunter Region at a Glance*, Maryville (Newcastle), 1976, p. 2 in Hunter Regional Council for Social Development (HRCSD), C720–750, University of Newcastle Cultural Collections (UNCC).
40 Rofe, From "Problem City" to "Promise City", pp. 195–196. The same point had been made by Metcalfe, Mud and Steel, p. 1.
41 Newcastle Port Corporation, *Annual Report for the Period 2007–2008*, p. 7 & Newcastle Port Corporation, *Annual Report for the Period 2013–2014*, p. 3.
42 Independent Commission Against Corruption (ICAC), Spicer Enquiry, www.icac.nsw.gov.au/investigations/past-investigations/categorylist/12/203 [accessed 10 August 2016]. & Select Committee on the Planning Process in Newcastle and the Broader Hunter Region, The Planning Process in Newcastle and the Broader Hunter Region Final Report, March 2015, www.parliament.nsw.gov.au/committees/DBAssets/InquiryReport/ReportAcrobat/5748/Final%20Report%20-%20The%20planning%20process%20in%20Newcastle%20a.pdf [accessed 23 April, 2015].
43 Judith Alfrey and Tim Putnamhe (eds), *Industrial Heritage: Managing Resources and Uses*, Routledge, London, 1992 and Chris Landorf, A Framework for Sustainable Heritage Management: A Study of UK Industrial Heritage Sites, *International Journal of Heritage Studies*, Volume 15, Issue 6, pp. 494–510, DOI: 10.1080/13527250903210795.
44 For a good summary of this history and the issues confronting the Fort, see *Fort Scratchley Historic Site – Heritage Management Plan*, Suters Architects and Dawbin Architects Newcastle, 2008, http://nag.org.au/__data/assets/pdf_file/0010/227548/FortHMPFinalSubmissionRevH.pdf [accessed 1 August 2016].
45 See Newcastle Post Office, NSW State Heritage Register Entry, www.environment.nsw.gov.au/heritageapp/ViewHeritageItemDetails.aspx?ID=5051298 [accessed 10 July 2016]. & *The Herald*, New Look for Newcastle's Historic Post Office, 9 June 2016, www.abc.net.au/news/2016-06-09/newcastle-historic-post-office-redesign/7496404 [accessed 20 July 2016].
46 For its website, which also lists the object of the Association, see www.niha.org.au/ [accessed 11 August 2016].
47 ABC News, Former Newcastle Steelworks Buildings Spared from Wrecking Ball, www.abc.net.au/news/2014-09-30/former-newcastle-steelworks-buildings-spared-from-wrecking-ball-/5778096 [accessed 10 July 2016]. The reprieve for these buildings was only temporary and they were finally demolished in 2015.
48 Coal River State Heritage Register Entry, www.environment.nsw.gov.au/heritageapp/ViewHeritageItemDetails.aspx?ID=5053900 [accessed 12 June 2016].

49　These four nominations can be accessed at https://hunterlivinghistories.com/ [accessed 30 July 2016].
50　Mark Maclean, Farewell Old Mate, https://hamiltonnorth.wordpress.com/2015/09/16/farewell-old-friend/ [accessed 12 June 2015]. Thanks to Mark Maclean for granting permission to cite this entry. Alice Mah found similar responses in an industrial suburb of Newcastle (UK). See her Memory, Uncertainty and Industrial Ruination: Walker Riverside, Newcastle upon Tyne, *International Journal of Urban and Regional Research*, 25 March 2010, DOI: 10.1111/j.1468–2427.2010.00898
51　Deborah Stevenson, Reflections of a "Great Port City": The Case of Newcastle, Australia, *Environment and Planning D: Society and Space*, Volume 17, Issue 1, February 1999, pp. 105–119, DOI: 10.1068/d170105
52　See Nancy Cushing, Remembering BHP: Memory and Industrial Heritage, *Workers' Online*, Issue No. 13, 14 May 1999, http://workers.labor.net.au/13/c_historicalfeature_bhp.html [accessed 6 June 2015].

Bibliography

ABC News. Former Newcastle Steelworks Buildings Spared from Wrecking Ball. www.abc.net.au/news/2014-09-30/former-newcastle-steelworks-buildings-spared-from-wrecking-ball-/5778096

ABC News. Newcastle Post Office Redesign. www.abc.net.au/news/2016-06-09/newcastle-historic-post-office-redesign/7496404

Alfrey, Judith & Putnamhe, Tim. (eds). *Industrial Heritage: Managing Resources and Uses*. Routledge, London, 1992.

Atkinson, Alan. *The Europeans in Australia: A History Volume One: The Beginning*. Oxford University Press, Melbourne, 1997.

Ballarat Historic Urban Landscape. 'Historic Urban Landscape Ballarat'. www.hulballarat.org.au

Bennett, James, Cushing, Nancy & Eklund, Erik. (eds). *Radical Newcastle*. New South, Sydney, 2015.

Bodnar, John. *Remaking America: Public Memory, Commemoration, and Patriotism in the Twentieth Century*. Princeton University Press, Princeton, NJ, 1994.

Branagan, David. *Geology and Coal Mining in the Hunter Valley, 1791–1861*. Newcastle Public Library, Newcastle, NSW, 1972.

The Bleak Future Facing Newcastle and its Hinterland, *Canberra Times*, 9 October 1976 p. 2.

Census of NSW, 1901, Habitations, Table VII: The Population and Number of Inhabited Dwellings in Each Municipality in 1891 and 1901, *Census of the Commonwealth of Australia*, 1901. http://hccda.anu.edu.au/pages/NSW-1901-census-02_481

Commonwealth Department of the Environment and Energy. National Heritage List Criteria. www.environment.gov.au/heritage/about/national/national-heritage-list-criteria

Cushing, Nancy. Remembering BHP: Memory and Industrial Heritage. *Workers'Online*, Issue No.13, 14 May 1999, http://workers.labor.net.au/13/c_historicalfeature_bhp.html

Cushing, Nancy. Revisiting "Living History: The City of Newcastle as a Museum". Revised version of paper presented to Hunter Heritage Network Symposium, 30 September 2011. http://hunterheritagenetwork.org/wp-content/uploads/2011/10/nancy-cushing-paper_newcastle-as-a-museum-revisited1.pdf

Docherty, James. *Newcastle: The Making of an Australian City*. Allen & Unwin, Sydney, 1983.

Douet, James. (ed). *Industrial Heritage Retooled*. Carnegie Publishing, Lancaster, UK, 2013.

Dunn, Kevin, McGuirk, Pauline & Winchester, Hilary. Place Making: The Social Construction of Newcastle. *Geographical Research*, October, 1995, DOI: 10.1111/j.1467-8470.1995.tb00691.x

Eardley, Gifford H. *The Railways of the South Maitland Coalfields*. Australian Railway Historical Society, NSW Division, Sydney, 1969.

Eklund, Erik. Managers, Workers, and Industrial Welfarism: Management Strategies at ER&S and the Sulphide Corporation, 1895–1929. *Australian Economic History Review*, Vol.37, No.2, July 1997, DOI: 10.1111/1467-8446.00010

Fort Scratchley Historic Site – Heritage Management Plan, Suters Architects & Dawbin Architects, Newcastle, 2008, http://nag.org.au/__data/assets/pdf_file/0010/227548/FortHMPFinalSubmissionRevH.pdf

Fredman, Lionel E. Goninan, Alfred (1865–1953) and Ralph Williams Goninan (1874–1948), Engineers. In Ritchie, John (ed.), *Australian Dictionary of Biography*. Vol. 14. Melbourne University Press, Melbourne, 1996, pp. 291–292.

Gascoigne, John. *The Enlightenment and the Origins of Australia*. Cambridge University Press, New York, 2002.

Herald, The. New Look for Newcastle's Historic Post Office. 9 June, 2016, www.abc.net.au/news/2016-06-09/newcastle-historic-post-office-redesign/7496404

Hunter Valley Research Foundation. *Diversification of the Hunter Economy Post-BHP*. Hunter Valley Research Foundation, Maryville (Newcastle), 2011.

Hunter Valley Research Foundation. *The Hunter Region at a Glance*. Hunter Valley Research Foundation, Maryville (Newcastle), 1976.

Independent Commission against Corruption (ICAC). Spicer Enquiry. www.icac.nsw.gov.au/investigations/past-investigations/categorylist/12/203

Jones, Roy & Birdsall Jones, Christina. The Contestation of Heritage: The Colonizer and the Colonized in Australia. In Graham, Brian and Howard, Peter (eds.), *The Ashgate Research Companion to Heritage and Identity*. Ashgate Publishing Limited, New York, 2008, pp. 365–440.

Landorf, Chris. A Framework for Sustainable Heritage Management: A Study of UK Industrial Heritage Sites. *International Journal of Heritage Studies*, Vol.15, No.6, pp. 494–510, DOI: 10.1080/13527250903210795

Maclean, Mark. Farewell Old Mate. https://hamiltonnorth.wordpress.com/2015/09/16/farewell-old-friend/

Mah, Alice. Memory, Uncertainty and Industrial Ruination: Walker Riverside, Newcastle upon Tyne. *International Journal of Urban and Regional Research*, 25 March 2010, DOI: 10.1111/j.1468-2427.2010.00898

Metcalfe, Andrew. Mud and Steel: The Imagination of Newcastle. *Labour History*, No.64, May 1993, pp. 1–16.

Moses, Dirk. *Genocide and Settler Society: Frontier Violence and Stolen Indigenous Children in Australian History*. Berghahn, New York, 2004.

Nevell, Michael. Editorial – Industrial Heritage at Risk. *Industrial Archaeology Review*, Vol.33, No.2, November 2011, pp. 79–80.

Newcastle City Council. Newcastle City-Wide Heritage Study, 1996–1997: Volume 3. 1997. https://coalriver.files.wordpress.com/2008/02/1997-nhs-v3-images-m-w.pdf

"Greater Newcastle", *The Newcastle Herald and Miners Advocate*, 10 July, 1917, p. 7.

Newcastle Industrial Heritage Association. Objectives of the Association. www.niha.org.au/staticpages/index.php?page=20040207150655226

Newcastle Port Corporation. *Annual Report for the Period 2007–2008*. Newcastle Port Corporation, Newcastle, 2009

Newcastle Port Corporation. *Annual Report for the Period 2013–2014*. Newcastle Port Corporation, Newcastle, 2015.
New South Wales State Heritage Register. Entry for the Civic Railway Workshops. www.environment.nsw.gov.au/heritageapp/ViewHeritageItemDetails.aspx?ID=5044977
New South Wales State Heritage Register. Entry for the Coal River Precinct. www.environment.nsw.gov.au/heritageapp/ViewHeritageItemDetails.aspx?ID=5053900
New South Wales State Heritage Register. Entry for the Earp Gillam Bond Store. www.environment.nsw.gov.au/heritageapp/ViewHeritageItemDetails.aspx?ID=5044982
New South Wales State Heritage Register. Entry for the Newcastle Post Office. www.environment.nsw.gov.au/heritageapp/ViewHeritageItemDetails.aspx?ID=5051298
Official Yearbook of the Commonwealth of Australia, No.53, Commonwealth Bureau of Census and Statistics, Canberra, 1967
Oliver, Bobbie. More Than Just Locomotives: Re-Discovering Working Lives at the Midland Railway Workshops. *Historic Environment*, Vol.21, No.2, 2008, pp. 20–24.
Peter-Little, Frances, Curthoys, Ann & Docker, John. (eds). *Passionate Histories: Myth, Memory and Indigenous Australia*. ANU E Press, Canberra, 2010.
Richmond Vale Railway Museum. www.richmondvalerailwaymuseum.org/
Roberts, David & Eklund, Erik. Australian Convict Sites and the Heritage of Adaptation: The Case of Newcastle's Coal River Heritage Precinct. *Australian Historical Studies*, Vol.43, No.3, 2012, pp. 363–380.
Roberts, David & Ford, Lisa. New South Wales Penal Settlements and the Transformation of Secondary Punishment in the Nineteenth-Century British Empire. *Journal of Colonialism and Colonial History*, Vol.15, No.3, http://dx.doi.org/10.1353/cch.2014.0038
Rofe, Mark. From "Problem City" to "Promise City": Gentrification and the Revitalisation of Newcastle. *Australian Geographical Studies*, Vol.42, No.2, June 2004, pp. 193–206.
Royal Commission of Inquiry as to the Areas in New South Wales Suitable for Self-Government as States in the Commonwealth of Australia: Also List of Exhibits. *New States Royal Commission*. (H.S. Nicholas), New South Wales. Parliament. Legislative Assembly. Alfred James Kent, Government Printer, Sydney, 1935.
Select Committee on the Planning Process in Newcastle and the Broader Hunter Region. The Planning Process in Newcastle and the Broader Hunter Region Final Report. March 2015. www.parliament.nsw.gov.au/committees/DBAssets/InquiryReport/ReportAcrobat/5748/Final%20Report%20-%20The%20planning%20process%20in%20Newcastle%20a.pdf
Shortland, Jun. to Shortland, Sen. HMS Reliance, Sydney Cove, Port Jackson, *Historical Records of New South Wales*, Vol.3, pp. 481–482.
Smith, Laurajane. *The Uses of Heritage*. Routledge, London and New York, 2006.
Spearitt, Peter. Money, Taste and Industrial Heritage. *Australian Historical Studies*, Vol.23, No.96, 1991.
Stevenson, Deborah. Reflections of a "Great Port City": The Case of Newcastle, Australia. *Environment and Planning D: Society and Space*, Vol.17, No.1, February 1999, pp. 105–119, DOI: 10.1068/d170105
Storm, Anna & Olsson, Krister. The Pit: Landscape Scars as Potential Cultural Tools. *International Journal of Heritage Studies*, Vol.19, No.7, 2013, pp. 692–708.
Taksa, Lucy. Machines and Ghosts: Politics, Industrial Heritage and the History of Working Life at the Eveleigh Workshops. *Labour History*, No. 85, November 2003, pp. 65–88.
Turner, John W. *Coal Mining in Newcastle, 1801 to 1900*. Newcastle City Council, Newcastle, 1982.

UNESCO. Historic Urban Landscape Approach Explained. http://whc.unesco.org/en/news/1026/

Wilkinson, John. Manufacturing and Services in New South Wales. *NSW Parliamentary Library Research Service*, Paper No.3/07. www.parliament.nsw.gov.au/researchpapers/Documents/manufacturing-and-services-in-nsw/ManuFINALandINDEX.pdf

Wright, Chris. The Formative Years of Management Control at the Newcastle Steelworks, 1913–1924. *Labour History*, No.55, November 1988, pp. 55–70, 175.

9 From mills to malls

Industrial heritage and regional identity in metropolitan Pittsburgh

Allen Dieterich-Ward

When employees first erected the Homestead Works' enormous 12,000-ton forging press in 1903, they stood at the center of the world's greatest steel-producing area. Originally built upon a mercantile framework of river cities spread throughout the Upper Ohio River Valley, by the late 19th century heavy industry formed the core of the region's economic life and cultural identity. After being rebuilt during World War II, the 12,000-ton press went on to produce armor plates for U.S. Steel's shipbuilding program through the Korean conflict and America's War in Vietnam. But, the fortunes of metropolitan Pittsburgh's steel industry declined during the postwar years, and by the late 1980s the iconic Homestead Works had been shuttered and largely demolished.

In 1991, the press was left exposed to the elements, standing in the same spot amidst the social and environmental problems of deindustrialization. However, this is not just a narrative of decline. A large real estate company announced plans in 1997 to remake the site into a regional shopping center along the Monongahela River. Dubbed The Waterfront, the automobile-oriented maze of 'big box' retailers situated in the midst of vast parking lots catered to the region's middle-class consumers who often worked in universities, hospitals and other service sector industries. Today the refurbished 12,000-ton press serves as a backdrop for the shoppers milling at its base, though its less-than-ideal location in a parking lot behind a chain home improvement store also suggests the contested nature of industrial heritage in shaping identity in the Pittsburgh metropolitan region (see Figure 9.1).[1]

The phoenix-like tale of the Homestead Works is an apt starting point for this story of a region transformed physically and symbolically. At the beginning of the 20th century, Pittsburgh and its hinterland in southeastern Ohio, southwestern Pennsylvania and northern West Virginia were celebrated examples of America's industrial power. "What energy, what a fury of industry! All Pittsburg at work before the dawn of day!" observed journalist James Parton in 1868, while 30 years later historian Reuben Gold Thwaites declared of a trip down the Monongahela River that mill towns were "literally abutting one upon the other all of the way down to Pittsburg [and] the ear is almost deafened with the whirr and bang of milling industries." Issues both economic and environmental eventually derailed regional prosperity as changes in production lessened locational advantages, while the rugged landscape and pollution problems made much of the area

Figure 9.1 Homestead's 12,000-ton press. Originally part of U.S. Steel's Homestead Works, the press was one of a handful of large artifacts retained when the site was demolished beginning in the late 1980s. The press now stands in the back parking lot of a chain home improvement store.

Photograph by Amanda Dieterich-Ward.

unsuitable for postwar growth industries. As a result of these limitations, by the 1990s abandoned mines and mills stood silent sentinels over a scarred landscape and aging communities wracked by rampant poverty, massive unemployment, and high out-migration particularly among the young and educated.[2]

In the face of economic stagnation and environmental catastrophe, after World War II some business and political leaders in Pittsburgh sought to refashion the city and region in ways that better suited the needs of corporate executives. Spearheaded by the elite Allegheny Conference on Community Development, a central component of this Pittsburgh Renaissance, as it became known, was the new cultural narrative of a city reborn with cleaner air, efficient highways and corporate skyscrapers in the downtown Golden Triangle. "The city welcomed tomorrow, because yesterday was hard and unlovely," Pittsburgh Mayor David Lawrence famously declared. "The town took pleasure in the swing of the headache ball and the crash of the falling brick." From the 1950s to the 1980s, the only "sure irritant" marring the city's "rebirth" was a lingering image problem, "a reference to 'The Smoky City' [with which] no Pittsburgher would be patient." Consequently, the dominant urban planning paradigm throughout the region shifted to erasing the 19th-century industrial landscape in favor of the modernist, highway-oriented framework that urban critic and activist Jane Jacobs famously derided as creating a lifeless "ersatz suburb."[3]

After decades of overall decline, metropolitan Pittsburgh's steel and coal industries collapsed in the 1980s. For the next 20 years, advocates for what we might call a post-industrial vision of regional identity battled for the region's soul with those focused on reopening the shuttered steel mills. Supporters of industrial heritage were forced to walk a tightrope between those who wished to erase the most visible landmarks of the industrial past and those who felt any attempt to memorialize such sites implicitly accepted that the region would never be reindustrialized. In addition to this question of what to remember and how to remember it, the emerging model of neoliberal urbanism that heritage advocates in the City of Pittsburgh itself were able to use to their advantage proved especially difficult for smaller communities in the regional hinterland that once served as important sites of industrial production, such as Wheeling, West Virginia and Homestead, Pennsylvania. Consequently, while adaptive reuse of industrial age sites has become a key organizing principle for economic and community development, the relationship between regional identity and industrial heritage in the early 21st century remains fraught and contested.

The vertically integrated region

Urban development in metropolitan Pittsburgh during the early 19th century spread up from the Ohio River and its tributaries, with wharfs and merchant warehouses giving way to retail establishments and central business districts and finally residential neighborhoods, which often spread to the lower slopes of the surrounding hills. The broken topography of mountains and river valleys tended to concentrate the population in the narrow flatlands as well as foster the growth of numerous, politically independent communities divided by the terrain. Beginning in the 1870s, the transformation from small craft-based industries to enormous integrated mills requiring river and rail access increasingly pushed companies to search for outlying sites for new facilities. As new mills and mines sprang up throughout the rapidly urbanizing river valleys and increasingly industrialized rural countryside, manufacturers, political leaders and engineers developed an extensive railroad system that spread throughout the region. Trunk lines and regional carriers connected the major cities, coal trains linked mill towns to mining camps, and inter-urban lines and streetcars enabled speedy movement within communities and out to their growing hinterlands.[4]

Despite an early reputation as an industrial powerhouse, between 1850 and 1870 the region's manufacturing facilities remained generally small affairs with the stages of production taking place in separate, often independently owned operations. After the financial stimulus provided by the American Civil War, vertical integration grew out the desire to lower unit costs by producing more goods

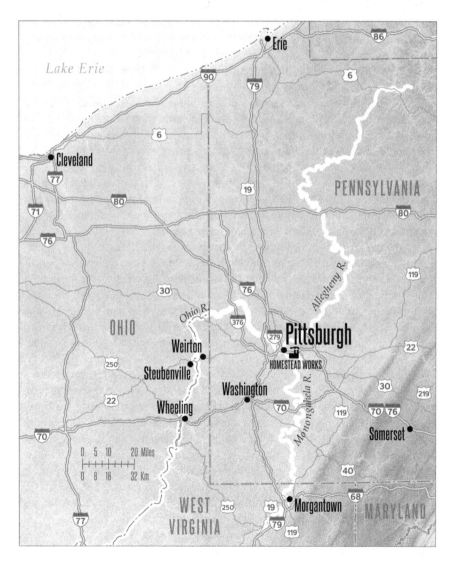

Figure 9.2 The Pittsburgh Metropolitan Region. Map created by Dr. Scott Drzyzga, Department of Geography and Earth Science, Shippensburg University

per investment dollar and cutting labor expenses. Industrialist Andrew Carnegie's first fully integrated steel mill, the Edgar Thomson Works (ET) just up the Monongahela River from Homestead, was a key example of this process in action. As opposed to the traditional separation of processes in the existing iron industry, the plans for ET combined the making of steel using the Bessemer process with the fabrication of steel rails in an integrated method based on cost-data analysis. When it opened in 1875, ET featured a plant with two 5-ton Bessemer converters and a mill capable of producing 225 tons of steel rails daily, an amount that increased to 3,000 tons later in the century. The addition of an onsite blast furnace in 1880 made it possible to transform raw iron ore and coke into finished steel rails all at one facility. ET's success, as one contemporary observer commented, was in the "wonderful power and perfection of the machinery" that made the process continuous and relatively independent of skilled labor.[5]

Between 1872 and 1901 when he sold his company to financier J. P. Morgan as the core of the new U.S. Steel, Carnegie created a vast industrial empire, centered in Pittsburgh, with an enormous array of iron and coal mines, railroad links, furnaces and rolling mills that allowed for the transformation of raw materials into finished products all by Carnegie-controlled companies. Following an infamous labor battle in 1892 at the Homestead Works, Carnegie systematically destroyed the region's once-powerful unions, removing any barrier to management's prerogative of vertical integration. The repercussions of this consolidation spread throughout the Upper Ohio Valley, pulling in hundreds of thousands of new residents, reshaping community bonds and transforming the physical landscape – in effect creating a new regional economy forged around heavy industry that displaced even if it did not fully supersede earlier social structures.[6]

While broadly representative of manufacturing areas more generally, from the 1890s to the 1980s metropolitan Pittsburgh featured two distinctive attributes – a high degree of specialization in basic manufacturing and the domination of a few very large, multidivisional industrial corporations – that together set the stage for its meteoric rise and subsequently hampered efforts at economic diversification. Despite a narrative of industrial dominance promulgated by business leaders and residents alike, few mills opened or expanded in the region after 1920, while air pollution and a devastating flood in 1936 contributed to the growing sense of unease and a negative view of Pittsburgh on the national level. "At worried board meetings," reported the *Atlantic Monthly*, "there was more and more talk of 'leaving Pittsburgh,' and no plans for postwar expansion lay on executive desks." In response, following World War II, Pittsburgh's Republican business elite and Democratic political leaders developed an ambitious program of pollution control and infrastructure development. In addition to clearing the city's notoriously smoky skies, this new public-private partnership made possible the razing and rebuilding of the central business district's Golden Triangle, which became a national model for downtown revitalization in the 1950s and 1960s (see Figure 9.3).[7]

The growth coalition behind the Pittsburgh Renaissance pursued nothing less than the selective erasure of the existing social and physical environment in favor of a modernist, functionally divided landscape: a conceptual goal other aging

Figure 9.3 Pittsburgh's Golden Triangle. Note the fountain and remains of Fort Pitt/ Duquesne at the point where the Monongahela and Allegheny rivers meet to create the Ohio River. City and state officials partnered with business leaders in erasing a dense industrial landscape to create Point State Park and the adjacent skyscrapers of Gateway Center during the Pittsburgh Renaissance.

Photograph by Amanda Dieterich-Ward.

cities widely copied. Emboldened by new downtown skyscrapers, hilltop commuter suburbs and highways blasted through rough terrain, the business-backed Allegheny Conference on Community Development and its local, state and federal allies also sought to refashion the broader region into a form they felt would be more attractive to corporate investment and white-collar workers. However, the social and physical landscapes of the industrial age formed an integrated framework that proved impossible for political leaders and business executives to fully overcome on a regional level. As the authors of the influential *Economic Study of the Pittsburgh Region* explained in 1963,

> it is a long step from a coal miner to an electronics technician: from an obsolete steel mill to a modern industrial park; from a giant corporation to a multitude of innovators and ambitious small entrepreneurs; from Sharpsburg or a Turtle Creek to a Santa Monica.[8]

The growing disconnect among various communities in this "region of contrasts" meant that even as a "brawny city" got ready to put "on a silk shirt," in the words of one *New York Times* reporter, significant questions remained about the viability of a post-industrial identity beyond select neighborhoods and commuter suburbs in the metropolitan core.[9]

Unlike in countries with more centrally-planned industrial policies, the extreme administrative fragmentation of metropolitan Pittsburgh meant that economic development initiatives were scattered across three states, more than a dozen counties, and hundreds of separate municipalities. Hyper-local loyalties and parochial concerns competed with an oftentimes weak sense of regional identity further complicating collaborative responses to industrial decline. Within this context, Wheeling provides a good example of the successes and failures of the Renaissance model in the region's smaller cities. Located about 60 miles southwest of Pittsburgh along the Ohio River, Wheeling began its history in competition with its larger rival, but ended the 19th century as an industrial satellite and secondary service hub. As one local businessman put it in a letter to Andrew Carnegie, "Pittsburg concerns had capital, transportation, business facilities and successful management, which could not be equaled here; and when Pittsburg's real growth began, Wheeling died."[10]

Following World War II, civic leaders sought guidance from Pittsburghers in remaking their downtown, formed a Wheeling Area Conference on Community Development patterned on the Allegheny Conference, and launched their own Wheeling Renaissance. By the mid-1960s, the city's Urban Renewal Authority had cleared riverfront neighborhoods to build parking garages, engineers had built new highways, a bridge and a tunnel to conquer the unruly landscape, and plans were in the works to replace much of the aging central business district with a new enclosed shopping center. However, the smaller city had neither Pittsburgh's economic base nor its powerful political machine, and after a referendum eliminated the urban renewal authority, in the early 1970s Wheeling's Renaissance sputtered to a halt leaving behind a score of empty lots and no administrative capacity to do much about them.[11]

Rust and response

Through the mid-1950s, the overall region shared in the economic prosperity enjoyed by the U.S. as a whole despite a wave of strikes in the coal and steel industries. Though dwindling mining jobs spurred population loss in many rural areas and helped keep unemployment rates above the national average, it was not until the recession of 1957–1958 that the region's political and economic elite really began to worry about deeper structural challenges to prosperity. Even as the national economy began to recover in 1959, southwestern Pennsylvania's unemployment rate remained stubbornly high with a spike of 10.7 per cent in 1961 when the national average was at 6.7 per cent. Limited economic opportunities resulted in a nearly 4 per cent drop in the region's population between 1960 and 1980 during a period when the nation grew by a quarter and metropolitan areas increased more than 40 per cent. "Increasingly the farmsteads are deserted; and in the coal towns unemployed miners wait to see if the pits will ever reopen," one report concluded. "Along the rivers the mills towns are built around factories half a century old; and some of these factories stand bleak and empty while the furloughed workers worry about their futures."[12]

This slow decline in manufacturing accelerated rapidly beginning in the late 1970s. In addition to the closure of most U.S. Steel mills in the region, dozens of smaller manufacturers, too, shut down or dramatically downsized; LTV Steel (formerly Jones & Laughlin) closed most of its Pittsburgh and Aliquippa plants in 1985, the same year that Wheeling-Pittsburgh Steel declared bankruptcy. The passage of revisions to the federal Clean Air Act in 1990 also capped a decade of turmoil in the coal industry, with mines supplying electrical power plants operating at an increasing disadvantage to low sulfur coal suppliers in other regions. Between 1988 and 1996 mining employment remained virtually unchanged in western states, but declined by nearly 50 per cent in Ohio and Pennsylvania and nearly 30 per cent in West Virginia. As a consequence, while metropolitan Pittsburgh declined by an average of nearly 6,000 residents annually between 1960 and 1980, more than 20,000 residents left the region every year during the 1980s.[13]

Responses to deindustrialization generally took one of two broad forms. First, as early as the 1950s some corporate and university officials began laying the foundations for a post-industrial economy centered on business services, higher education and healthcare. The 1962 selection of Robert H. Ryan, a graduate of Harvard Business School and vice president of the Boston Development Authority, as president of the nonprofit Regional Industrial Development Corporation signaled a desire to build on existing research and development activities at companies such as Westinghouse and institutions such as Carnegie Mellon University. Ryan's vision of "invent[ing] new ways for industry to grow," "especially ... the kinds of industries [that] didn't even exist 10 years ago ... with two guys out of a research lab in a garage" undergirded the decision in the late 1980s to transform part of LTV Steel's abandoned Pittsburgh Works along the Monongahela River into the Pittsburgh Technology Center (see Figure 9.4). Just a year and a half after the closure of the nearby Homestead Works, the site was completely cleared with advocates declaring a "readiness for real growth in technology companies and jobs. It is time to develop a strategy to make the Greater Pittsburgh region itself a Technology Park."[14]

Even as employment growth in health, business and educational services continued in what boosters celebrated as a "collective career change," modest post-industrial successes existed side-by-side with the reality of a deindustrializing region. It was a long step from steel workers and coal miners to nurses and secretaries, a process that involved a transformation of deeply ingrained notions of masculinity as well as expensive and extensive retraining over a period of years. Despite a stated desire to "shift people and physical resources from one activity to another, and to train and retrain individuals for changing and altogether new tasks," day-to-day needs often preempted training for a better position, while the massive layoffs in manufacturing created an imbalance between job seekers and available positions, even for those who obtained a college degree. Race, class and gender distinctions also shaped the distribution of wealth in post-industrial Pittsburgh. As a result, while Pittsburgh's unemployment rate fell to 6.9 per cent for white men and 4.4 per cent for white women during the early 1990s, it remained at 14.3 per cent for black women and nearly 20 per cent for black men.[15]

Consequently, a focus on restarting closed mills formed an important alternative to the post-industrial strategy. Advocates of reindustrialization scored perhaps

Figure 9.4 Clearing Ground for the Pittsburgh Technology Center, 1993. Note the shuttered mills of the South Side portion of the LTV facility across the Monongahela River. Attribution: Lowe, Jet, "View of Jones and Laughlin from Oakland Looking South."

Photograph: Historic American Engineering Record, National Park Service, U.S. Department of the Interior, 1979. From Prints and Photographs Division, Library of Congress (HAER LA,29-THIB,1A—3).

their most important victory in the employee buyout of National Steel's mill in Weirton, West Virginia. To pay for the deal, workers gave up a substantial portion of their wages and benefits in exchange for profit sharing, a relationship known as an Employee Stock Ownership Plan (ESOP). The new company was immediately profitable and for much of the 1980s employment remained above 8,000. More radical groups such as the Tri-State Conference on Steel led reindustrialization campaigns at Crucible Steel in Midland, Mesta Machine Company in West Homestead, and Westinghouse Air Brake among many others. In January 1985, more than five hundred people participated in a rally to save the Dorothy Six blast furnace at U.S. Steel's Duquesne Works, with speakers including union president Lynn Williams, Pittsburgh Mayor Richard Caliguiri and the Rev. Jesse Jackson, who declared the Mon Valley "the Selma of the plant shutdown movement." Indeed, even as civic boosters touted their status as America's "Most Livable City" and national newspapers ran stories with titles like "Brawn Forged into Brain," the widespread appearance of "Save Dorothy" bumper stickers, t-shirts and coffee mugs revealed the persistence of a regional identity rooted in blue-collar work.[16]

One of the most sustained and visible attempts to implement community-led reindustrialization focused on the LTV mill site across the Monongahela River from what would become the Pittsburgh Technology Center. Efforts to restart the city's last integrated mill after the closure of the South Side Works in 1985 were led by the newly formed Steel Valley Authority (SVA) composed of eight smaller communities and the City of Pittsburgh. While SVA officials were able to delay the demolition of much of the South Side Works, the supporters of reindustrialization faced serious economic obstacles. Local and state governments proved unwilling (or unable) to commit the hundreds of millions need to restart the mill and private capital was not available at a time of oversupply in the basic steel industry. With this basic scenario repeating itself throughout the region and the broader Rust Belt, as the 1980s drew to a close, a deindustrializing metropolitan Pittsburgh continued to hemorrhage both jobs and residents.[17]

Forging a regional identity

The two former LTV mill sites facing each other across the Monongahela River in Pittsburgh became potent symbols of a broader struggle over regional identity. Historically, the Upper Ohio Valley's location at the intersection of the cultures and economies of the U.S. Northeast, Midwest and Appalachian regions made it difficult at times to discern a distinct regional identity, as the unifying factors of a shared geography and economy vied with the various political and administrative boundaries inherent in a multi-state region. Nevertheless, by the late 19th century a system of rural coal mines and industrial mill towns connected via an extensive network of railroads and administered by corporate executives in Pittsburgh, Wheeling and other smaller cities formed the foundation for a common economy and culture. The rugged, mountainous topography separated and distinguished the region's communities from those in other areas, while creating similar problems and opportunities for residents. The Ohio River and its tributaries were also a constant presence whether commuters were on bridges, miners were loading coal onto barges, residents were dealing with water pollution, or boaters were enjoying a sunny day on the water.

During the eighteenth and nineteenth centuries, the Pittsburgh area emerged first as an imperial frontier, then as a riverine mercantile community, and finally as the industrial Steel Valley, with shifting borders, economic foundations and cultural imagery. This is not to suggest that there is anything inherently linking the major cities of the area outside of historical contingency – residents' identities as living in a shared region ebbed and flowed according to broader economic and political patterns. Indeed, during the 19th century Steubenville, Pittsburgh and Wheeling were fierce competitors, with the latter rivalry becoming particularly bitter during the infamous bridge war of the 1840s and 1850s. That said, by the 1890s Pittsburgh had eclipsed its neighbors, drawing them into a metropolitan orbit and making of them industrial satellites. Transportation infrastructure served as an important indicator of this changing framework as rivers, canals and later railroads bound the region, separating it from other early corridors such as the Great Lakes or the Cumberland Gap. The construction of railroads and trolleys reinforced an urban development pattern that began at the riverfront, extended up the surrounding hills and connected through a dense network of tracks to the mining towns and rural hamlets in the surrounding countryside.[18]

On the other hand, following World War II, links between the Steubenville/ Wheeling and greater Pittsburgh portions of the region actually decreased due to a number of political and economic factors. The powerful pro-growth coalition in southwestern Pennsylvania responsible for the Pittsburgh Renaissance successfully attracted millions in state and federal road dollars, for example, but the growing network of highways stopped at the state line because the smaller populations of Steubenville and Wheeling failed to generate equivalent support from Columbus and Charleston. In effect, the decline of the railroads increased the *relative* distance between Pittsburgh and its smaller neighbors in the industrialized river valleys, challenging the bonds of both culture and commerce. Further, the increasing economic disparities between communities due to deindustrialization threatened to break down the economic and cultural bonds that had unified the region. By the 1980s metropolitan Pittsburgh was, in effect, two regions; one, in the industrialized river valleys and on the rural periphery, featured a continued reliance on the mills and mines, low education levels, high out-migration and increasing poverty – the other, in select urban neighborhoods and highway-oriented suburbs, focused on universities and healthcare, two sectors that had received generous state subsidies.[19]

Pittsburgh's regional identity had long rested on a cultural construction of the region's environment, both human and manmade, that centered on heavy industrial production and extractive industries. During the late 19th century, communities faced away from rivers that became sewers and canals, mills and mines refashioned the contours of the earth itself, and smoke that became a signature of economic prosperity filled the air. A century later, however, economic development officials as well as residents employed in the region's expanding research and service sectors increasingly saw traditional imagery rooted in the dirty, blue-collar mills of the industrialized river valleys as "a barrier to recruiting talent, attracting businesses, and giving the Pittsburgh market area the economic stature it deserves." The Allegheny Conference's chief marketing official even joked that the Pittsburgh Steelers should change their name to the "Pittsburgh Softwares" in order to encourage new investment.[20]

Other residents, particularly steelworkers and their families, met attempts to separate the region's economy and imagery from heavy industrial production with skepticism and alarm, especially during the economic upheaval of the 1980s. "Pittsburgh looks beautiful," declared AFL-CIO labor union president Lane Kirkland on a visit to the Monongahela Valley in 1985. "But I'd like to see it a little dirtier, a little more smoke. The most environmentally offensive thing I see is the shutdown mills." As they discussed the region's problems many of those on the rural periphery, too, linked increasing unemployment with new environmental regulations, particularly the Clean Air Act, and envisioned a return to the industrial past. "The whole bottom line is: knock the EPA out!" railed one resident. "We want work. We don't want the clean air. We want the factories back. We want the mines back."[21]

As job losses intensified in the late 1980s, debates over economic policy were thus intimately intertwined with a more fundamental battle over metropolitan

Pittsburgh's regional identity. "Image is terribly important [and] ours is more negative than it should be," complained one advertising executive. While postindustrial boosters insisted they "were not trying to put the knock on steel," they celebrated a narrative of the Pittsburgh Technology Center where "the city's steelmaking past [was] being buried under 90,000 cubic yards of dirt to prepare for a future shaped by robots and miracle drugs."[22] In response, campaigners associated most closely with unemployed steelworkers and their families undertook controversial direct action campaigns such as depositing fish in safety deposit boxes and dumping pennies in the lobbies of banks accused of disinvestment in the steel industry. In response to challenges that their tactics were "keeping out the very people who might be able to bring some hope," one local minister and activist replied, "They can have their image back as soon as they deliver for the people."[23]

"The past *must* have a place in the total picture of the city"

Even as the very public battle over post- versus reindustrialization was in full swing, the first major site to embrace industrial heritage as a tool for economic and community development was emerging near the LTV site on Pittsburgh's South Side. Back in the mid-1960s, some residents had begun to criticize the focus of the Pittsburgh Renaissance on razing the existing built environment and instead advocated the adaptive reuse of industrial age structures. In 1964, two architectural enthusiasts and their supporters founded the Pittsburgh History and Landmarks Foundation (PHLF), an organization that would play a key role on the local, regional and national levels. Heritage advocates lambasted urban renewal for being "too much involved with tearing down, building and relegating the labor and money investment of the past to the dump heap." Instead, PHLF founders Arthur Ziegler and James Van Trump argued, "the past *must* have a place in the total picture of the city."[24]

PHLF's initial activities focused on preserving a few important sites and rehabilitating Victorian-era housing, but in 1976 the group used a $5-million foundation grant and a $2-million investment by an outside restauranteur to purchase the old Pittsburgh and Lake Erie Railroad Terminal on the city's South Side. The transformation of the 52-acre site into a mixed-use development known as Station Square marked the region's first major articulation of heritage-based economic and community development and formed a key example of the role of industrial heritage in shaping regional identity. The Express House opened as a three-story office building in 1977, followed by the 550-seat Grand Concourse restaurant (1978), Bessemer Court (1979), Freight House shops (1979) and Commerce Court (1982). In 1981, a national advertising campaign highlighting how Pittsburgh was "a city where historic neighborhoods are renewing themselves [and] classic architecture combines with contemporary living," featured Station Square prominently. By 1994, the year PHLF sold the site to finance new projects, the 134 shops, offices and restaurants overlooking the Monongahela River received more than 3 million visitors a year and created an estimated 3,000 jobs (see Figure 9.5).[25]

Figure 9.5 Station Square. A festival marketplace developed by the Pittsburgh History and Landmarks Foundation on the site of the former Pittsburgh and Lake Erie Railroad Terminal. Note the prominent placement of the industrial artifact at the entrance to Bessemer Court.

Photograph by Alexander Klyuch via Wikimedia Commons.

There are two key ideas here to focus on; first, the success of Station Square and its symbolic inclusion in a new round of urban renewal in the 1980s, which boosters dubbed Renaissance II, highlighted the increasing role of foundations and community development corporations in conceiving and nurturing new approaches to development within a context of 'neoliberal urbanism.'[26] Second, the success of Station Square in using heritage principles to re-imagine an abandoned riverfront industrial site flew in the face of the dominant trope of raze and rebuild urban renewal. This framework, which we can see beginning with the Renaissance and accelerating through the massive projects of the 1960s, largely ignored both the existing built infrastructure and the rivers in favor of modernist-inspired buildings and suburban-style land use planning that essentially viewed brownfields as expensive greenfields in the making.[27]

However, Station Square's model of adaptive reuse was adopted only in fits and starts by municipal officials in the 1980s as other high profile projects continued the earlier tower-in-the-park model that saw industrial age infrastructure as both a symbolic and physical obstacle to be overcome. A good example of this is the Pittsburgh Technology Center built on part of LTV Steel's shuttered mill, which makes no reference in its site design to either industrial heritage or even the adjacent riverfront. On the other hand, beginning in the mid-1990s some Pittsburgh officials, including Mayor Tom Murphy (1994–2005) championed the conversion of abandoned rail lines into recreational trails, poured municipal resources into the remediation of polluted brownfield sites, and advocated for offices, museums, theaters and sports stadiums, some of which adaptively reused existing buildings, that embraced rather than ignored the rivers and prioritized some heritage-oriented renovation, including the transformation of the Chautauqua Lake Ice Company Building into the Heinz History Center.[28]

While his relationship with preservation groups such as PHLF was often rocky, Murphy generally articulated a vision of industrial heritage as central to regional identity, such as when he declared a new Three Rivers Heritage Trail created from abandoned railroad rights-of-way, "A Twelve Mile Story of Who We Are." As a result, from the Murphy Administration on there was a broad agreement among Pittsburgh city officials that post-industrial transformation was often compatible with promoting industrial heritage. Indeed, following the 2002 publication of *Rise of the Creative Class* by urban theorist Richard Florida, at the time a professor at Carnegie Mellon University, innovative reuse of industrial age sites in the city became closely associated with fostering the dynamic urban environment sought by young, urban professionals.[29]

However, the problem with beginning and ending the discussion with Pittsburgh itself is that so many of its industrial sites had long been demolished as corporate executives moved away from using the central city as a site of actual industrial production in the 20th century. Further, Pittsburgh was an outlier in terms of having extraordinary access to the financial and political capital that was simply unavailable to the region's smaller communities. Once again, a good comparison is with Wheeling, where in the late 1980s, local advocates also joined forces with the business community and municipal officials with the goal of using heritage preservation as an economic development tool. Despite a timely grant from a Pittsburgh-based foundation, the reality was that Wheeling had neither the private funding nor the public administrative capacity to carry out on their own even a modest version of what Pittsburgh achieved during the same period. Fortunately, the city had an advocate in West Virginia Senator Robert C. Byrd, who introduced legislation in August 1993 to create a National Heritage Area in Wheeling, secured $4.7 million dollars for development projects in the city, and earmarked $3 million more for future use. This 'early Byrd' money, as supporters later dubbed it, made possible a raft of investments that carried downtown revitalization through the early 21st century, including the 13.1 mile Heritage Rail-Trail, an amphitheater and marina dubbed the Heritage Port, a parking garage that housed a modest visitor's center, and the $6 million Wheeling Artisan Center featuring exhibits, an arts and crafts retail shop, art gallery and a (financially-shaky) brew-pub (see Figure 9.6).[30]

While the creation of these attractions seemed to provide a focal point for recreating regional identity, in terms of promoting industrial heritage the Wheeling National Heritage Area had significant drawbacks. From the perspective of the National Park Service, Wheeling's national importance was as a 'Gateway to the West' in the early 19th century and as a center of artisanal rather than vertically integrated production. As a result, it proved difficult to craft a coherent message that could both define the city for outsiders as well as resonate with the self-image of residents. Further, the scope of the National Heritage Area was quite small as the state boundary of the Ohio River limited its scale to the city itself. Consequently, the historical significance of an integrated industrial process that linked the central city to mill towns and mining camps was largely lost in an overwhelmingly local narrative.[31]

Figure 9.6 Wheeling Artisan Center. An adaptive reuse of an 1868 warehouse, the federally funded Artisan Center opened in 1999 as a centerpiece of the Wheeling National Heritage Area. It contains a first-floor restaurant, a heritage-themed gift shop, banquet facilities and office space.

Photograph by Allen Dieterich-Ward.

Despite modest successes, the city's public-partnership really struggled in an atmosphere of neoliberal urbanism to maintain even a dramatically scaled back development program as there were simply no public or private resources that could compensate for the trailing off of federal funds in the first decades of the 21st century. And this is a problem, because the basic premise of National Heritage Areas was to prime-the-pump of local investment so that local organizations could be self-sufficient in the long run. As changes on the federal level made it increasingly difficult for Senator Byrd to channel money to the city, local officials pinned their hopes for revitalizing downtown on plans for a Victorian-themed shopping area that had little to do with industrial heritage even as the area's industrial-age infrastructure continued to crumble for lack of interested buyers.[32]

We see a similar set of challenges, but a very different conceptual and administrative framework if we turn to metropolitan Pittsburgh's other National Heritage Area – Rivers of Steel, headquartered in Homestead. Following the closure of the Homestead Works, in 1987 U.S. Steel sold the site to the Park Corporation, a Cleveland-based industrial salvager. Local residents spent the next decade watching the region's rusted heart being cleared and sold for scrap, even as the borough itself entered the state's distressed communities program in 1993. Despite the formation of a Steel Industry Heritage Task Force that advocated for the creation of a large park showcasing the region's "proud and nationally significant" industrial history, the company demolished much of the site during the early 1990s. In 1997, the portion of the site in Homestead along the south side of the Monongahela opened as a large shopping area called The Waterfront, that retained a few decontextualized industrial artifacts, such as the iconic Open Hearth Stacks, a modest interpretive building at the site of the infamous 1892 labor battle, and the 12,000-ton press.[33]

As in Wheeling, the costs associated with transforming the riverfront site dwarfed the available local resources as proponents looked to state and federal agencies for funding. Similar to Senator Byrd, U.S. Senator John Heinz introduced a series of measures that helped fund National Park Service planning studies in Homestead. Further, unlike the very modest support Wheeling received from the state of West Virginia, Pennsylvania developed a state Heritage Areas program, creating a bureaucratic and funding framework on which local heritage proponents would build. With backing from Pittsburgh foundations, in 1990 the Steel Industry Task Force hired August Carlino as executive director and he continued through the formation of the Steel Industry Heritage Corporation and is still at the helm today. The corporation acquired and began restoring the Bost Building, a former hotel in Homestead that served as union headquarters during the infamous 1892 labor unrest, as an archive, museum and visitor's center. In April 1996 Rivers of Steel was designated as the state's eighth 'heritage park' and later that year President Clinton signed the bill designating the region a National Heritage Area.[34]

For a variety of reasons, the folks at Rivers of Steel ended up taking a different approach to industrial heritage than either Pittsburgh or Wheeling, which resulted in a different set of successes and failure. With their efforts to create a grand industrial museum out of the Homestead Works stymied, Carlino and his allies began to reevaluate their strategy in terms of both regional development and community empowerment. Homestead's central location coupled with Pennsylvania's proactive state heritage areas program allowed Rivers of Steel to scale up their activities to a regional level, acting as a coordinating body between government agencies and private businesses within the emerging framework of neoliberal urbanism. Over time, this allowed for the creation of a regional coalition that linked preservationists to a range of community development corporations throughout southwestern Pennsylvania.[35]

According to Carlino, staff members would "go as community organizers with the philosophy that they weren't going to do project themselves, but needed to find people in those communities that would come to the table willing to do it."[36] For advocates, making a place for the industrial past in the post-industrial future was about more than attracting tourists. What we "were saying is that this region has a very unique, iconic image and it's one that no place else can claim," Carlino explained. In terms of shaping regional identity, this actually brought them into conflict at times with civic boosters. Carlino explained that they had "a huge battle" with the Allegheny Conference on Communality Development because of the focus by business groups on "rebranding Pittsburgh" in the 1990s. For Carlino, it seemed like regional marketers were saying that the region's industrial "heritage and anyone that worked in mining or manufacturing or a job related to that wasn't important to the new Pittsburgh." Instead, he argued, the goal of heritage advocates was to say "look who we were, look who we are. We still are that way even though all of this deindustrialization occurred and that is to be proud of [and] built on."[37]

Conclusion: "this old stuff is what the millennials love"

As the nascent vision of a regional identity that combined heritage and high-tech began to take shape in the early 21st century, the ongoing impasse over the preservation of the Carrie Furnaces remained a symbol of the pragmatic difficulties faced by preservationists in forming effective public-private partnerships to preserve industrial sites, especially outside of Pittsburgh itself. Finally, in 2005 county officials announced agreement on a plan to purchase the 137 acres north of the river for $5.75 million. The next year, the National Park Service finally declared the Carrie Furnaces a National Historic Landmark more than 25 years after advocates began working to create a great museum of Pittsburgh's steel industry. Rivers of Steel's eventual success in saving the site, which is currently being developed in tandem with a broader mixed-use site plan that is integrated with the surrounding communities, suggests the potential, however fraught, of heritage preservation in creating powerful symbols around which diverse coalitions can be assembled within the market-driven framework of neoliberal urban policy. "This old stuff is what the millennials love," one heritage advocated proudly declared. "It's got this authentic element to it that kids, twenty-somethings, find cool (see Figure 9.7)."[38]

Wheeling, too, has had some success in framing economic development initiatives around heritage themes, though industrialization is still only one among several narratives shaping regional identity. The city scored a coup in 2001 when community leaders recruited the San Francisco-based law firm of Orrick, Herrington & Sutcliffe to establish its global operations center in the former Wheeling Stamping Building a few blocks away from the beautifully renovated Baltimore and Ohio Railroad Station that reopened as a community college. Currently, loft apartments are being built nearby in another late 19th century warehouse creating an urban space that looks a lot like some vibrant neighborhoods in Pittsburgh. On the other hand, in much of the city a lack of demand has meant that dozens of Victorian houses and other historic properties are razed each year. This includes the recent demolition of the iconic LaBelle Iron Works, which operated from 1852 to 2010, and gave Wheeling its nickname of "Nail City." "This place has so much historic value, it's unbelievable," lamented one former mill employee. "I don't know if anyone realizes that."[39]

Finally, these themes also continue to play out in Pittsburgh itself where many residents are struggling to come to terms with their new status as a hip, high-tech destination that has recently attracted the likes of Uber and Google to repurposed industrial sites in neighborhoods such as East Liberty and Lawrenceville. Here the region's industrial heritage is both widely embraced and contested terrain as the adaptive reuse of industrial-era buildings can often become a sort-of stand-in for evaluating the extent to which the existing population of local areas can

From mills to malls 207

Figure 9.7 Carrie Furnaces, 2015. Built in 1907, the blast furnaces on the north side of the Monongahela River produced iron for the Homestead Works until 1978. Much of the site was demolished before being purchased by Allegheny County in 2005. Furnaces 6 and 7 were declared a National Historic Landmark in 2006 and are now part of the Rivers of Steel National Heritage Area.

Photograph by Amanda Dieterich-Ward.

benefit from the influx of new jobs that often require college degrees for anything approaching a living wage. Once again the former LTV mill along the Monongahela River has an important role to play as the final production facility on the site, a coke works, closed in 1997 – leaving the 178-acre site as the last major undeveloped area in the city. While the coalition of nonprofit foundations that purchased the mill razed most of the property in preparation for new development, in a departure from the Renaissance model of erasing the past, they retained one enormous former mill building and a historic railroad roundhouse slated to become the site's centerpieces. "This site was the cradle of innovation in steelmaking," the site developer declared in a demonstration of how central industrial heritage has become to the region's identity, "and today it's going to be the cradle of innovation in the next industries that drive Pittsburgh. . . . This is the building that they are going to show to showcase the new Pittsburgh."[40]

Notes

1 For a fuller analysis of the topics covered in this chapter, see Allen Dieterich-Ward, *Beyond Rust: Metropolitan Pittsburgh and the Fate of Industrial America* (Philadelphia, 2016).

2. James Parton, Pittsburg, *Atlantic Monthly*, Jan. 1868, 21; Reuben Gold Thwaites, *Afloat on the Ohio: An Historical Pilgrimage of a Thousand Miles in a Skiff from Redstone to Cairo* (New York, 1900), 13.
3. David Lawrence, Rebirth, in Stefan Lorant, *Pittsburgh: The Story of an American City* (Garden City, 1999), 373; Jane Jacobs, Downtown Is for People, in William H. Whyte, Jr., ed., *The Exploding Metropolis* (Berkeley, 1993), 159.
4. Edward Muller and Joel Tarr, The Interaction of Natural and Built Environments in the Pittsburgh Landscape, in Joel A. Tarr, ed., *Devastation and Renewal: An Environmental History of Pittsburgh and Its Region* (Pittsburgh, 2003).
5. John Ingham, *Making Iron and Steel: Independent Mills in Pittsburgh, 1820–1920* (Columbus, 1991), 48; Edward Steven Slavishak, *Bodies of Work: Civic Display and Labor in Industrial Pittsburgh* (Durham, 2008), 28.
6. Harold Livesay, *Andrew Carnegie and the Rise of Big Business* (New York, 2007); Paul Krause, *The Battle for Homestead, 1880–1892* (Pittsburgh, 1992).
7. Sherie R. Mershon, *Corporate Social Responsibility and Urban Revitalization: The Allegheny Conference on Community Development, 1943–1968* (Ph.D. thesis, Pittsburgh, Carnegie Mellon University, 2004). Quote is from Karl Schriftgiesser, The Pittsburgh Story, *Atlantic Monthly*, May 1951.
8. Max Nurnberg, *Economic Study of the Pittsburgh Region, Vol. III: Region with a Future* (Pittsburgh: University of Pittsburgh Press, 1963), 267.
9. Max Nurnberg, *Economic Study of the Pittsburgh Region, Vol. III: Region with a Future* (Pittsburgh, 1963), 267; Southwestern Pennsylvania Regional Planning Commission, *Issues in a Region of Contrasts* (Pittsburgh, 1968); Douglas Kneeland, Pittsburgh: A Brawny City Puts on a Silk Shirt, *New York Times*, Oct. 3, 1970.
10. Nelson C. Hubbard, to Hon. Andrew Carnegie, Letter, Wheeling, WV, May 12, 1899, copy in author's possession.
11. For more on postwar urban renewal in Wheeling, see Allen Dieterich-Ward, "Live on the Hills and Work in the City": Rise and Fall of Renaissance in Pittsburgh's Regional Hinterland, *Journal of Urban History* 41, no. 1 (Jan. 2015).
12. U.S. Bureau of the Census and Inter-University Consortium for Political and Social Research, *County and City Data Book* (Ann Arbor, MI: ICPSR, 1947–1983); U.S. Bureau of the Census, *Statistical Abstract of the United States*, 117th ed. (Washington, DC, 1997); Ira S. Lowry and Pittsburgh Regional Planning Association, *Economic Study of the Pittsburgh Region, Vol. II: Portrait of a Region* (Pittsburgh, 1963), 33, 48–49.
13. John P. Hoerr, *And the Wolf Finally Came: The Decline of the American Steel Industry* (Pittsburgh, 1988), 11; Jonathan P. Hicks, Bankruptcy Helps a Steelmaker, *New York Times*, Jul. 19, 1990, D1; David McDermott, Coal Mining in the U.S. West: Price and Employment Trends, *Monthly Labor Review*, Aug. 1997, 18–23; U.S. Bureau of the Census and Inter-University Consortium for Political and Social Research, *County and City Data Book*.
14. William Allan, Plan to Gain Industry Told by RIDC Chief, *Pittsburgh Press*, Feb. 15, 1962, 1, 14; Donald Miller, Building the Future on the Past, *Pittsburgh Post-Gazette*, Mar. 2, 1993, D1; Working Together Consortium, *The Greater Pittsburgh Region: Working Together to Compete Globally*, Nov. 1994.
15. Editorial Board, High-Promise High-Tech, *Pittsburgh Post-Gazette*, Nov. 28, 1990, C2; Nurnberg, *Region with a Future*, 232; Ralph L. Bangs and Vijai P. Singh, *The State of the Region: Economic, Demographic and Social Trends in Southwestern Pennsylvania* (Pittsburgh: University Center for Social Research, 1988), 98; Ralph L. Bangs and J.H. Hong, *Black and White Economic Conditions in the City of Pittsburgh* (Pittsburgh: University Center for Social Research, 1995).
16. David T. Javersak, *History of Weirton, West Virginia* (Virginia Beach, 1999); Associated Press, In Strife-Torn Valley, a Quiet Effort to Save Jobs, *Philadelphia Inquirer*, Jan. 8, 1985, B2; Mike Stout, Reindustrialization from Below: The Steel Valley Authority, *Labor Research Review* 1, no. 9 (1986), 25; Marty Willis, Jackson Seeks

"New Formula" *New Pittsburgh Courier*, Feb. 2, 1985, 1, 3; Dale Russakoff, Brawn Forged into Brain, *Washington Post*, Apr. 12, 1987, A1; Lindsey Gruson, Clean Pittsburgh Air Symbolizes Economic Shift, *New York Times*, May 10, 1987, 18; Peter Perl, Union Leaders Tour Rusted "Mon Valley", *Washington Post*, Aug. 13, 1985, A4; Christopher Briem, Parsing the "New Pittsburgh" Narrative, editorial, *Pittsburgh Post-Gazette*, Mar. 1, 2015, D1.

17 Mary Kane, Steel Valley Panel Facing Tough Road in Plant Takeover, *Pittsburgh Press*, Dec. 13, 1987, A8; Thomas Buell, Jr., Steel Venture's Chances of Success Dim with Time, *Pittsburgh Press*, Aug. 19, 1990, D18.

18 Edward Slavishak, *Bodies of Work: Civic Display and Labor in Industrial Pittsburgh* (Durham, 2008); Muller and Tarr, The Interaction of Natural and Built Environments in the Pittsburgh Landscape.

19 Andrew T. Simpson, Health and Renaissance: Academic Medicine and the Remaking of Modern Pittsburgh, *Journal of Urban History* 41, no. 1 (Jan. 2015), 19–27.

20 Allegheny Conference on Community Development, *A Strategy for Growth: An Economic Development Program for the Pittsburgh Region* (Pittsburgh, 1984); Don Oldenburg, The Selling of American Cities, *Washington Post*, Dec. 17, 1985, B5.

21 Perl, Union Leaders; Jim McPharlin, prod., "The Ohio Remote: American Dreams Shattered," in *The Oprah Winfrey Show* (USA: WLS-TV, 1988). EPA refers to the Environmental Protection Agency, the federal government agency tasked with implementing environmental laws.

22 Dan Fitzpatrick, Stuck with Steel, *Pittsburgh Post-Gazette*, Nov. 3, 2002, D1.

23 Dan Fitzpatrick, Stuck with Steel, *Pittsburgh Post-Gazette*, Nov. 3, 2002, D1; Associated Press, Rust Belt Cities Are Trading in Old Economies, *Philadelphia Inquirer*, Nov. 26, 1987, J1; Michael Drayton, A New Ballgame, *Tampa Tribune*, Dec. 14, 1992, 1; Christopher H. Marquis, Radical Ministers Make Waves Over Joblessness in Pittsburgh, *Christian Science Monitor*, Sep. 30, 1985, 1.

24 Arthur P. Ziegler, Jr., Observations, *Charette, Pennsylvania Journal of Architecture* 46, no. 8 (Aug. 1966), 4; James D. Van Trump, *1300–1335 Liverpool Street, Manchester, Old Allegheny, Pittsburgh* (Pittsburgh: Pittsburgh History & Landmarks Foundation, 1965), 5, 20.

25 Roberta Brandes Gratz, *The Living City: How America's Cities Are Being Revitalized by Thinking Small in a Big Way* (New York, 1994), 286–288; Walter Kidney, *A Past Still Alive: The Pittsburgh History and Landmarks Foundation Celebrates Twenty-Five Years* (Pittsburgh, 1989), 126–130; Joyce Gannon, Rolling Down the River, *Pittsburgh Post-Gazette*, Nov. 18, 1997, F1. Quote is from Penn's Southwest Association, *Dynamic Pittsburgh: It's a Vital, Vibrant, Historic, Sporting, Bright, Breakthrough, Resourceful Place to Live and Work* (Pittsburgh, 1981), 23.

26 The term "neoliberal urbanism" refers broadly to changes in the public policy framework of American cities since the 1970s, which includes such activities as the privatization and dismantling of public services, the increasing use of tax credits and other novel financing instruments, and the expanded role of public-private partnerships. See Jason Hackworth, *The Neoliberal City: Governance, Ideology, and Development in American Urbanism* (Ithaca, 2006); Jamie Peck, Nik Theodore and Neil Renner, Neoliberal Urbanism: Models, Moments, Mutations, *SAIS Review* 19, no. 1 (Winter-Spring 2009), 49–66. For a comparative study of urban renewal and image-making during this period in Pittsburgh and Hamilton, Ontario, see Tracy Neumann, *Remaking the Rust Belt: The Postindustrial Transformation of North America* (Philadelphia, 2016).

27 For more on brownfield redevelopment in Pittsburgh, see Justin B. Hollander, *Polluted and Dangerous: America's Worst Abandoned Properties and What Can Be Done about Them* (Burlington, 2009), 118–148.

28 Jon Schmitz, Golden Crossroads, *Pittsburgh Post*-Gazette, Aug. 2, 1995, A1; James P. DeAngelis and Sabina Deitrick, *The Regional Economic Development Bibliography and Data Base (TRED/Biblio)*, Dec. 1994.

29 Carmen J. Lee, Riverside Path for Hiking and Cycling Proposed, *Pittsburgh Post-Gazette*, Dec. 6, 1990, 1, 6; Don Hopey, Bike Trail Rolls $14 Million into Local Economies, *Pittsburgh Post-Gazette*, Feb. 23, 1999, A12; Richard L. Florida, *The Rise of the Creative Class: And How It's Transforming Work, Leisure, Community and Everyday Life* (New York, 2002). This has become even more the case in recent years with the association of so-called Rust Belt chic with younger urban residents. See Will Doig, Rust Belt Chic: Declining Midwest Cities Make a Comeback, *Salon.com*, May 12, 2012, www.salon.com/2012/05/12/rust_belt_chic_declining_midwest_cities_make_a_comeback/; Dan Majors, Pittsburgh's Youth Exodus Reverses: Millennials Are Being Drawn to the City, *Pittsburgh Post-Gazette*, Aug. 8, 2016, A1.

30 George Hohmann, A Downtown Turnaround, *Charleston Daily Mail*, Dec. 14, 1998, D1; ICON Architects, Inc., *Management Plan for the Wheeling National Heritage Area*, May 2004, B1; Robert C. Byrd, *Robert C. Byrd: Child of the Appalachian Coalfields* (Morgantown, 2005), 499, 525, 540–541, 564, 710–711.

31 Ian Hicks, WNHAC's Master Plan, 20 Years Later, *Wheeling Intelligencer*, May 28, 2012. On the dissonance between the values of historians tasked with explaining the significance of a community's story and those elements of history important to local identity at another federally financed historical park, see Cathy Stanton, *The Lowell Experiment: Public History in a Postindustrial City* (Amherst, 2006).

32 John McCabe, Industrial Park Expected to be Ready by Next Fall, *Wheeling Intelligencer*, Oct. 13, 1997; Carley Amico, Too Many Hurdles in Way for Outlets, *Wheeling Intelligencer*, Jan. 10, 2004. Ian Hicks, Dilapidated Houses to be Torn Down, *Wheeling Intelligencer*, Jan. 14, 2015; Ian Hicks, WNHAC's Master Plan, 20 Years Later, *Wheeling Intelligencer*, May 28, 2012.

33 Historical Society of Western Pennsylvania, *Preliminary Report on Steel Historic Site Evaluation to the Steel Heritage Task Force* (Pittsburgh 1988); Suzanne Elliott, Homestead Set to Benefit from the Promise of Waterfront Development, *Pittsburgh Business Times*, Jul. 15, 2001.

34 Bill Steigerwald, Mill-Site Museum Backed by Heinz, *Pittsburgh Post-Gazette*, Jun. 29, 1989; P-G Staff, Group Saves Bost Building, *Pittsburgh Post-Gazette*, Aug. 1, 1991, S7; P-G Staff, Clinton Signs Measure Designating Region a National Heritage Area, *Pittsburgh Post-Gazette*, Nov. 14, 1996, C10.

35 A series of driving tours demonstrated how organizers framed Homestead as a nexus linking a whole range of industrial, mining, financial and other activities that, they argue, continue to frame regional development even in the so-called post-industrial era. See www.riversofsteel.com/routestoroots/index.html

36 Author's Interview with August Carlino and Edward Muller, June 4, 2014.

37 Interview with Carlino and Muller.

38 Carlino and Muller Interview. Quote is from Edward Muller.

39 Joyce Gannon, Law Firm's Operations Center Helps Restore an Old Building, Revitalizes West Virginia Mill Town, *Pittsburgh Post-Gazette*, Aug. 13, 2012; Pieces of Wheeling History Sold in Auction, Sep. 12, 2016, www.yourohiovalley.com/story/30016780/pieces-of-wheeling-history-sold-off-in-labelle-nail-factory-auction

40 Patrick Doyle, From Red-Hot Steel to Red-Hot Tech: Reinventing an Old Industrial Site, *NewsWorks*, Jul. 12, 2016, www.newsworks.org/index.php/local/reinvention/95308-from-red-hot-steel-to-red-hot-tech-reinventing-an-old-industrial-site.

Bibliography

Allan, W. (1962) Plan to Gain Industry Told by RIDC Chief. *Pittsburgh Press*, Feb. 15, 1962, pp. 1, 14.

Allegheny Conference on Community Development. (1984) *A Strategy for Growth: An Economic Development Program for the Pittsburgh Region*. Pittsburgh, The Conference.

Amico, C. (2004) Too Many Hurdles in Way for Outlets. *Wheeling Intelligencer*, Jan. 10, 2004.

Associated Press. (1985) In Strife-Torn Valley, a Quiet Effort to Save Jobs. *Philadelphia Inquirer*, Jan. 8, 1985, p. B2.

Associated Press. (1987) Rust Belt Cities Are Trading in Old Economies. *Philadelphia Inquirer*, Nov. 26, 1987, p. J1.

Associated Press. (1994) Wheeling Site among Heritage Areas. *Charleston Gazette*, Oct. 6, 1994.

Bangs, R.L. and Hong, Jun Hyun. (1995) *Black and White Economic Conditions in the City of Pittsburgh*. Pittsburgh, University Center for Social and Urban Research.

Bangs, R.L. and Singh, Vijai. (1988) *The State of the Region: Economic, Demographic and Social Trends in Southwestern Pennsylvania*. Pittsburgh, University Center for Social and Urban Research.

Briem, C. (2015) Parsing the "New Pittsburgh" Narrative. *Pittsburgh Post-Gazette*, Mar. 1, 2015, p. D1.

Buell, T. (1990) Steel Venture's Chances of Success Dim with Time. *Pittsburgh Press*, Aug. 19, 1990, p. D18.

Byrd, R.C. (2005) *Robert C. Byrd: Child of the Appalachian Coalfields*. Morgantown, West Virginia University Press.

DeAngelis, J.P. and Deitrick, S. (1994) *The Regional Economic Development Bibliography and Data Base (TRED/Biblio)*. Pittsburgh, City of Pittsburgh and Allegheny County Service Consolidation Task Force on Economic Development.

Dieterich-Ward, A. (2015) "Live on the Hills and Work in the City": Rise and Fall of Renaissance in Pittsburgh's Regional Hinterland. *Journal of Urban History*, 41 (1): 28–34.

Dieterich-Ward, A. (2016) *Beyond Rust: Metropolitan Pittsburgh and the Fate of Industrial America*. Philadelphia, University of Pennsylvania Press.

Doig, W. (2012) Rust Belt Chic: Declining Midwest Cities Make a Comeback, *Salon.com*, May 12, 2012, www.salon.com/2012/05/12/rust_belt_chic_declining_midwest_cities_make_a_comeback/

Doyle, P. (2016) From Red-Hot Steel to Red-Hot Tech: Reinventing an Old Industrial Site, *News Works*, Jul. 12, 2016, www.newsworks.org/index.php/local/reinvention/95308-from-red-hot-steel-to-red-hot-tech-reinventing-an-old-industrial-site

Drayton, M. (1992) A New Ballgame. *Tampa Tribune*, Dec. 14, 1992, p. 1.

Editorial Board. (1990) High-Promise High-Tech. *Pittsburgh Post-Gazette*, Nov. 28, 1990, p. C2.

Elliott, S. (2001) Homestead Set to Benefit from the Promise of Waterfront Development. *Pittsburgh Business Times*, Jul. 15, 2001.

Fitzpatrick, D. (2002) Stuck with Steel. *Pittsburgh Post-Gazette*, Nov. 3, 2002, p. D1.

Florida, R.L. (2002) *The Rise of the Creative Class: And How It's Transforming Work, Leisure, Community and Everyday Life*. New York, Basic Books.

Gannon, J. (1997) Rolling Down the River. *Pittsburgh Post-Gazette*, Nov. 18, 1997, p. F1.

Gannon, J. (2012) Law Firm's Operations Center Helps Restore an Old Building, Revitalizes West Virginia Mill Town. *Pittsburgh Post-Gazette*, Aug. 13, 2012.

Gratz, R.B. (1994) *The Living City: How America's Cities Are Being Revitalized by Thinking Small in a Big Way*. New York, Wiley.

Gruson, L. (1987) Clean Pittsburgh Air Symbolizes Economic Shift. *New York Times*, May 10, 1987, p. 18.

Hackworth, J. (2006) *The Neoliberal City: Governance, Ideology, and Development in American Urbanism*. Ithaca, Cornell University Press.

Hicks, I. (2012) WNHAC's Master Plan, 20 Years Later. *Wheeling Intelligencer*, May 28, 2012.

Hicks, I. (2015) Dilapidated Houses to be Torn Down. *Wheeling Intelligencer*, Jan. 14, 2015.

Hicks, J.P. (1990) Bankruptcy Helps a Steelmaker. *New York Times*, Jul. 19, 1990, p. D1.

Historical Society of Western Pennsylvania. (1988) *Preliminary Report on Steel Historic Site Evaluation to the Steel Heritage Task Force*. Pittsburgh, The Society.

Hoerr, J.P. (1988) *And the Wolf Finally Came: The Decline of the American Steel Industry*. Pittsburgh, University of Pittsburgh Press.

Hohmann, G. (1998) A Downtown Turnaround. *Charleston Daily Mail*, Dec. 14, 1998, p. D1.

Hollander, J.B. (2009) *Polluted and Dangerous: America's Worst Abandoned Properties and What Can be Done about Them*. Burlington, University Press of New England.

Hopey, D. (1999) Bike Trail Rolls $14 Million into Local Economies. *Pittsburgh Post-Gazette*, Feb. 23, 1999, p. A12.

ICON Architects, Inc. (2004) *Management Plan for the Wheeling National Heritage Area*. Wheeling, Wheeling National Heritage Area, Inc.

Ingham, J. (1991) *Making Iron and Steel: Independent Mills in Pittsburgh, 1820–1920*. Columbus, Ohio State University Press.

Javersak, D.T. (1999) *History of Weirton, West Virginia*. Virginia Beach, The Donning Company.

Kane, M. (1987) Steel Valley Panel Facing Tough Road in Plant Takeover. *Pittsburgh Press*, Dec. 13, 1987, p. A8.

Kidney, W. (1989) *A Past Still Alive: The Pittsburgh History and Landmarks Foundation Celebrates Twenty-Five Years*. Pittsburgh, Pittsburgh History & Landmarks Foundation.

Kneeland, D. (1970) Pittsburgh: A Brawny City Puts on a Silk Shirt. *New York Times*, Oct. 3, 1970, p. 33.

Krause, P. (1992) *The Battle for Homestead, 1880–1892*. Pittsburgh, University of Pittsburgh Press.

Lee, C.J. (1990) Riverside Path for Hiking and Cycling Proposed. *Pittsburgh Post-Gazette*, Dec. 6, 1990, pp. 1, 6.

Livesay, H. (2007) *Andrew Carnegie and the Rise of Big Business*, 3rd ed. New York, Pearson Longman.

Lorant, S. (1999) *Pittsburgh: The Story of an American City*, 5th ed., updated and enlarged, Millennium ed. Pittsburgh, Esselmont Books.

Lowry, I.S. (1963) *Economic Study of the Pittsburgh Region, Vol. II: Portrait of a Region*. Pittsburgh, University of Pittsburgh Press.

Majors, D. (2016) Pittsburgh's Youth Exodus Reverses: Millennials Are Being Drawn to the City. *Pittsburgh Post-Gazette*, Aug. 8, 2016, p. A1.

Marquis, C.H. (1985) Radical Ministers Make Waves Over Joblessness in Pittsburgh. *Christian Science Monitor*, Sep. 30, 1985, p. 1.

McCabe, J. (1997) Industrial Park Expected to be Ready by Next Fall. *Wheeling Intelligencer*, Oct. 13, 1997.

McDermott, D. (1997) Coal Mining in the U.S. West: Price and Employment Trends. *Monthly Labor Review*, Aug. 1997, pp. 18–23.

McPharlin, J. (prod.) (1988) The Ohio Remote: American Dreams Shattered. In *The Oprah Winfrey Show*. USA, WLS-TV.

Mershon, S.R. (2004) *Corporate Social Responsibility and Urban Revitalization: The Allegheny Conference on Community Development, 1943–1968* (PhD). Pittsburgh, Carnegie Mellon University.

Miller, D. (1993) Building the Future on the Past. *Pittsburgh Post-Gazette*, Mar. 2, 1993, p. D1.
Neumann, T. (2016) *Remaking the Rust Belt: The Postindustrial Transformation of North America*. Philadelphia, University of Pennsylvania Press.
Nurnberg, M. (1963) *Economic Study of the Pittsburgh Region, Vol. III: Region with a Future*. Pittsburgh, University of Pittsburgh Press.
Oldenburg, D. (1985) The Selling of American Cities. *Washington Post*, Dec. 17, 1985, p. B5.
Peck, J., Theodore, N. and Renner, N. (2009) Neoliberal Urbanism: Models, Moments, Mutations. *SAIS Review*, 19 (1): 49–66.
Penn's Southwest Association. (1981) *Dynamic Pittsburgh: It's a Vital, Vibrant, Historic, Sporting, Bright, Breakthrough, Resourceful Place to Live and Work*. Pittsburgh, The Association.
P-G Staff. (1991) Group Saves Bost Building. *Pittsburgh Post-Gazette*, Aug. 1, 1991, p. S7.
P-G Staff. (1996) Clinton Signs Measure Designating Region a National Heritage Area. *Pittsburgh Post-Gazette*, Nov. 14, 1996, p. C10.
Pieces of Wheeling History Sold in Auction, Sep. 12, 2016, www.yourohiovalley.com/story/30016780/pieces-of-wheeling-history-sold-off-in-labelle-nail-factory-auction
Russakoff, D. (1987) Brawn Forged into Brain. *Washington Post*, Apr. 12, 1987, p. A1.
Schmitz, J. (1995) Golden Crossroads. *Pittsburgh Post-Gazette*, Aug. 2, 1995, p. A1.
Schriftgiesser, K. (1951) The Pittsburgh Story. *Atlantic Monthly*, May 1951, pp. 66–69.
Simpson, A.T. (2015) Health and Renaissance: Academic Medicine and the Remaking of Modern Pittsburgh. *Journal of Urban History*, 41 (1): 19–27.
Slavishak, E.S. (2008) *Bodies of Work: Civic Display and Labor in Industrial Pittsburgh*. Durham, Duke University Press.
Southwestern Pennsylvania Regional Planning Commission. (1968) *Issues in a Region of Contrasts*. Pittsburgh, The Commission.
Stanton, C. (2006) *The Lowell Experiment: Public History in a Postindustrial City*. Amherst, University of Massachusetts Press.
Steigerwald, B. (1989) Mill-Site Museum Backed by Heinz. *Pittsburgh Post-Gazette*, Jun. 29, 1989.
Stout, M. (1986) Reindustrialization from Below: The Steel Valley Authority. *Labor Research Review*, 1 (9): 18–33.
Tarr, J.A. (ed.) (2003) *Devastation and Renewal: An Environmental History of Pittsburgh and Its Region*. Pittsburgh, University of Pittsburgh Press.
U.S. Bureau of the Census. (1997) *Statistical Abstract of the United States*, 117th ed. Washington, DC, U.S. G.P.O.
U.S. Bureau of the Census and Inter-University Consortium for Political and Social Research. (1947–1983) *County and City Data Book*. Ann Arbor, The Consortium.
Van Trump, J.D. (1965) *1300–1335 Liverpool Street, Manchester, Old Allegheny, Pittsburgh*. Pittsburgh, Pittsburgh History & Landmarks Foundation.
Whyte, W.H. (1993) *The Exploding Metropolis*. Berkeley, University of California Press.
Willis, M. (1985) Jackson Seeks "New Formula". *New Pittsburgh Courier*, Feb. 2, 1985, pp. 1, 3.
Working Together Consortium. (1994) *The Greater Pittsburgh Region: Working Together to Compete Globally*. The Consortium. November 1994.
Ziegler, A.P. (1966) Observations. *Charette, Pennsylvania Journal of Architecture*, 46 (8).

10 Regions of heavy industry and their heritage – between identity politics and 'touristification'
Where to next?[1]

Stefan Berger and Paul Pickering

Introduction

> More than anyone else, perhaps, the miner can stand as the type of the manual worker, not only because his work is so exaggeratedly awful, but also because it is so vitally necessary and yet so remote from our experience, so invisible, as it were, that we are capable of forgetting it as we forget the blood in our veins. In a way it is even humiliating to watch coal-miners working. It raises in you a momentary doubt about your own status as an 'intellectual' and a superior person generally. For it is brought home to you, at least while you are watching, that it is only because miners sweat their guts out that superior persons can remain superior. You and I and the editor of the *Times Lit. Supp.*, and the poets and the Archbishop of Canterbury and Comrade X, author of *Marxism for Infants* – all of us *really* owe the comparative decency of our lives to poor drudges underground, blackened to the eyes, with their throats full of coal dust, driving their shovels forward with arms and belly muscles of steel.[2]

Among the many confronting and memorable descriptions in George Orwell's pioneering social investigation into the lives of working people in the industrial heartlands of northern England is that of the labor of coal miners. His account was based not on second-hand testimony; in fact, he had descended with the miners half a mile underground and crawled on hands and knees for two to three miles along a seam to the coal face. He understood the importance of visiting the coal face when the 'fillers' were at work. "The time to go there", he wrote, "is when the machines are roaring and the air is black with coal dust, and when you can actually see what the miners have to do". "At those times the place is like hell, or at any rate like my own mental picture of hell", he continued,

> Most of the things one imagines in hell are there – heat, noise, confusion, darkness, foul air, and, above all, unbearably cramped space. Everything except the fire, for there is no fire down there except the feeble beams of Davy lamps and electric torches which scarcely penetrate the clouds of coal dust.[3]

Orwell's account is a sage reminder to those of us interested in the preservation, curation and narration of industrial heritage of the complexity of our task. Orwell came up from a working mine knowing that he would never have to go down again; it took him ten minutes to wash the coal dust from under his eyelids but he knew that it was not something he'd have to do six days a week for the remainder of his working life, however short. Orwell's use of 'heroic' colliers to typify the experience of the English working class has rightly been criticized for overlooking gender and community more generally, including in the mining industry.[4] A well-known street ballad in circulation from the 1790s to well into the 20th century – *The Collier Lass* – anticipated his critics by many decades. It tells the story of 'Polly Parker' of Worsely near Manchester:

> By the greatest of dangers each day I'm surrounded,
> I hang in the air by a rope or a chain,
> The mine may fall in, I may be killed or wounded,
> May perish by damp, or the fire of a train.
> And what would you do, if not for our labour?
> In wretched starvation your days they would pass
> While we can provide you with life's greatest blessing,
> O do not despise a poor collier lass.[5]

Nevertheless, the broader point stands. Almost all of the chapters in this volume engage with physical sites in one way or another and these industrial 'museums' offer an affective experience that is barely a faint echo of the past. One noisy machine – however loud – cannot stand in for forty roaring simultaneously; wandering along mining tunnel 3 meters by 3 meters square tells us little or nothing about the experience of crawling into a space just wide enough to swing a pick where the act of labor itself produces noxious fumes, carcinogenic dust and the ever-present threat of a cave-in. Visitors to industrial sites do not hang like Polly on a chain over a chasm. Of course, this issue of visitor experience is further complicated by the fraught concept of memory. Industrial heritage has, in many cases, not passed beyond the realm of living memory and these sites, all be they physically *faux*, are often interpreted by those who spent their working lives there. Here is the possibility of access to what, in the 1920s, Maurice Halbwachs called "frameworks of social memory".[6] For all that it might appear self-evident to say it, our deliberations must begin with a recognition of the limits and potential of heritage sites and be shaped by an appreciation of the implications of it. Where to next?

For us, the case studies presented in this volume generate, *inter alia*, four key themes worthy of reflection. The first is the importance of a comparative perspective on the history of de-industrialization to provide an international context against which industrial heritage initiatives began to develop from the 1950s onwards. How did the specifics of such de-industrialization processes impact on the emergence and shape of industrial heritage initiatives in different parts of the de-industrializing West? The second major theme is the critical role of key actors to the success or failure of industrial heritage initiatives. Which agents were active on behalf of industrial heritage, what was their intention and what resources were at their disposal? Moreover, what alliances were at play in the pursuit of industrial heritage initiatives? The third key theme is the importance of industrial heritage to a range of identity politics that have often been used to put forward particular narratives of region and of class. In turn, these were invariably related to narratives of national and transnational identities as well to narratives of religion, of culture, of ethnicity/race and of gender. What were the most influential narratives dominating the discourses and practices of industrial heritage in different former regions of heavy industry? Finally, the fourth significant theme to be explored here is the impact of what we might call the 'touristification' of industrial heritage. To what extent has industrial heritage been commercialized and utilized for the generation of a new tourist industry in regions formerly dominated by iron, steel and coal? What factors determined whether these strategies were successful or not in terms of actually attracting tourists? And what impact did success have on these locations' self-understanding and representation? It is in this final part that we shall also come back to the repercussions of the gap between the actual experience of a working mine or steel plant and the post-industrial heritage site that we referred to in our opening references to George Orwell and 'Polly Parker'.

Of course, the questions that we raise here in relation to the four themes cannot be comprehensively answered as yet – at least not in global comparative perspective. Much more comparative and transnational research will be necessary in order to explore these issues further. The current volume intends to develop these themes and, as individual contributions to it make clear, it can build on a considerable literature. But much of that literature remains focused on individual regions and places. What is therefore needed is a broader comparative and transnational examination of industrial heritage, including the non-Western world. In parts of China, India and Latin America and perhaps elsewhere processes of rapid industrialization go hand in hand with processes of de-industrialization as we write. If we take the example of China, vast provinces that were once the strongholds of coal and steel industries, such as the North-East of the country or Shaanxi province, have experienced processes of de-industrialization, whilst other parts of China are booming.[7] A day in Beijing reminds the reader of a plethora of accounts of sooty Manchester from the 1840s to the 1950s. Similarly, if we take the case of Monterey in Mexico, de-industrialization has hit the steel industry and forced workers to confront new neo-liberal challenges.[8] Eventually it will be vital to include those non-Western experiences in a truly global history of industrial heritage initiatives.[9] However, in this volume we have focused on the West, which is also a global West, ranging from Japan to North America and from Europe to Australia. Here a shift in the production patterns of global capitalism has meant that heavy industry, principally coal and steel, has increasingly no space in their economies.[10] The coal crises hit the West from the late 1950s onwards and steel followed suit in the 1970s. In both cases cheaper imports of coal and steel from the non-Western world played a crucial role in making Western coal and steel uncompetitive and forcing it out of globalized markets.[11] The story is a different one in Communist countries during the Cold War. The eastern bloc had its own internationalized economic system, but unlike the globalized capitalist economies, heavy industry was state-protected from the vagaries of the market, even if it was terribly unproductive. Moreover, unlike those miners demonized in Thatcher's Britain, miners (and steel-workers) in the east were lionized in officially-sanctioned state narratives. These were the archetypal proletarians, the vanguard of the successful class struggle for social justice.[12] Communist Eastern Europe therefore often followed very different trajectories from those of the capitalist west during the Cold War. There are, for sure, many different edges to this story of de-industrialization, and the chapters in this volume tell some of them.

Towards a comparative history of de-industrialization

If the birth of the industrial revolution took place in Great Britain, it was also one of the first Western countries to experience massive crises in those industries that had made it the workshop of the world. From a peak of production in 1912, when 8 billion yards of cloth was manufactured in north-west England, for example, the cotton industry collapsed. Between the wars 800 mills closed. Similarly, in the interwar period it seemed to some observers that there was no future for the heartlands of mining. For Thomas Jones, writing in the *New Statesman* in 1935, a fitting way to lament the inexorable decline of the South Wales coalfields, for example, was to invoke the idea of a sprawling tourist site. "If we want to turn South Wales into an industrial museum", he wrote with his pen dripping with sarcasm, "there's no shortage of blueprints":

> Consider this one: "Details of the best way of laying out the National Ruin so as to make it attractive to American tourists and remunerative to the transport and catering companies may be left to be worked out by a committee. . . . The Rhymney valley might be flooded and made into a lake. . . . For the Rhondda and Merthyr area we urge . . . an irrevocable Standstill Order, once all human beings have been evacuated to the Hounslow/Dagenham green belt. The Office of Works should then proceed to protect all approaches from souvenir hunters and should invite His Majesty to declare the area an open Museum . . . to illustrate the Industrial Revolution. Some winding engines should be kept in open repair and enable visitors to descend the pit shafts and explore the subterranean galleries, an experience which should be no less thrilling than a visit to the catacombs of Rome".[13]

This was only a slightly overdramatic glimpse of the future to come. It was also too soon. In fact, the coal and, especially, the steel industry, seemed to be booming at the end of the Second World War, as they did throughout much of Western Europe in the 1950s and 1960s, with new modern steel factories being opened, such as Llanwern near Newport or the Port Talbot steelworks that opened in 1951.[14]

By the mid-1950s Jones's prognostications seemed to be coming to fruition but again not for the reason he cited, at least in the first instance. Britain was a pioneer in industrial heritage initiatives, but this had as much to do with the prominence of the industrial revolution in the national imaginary as it did with economic and social developments summarized under the rubric of de-industrialization. The discipline of industrial archaeology was more or less invented in Britain with early pioneers, such as Michael Rix, writing about industrial archaeology as early as the late 1950s, and the first survey being published by British journalist Kenneth Hudson in 1963.[15] The *Journal of Industrial Archaeology* was founded in Britain in 1964. Ironbridge in Shropshire, a site of the early iron industry in Britain, became the first industrial heritage site to be ennobled with the world heritage stamp in 1986.[16] It also hosted the first major international conference of industrial archaeologists in 1973.[17] In other words, just as Britain had been the paragon of the industrial revolution, it had become the shining example of industrial heritage initiatives before that glory had faded. However, the prolonged economic crisis of the 1960s and 1970s changed much of context in which representations of industrial heritage were framed. When Britain became widely known as the economic 'sick man' of Europe, its ailing coal and steel industries, which had been nationalized at the end of the Second World War, became key symbols of economic decline. No longer were they something of which to be proud; they represented a problem, maybe even an embarrassment to the nation.

When the self-appointed champion of neoliberalism, Margaret Thatcher, took on what was widely perceived to be the most powerful trade union in the country, the miners' union, in a strike that lasted for more than a year and brought the country to the brink of civil war, she did not only want to break the back of the union movement but also to sound the death-knell of the coal industry. For free marketers like Thatcher, the domestic coal industry could not survive in competitive global markets. As one of the present authors has argued elsewhere, it is the bitterness of this conflict that set the stage for the scarcity of industrial heritage initiatives in former coal and steel regions of Britain.[18] Most of the mines were quickly closed in 1985, demolished and replaced with parks, sporting facilities, cultural centers or shopping malls. The memory of this industry and those that worked in it was, by and large, preserved by initiatives countering the dominant neo-liberalism of the 1980s.

The story of de-industrialization is rarely as dramatic as it has been in Britain. On a spectrum the German experience in the Ruhr, described here by Stefan Berger, Christian Wicke and Jana Golombek, is perhaps furthest removed from that of Britain. The Rhenish capitalist model that developed in West Germany after the end of the Second World War relied on corporatist structures that brought the state, employers and trade unions together in various attempts to address the coal and steel crises together. In the case of coal, a long-term strategy was devised that phased out the industry over 50 years. Made possible by public subsidies, no miner was made forcibly redundant and many benefited from social plans allowing them to retire early on generous pensions. Mine after mine was closed and the workforce reduced but in a way that left no one in the industry behind. Such a major act of social solidarity was not repeated in the steel industry, yet when a major crisis hit, such as in Duisburg Rheinhausen in the mid-1980s, community activities that mobilized whole cities and populations in the Ruhr, ensured a political outcome of the crisis which cushioned the effect of de-industrialization, even if it could not prevent forcible redundancies. The successful mastering of de-industrialization in the Ruhr was arguably also the precondition for the valorization of industrial heritage in the region. The history of the region as the heartland of German (and indeed the European) coal and steel industries that had been the driver of the first industrial revolution, and which played a major economic role for much of the 20th century, was ultimately connected to a largely positive experience of de-industrialization and provided a positive basis for industrial heritage.

Elsewhere, as the contributions to this volume indicate, the experience of de-industrialization lay somewhere in between that of Britain and Germany. In France, like in Britain, the mining industry was nationalized after the Second World War. Unlike in Britain, the government was actively involved in making plans for the structural change of the French coal-mining regions from the 1950s onwards. Nevertheless, these plans did not prevent the social hardship that came with the closing of the mines. When many places in the world embarked on a period of neo-liberalism in the early 1980s, France seemed out of step with the election of a Socialist president and a coalition government of Socialists and Communists promising the structural industrial renewal of coalmining regions. However, as Marion Fontaine details in her chapter, the promises of renewal were not followed up with concrete programes and hence soon rang hollow in coal-mining communities ravaged by the closure of mines.

In Japan, here analyzed by Regine Mathias, the timing of both the coal and the steel crisis exactly parallels the timing in Europe and, as we shall see, North America – with coal slipping into decline from the late 1950s and steel from the 1970s onwards. The experience of Japan is closer to that of Britain, with unions, where they were strong, putting up significant resistance (also going on strike for over a year) but ultimately losing out to the employers who pushed through rationalization measures, which left thousands unemployed and wreaked havoc to many mining communities. Over a period of ten years, most of the coalmines were shut or continued as a pale imitation of their former glory.

In the land of the free (markets), the decline of the coal and steel industries in Pittsburgh, covered here by Allen Dieterich-Ward's chapter, was also unmitigated by any government intervention worth its name and by the 1990s the former industrial powerhouse was a shadow of its former self, with unemployment rampant and whole city quarters derelict 'no-go' zones. The form that de-industrialization took in Pittsburgh left those looking for a 'renaissance' initially little else than to sharply demarcate themselves from a past that had been engulfed by an economic and ecological disaster.

For much of the 20th century the local economy of Newcastle in the Hunter Valley region of New South Wales in Australia was also based on a combination of coal mining for export and heavy industry. Focussing again on steel, rather than on coal, the chapter by Erik Eklund also tells a tale of de-industrialization starting in the early 1960s and continuing until the late 1990s, concluding with the closure of the large steel-mill that had dominated city life in Newcastle for so long.

Considerable job losses and high unemployment inevitably accompanied de-industrialization and devastated working-class communities. Like in Pittsburgh, the strategy pursued following de-industrialization was to draw a line under the industrial past, a radical break with what was seen as an overwhelmingly negative legacy.

Rubén Vega García's chapter on Asturias deals with a region that, like the Ruhr, was similarly based on both coal and steel. Due to the protected nature of the Spanish economy under Francoism, the economic crisis affected the Spanish coal and steel industries slightly later than in the rest of Western Europe. When it did hit in the 1980s however, it had dire consequences for the workers employed in those industries. Here we encounter a case where strong unions, unlike in Britain and Japan, did not put up a fight against employers and the government. They themselves managed the de-industrialization process that ultimately led to the slow disappearance of heavy industry from the region, but in a way that often allowed employees to benefit from early retirement packages and good pension provisions. It was in particular the young who were left with few employment prospects as a result of de-industrialization without structural transformation. Yet, the young had often benefitted from excellent educational opportunities denied to their parents and grandparents. Thus, they were less reliant on finding jobs in the same industries that had sustained their forefathers.

If the clock of de-industrialization ticked slightly differently in Spain to elsewhere in Western Europe, it followed a different periodization altogether in the Communist Eastern Bloc countries of central and eastern Europe, an example of which – the Jiu Valley in Romania – is presented in this volume by David Kideckel. Protected, nurtured and privileged by the Communist government in Romania until the early 1990s, the miners had to face capitalist transformation (privatization), EU regulation (after Romania joined the EU) and significant ecological concerns. Taken together, these ill winds resulted in a rapid and terminal decline of the coal industry in Romania. The public image of the miners had been darkened by the so-called mineriade, a demonstration of miners' power in favor of the post-Communist regime of Iliescu that many Romanians remembered very poorly. A second Eastern European example, presented in this volume by György Németh, is that of the Borsod industrial area in Hungary, where significant industrialization occurred around railway, iron/steel and mining industries from the last third of the 19th century onwards. The Communist regime developed the heavy industry of the Borsod region systematically after 1948. Like in Romania, it hit a terminal crisis only in the post-Communist 1990s, when its low productivity, obsolete technology and high energy consumption made it uncompetitive in international markets. The combined pressure of privatization and a necessary re-orientation of markets away from former Comecon states led to the collapse of heavy industry in the Borsod region. The workers that had been employed there were no longer represented as heroic archetypal proletarians, but as left-overs and at best victims of a post-Communist and post-industrial age. Even today the association of heavy industry with Communist regimes is a major hindrance to the development of industrial heritage across the former Eastern Bloc. Overall, then, de-industrialization in the West followed recognizable economic patterns, but the political frameworks and answers to economic crises were vastly different across different regions of heavy industry.

Agents of industrial heritage

Taken together the chapters here identify numerous 'constituencies' involved in industrial heritage. From heritage professionals, conservators, curators and other gatekeepers of the recent past to property developers and corporate barons seeking to sanitize a traumatic history; from Tammany Hall politicians and State legislators to community activists and academics of various stripes; from workers and their representatives, notably in the trade union movement, to those who have embraced change to exercise a potent form of assertive pedagogy over the curation of their collective memories. The institutionalization of industrial heritage initiatives has catapulted into prominence in particular heritage professionals in museums and at heritage sites who significantly shape the discourses and practices surrounding that heritage. These professionals have become significantly internationalized, in particular in the form of The International Committee for the Conservation of the Industrial Heritage (TICCIH), which has become a powerful forum for promoting industrial heritage world-wide.[19]

For many of the social actors discussed in these chapters (and for some of their authors) the preservation of the site is paramount but even on this point we learn of considerable disagreement over issues of originality and authenticity, almost inevitably revolving around the threshold question of what to do with it. In many cases the remains of factories are toxic husks on the verge of collapse and in need of remediation. Of course, any change to the site inevitably alters its ontological status; in fact, the passage of time has already compromised it. Notwithstanding, there is considerable scope for debate about the extent of remediation of the original site that ought to be undertaken. Should the industrial landscape be restored just enough to render it safe to visit or should derelict factories be returned to 'pristine' condition? Is a new industrial landscape emerging in and around post-industrial ruins, in which nature and industry form a new symbiosis and how is that new symbiosis endowed with meaning?[20] As Greg Dickinson, Carole Blair and Brian Ott have noted, places of public memory quickly come to have their own history independent of that they seek to memorialize.[21] Inevitably, this debate is cross-cut both by museological theory and practice as well as ideology, emotion and nostalgia.[22]

But the question of the sites and what to do with them is also invariably linked to the question with what meaning to endow them. Which narratives have been constructed around those sites by whom and with what intention? In the Ruhr, which emerges in this volume as the region where the most impressive industrial landscape has been preserved because of a unique combination of actors and their narrative strategies that gave meaning to those sites. The earliest heritage activists were intellectuals, artists and 'history from below' practitioners, who argued vehemently against the demolition of sites associated with the coal and steel industries. The community initiatives that resulted were very successful, because they were picked up, after some initial conflict, by powerful politicians, businessmen and trade unionists who made industrial heritage part and parcel of a tripartite consensus on how to facilitate structural change in the Ruhr.

In Pittsburgh, the first efforts to save sites of industrial heritage also came from below in the mid-1960s, when architectural enthusiasts formed the Pittsburgh History and Landmarks Foundation. This organization subsequently formed an important voice in community heritage projects. Although industrial 'heritage from below'[23] was reluctantly and selectively embraced by municipal officials in the 1980s, things began to change under the leadership of long-serving Democrat politician and urban planner, Mayor Tom Murphy, who helped to develop a vision of regional identity in which industrial heritage took pride of place. With assistance from Federal and State heritage programes, some businessmen and State Senators, the industrial heritage movement gained in prominence from the second half of the 1990s onwards. Yet, by comparison to the Ruhr, the relative limits of state funding and the need to forge difficult-to-generate public-private partnerships for the preservation of industrial heritage put tight restrictions on the kind of industrial landscape that could be maintained.

In Britain, the national government, in conjunction with the employers such as the National Coal Board, were trenchant opponents of industrial heritage initiatives. Put simply they wanted to consign the memory of those industries and its deeply conflictual ending to oblivion. Hence it was left to community initiatives involving trade unionists and former miners who, sometimes in alliance with local councils, ensured the survival of at least some industrial heritage that was subsequently conceptualized and narrated very much in opposition to the neoliberal policies that had ensured its rapid and catastrophic demise. The slogan that heads a list of all coal collieries in South Wales at the end of the little museum that is part of the Big Pit world heritage site in Blaenavon reads: "We will be back". Such defiance is a reminder of Laurajane Smith's description of community-based industrial heritage as a process linked to class and the quest for social justice. In this case the memory of the bitter struggle in defense of livelihoods and communities is a clear case of the participants speaking for themselves (to borrow her words), fusing the history of a struggle with its meaning in and for the present.[24] In an important sense then the sign is more important than the site.

The other cases described in this volume also highlight the importance of agents fostering industrial heritage initiatives. In Japan, architects and engineers were among the first to draw attention to the value of industrial heritage, and it took the best part of two decades before the national government began to take an interest, largely because it saw in industrial heritage a strategy of reviving those ailing regions of heavy industry by replacing it with tourism. The world heritage stamp was seen as a vital ingredient of the touristification of former regions of heavy industry.

In the Jiu valley there is very little political support for industrial heritage. Ultimately bottom-up initiatives dominate the scene. The agents include artists, architects, journalists and students claiming to speak on behalf of the community against the mining companies and seeking to build alliances with former miners and their families. Local political support is haphazard and unreliable, and there are hardly any heritage professionals in the region to support those bottom-up initiatives. Hence many collections of heritage-related items are in private hands and many sites are re-appropriated by private businessmen, transforming them into restaurants, warehouses and clubs.

Whereas in the post-Communist Jiu valley, miners, in alliance with middle-class intellectuals, played some role in industrial heritage initiatives, workers were completely absent from any such initiatives in the Borsod area of Hungary. Here the Communist regime had started developing industrial heritage initiatives from the 1950s onwards. It had inscribed its own ideological readings into that heritage. After the fall of Communism this made industrial heritage suspect to many in Hungary. Nevertheless, from the late 1990s onwards a motley assembly of largely middle-class associations of historians, architects and professionals, including heritage professionals organized in TICCIH Hungary and ICOMOS Hungary, tried to mobilize support for industrial heritage initiatives. Yet, as Németh argues in her chapter, the prospects of success of such initiatives are bleak, as industrial heritage is disappearing fast from erstwhile industrial landscapes in Hungary.

In Newcastle in the Hunter Valley former workers in steel plants and coalmines, as well as a motley assembly of heritage activists, from museum professionals, academics and school teachers to union officials, have also been active in promoting the industrial heritage of the region and preserving the memories of its working-class communities, but on the whole they have lacked powerful allies in politics and administration to realize their ideas. In addition, property developers saw an opportunity make a lot of money by redeveloping former industrial sites into attractive flats and living spaces (as it was, in the case of the major steel plant discussed in Eklund's chapter, near the seaside). Industrial heritage was seen here as standing in the way of redevelopment. This is also a striking contrast to the Ruhr, where a combination of a declining population and cheap house prices meant that property developers did not exactly queue up to buy and develop former industrial sites. The proactive role of the federal government in buying up sites ensured a breathing space where proper thought could be given how to redevelop them. With the increasing valorization of industrial heritage, retaining as much as possible became the standard response.

In Northern France it was not so much the property developers but the local administration and local politicians who were at the forefront of erasing all traces of the industrial past of the region. Mayors and city officials pursued their dreams of getting rid of former coalmines and steelworks, which they regarded to be polluted eyesores. Instead they sought to redevelop their towns and regions as modern, forward-looking post-industrial spaces investing in new infrastructure and hoping to attract new industries. Whilst there was some difference with regard to specific political parties (the Communists, who had a large following among miners, were more pro-heritage than the Socialists), Northern France is a far cry from the massive political consensus in the Ruhr region of the enormous value of industrial heritage. This was, of course, not always the case and it needed a learning curve. Increasingly from the 1980s however, highlighting the industrial heritage of the region and making it the anchor point of redevelopment became an all-party consensus.

Rubén Vega García's chapter on Spain also highlights the important role of cultural production, specifically the arts and popular music, in Asturias. The complexity is worthy of emphasis. On the one hand, the narratives of a heroic past are promulgated in what is effectively a 'post-industrial' youth culture. This valorizing sits uneasily with their stories of loss and social problems in a de-industrialized present let alone their pessimism about the future. In turn, these views are discordant with narratives articulated by other key players in the region, such as the state-owned coal company, which stress the technical and engineering successes of the industry in difficult terrain, as well as the unions, who have negotiated the deals endorsing the closure of mines and de-industrialization more generally.

It is truly striking how important bottom-up initiatives have been in all cases under discussion in this volume. Without them, the transition from industry to industrial heritage would not have happened. Equally striking is the extent to which their successes were made easier by the alliances they could forge with political bodies, businesses and trade unions. This allowed them to draw on a range of resources. If, and to what extent, those alliances changed the bottom-up initiatives and made them less independent from 'official' industrial heritage narratives is a subject worthy of further exploration in future research involving the diverse case studies in this volume. Whether motivated by profit, public policy or professional curiosity, many of the active agents in the industrial heritage industry discussed here are 'outsiders'. For them the 'age of industry' is not (in Clifford Geertz's sense) 'experience-near'.[25] Rendering rusting ruins safe enough to visit, making them shiny new, enveloping them within the walls of an institution called a 'museum' or even endeavoring to 'save' their occupants' stories from the "enormous condescension of posterity" (to invoke E. P. Thompson's well-known aim),[26] is an act of appropriation. It goes without saying that when events pass beyond the realm of living memory there is no one left to complain. The chapters in this book, however, demonstrate that in these cases there are millions for whom 'the age of industry' was lived-experience. Some of the heroes of the stories told in these chapters are those who assert authority over their stories. For all that there is evidence of loss and despair, the reader will find numerous overt expressions of pride not only in individual skill but also in the importance of community and tenacity of the values that underpinned. As Erik Eklund demonstrates in his chapter on Newcastle, one of the key sources of what he describes as "a vernacular or dissenting view of industrial heritage, which can challenge and disrupt an official focus on development, refashioning and above all removing tangible expressions of the industrial past from the regional landscape", are retired workers. They "share a commitment to see their workplace as significant both locally and nationally"; they "wish to see their workplace as a place that made a difference. They have an investment in making sense of their working lives". As Leighton James shows, many aging museum volunteers worry about who will curate and narrate their stories in years to come. In the end, these chapters compel the reader to reconsider any lingering suspicion of nostalgia. On the contrary, as Laurajane Smith has suggested, nostalgia can be a positive force, that has less to do with the physical remnants of the apotheosis of this or that industry than the values that animated the lives of those who populated it. It is clear here, however, that for all that it is complex; the division between 'insider' and 'outsider' is less of a profound caesura than a productive tension. Professionalizing, giving official sanction to, and even making money from industrial heritage attributes value to it.

Industrial heritage as identity politics

The agents of industrial heritage appear to be similar in different locations, even if their alliances vary considerably across the cases introduced by this volume. The narratives that are being shaped by those actors also have a good deal in common, although they put the emphasis and the accents of their stories all slightly differently. In some cases, like the Ruhr, the spatial regional identity is a paramount structuring device in many of its industrial heritage initiatives, whilst other elements, in particular those of class, are downplayed. The industrial heritage sites give meaning, above all, to the region known as the Ruhr. This is a place that did not exist as such before the onset of industrialization. The fact that it was shaped by industrialization adds especial gravitas to the question what will happen to it, as a region, after the industries that gave meaning to it have finally disappeared. Many of the heritage initiatives therefore attempt to anchor the region in a past that includes the processes of structural transformation which continue even today. Moreover, as noted, the heritage sites now have their own history, which promotes stability. Taken together then the industrial history of the Ruhr, its heritage industry and the history of its heritage industry provide surety in a changing world. They re-assure the populace of their connectedness in a proud past, where the future seems daunting and unclear, albeit manageable and directed.

The issues of class and social status more generally are almost invariably present in the chapters. As noted, the heritage consensus has muted references to class in the dominant narrative. Ruhr miners had been protected by the Prussian state before the privatization of mining around the middle of the 19th century.[27] They enjoyed a relatively high social status and privileges that remained part of their cultural memory long after the mines had passed into private ownership. The legacy of recognition and support from the State gave miners a particular pride which led them to coalesce against those employers who they saw as violating their customary rights. Any collective memory of a once high and now lost social status was completely absent in Japan, where mining was always seen as work for the wretched of the earth. From that position it was far more difficult to build up narratives of pride and self-worth that could contribute to the building of strong unions and the mobilization of resistance against exploitation. Nevertheless, the mining communities in Japan like elsewhere in the world, were close-knit and seemed to move closer together in the face of discrimination and a negative perception by outsiders.

Newcastle and the Hunter Valley in Australia form an interesting counter-point to the Ruhr, in that here the revival of the fortunes of the coal industry led to growing hostility to heritage efforts, which seemed to consign coal to the past, when in fact it was again booming. As Erik Eklund notes, this gave credence to a narrative that juxtaposed development to heritage. The latter came to mean standstill, decline and degradation whereas development meant either continuation with (working) heavy industries or a radical departure from those industries that had to be replaced with something else. Similarly, whilst there had been a good deal of class conflict in Newcastle and the Hunter Valley more generally, there were very few prominent representatives who wanted to translate the memory of it by turning it into heritage. Admittedly, some retired workers in conjunction with heritage activists did try to find ways to articulate the experience of working in heavy industry and maintaining the stories associated with its communities, but they lacked powerful allies to realize their ideas.

Not unlike the Hunter Valley, the case of Pittsburgh is an example of the extent to which the development of industrial heritage initiatives can get caught up in the cross fire in the drawn-out debates between those championing a post-industrial future and those advocating a re-industrialization strategy for the city. Powerful community-led forces, including many former workers who cherished the vision of the return of the smoke of heavy industry over the city, fought heritage practices and discourses tooth-to-nail as they were seen as the vanguard of a post-industrial vision of the city. In other words the creation of a heritage industry (and other re-industrialization projects) was seen as a death knell; an admission that the past was past. In this respect it is easier to understand the appeal of Donald Trump's 2016 election promise to "Make America Great Again" by re-opening the coal mines and steel mills in America's Midwest to many of those whose sense of self had been given meaning by their role in heavy industry.

Class and class conflict also often stand at the center of narrative constructions of industrial heritage in Asturias. It is the memory of a Red Asturias, where miners provided the shock-troops of revolutionary endeavors, such as the 1934 proletarian rising, or of anti-fascist activities against Francoism. These memories combine with tales of an unruly and rebellious people with their own ancient kingdom that has never been conquered and subdued. Unlike other regions of Spain, such as Catalonia or the Basque Country, these narratives have not gelled around a strong separatist and nationalist movement but rather they were integrated into a powerful proletarian narrative. Nevertheless, tensions appeared in that account when the powerful union movement, itself one of the progenitors of the trope, took a leading role in negotiating the demise of the coal industry – allegedly to the benefit of its members. Indeed, such 'class collaboration' sits uneasily with the dominant sense of class-consciousness in the region, which might also be the reason why some of the industrial heritage museums in the region lack a strong narrative framing around issues of class.

At the same time that the language of class in Spain was being revived in the post-transition period from Francoist dictatorship to democracy, and as the memory of anti-fascism reinforced class identities, the collapse of communism in Eastern Europe discredited the class narratives, which had sustained the legitimacy of the Communist dictatorships. As noted, in Romania the widely-held negative perception of the working-class, and in particular the archetypal proletarian, the miner, was exacerbated by the support of the miners for the Communist transition government of Iliescu in the so-called mineriade of the early 1990s. As a result, no coherent class-based narrative has emerged around industrial heritage initiatives in the Jiu valley. At the same time local rivalries and conflicts also make it impossible to tie industrial heritage to regional identity. Consequently the nascent industrial heritage movement in the Jiu Valley struggles to find a narrative frame for its future. Similar developments were at play in the Borsod region of Hungary, where post-Communist rejection of the industrial heritage narratives of Communism made it near impossible to mobilize support for the preservation of that heritage. In post-Thatcherite Britain, class was declared dead as an analytical category and a sociological actuality. In post-Blairite Britain, however, class is no longer a dirty word, in some circles at least. But the reality is that in vast areas of the British Isles – South Wales, the English Midlands, Lancashire and Yorkshire, the North East and South West Scotland – 'class' never went away. However, it is now less invested in the toil of women and men than it is in the memory of that labor. In many areas the collective narratives associated with the working-class communities have now become heritage and are often directly counter-hegemonic.

In France the basis for the promotion of industrial heritage was scientific, technical and entrepreneurial, with representatives of the coal company and engineers lending a powerful voice to heritage initiatives. They did so in the face of implacable opposition from the Communist miners' trade union for whom every move towards heritage was another lost job. Later Communists and Socialists became more favorably inclined to promoting heritage initiatives as part and parcel of redeveloping areas of heavy industry into regions of tourism, where new cultural facilities, such as the Louvre Lens in the north of the country, were supposed to give a boost to the tertiary sector of the industry. Yet the heritage initiatives were not successful in representing the specific working-class identities underpinning the former regions of heavy industry, which might also explain why the official heritage discourse has been unable to stem the tide of support in those regions (including among former miners and steelworkers) for the right-wing National Front.

The chapters in this volume all testify to the multiplicity of voices emerging from heritage discourses. Such veritable cacophonies cannot easily be put into binaries such as 'authorized' and 'unauthorized', even if it can be very helpful to think about the extent to which such heritage tropes are in the service of a dominant ideology or allied with powerful interests. Inversely, it is interesting to explore the oppositional potential of industrial heritage initiatives vis-à-vis dominant and powerful 'others' that they address. Ultimately, however, scholars of industrial heritage will have to pay closer attention to the specificities of particular narratives and practices of industrial heritage in specific chronological, spatial and non-spatial contexts. It may therefore be helpful to move the discussion of industrial heritage closer to the broader of memory, which provides an arsenal of useful theoretical and methodological insights that have not yet been fully exploited. After all, heritage politics and memory politics are surely opposite sides of the same coin. Studies of commemoration often identify memory cycles recurring over long periods of time.[28] As the practice of memorializing the industrial landscape continues to develop its own history, this concept will help us to think about the different conditions for remembering industrial pasts. Similarly,

Jan and Aleida Assmann's distinction between institutional and communicative memory is particularly useful for scholars of industrial heritage. So many of the initiatives under discussion fall into the category of communicative memory, that is, the memory of living generations, where the memories are direct and personal. At the same time, industrial heritage in many places has already been institutionalized in the form of museums and re-appropriated heritage sites. This institutionalized memory is sending out powerful messages of meaning into the communities and wider society about industrial pasts, producing an often productive but also frequently conflictual tension between communicative and institutional forms of memory. These tensions have a lot to tell us about the silences and omissions in existing heritage practices. Forgetting is an integral part of memory and the stories that are forgotten in existing heritage narratives are as important as the ones that are remembered and foregrounded. As long as there is still is access to communicative memory, heritage scholars are able to end specific silences and establish alternative memorial practices.[29]

The 'touristification' of industrial heritage

In many places processes of the memorialization of industrial heritage take place within the context of the emergence of a tourist industry. Tourism and economic issues more broadly, emerge from several essays as crucial determinants of the course of structural transformation. At some level, establishing industrial heritage sites has been nothing more (or less) than part of a strategy for economic recovery; a top-down attempt to tackle unemployment by providing livelihoods to displaced workers – creating a nation of museum attendants, as one of the contributors puts it. In some cases protecting industrial heritage does not go hand in hand with recovery for those affected by de-industrialization. For example, in his chapter on Pittsburgh, Dieterich-Ward shows that what he calls the "adaptive reuse of industrial-era buildings" has been controversial, because it has served as a crude index of the "extent to which the existing population of local areas can benefit from the influx of new jobs that often require college degrees for anything approaching a living wage". At the same time, turning factory sites into theme parks has been seen by some as a good business proposition, an opportunity to cash in on an emergent industry. In other cases, fostering a heritage industry is an attempt to obfuscate the scar tissue left by heavy industry. In her essay on the coal region of Northern Kyūshū in Japan, for example, Regine Mathias notes that museums and memorial parks funded by the former mining companies are part of a local tourism strategy explicitly aimed at "wiping out the gloomy picture". In northern France, as Marion Fontaine shows in her chapter, the belated conversion of those in political power to promoting industrial heritage initiatives in a bid to revive the depressed former regions of heavy industry through the injection of high doses of culture, did not generate an industrial heritage that could underpin regional working-class identities in those regions. Here 'touristification' spelt alienation and the promotion of alternative heritage and political identities through support for the National Front. In each case the intrinsic 'value' of the industrial heritage itself can be regarded as marginal or incidental or simply a reflection of something else. Here the words of Slavoj Žižek are apposite. In relation to "New Urbanism", he suggests that the rebuilding of "small family houses in small towns, with front porches, recreating the cosy atmosphere of the local community" is a case of "architecture as ideology"; a "solution to a real social deadlock which has nothing to do with architecture and everything to do with late capitalist dynamics".[30] Taken to its logical conclusion, this argument suggests that, despite the best intentions of all concerned (including us), we are all engaged in a business coterminous with capitalism: tourism.

The marketing of industrial heritage sites as magnets for tourists often means the aestheticization of the former sites. In these cases the machines are cleaned, the shafts become fit for modern safety regulations in the tourism industry, the air is monitored, cafes and restaurants look after the wining and dining needs of visitors, and the sites are presented in their 'Sunday best' to make as positive an impression on visitors as possible. The end result is the production of what Jörn Rüsen has called an "aesthetic glow" of industrial heritage.[31] It represents a sanitized version of industrial history that results in nostalgic glimpses into a past that never was. The hard toil, the exploitation, the dangers, the sweat, the disappointments and the dirt of the work that was once performed at those sites are eschewed. The gap between actual experiences and representations of those experiences in heritage might be un-bridgeable, but in many cases we see the introduction of mechanisms for self-reflection about this gap, to encourage visitors to think about the difference. Re-enactors are often utilized in historical sites as 'time-travelers' in order to *pique* the affective experience,[32] but in the case of industrial heritage the sites are often narrated by former workers. Clearly, this serves to narrow the gap between past and present.

Some of the essays in the present volume that deal with Europe and the US highlight that the remnants of industrial heritage have, and continue to be, insouciantly scraped away in the search for fragments of a medieval castle keep or a Roman fort preserved in deeper layers of time. In Asturias, pre-Romanesque churches combine again with beautiful landscape, and in both cases tourist managers might well ask what industrial heritage will add to the mix and whether it is actually beneficial in attracting greater numbers of tourists. Yet it can also be argued that, in a region of Spain not known for its reliable sunshine, museums and sites of industrial heritage can act as a welcome addition to a touristic program otherwise centered on nature (and older layers of history, including the ancient kingdom of Asturias and its pre-Romanesque churches). In Australia, as Eklund has shown, this is also true of the quest to uncover traces of indigenous culture. Moreover, in many regions there are important alternatives to marketing the built environment: often factories and mines have to compete with places of sublime natural beauty as the basis of a vibrant tourist industry. In some places, like in the Jiu valley in Romania or the Borsod region of Hungary, the vision of rejuvenating the region through tourism explicitly excludes mining heritage, as it would detract the visitor from the beauty of the valley. The immediate consequence of this would be to erase the past in the name of a touristic future.

Nevertheless, it is difficult to argue that the 'age of industry', which shaped the lives of hundreds of millions of people in the global West, from the middle of the 18th century to the *fin de siecle* of the 20th, is not deserving of study and memorialization as much as the Middle Ages and the age of antiquities. Among the rusting carcasses of the 'palaces of industry' across Europe are buried many stories of many lives worthy of telling. Several of the places under discussion in the present volume have been designated by UNESCO as World Heritage Sites and others have attracted significant funding from government agencies – local, regional and national. This indicates that industrial heritage is to a modest extent being taken seriously enough to be incorporated into what Laurajane Smith has dubbed the "authorised heritage discourse".[33] There is still a long way to go: as Smith notes, of nearly 1000 World Heritage Sites less than fifty relate to mining, manufacturing or heavy industry.

Even where they may not be attractive alternatives upon which to base a tourism industry, there is often still opposition to the 'touristification' of industrial heritage. In Pittsburgh, for example, some of the key proponents of industrial heritage in the city were open about having different motives than those of encouraging tourism. And in the Ruhr, many voices have been raised against the cheap commodification of industrial heritage as what is at the end of the day a form of entertainment. This is all the more striking in the Ruhr which once again serves as a contrasting example. In reality there is nothing else to develop in terms of tourism than its industrial heritage, and making the latter the unique single most important characteristic of tourism in the Ruhr therefore makes a lot of sense to those wishing to market the region for tourism.

Conclusion

Hegel famously wrote that the owl of Minerva only flies out at dusk. The concern with heavy industries and the way in which they shaped landscapes and communities only fully came into its own with the terminal demise of those industries. Industrial heritage began when industry was about to come to an end. Indeed, in all of the cases reviewed in this volume, there is a time gap between the recognition that an industry was in inexorable decline and the flowering of industrial heritage initiatives. Of course, the contributions here are also a powerful reminder that industrial heritage took off in some places more than in others, but we can find initiatives and concerns everywhere. What is more, the time gap seems to be pretty consistently the gap of one generation, around twenty years, between the perception of crisis and the endorsement (to varying degrees) of heritage. This time gap is important not least because in these years, much of what the industry left behind was destroyed. By the time the owl is ready to fly, it flies over a territory that tends to be only a dim shadow of what it once was. To what extent the transformation of industrial landscapes into industrial shadowlands influenced the subsequent revivification of parts of those shadowlands into industrial simulacra is an intriguing question that still has to be addressed by scholars of industrial heritage. We need to know more about physically rebuilding the recent past.

Comparing the different cases that are represented in this volume, it is hard to avoid the impression that the Ruhr is somewhat of a special case among former regions of heavy industry. Nowhere else is the industrial heritage landscape as densely reclaimed, curated and narrated. Nowhere else do we find the fortuitous combination of circumstances that gave such prominence to industrial heritage. Firstly, the peculiar form of German corporatism, also known as Rhenish capitalism, provided a stable framework for the development of industrial heritage initiatives. This provided a platform for all players – government, employers and the unions – to embrace the concept. Secondly, a strong alliance between heritage and museum professionals, academics, artists and intellectuals on the one hand and former workers who were committed to the preservation of the memory of the industries that had had a massive influence on the region's development, served as a powerful 'bottom-up' force. Notably, this coalition in favor of industrial heritage preceded the official endorsement of industrial heritage. Once industrial heritage had become part and parcel of the official discourse of the region, it was able to draw upon manifold channels of financial support and other resources. Thirdly, the strong federalism, which underpins the structure of the Republic, meant that the key agencies of the State government of North-Rhine Westphalia were far closer to the region than the national government. The State and regional administrative bodies, above all the Regionalverband Ruhr and its predecessor, were vital agencies advocating on behalf of industrial heritage. Fourthly, the restructuring of the coal industry that led to the formation of a heavily state-subsidized single company, the Ruhrkohle AG (RAG), ensured the realization of a long-term strategy for the coal industry that avoided social conflict and social misery as part of a de-industrializing experience. The company itself developed a keen interest in playing a positive role in the structural transformation of the Ruhr and came to see the promotion of industrial heritage as key way of doing so. Fifthly, the mining unions that achieved considerable influence within the RAG (it could perhaps be said with some justification that the unions set the agenda for the coal industry from the late 1960s onwards) also came to regard industrial heritage as means of providing a lasting legacy to their own achievements on behalf of miners. Finally, the overwhelming support for industrial heritage that had been building throughout the 1980s came together in a decade-long project, the International Building Exhibition (IBA) Emscher Park, led by an inspired director who could draw on massive financial resources. This project created many of the iconic sites of industrial heritage in the Ruhr and led to a multiplication of heritage sites in the years that followed the IBA.

Even if, as we have seen, many of the actors that played such an influential role in the Ruhr, were present elsewhere in regions of heavy industry, the happy conjuncture of conditions that we have been able to list for the Ruhr above were not present. In post-Communist societies, such as Romania, the legacy of the Communist discourses on heavy industry loomed large, creating a pervasive negative perception. In Western capitalist societies where the heavy industry was nationalized after the Second World War, such as France and Britain, antagonistic social relations between mining unions and the state, in the case of Britain, and the failure of state-led planning initiatives in France, led to conditions in which much of the industrial heritage was seen more as a liability than a vital part of the regeneration process. In Western capitalist countries, where heavy industry was part of the free market, such as in the US and Australia, the promoters of bottom-up industrial heritage initiatives often did not find powerful-enough allies to realize their ambitious plans for industrial heritage landscapes. In Japan, the national government took on board industrial heritage initiatives in order to promote tourism as a means of regenerating ailing regions of heavy industry, but often without the dense local networks of supporters who could have given deeper meaning to that heritage for regional forms of identity. The final case presented in this volume, that of Spain, is one where the post-Francoist de-industrialization process in Asturias was influenced to a remarkable extent by left-wing unions, who bargained the closure of the mines against generous pensions and social plans. Yet, their success was not paralleled by a vigorous interest in retaining the heritage of the industry, although struggles surrounding the construction and retention of industrial heritage landscapes in Asturias are ongoing and it may therefore be too early to come to a conclusion here.

Whilst the Ruhr, because of a unique confluence of factors, has become the world's leading region in promoting its industrial heritage on a large scale, such status also produces industrial heritage narratives that are remarkably consensual and uniform, perhaps overly so. It underpins, above all, regional identity, and de-emphasizes class (in line with the self-image of West German official discourse as a 'class-less society'), whereas much of the less official industrial heritage in other parts of the world, including Britain, Australia and Spain foregrounds narratives of class and class conflict (often embedded in a counter-cultural strategy and speaking from a position of weakness rather than strength). In this way one of the interesting questions to pursue from a comparative perspective is what is lost in making industrial heritage part and parcel of an 'official discourse' that accompanies structural transformation. Orwell once lamented the fact that we know very few of the names of the countless slaves, "on whose backs civilization rested generation after generation", in the ancient world. "I can think of two, or possibly three", he continued, "The rest have gone down into utter silence".[34] The 'age of industry' also rested on the backs of millions of workers – women and men – some of whom are still alive. How many of their names (and their voices) are in danger of being lost, distorted or disregarded, whether local industrial heritage is ignored causally, opposed actively or embraced successfully? In sum then, the essays in this volume highlight a pressing need not only for more cases studies (including those outside of the global West) but also for a comprehensive transnational and comparative approach.

Notes

1 Our chapter draws upon examples in the chapters in this volume, which are clearly attributed to their author in the text. We are very grateful to the authors with furnishing us with their work.

2. George Orwell, *The Road to Wigan Pier*, London: Victor Gollancz Limited, 1937, chapter 2.
3. Ibid, p. 18.
4. See for example, Raphael Samuel, *Island Stories: Unravelling Britain*, Vol. 2, London: Verso, 1998, pp. 153–171.
5. The Bodleian ballad collection contains several editions. See http://ballads.bodleian.ox.ac Bod10216, V7863, V501, Bod1316.
6. Maurice Halbwachs, *On Collective Memory, 1925*, Chicago: University of Chicago Press, 1992. See also Paul Connerton, *How Societies Remember*, Cambridge: Cambridge University Press, 1989.
7. Cheng Li, China's Northeast: From Largest Rustbelt to Fourth Economic Engine, in: *China Leadership Monitor* 9 (2004), pp. 1–15.
8. Michael Snodgrass, New Rules for the Unions: Mexico's Steelworkers Confront Privatization and the Neo-Liberal Challenge, in: *Labor* 4:3 (2007), pp. 81–103; see also idem, *Deference and Defiance in Monterrey: Workers, Paternalism and Revolution in Mexico, 1890–1950*, Cambridge: Cambridge University Press, 2003.
9. The work in progress of Yujie Zhu, at the Centre for Heritage and Museum Studies at the Australian National University, on the anthropology of tourism in China promises to offer important preliminary insights.
10. Ramana Ramswamy and Bob Rowthorn, Deindustralisation: Causes and Consequences, IMF Working Paper (April 1997).
11. Mike Parker, *The Politics of Coal's Decline: The Industry in Western Europe*, London, Earthscan Publications, 1994; Yves Mény and Vincent Wright (eds), *The Politics of Steel: Western Europe and the Steel Industry in the Crisis Years, 1974–1984*, Berlin: de Gruyter, 1987.
12. See the articles dealing with the economic legacies of Communism in Mark R. Beissinger and Stephen Kotkin (eds), *Historical Legacies of Communism in Russia and Eastern Europe*, Cambridge: Cambridge University Press, 2014.
13. Thomas Jones, in: *New Statesman*, July 1935.
14. Louise Miskell, Doing It for Themselves: The Steel Company of Wales and the Study of American Industrial Productivity, 1945–1955, in: *Enterprise and Society* 18:2 (2017), pp. 184–213.
15. Kenneth Hudson, *Industrial Archaeology: An Introduction*, London: John Baker, 1963.
16. Judith Alfrey and Catherine Clark, *The Landscape of Industry: Patterns of Change in the Ironbridge Gorge*, London: Routledge, 1993.
17. G. Neumann and Wolfhard Weber, Bericht über den ersten Internationalen Kongress zur Erhaltung von industriellen Denkmälern in Ironbridge, in: *Technikgeschichte* 3 (1973), p. 279 f.
18. Stefan Berger, Representing the Industrial Age: Heritage and Identity in the Ruhr and South Wales, in: Peter Itzen and Christian Müller (eds), *The Invention of Industrial Pasts: Heritage, Political Culture and Economic Debates in Great Britain and Germany, 1850–2010*, Augsburg: Wiessner, 2013, pp. 14–35.
19. See http://ticcih.org/ [accessed 11 July 2017].
20. For the Ruhr, see Pia Eiringhaus, Industrie wird Natur – postindustrielle Repräsentationen von Region und Umwelt im Ruhrgebiet, University of Bochum MA thesis, 2017.
21. Greg Dickinson, Carole Blair and Brian Ott, *Places of Public Memory: The Rhetoric of Museums and Memorials*, Tuscaloosa: University of Alabama Press, 2010.
22. Dirk Schaal, Museums and Industrial Heritage: History, Functions, Perspectives, in: Heike Oevermann and Harald A. Mieg (eds), *Industrial Heritage Sites in Transformation: Clash of Discourses*, London: Routledge, 2015, pp. 146–153.
23. Iain Robertson (ed), *Heritage from Below*, London: Routledge, 2016.
24. See Laurajane Smith, *Heritage, Labour and the Working Classes*, London: Routledge, 2011.

25 Clifford Geertz, *"From the Native's Point of View": On the Nature of Anthropological Understanding, Reprinted in Local Knowledge*, New York: Basic Books, 1993, p. 58.
26 Edward P. Thompson, *The Making of the English Working Class*, London: Penguin, 1978.
27 Klaus Tenfelde, *Sozialgeschichte der Bergarbeiterschaft an der Ruhr im 19. Jahrhundert*, Bonn: J.W.H. Dietz, 1977.
28 See for example, James Pennebaker, Dario Paez and Bernard Rimé (eds), *Collective Memory of Political Events: Social Psychological Perspectives*, Mahwah: Lawrence Erlbaum Associates, 1997.
29 The literature on the history of memory is vast. For an introduction, see Stefan Berger and Bill Niven (eds), *Writing the History of Memory*, London: Bloomsbury, 2015; Paul Pickering and Alex Tyrrell, *Contested Sites, Contested Sites: Commemoration, Memorial and Popular Politics in Nineteenth Century Britain*, Aldershot: Ashgate Publishing, 2004, chapter 1; see also Aleida Assmann, *Cultural Memory and Western Civilisation: Arts of Memory*, Cambridge: Cambridge University Press, 2011.
30 Slavoj Žižek, *Living in the End Times*, London: Verso, 2010, pp. 461–462. Paul Pickering has work in progress on the evolving industrial landscape and the heritage industry in Manchester, 1840–2015, which will appear as a volume in the Routledge *Museums in Focus* series edited by Kylie Message.
31 Jörn Rüsen, Industriedenkmale und Geschichtskultur im Ruhrgebiet, in: *Industriedenkmalpflege und Geschichtskultur* 2 (1998), p. 4.
32 See Iain McCalman and Paul Pickering (eds), *Historical Re-Enactment: From Realism to the Affective Turn*, Basingstoke: Palgrave, 2010.
33 Laurajane Smith, *The Uses of Heritage*, London: Routledge, 2006, p. 29.
34 George Orwell, *Looking Back on the Spanish Civil War*, London: New Road, June 1943.

Bibliography

Alfrey, Judith and Catherine Clark: *The Landscape of Industry: Patterns of Change in the Ironbridge Gorge*, London: Routledge, 1993.

Assmann, Aleida: *Cultural Memory and Western Civilization: Functions, Media, Archives*, New York: Cambridge University Press, 2011.

Berger, Stefan: Representing the Industrial Age: Heritage and Identity in the Ruhr and South Wales, in: Peter Itzen and Christian Müller (eds): *The Invention of Industrial Pasts: Heritage, Political Culture and Economic Debates in Great Britain and Germany, 1850–2010*, Augsburg: Wiessner, 2013, pp. 14–35.

Berger, Stefan and Bill Niven (eds): *Writing the History of Memory*, London: Bloomsbury, 2015.

Blair, Carole, Greg Dickinson and Brian Ott: *Places of Public Memory: The Rhetoric of Museums and Memorials*, Tuscaloosa: University of Alabama Press, 2010.

The Bodleian ballad collection contains several editions. See http://ballads.bodleian.ox.ac Bod10216, V7863, V501, Bod1316.

Connerton, Paul: *How Societies Remember*, Cambridge: Cambridge University Press, 1989.

Coser, Lewis A. (ed): *Maurice Halbwachs: On Collective Memory*, Chicago: University of Chicago Press, 1992.

Eiringhaus, Pia: *Industrie wird Natur – postindustrielle Repräsentationen von Region und Umwelt im Ruhrgebiet*, Ruhr: University of Bochum MA Thesis, 2017.

Geertz, Clifford: *"From the Native's Point of View": On the Nature of Anthropological Understanding, Reprinted in Local Knowledge*, New York: Basic Books, 1993.

Hudson, Kenneth: *Industrial Archaeology: An Introduction*, London: John Baker, 1963.
Jones, Thomas, in: *New Statesman*, July 1935.
Kotkin, Stephen and Mark R. Beissinger (eds): *Historical Legacies of Communism in Russia and Eastern Europe*, Cambridge: Cambridge University Press, 2014.
Li, Cheng: China's Northeast: From Largest Rust Belt to Fourth Economic Engine, in: *China Leadership Monitor* 9 (2004), pp. 1–15.
McCalman, Iain and Paul Pickering (eds): *Historical Re-Enactment: From Realism to the Affective Turn*, Basingstoke: Palgrave, 2010.
Mény, Yves and Vincent Wright (eds): *The Politics of Steel: Western Europe and the Steel Industry in the Crisis Years (1974–1984)*, Berlin: de Gruyter, 1987.
Miskell, Louise: Doing It for Themselves: The Steel Company of Wales and the Study of American Industrial Productivity, 1945–1955, in: *Enterprise and Society* 18(2) (2017), pp. 184–213.
Neumann, G. and Wolfhard Weber: Bericht über den ersten Internationalen Kongress zur Erhaltung von industriellen Denkmälern in Ironbridge, in: *Technikgeschichte* 3 (1973), pp. 279–280.
Orwell, George: *The Road to Wigan Pier*, London: Victor Gollancz Limited, 1937.
idem: *Looking Back on the Spanish Civil War*, London: New Road, 1943.
Paez, Dario, James Pennebaker and Bernard Rimé (eds): *Collective Memory of Political Events: Social Psychological Perspectives*, Mahwah: Lawrence Erlbaum Associates, 1997.
Parker, Mike: *The Politics of Coal's Decline: The Industry in Western Europe*, London: Earthscan Publications, 1994.
Pickering, Paul and Alex Tyrrell: *Contested Sites, Contested Sites: Commemoration, Memorial and Popular Politics in Nineteenth Century Britain*, Aldershot: Ashgate Publishing, 2004.
Ramswamy, Ramana and Bob Rowthorn: Deindustrialization: Causes and Implications, IMF Working Paper WP/97/42, 1997.
Robertson, Iain (ed): *Heritage from Below*, London: Routledge, 2016.
Rüsen, Jörn: Industriedenkmale und Geschichtskultur im Ruhrgebiet, in: *Industriedenkmalpflege und Geschichtskultur* (2) (1998), p. S. 4.
Samuel, Raphael: *Island Stories: Unravelling Britain*, Vol. 2, London: Verso, 1998.
Schaal, Dirk: Museums and Industrial Heritage: History, Functions, Perspectives, in: Harald A. Mieg and Heike Oevermann (eds): *Industrial Heritage Sites in Transformation: Clash of Discourses*, London: Routledge, 2015, pp. 146–153.
Smith, Laurajane: *The Uses of Heritage*, London: Routledge, 2006.
idem: *Heritage, Labour and the Working Classes*, London: Routledge, 2011.
Snodgrass, Michael: *Deference and Defiance in Monterrey: Workers, Paternalism and Revolution in Mexico, 1890–1950*, Cambridge: Cambridge University Press, 2003.
idem: "New Rules for the Unions": Mexico's Steelworkers Confront Privatization and the Neo-Liberal Challenge, in: *Labor* 4(3) (2007), pp. 81–103.
Tenfelde, Klaus: *Sozialgeschichte der Bergarbeiterschaft an der Ruhr im 19. Jahrhundert*, Bonn: J.W.H. Dietz, 1977.
Thompson, Edward P.: *The Making of the English Working Class*, London: Penguin, 1978.
Žižek, Slavoj: *Living in the End Times*, London: Verso, 2010.

Index

Note: Page numbers in italics refer to figures.

Agency for Cultural Affairs (Japan) 150
Albrecht, Karl 84
Allegheny Conference on Community Development 192, 200, 205
Almási, Tamás 102
Antuña, Gonzaga G. 43
archaeology, industrial 3, 14, 20, 78–79, 218
Architectural Institute of Japan (AIJ) 150
Argentinian Chaco 120
Arima Manabu 154, 155
Arma X (hip-hop singer) 43
Arnao Coalmine Museum 40
artistic creation: in Asturias 40–45; commemorative art 45–47, *48–50*; concept art 47; filmmaking 42, 44–46, 102, 145; literary 44; multimedia installations 46; musical 41–42, 43; photography 78–79, 145, 155, 157; theatrical 43–44, 46–47; works of remembrance 45, 46, 77
Asturian language 47
Asturian Museum of Mining 40
Asturias: coal industry in 32–35; commemorative art in 45–47, *48–50*; Communism in 37; cultural and artistic creation in 40–45; de-industrialization in 6, 33–35, 37–38, 220; filmmaking in 42, 44–45; heritage sites in 52n12; history of 36–37; industrial decline in 32; industrial heritage in 35–40, 223–224, 226; industrialization in 33–35, 39; labor unions in 32, 34, 36, 37, 41, 45, 220, 224, 226; map of *51*; musical heritage of 33, 37, 41, 42–43; nationalism in 38; regional identity in 6, 35–40; regionalism in 38; state-owned industry in 34; steel industry in 33–35; tourism industry in 39–40, 229; working-class history of 41–43; *see also* Spain
Australia: Aboriginal heritage in 175–176; convict settlements in 169–170, 176–177; industrial heritage in 168–169, 223, 225–226; labor unions in 173, 223; regional identity in 8; as settler society 168–169, 175; *see also* New South Wales
Austro-Hungarian Compromise 96
Austro-Hungarian Railway Company 97
authorized heritage discourses (AHD) 15, 28, 230

Baltimore and Ohio Railroad Station 206
Barbu, Ion 128
Bartók Plus Operafestival 107
Basque language 47
Bassin Minier UNESCO 68
Becher, Bernd 78
Becher, Hilla 78
Berger, Stefan 5
Big Pit National Coal Museum (Blaenavon, South Wales) 5, 13, *14*, 15–16, 222; government funding for 27–28; tour guides at 23, 25–26, 28; visitor survey 24–25, 28; visitors to 22–24; and working-class identity 21–27
Blaenavon Ironworks 21, 23
Bochumer Verein 5
Bodnar, John 169
Borchers, Günter 82
Borsdorf, Ulrich 77–78
Borsod Industrial Area 7, 95; coal industry in 95; de-industrialization in 98–100, 107; history of industrialization in 95–98; industrial heritage in 103–107; industrialization in 95–98, 107; iron

238 Index

industry in 95–96; map of *108*; regional identity in 7, 100–103, 105–107; steel industry in 95, 96; urban development in 95–98
Borsod Mining Corporation 96
Britain: coal industry in 218; de-industrialization in 217–218; industrial heritage in 222; labor unions in 218, 222, 231–232; *see also* South Wales
Broken Hill Proprietary Ltd (BHP) 170, 180
Brooks, Aubrey 180
Brüggemeier, Franz-Josef 78
Buddensieg, Tilmann 77
Burra Charter 175
Byrd, Robert C. 203, 204

CADW 20
Caliguiri, Richard 198
capitalism 216–217, 220, 229; Rhenish 1, 76, 218, 231–232
Cardiff Museum 18
Carlino, August 205–206
Carnegie, Andrew 194
Carnegie Mellon University 197
Carrie Furnaces 206, *207*
Catalan language 47
Cazinoul Funcţionarilor (Mine Functionaries' Club) 123
Cazinoul Muncitoresc (Workers' Club) 123, 127
Cefn Coed Colliery Museum 21
Central Foundry Museum 103, 106
Centre Historique Minier de Lewarde (CHM, Historic Mining Centre) 63, 68
charcoal blast furnaces 95, 103, 105, 106, *109*
Chichen Itza (Mexico) 121
Chikuhō area 138, 140, 141, 142, 143–145, *143*, 146, 151–152, 154, 155, 156–157; regional identity in 147–148
China, de-industrialization in 216
Church of Wales 17
CILAC (*Comité de liaison et d'information sur l'archéologie industrielle*) 63
class conflict 15, 29, 34, 226
class-consciousness 226
Clean Air Act (US) 197, 200
coal industry 1–2, 4, 5, 214–215; in Asturias 32–35; in Borsod Industrial Area 95; in Britain 218; decline in 99, 143–147, *144*; housing for miners 141–142, *143*, 152; in Japan 137–138, 154; in Jiu Valley 123–127; in New South Wales 168, 169, 178–179; in Northern Kyūshū 136–167, 138, *139*, 140–143, 151–152; open-pit mining 168; in Romania 119; in the Ruhr region 76, 231; in South Wales 5–6, 13, 16, 17–18; *see also* mining industry
Coal Industry and Science Museum (Japan) 157
Coal Memorial Park (Tagawa) 156
coal mining *see* coal industry; mining industry
Coal River historic precinct 176–177, 181
The Collier Lass 215
Combinatul Carbonifer Valea Jiului (Jiu Valley Carbon Combine) 124
Comecon (Council for Mutual Economic Assistance) 99
commemorative art 45–47, *48–50*; *see also* artistic creation
Committee on Historical Studies on Civil Engineering (JSCE) 150
Communism: in Asturias 37; in France 58–59, 62, 219, 223; and heavy industry 105, 216–217, 219–220, 223, 226–227; in Hungary 97–98, 101–102, 105–106, 107, 220, 223; in Romania 119, 124, 220, 223
Complexul Energetic Hunedoara (CEH) 122, 126
concept art 47; *see also* artistic creation
conservationism 9
constructivism 2
Convention for the Safeguarding of the Intangible Cultural Heritage (UNESCO) 177
Coupland, Bethany 25–26, 28
Cozma, Miron 124
Crucible Steel 198
cult of labor 124
cultural events 105; *see also* artistic creation
cultural landscapes 56
cultural trauma 32, 51n2
cultural heritage 6, 95, 106, 107, 121, 125, 152, 155
cultural production 223–224
Cultural Properties Law (Japan) 150
culture, material 4, 7, 95

Davies, Rhys 19
de-industrialization 1–2, 4, 5, 15, 26, 103, 228; in Asturias 6, 33–35, 37–38, 220; in Borsod Industrial Area 98–100, 107; in Britain 217–218; in China 216; comparative history of 217–221; in France 219; in Germany 218–219;

history of 215; in Hungary 220; in Japan 143–147, 218–219; in New South Wales 168, 171, 219–220; in Pittsburgh 190, 197, 205; in Romania 220; in the Ruhr region 74, 76; in South Wales 13, 217
Department of Industry (Wales) 20
Desakato (rock band) 41
Destruys, Alexis 63
Deutsche Werkbund 77
Dicks, Bella 20, 22, 23, 28
Diósgyör ironworks 105
Diósgyör Machine Tool Factory 98
Dixebra (rock band) 43, *50*
Duisburg Landschaftspark 77, 82

Edgar Thomson Works (ET) 194
Edwards, H.W.J. 19
Eisenheim workers' quarters (Oberhausen) 79
Employee Stock Ownership Plan (ESOP) 198
Emscher zone 82, 95, 231
entertainment culture 85
environmental rehabilitation 9
Erice, Francisco 36
European Labour History Network 5
European Union 34, 99, 125

Fazola, Frigyes 106
Fazola, Henrik 106
Fazola Festival 106, *109*
Federal Mining Law (*Bundesberggesetz*) 81
Fernánadez, Xandru *49*
Filanda (musical group) 42
filmmaking 42, 44–46, 102, 145
Florida, Richard 203
Flynn, Kathryn 21
Fort Scratchley 176, 180
France: communism in 58–59, 62, 219, 223; de-industrialization in 219; industrial heritage in 223, 227; labor unions in 59, 63, 227, 231; regional identity in 6; *see also* Nord-Pas-de-Calais
Fresno, Francisco *48*
Front national 56, 227, 228

Galician language 47
Ganser, Karl 82
Garfias, Pedro 41
Gasometer 77, 82
gentrification 8
German Mining Museum (Bochum) 80
Germany: de-industrialization in 218–219; industrial heritage in 221–222; mining industry in 218–229; regional identity in 6–7; steel industry in 218; *see also* Ruhr region
Gerö, Ernö 97
Glaser, Hermann 77
globalization 1, 3, 68, 120, 216
Glover, Thomas B. 153
Goch, Stefan 85
Golden Triangle (Pittsburgh) 192, 194, *195*
Gonians 170
Gordillo, Gaston 120, 121
Graffiti Tenneco Strike (street art) *48*
Grieska (album) *50*
Gunkanjima craze 157–158
Günter, Roland 79
gwerin identity 19–20, 22, 28

Halbwachs, Maurice 215
Hashima Association 149
Hashima island 141–142, *142*, 146, 149, 151, 157–158
Heinz, John 205
Heinz History Center 203
heritage: as process 120, 121; regional 128; *see also* cultural heritage; industrial heritage; mining heritage
heritage movement 22
heritage sites 52n12; *see also* UNESCO World Heritage Sites
Heritage Act (New South Wales) 174
Heritage Areas program (Pennsylvania) 205
heritage industry 228
heritage initiatives, role of key actors in 215–216
Heritage of Industrial Modernization (Japan) 150, 151
Heritage Rail-Trail (Wheeling, WV) 203
Hewison, Robert 13–14
Historic Urban Landscape (HUL) initiative 175
history, public 74, 77
histotainment 85
Homestead Works (U.S. Steel) 190, *191*, 197, 204
Hungarian Historical Association 104
Hungarian Mining and Metallurgical Society 100, 101, 104
Hungarian Mining and Metallurgical Industry 123
Hungary: and the Austro-Hungarian Empirre 96–97; under Communism 97–98, 101–102, 105–106, 107, 220, 223; de-industrialization in 220; industrial heritage in 223, 227; iron industry in *108*, *109*; steel industry in *108*, *109*; switch to

240   Index

market economy 98–101, 102–103, 106; tourism industry in 229
Hunter Valley (New South Wales) 182; coal mining in 169, 170; industrial and Indigenous heritage in 176; regional identity in 172–174, 178–182; steel industry 170–171; *see also* New South Wales

ICOMOS Hungary 104, 223
Idegawa Yasuko 148
identity: Asturian 33, 38, 47; in Asturias 33; Basque 32, 38, 39, 47, 226; Catalonian 32, 38, 39, 47, 226; construction of 74, 85; formation of 148–149, 190; Galician 47; industrial 35, 95; and the industrial past 32; and industrial heritage 190; of ironworkers 102; mining 38, 41, 102, 123–125; national 1, 15–16, 18, 69; post-industrial 196; as process 121; related to heritage 2–3, 119, 120; Welsh 17, 19, 21; working-class 20, 21–27, 35, 36, 124, 174; *see also* regional identity
identity politics, and industrial heritage 216, 225–228
Independent Commission Against Corruption (ICAC) 179
Indigenous heritage, and industrial heritage 175–176
industrial archaeology 3, 14, 20, 78–79, 218
Industrial Archaeology Society (Japan) 8
industrial buildings, demolition of 103–104, 107
industrial heritage 3; agendas of 28; agents of 221–225; in Asturias 35–40, 223–224, 226; in Australia 168–169, 223, 225–226 (*see also* New South Wales); in Borsod Industrial Area 103–107; in Britain 222 (*see also* South Wales); as casualty 119; challenges of 23; under Communism 97, 101–102, 105–106, 231–232; community control of 15; contestation of 14–16; criticism of 84; and discrimination 225; dissenting view of 180–181; in France 69, 223, 227 (*see also* Nord-Pas-de-Calais); in Germany 6–7, 77–83, 221–222, 225, 231–232 (*see also* Ruhr region); as historic monument 15; in Hungary 223, 227; and identity 190; as identity politics 216, 225–228; and Indigenous heritage 175–176; in Jiu Valley 120–125, 128–129; mainstreaming 81–83; negative view of 107; in Newcastle 176; in New South Wales 174–175; in Pittsburgh 201–207, 222, 226; questions of accuracy 14; recent trends and debates 84–85; and regional identity 76–77, 105, 154–159, 178–182, 203; in Romania 222–223, 226–227; of South Wales 15, 18–19, 20, 27–28; touristification of 216, 228–230; *see also* Japanese industrial heritage
Industrial Heritage Route (Ruhr region) 83
industrialization 1–2, 107, 225; in Asturias 33–35, 39; in Borsod Industrial Area 95–98, 107; in Japan 137–138; in New South Wales 169–171; in Nord-Pas-de-Calais 58–59, 61–62; in the Ruhr region 74, 76; in Spain 32
industrial monuments 77
industrial museums: Arnao Coalmine Museum 40; Asturian Museum of Mining 40; Cardiff Museum 18; Cefn Coed Colliery Museum 21; Central Foundry Museum 103, 106; Coal Industry and Science Museum 157; and Communist ideology 105; Duisburg Landschaftspark 77, 82; German Mining Museum 80; in Hungary 103, 104; Jiu Valley Mining Museum 122; National Museum of Wales (NMW) 18, 20–21; Petroşani Minimg Museum 126–127; Rhenish Industrial Museum 80; Richmond Vale Railway Museum 177; Ruhr Museum 77–78; Samuño Valley Museum 40; South Wales Miners' Museum 13, 21, 23; Welsh Industrial and Maritime Museum (WIMM) 20; Westphalian Industrial Museum 80; *see also* Big Pit National Coal Museum
industrial revolution 1, 8, 15, 137, 138, 174, 217–219
industrial tourism 151; *see also* tourism industry
Industriekultur 77
INSEMEX 124
International Building Exhibition (IBA) Emscher Park 82, 95, 231
International Committee for the Preservation of Industrial Heritage (TICCIH) 103–104, 150, 157, 221, 223
Ironbridge (Shropshire) 218
iron industry: in Borsod Industrial Area 95–96; and Communist propaganda 105; decline in 99; in Miskolc *108*; in New South Wales 168, 170; in Ózd *109*

Jackson, Jesse 198
Jameson Cinefest 107
Japan: coal industry in 137–138, 154; de-industrialization in 218–219; industrial

heritage in 149–154, 151, 222, 225; industrialization in 137–138; labor unions in 138, 145, 160n34, 219, 225; mining heritage in 148; modernization in 137, 155, 158; regional identity in 8, 147–149; steel industry in 138, 142; tourism in 157–158, 228; urban development in 137–138; *see also* Northern Kyūshū

Japanese industrial heritage 149–154, 222, 225; Arao 141, 146, 152, 157; Chikuhō area 138, 140, 141, 142, 143–145, *143*, 146, 151–152, 154, 155, 156–157; Fukuoka prefecture 138, 140–141; Hashima island 140, 141–142, 146, 149, 151, 153–154, *154*, 157–158; Hokkaidō 137, 154; Iizuka 141, 152, 154, 155; Kitakyūshū 138; Kurate 155; Nagasaki prefecture 140, 141, 146, 152, 155, 157; Nagoya 137; Nōgata 141, 152, 155; Ōmuta 141, 145–146, 149, 152, 157; Ōsaka/Kyōto 137; Sonogi region 136, 140, 141, 149, 151; Tagawa 141, 152, 155; Takashima island 140, 146, 151, 152–153, 157; Tōkyō/Yokohama 137; Yawata 141–142; *see also* Northern Kyūshū

Japanese Society of Civil Engineers 154
Japan Industrial Archaeology Society (JIAS) 136, 149–150
Japan Society of Mechanical Engineers (JSME) 150
Jenkins, J. Geraint 14
Jiu Valley 7–8; coal industry in 123–127; development of 123–125; end of coal production in 125–127; industrial heritage and identity in 120–123, 128–129; labor unions in 122, 125–127; regional identity in 7–8, 119, 123–125; *see also* Romania
Jiu Valley Mining Museum 122
Jones, Andrew 21
Jones, Carwyn 27
Jones, Thomas 13, 217
Jones & Laughlin steel 197

Kawamata Tadashi 155
Ken, Domon 145
Kimura Shisei 158
Kirkland, Lane 200
Kumagai Hiroko 145
Kyushu Heritage tourist guidebook 151

LaBelle Iron Works 206
labor unions 221, 224; in Asturias 32, 34, 36, 37, 41, 45, 220, 224, 226; in Australia 173, 223; in Britain 218, 222, 231–232;
in France 59, 63, 227, 231; in Japan 138, 145, 160n34, 219, 225; in Jiu Valley 122, 125–127; in Pittsburgh 194, 205; in the Ruhr region 76, 80, 87n32, 218, 222; in South Wales 17, 226
labor force, rural 101; *see also* migrant labor
Labour Party 17
"Law on Special Measures to Promote Coal mine Regions" 145
Lawrence, David 192
La Xata la Rifa (theater group) 46–47
leisure culture 84
Lenin Metallurgical Works 97, 98, 105
Lewis, Russell 17–18
Lewis Merthyr colliery 14, 22, 217
Liberal Party 17
liberalism, economic 15
Lib-Labism 17
Lopez, Sara 46
Louvre Lens 67
LTV Steel 197, 199, 201, 202, *207*

Maclean, Mark 181
Manuel, Victor 41
Marxism 79
Mason, Rhiannon 18
material culture 4, 7, 95
Meana, Fran 47
Medina, Pablo Rodriguez 41–42
memory: collective 1, 32, 41, 42, 46, 47, 225; communal 1; communicative 228; cultural 25, 27, 225; historical 85; industrial 46; institutional 228; politics of 2, 227; public 4, 221; social 83, 215; territories of 32; traumatic 44, 47
Menckens, Frederick 176
Merino, Marcos 41–42
Mesta Machine Company 198
Meyer, Laurenz 84
migrant labor 39, 76; in Wales 16, 123; in Japan 141
mineriade 119, 121–122, 125
Miners' Cultural Palace (Lupeni) 123
mining industry 214–215; divided legacy of 67–69; in Germany 218–219; and industrial identity 35–36; negative view of 60–61; stigmatization of 67–68, 77; *see also* coal industry
mining sites, historically sensitive conversion of 81
mining heritage 126–127; in Japan 148
Ministry of Economy, Trade and Industry (METI; Japan) 151
Miskolc-Diósgyör ironworks 106
Mitsubishi Corporation 146, 149, 153

Mitsui Corporation 141, 145, 149, 157
Mitsui Mining 141
modernization 67; heritage of 149–50; in Japan 137, 155, 158
Möhring, Bruno 78
Morgan, Prys 19
Morgan, J. P. 194
Móricz, Zsigmond 100
Morisaki Kazue 145
Morris, Samuel John 152
multimedia installations 46; *see also* artistic creation
Murphy, Tim 202, 203
Murphy, Tom 222
museological theory 221
Museum of Fine Arts of Asturias 46
museum work 105
museums *see* industrial museums

Nagayoshi Mamoru 157
National Coal Board (NCB) 21, 22
National Museum of Wales (NMW) 18, 20–21
National Trust (Great Britain) 81
National Coal Board (NCB) 222
National Front 56, 227, 228
National Heritage Area: in Pittsburgh 204–205; in Wheeling WV 203–204
National Heritage List (New South Wales) 181
National Historic Landmark 206
nationalization 20
nationalism, in Asturias 38
National Society for the Closing of Jiu Valley Mines (SNIMVJ) 126
National Steel 198
National Thermal Coal Company (CNH) 126
Nenyure (memorial to miners) 50
neoliberalism 1, 9, 218
neoliberal urbanism 202, 209n26
New Left 79
Newcastle (New South Wales) 182; coal mining in 168–169; and the Coal River historic project 176–177; as convict colony 170; de-industrialization in 171; industrial and Indigenous heritage in 175–176; railway heritage in 177–178; regional identity in 178–182; steel industry in 170–171; *see also* New South Wales
Newcastle Industrial Heritage Association 180
New South Wales: coal industry in 168, 178–179; Coal River historic precinct 176–177, 181; de-industrialization in 168, 171, 219–220; industrial heritage in 174–175; industrialization in 169–171; iron industry in 168, 170; railway heritage 177–178; regional identity in 8, 168, 172–174, 178–182; steel industry in 168, 170–171; suburbanization in 173; unemployment in 171; urbanization in 169–171; *see also* Australia; Hunter Valley; Newcastle
New South Wales State Heritage Register 177
new urbanism 229
Nicholas Royal Commission 172
Niethammer, Lutz 77
Nizhny Tagil Charter for the Industrial Heritage 3
Nonconformity 17
Nord-Pas-di-Calais 69; abandonment of mining heritage 61–62; aerial photo *57*; heritage discourse in 6; industrialization of 58–59, 61–62; as mining basin 56, 58–61; mining heritage in 63, 64–69; new identity for 67–69; tourism industry in 56; as UNESCO World Heritage site 56, 67; *see also* France
North Rhine-Westphalia (NRW) 77, 80
North-East Passage association 106
Northern Kyūshū 8, 154, 155, 158; Chikuhō area 138, 140, 141, 142, 143–145, *143*, 146, 151–152, 154, 155, 156–157; coal industry in 136–137, 138, *139*, 140–143, 151–152; de-industrialization in 143–147; Miike coalfield 140, 141, 145, 155; Nishi Sonogi coal beds 140, 146–147; regional identity in 147–149; steel industry in 136; tourism industry in 228; as UNESCO World Heritage site 136 (*see also* Japan; Japanese industrial heritage)
North-Rhine Westphalia Program 1975 80
nostalgia 221
NPO Omuta-Arao Coal Mining Fan Club 157

Open Hearth Stacks 205
Orwell, George 214–215
Overbeck, Willi 80

Parton, James 190
paternalism 100
Peate, Iowerth 18–19, 27
Petroşani Minimg Museum 126–127
Phare Cross-border Cooperation Programme of the European Commission 104

photography 78–79, 145, 155, 157; *see also* artistic creation
Pittsburgh 8–9; changing regional identity of 199–201; de-industrialization in 190, 197, 205; history of industry in 192–194; industrial heritage in 201–207, 222, 226; labor unions in 194, 205; map (Pittsburgh metropolitan region) *193*; National Heritage Area in 204–205; regional identity in 8–9, 199–201; re-industrialization in 197–199, 226; response to industrial decline 196–199; steel industry in 190–192, 194; as technology park 197; tourism industry in 228, 230; unemployment in 197, 200–201; urban development in 137–138, 192–196; urban renewal in 202
Pittsburgh and Lake Erie Railroad Terminal 201
Pittsburgh History and Landmarks Foundation (PHLF) 201, 203, 222
Pittsburgh Renaissance 192, 194–5; urban development in 192–196
Pittsburgh Technology Center 197, 198–199, *198*, 201, 202
Plus-Minus Foundation 128
Pom Mahakan (Bangkok) 121
post-industrialism 2, 6, 8, 69, 82, 168, 196, 203
preservation initiatives 106, 107, 126, 136, 149–150, 176, 202–203, 206; bottom-up 15, 222, 224, 231; points of contention 221; in the Ruhr region 231
privatization 15, 99, 102, 107, 170, 225
Projekt Ruhr GmbH 83
Proken Hill Propriety Ltd (BHP) 168
public-private partnerships 222

RAG Montan Immobilien 76
Railway Museum (Asturia) 40
railway heritage 177–178
Rákosi, Mátyás 98
regional identity: in Asturias 6, 35–40; in Australia 8; in Borsod Industrial Area 7, 100–103, 105–107; in Chikuhō area 147–148; and discrimination 148–149; in France 6 (*see also* Nord-Pas-di-Calais); in Germany 6–7 (*see also* Ruhr region); in Hunter Valley 172–174, 178–182; and industrial heritage 76–77, 105, 154–159, 178–182, 203; in Japan 8, 147–149 (*see also* Northern Kyūshū); meaning of 2–4; and negative images 148–149; in New South Wales 8, 168, 172–174,

178–182; in Pittsburgh 8–9, 199–201; post-Socialist 7; in Romania's Jiu Valley 7–8, 119, 123–125; in the Ruhr region 74, 76–77; in South Wales 5–6
regional heritage 128
Regional Industrial Development Corporation (Pittsburgh) 197
Regionalverband Ruhr (RVR) 76, 231
Reicher, Christa 76
re-industrialization, in Pittsburgh 197–199
Research Centre for Historical Sources on Coal Mining 155
Rhenish Industrial Museum 80
Rhondda Heritage Park (RHP) 13, 15, 22–23
Richmond Vale Railway Museum 177
Rima Steel Corporation 96
Rimamurány-Salgótarján Ironworks Company Ltd. 96, 97
Rivers of Steel 204–205
Rix, Michael 218
Romania: coal industry in 119; Communism in 119, 124, 220, 223; de-industrialization in 220; industrial heritage in 222–223, 226–227; under socialism 123–124; tourism industry in 122, 229; *see also* Jiu Valley
Romanian Workers' Party (PMR) 124
Ruhr Museum 77–78
Ruhr region: coal industry in 76, 231; de-industrialization in 74, 76; as European Capital of Culture 83; industrial heritage in 6–7, 77–81, 225, 231–232; industrial heritage sites in 80; industrialization in 74, 76; leisure culture in 84; labor unions in 76, 80, 87n32, 218, 222; map of *75*; preservation initiatives in 231; regional identity in 74, 76–77; steel industry in 76; tourism industry in 83, 84, 222, 228
Ruhr Triennale 83
Ruhrkohle AG (RAG) 76, 81, 83, 231
Ruhr-Universität-Bochum (RUB) 5
The Ruins (Xandru Fernánadez) *49*
Ruiz, Nacho 46
Runrgebiet Tourismus GmbH 83
Rüsen, Jörn 85
Ryan, Robert H. 197

Sala, Avelino 46
SALVAMIN 124
Samuel, Raphael 14–15
Samuño Valley Museum 40
Sârbu, I. D. 128
Schemnitz Mining Academy 103
Science Park (Gelsenkirchen) 82

Index

scrap-and-build policy 143, 145
settler societies 168–169, 175
shiny machine syndrome 20, 22
Sites of Japan's Meiji Industrial Revolution 136
Slotta, Delf 85
Smith, Laurajane 15, 169, 222
Socialism: in Asturias 220, 224, 226; in Britain 15; in Central and Eastern Europe 1; in France 59, 61, 62, 63, 66, 219, 223, 227; in Hungary 7, 95, 97, 98–99, 101–103, 105–106; in Japan 145; in Romania 7, 119, 121–122, 124–125
Sotón mine 40
South Side Works 198–199
South Wales: coal industry in 5–6, 13, 16, 17–18; de-industrialization in 13, 217; heritage initiatives in 18–21; industrial heritage in 15, 27–28; industrialization of 16–18; labor unions in 17, 226; mining industry in 5–6; national identity in 15–16; political life in 17; regional identity in 5–6; religious and cultural life in 17; tourism industry in 21; urbanization in 16–17; and visions of Wales 18–21; *see also* Big Pit (Blaenavon, South Wales); Britain
South Wales Miners' Federation (SWMF) 17
South Wales Miners' Museum 13, 21, 23
Spain: industrialization in 32; *see also* Asturias
Spanta la Xente 42
Spearritt, Peter 169
St Fagans National History Museum 18–20
Stalinism 98
Stația de Pompe-Dieu 128
State Heritage Preservation Law (NRW) 80
State Ironworks (Hungary) 97
State Heritage Register (New South Wales) 176
Station Square (Pittsburgh) 201–202, *202*
steel industry 1, 4, 5; in Asturias 33–35; Bessemer process 194; in Borsod Industrial Area 95, 96; in Germany 218; in Japan 138, 142; in Miskolc *108*; in New South Wales 168, 170–171; in Northern Kyūshū 136; in Ózd *109*; in Pittsburgh 190–192, 194; in the Ruhr region 76
Steel Industry Heritage Task Force 205
Steel Valley Authority (SVA) 199
Stiftung Industriedenkmalpflege und Geschichtkultur (Foundation for Industrial Heritage Protection and Historical Culture) 81
Stoned Atmosphere (musical group) 43

Storm, Anna 169
suburbanization 173
Sulphide Corporation Pty Ltd 170

Tagawa City Coal Mining Historical Museum 155
Tagawa Coal Mine Festival 156
Takashima island 140, 146–147, 149, 151, 152–153, 157–158
Tanigawa Gan 145
Techniquest 20
technology, history of 3, 78
Tetraeder (sculpture) 77
Thatcher, Margaret 218
Thatcherism 1, 15
Thomas, Brinley 16
Thompson, Ceri 20, 22, 26–27
Three Rivers Heritage Trail (Pittsburgh) 203
Thwaites, Reuben Gold 190
TICCIH (The International Committee for the Conservation of the Industrial Heritage) 103–104, 150, 157, 221, 223
tourism industry 81; in Asturias 39–40, 229; "dark" or "ruin" 157–158; in Hungary 229; industrial 151; and industrial heritage 216; in Japan 157–158, 228; in Nord-Pas-de-Calais 56; in Pittsburgh 228, 230; in Romania 122, 229; in the Ruhr region 83, 84, 222, 228; in Wales 21
Tower of Remembrance (Francisco Fresno) *48*
Tri-State Conference on Steel 198

Ueno Eishin 145
unemployment 56, 99, 102; in New South Wales 171; in Pittsburgh 197, 200–201
UNESCO Memory of the World Program 152
UNESCO World Heritage application 158
UNESCO World Heritage sites 56, 81, 82, 136, 155, 157, 230
urban development: in Borsod Industrial Area 95–98; in Japan 137–138; in Pittsburgh 137–138, 192–196
urbanism, neoliberal 9, 202, 209n26
urbanization: in New South Wales 169–71; in South Wales 16–17
urban renewal, in Pittsburgh 202
URUMP 124
U.S. Steel 194; "Dorothy Six" blast furnace 198; Homestead Works 190, *191*, 197, 204

Van Trump, James 201
vertical integration 192–196
virtual spaces 45

Wakelin, Peter 20
Wales *see* Britain; South Wales
The Waterfront (Pittsburgh) 190, 205
Weber, Wolfhard 78
Welsh Bygones collection 18–19
Welsh Development Agency 22
Welsh Folk Museum 14
Welsh Industrial and Maritime Museum (WIMM) 20
Welsh language 16, 19
Welsh Tourist Board (WTB) 21, 22, 24
Welsh Folk Museum 18–19
Westinghouse 197
Westinghouse Air Brake 198
Westpark (Bochum) 77
Westphalian Industrial Museum 80
Wheeling (West Virginia) 196, 199, 200, 203, 206
Wheeling Area Conference on Community Development 196
Wheeling Artisan Center 203, *204*

Wheeling-Pittsburgh Steel 197
Wheeling Stamping Building 206
Williams, Lynn 198
Witkowitz Mining and Iron Corporation 96
World Heritage Property application (Japan) 151–152, 154
Wright, Patrick 13

Yamamoto Sakubei 152, 155–156, *156*
Yamamoto Sakubei Collection 155
Yoshioka Hirotaka 148, 154

Zeche Carl (Essen) 80
Zeche Zollern machine hall 78, *78*, *79*, 80
Ziegler, Arthur 201
Zimmerman, P. 39
Zollverein Foundation 83
Zollverein mining complex 7, 77, 78, *78*, 81, 82, 83; as UNESCO World Heritage site 82, 83
Zöpel, Christoph 82